HABEAS DATA

habeas data

Privacy
vs. the Rise of
Surveillance
Tech

Cyrus Farivar

▲ MELVILLE HOUSE
BROOKLYN • LONDON

HABEAS DATA

Melville House Publishing
46 John Street
Brooklyn, NY 11201

and

8 Blackstock Mews
Islington
London N4 2BT

mhpbooks.com
facebook.com/mhpbooks
@melvillehouse

ISBN: 978-1-61219-646-6
EBook ISBN: 978-1-61219-647-3

Designed by Euan Monaghan
Printed in the United States of America

1 3 5 7 9 10 8 6 4 2

A catalog record for this book is available from the Library of Congress

To Nora and Kas,

I know you will see the world with your own eyes,
and make it better in your own way.

With love,
—Papa

The fantastic advances in the field of electronic communication constitute a great danger to the privacy of the individual; that indiscriminate use of such devices in law enforcement raises grave constitutional questions under the Fourth and Fifth Amendments; and that these considerations impose a heavier responsibility on this Court in its supervision of the fairness of procedures in the federal court system.

—CHIEF JUSTICE EARL WARREN
LOPEZ V. UNITED STATES (1963)

I just hate Fourth Amendment cases.

—JUSTICE ANTONIN SCALIA (2009)

CONTENTS

INTRODUCTION

I believe in big data. I believe that large scale aggregation changes our ability—that one plus one plus one can equal 23.

—PAUL ROSENZWEIG
DEPUTY ASSISTANT SECRETARY FOR POLICY
DEPARTMENT OF HOMELAND SECURITY (2005–2009)

On December 13, 2010, two men ran into a RadioShack on East Jefferson Avenue in Detroit, just blocks away from Chrysler's headquarters. One drew a gun, and demanded that the staff load up the latest smartphones into a few laundry bags. Within minutes, it was all over, and they'd made off with thousands of dollars worth of iPhones and Samsung handsets. Timothy "Little Tim" Carpenter sat in a nearby car, waiting for his accomplices to return.

Along with another man named Timothy "Big Tim" Sanders, Little Tim orchestrated a massive robbery ring, hitting T-Mobile and RadioShack stores in Michigan and Ohio. Eventually, some of the other robbers were caught, and they quickly flipped. Among the information that they gave to authorities was Little Tim's phone number. This proved crucial. With it, authorities quickly got a court order and served it upon Little Tim's cell phone company, MetroPCS. This court order, known as a d-order, for the portion of the 1980s-era Stored Communications Act, is routine. Companies respond to them all the time.

Under current law, no warrant is required to simply find out who called whom, when, and from where. Without batting an eye, MetroPCS turned over 127 days' worth of Carpenter's cell-site location data—effectively turning his own phone into a snitch. The 12,898 data points showed that yes, he was at the scene of the crime during the robberies. But the data also showed that he was at church many Sunday afternoons, and on occasion, spending the night somewhere that was not his known residence.

The case was successfully challenged all the way up to the Supreme Court. The question looms: Is it OK for law enforcement to obtain such a vast quantity of personal, intimate data about someone without a warrant?

On November 29, 2017, the nine justices heard oral arguments in *Carpenter v. United States*. Carpenter was represented by Nathan Freed Wessler, a thirty-five-year-old attorney with the American Civil Liberties Union (ACLU).

"At issue in this case is the government's warrantless collection of 127 days of Petitioner's cell site location information revealing his locations, movements, and associations over a long period," Wessler said.

Before Wessler could even utter his fourth sentence in his opening argument, Justice Anthony Kennedy jumped in.

"What is the rule that you want us to adopt in this case, assuming that we keep [*United States v.*] *Miller* and *Smith v. Maryland* on the books?"

Justice Kennedy, most often dubbed the court's crucial swing vote, was referring to two bedrock cases dating back to the 1970s, which enshrined the third-party doctrine. The idea of the third-party doctrine is that individuals relinquish their "reasonable expectation of privacy" when they transact via a third party, like a phone company. In other words, the data given up by Carpenter—not only what numbers he called, but where he was while doing so—can easily be obtained by the government.

In one short question, Kennedy was expressing the anguish that many judges have had to grapple with over the last half century: Where is the line between appropriate government action when it comes to the surveillance of its citizens? How much privacy do individuals have against the government's use of surveillance technologies, ranging from simple microphones, to wiretaps, to thermal imagers, to cell-site simulators, to drones, and beyond?

In Carpenter's case, rather than deploy humans to follow him or his fellow suspects, investigators simply went after his data at MetroPCS. Under the third-party doctrine, police did not need, much less try to obtain, a warrant. But to most ordinary citizens, myself included, this notion seems ludicrous. To the government, getting location data without a warrant is effectively the same thing as having a policeman make physical observations from the street. Modern technology has enabled so much data to be generated by all of us that it effectively has given the government superpowers.

"Although police could have gathered a limited set or span of past locations traditionally by canvassing witnesses, for example, never has the government had this kind of a time machine that allows them to aggregate a long period of people's movements over time," Wessler continued a few minutes later.

In other words, in the absence of a meaningful restraint, government authorities will continue to push as hard as they can.

Since the eighteenth century, some of the most aggressive law enforcement officers have known precisely where the legal limits were, and gone right up to them. Perhaps the most notable articulation of this idea in the twenty-first century came from General Michael Hayden, who served as both the head of the National Security Agency (NSA) and the Central Intelligence Agency. He has famously said since September 11, as a top intelligence official, he would play aggressively and fairly up to the line, so much so "that there would be chalk dust on my cleats." While Hayden, as a lifelong Pittsburgh Steelers fan, was referring to the national security state, the same logic often applies for federal and local law enforcement as well.

However, the problem with playing to the edge is that sometimes the judicial system is given an impossible task: serving as a backstop to years of government overreach.

Where and how one can meaningfully withdraw from the watchful eye of the government in the early twenty-first century remains an open question. A half-century ago, the Supreme Court ruled that if someone steps into a phone booth and closes the door, we have a "reasonable expectation of privacy," much in the same way that we do at home: in most cases the government needs a warrant first to legally surveil. But since that time, as technology has advanced incredibly quickly, the government has understandably adopted tools to its advantage.

When I first began as a professional reporter in 2004, I was largely dazzled by the excitement of new technology: Gmail was new. Facebook was just beginning. Ubiquitous Wi-Fi was just starting. Podcasts entered the lexicon. Rarely did I consider what impact all of this whizbang technology would have on society, and in particular, on law enforcement.

In 2005, I wrote my first story for Wired News about automated license plate readers (LPRs), and how they were being tested by the Los Angeles Sheriff's Department (LASD). These specialized devices have quietly become pervasive in American law enforcement over the last decade. They rapidly scan, at 60 plates per second, when and where a license plate was seen. That data can be kept indefinitely.

When I was a young reporter, and didn't really have the wherewithal to think about what it meant when then commander Sid Heal, of the LASD, told me that LPRs improved spotting stolen cars by "an order of magnitude."

"This makes us more efficient than we've been in the past," he said. "We would never check 12,000 license plates the conventional way."

That sounded great! Who doesn't want the police to retrieve more stolen cars? But, what I didn't fully realize at the time was just like when Gmail made deleting e-mails practically obsolete, LPR data can also be kept forever. Given a large enough sample size, a pattern can easily be discerned.

I was slowly coming to the same conclusion that many in law enforcement and government circles had come to long ago: that the gathering of all kinds of our data, whatever it might be, was incredibly precious.

Eventually, I found out that LPR collection began in the city where I live, Oakland, California, way back in 2006. An early police analysis showed that nearly all of the plates collected were not a hit. In April 2008, the department reported to the city council that after using just four LPR units for 16 months, it had read 793,273 plates and had 2,012 hits—a hit rate of 0.2 percent. In other words, nearly all of the data collected by an LPR system concerns people not currently under suspicion of a crime. In late 2014, the Oakland Police Department (OPD) expanded its LPR-enabled fleet from 13 vehicles to 33, rapidly increasing the amount of LPR data collected: currently, 48,000 records are collected every day.

Our data is valuable to companies that are trying to sell advertisements and other products, and it's attractive to the government, which is trying to hunt terrorists, miscreants, and scofflaws of all kinds. For the NSA and other federal agencies, that means using the most sophisticated tools against the most vicious of adversaries. For local law enforcement, it means catching car thieves, burglars, and other criminals.

Between April 2010 and April 2012, I lived and worked as a journalist in Bonn, Germany. From the former capital of West Germany, I was greeted almost immediately by the barrage of news about American tech companies. German public officials were generally not impressed: they were constantly berating American tech companies (usually Google and Facebook) over their practices.

I learned that in the decades since Nazism and the East German Stasi, Germans largely have been very sensitive to the type of data that the government can collect. As a result, German legal thinking about privacy originated from the central state of Hessen, which created the world's first data protection law in 1970. That law evolved into a federal version in 1979, a non-binding 1981 version from the Council of Europe, and was last updated in Germany in 2003.

One of Germany's most fundamental data protection principles describes practically the opposite of how we typically do things in America: "The collection, processing and use of personal data shall be admissible only if permitted or prescribed by this Act or any other legal provision or if the data subject has consented."

In the United States, no one gave Google permission to go down all the roads in America and take pictures of every home. The company just did it. That's why, when Street View arrived in Germany in 2010, politicians bent over backwards to show how opposed to Google they were. Notably, Guido Westerwelle, then the foreign minister, said, "I will do all I can to prevent it."

Google came up with a compromise: it would allow Germans to opt out of the service. To do this, they would have to input their name and address, and Google would blur their home, as it does with faces and cars. In the end, less than 3 percent of people covered did so. But Google gave up Street View in Germany—it hasn't updated its local photography there since the service's German debut in 2010. Google has never said explicitly why it stopped updating the images in Germany, but it seems likely that the company did not want to be bogged down in both German courts and the court of public opinion for years on end.

This background was on my mind when I first began reporting again about LPRs. What law or precedent gives law enforcement the authority to capture this kind of data? How was this surveillance technology acquired? Who governs its use? How long is the data kept? How are abuses mitigated? These were questions I could now internalize in a way that I couldn't previously.

In July 2013, I wrote a story about my efforts to learn what the police knew about me: I filed numerous public records requests with law enforcement agencies across California asking for records about my own car over the previous year. I discovered that the OPD scanned my car on May 6, 2013, at 6:38:25 PM at the corner of Mandana Boulevard and Grand Avenue.

This unremarkable hilly intersection boasts a 7-Eleven and a 76 gas station, although across the street is The Star, a hip Chicago-style pizza joint. It was just blocks away from the apartment that my wife and I had moved out of about a month earlier. It's a crossroads I drive through fairly frequently even now, and the OPD's LPR data bears that out.

I have lived in Oakland since 2005, other than my time abroad in late 2008 until early 2009 and again from 2010 until 2012. I have never been arrested. I have had nothing but positive and extremely brief interactions with police. I've been pulled over by the OPD exactly once—for accidentally not making a complete stop while making a right-hand turn at a red light back in 2009. Nevertheless, the OPD's LPR system captured my license plate 13 times between April 29, 2012, and May 6, 2013, at various points around the city, and it retained that data for years. During this period, my car was neither wanted nor stolen. I paid my state registration fees like everyone else. The OPD had no reason to keep tabs on my movements, and yet, it did. Worse still, there's no way to know if my license plate has been captured by a privately owned LPR system.

"Where someone goes can reveal a great deal about how he chooses to live his life," Catherine Crump, a former ACLU lawyer and current law professor at the University of California, Berkeley, told me in 2015. "Do they park regularly outside the Lighthouse Mosque during times of worship? They're probably Muslim. Can a car be found outside Beer Revolution a great number of times? May be a craft beer enthusiast—although possibly with a drinking problem."

As I continued to report on LPRs, I realized the same questions I had about this technology applied to so much more: telephone metadata, cell-site simulators (aka stingrays), body-worn cameras, drones, facial-recognition technology, autonomous cars, artificial intelligence, and more. There was a torrent of technology that was becoming more ubiquitous and cheaper by the day, with little standing in its way. Legislators have generally seemed unable or unwilling to halt the ever-advancing technological mission creep. Courts seemed to always lag behind—by the time a technology was finally raised at an appellate court or at the US Supreme Court, it was far out of date. Carpenter's criminal acts were committed in 2010 and 2011. His case didn't reach the Supreme Court until late 2017. How much better has the smartphone in your pocket gotten during that time?

Many people say, "Yeah, whatever, I have nothing to hide." But there's probably something that you do (or have done), that you wouldn't want known by anyone outside of a tight circle. Maybe you're pregnant. Maybe you're a gun owner. Maybe you ditched work yesterday to go to a baseball game. Whatever it is that you're doing, what business is it of the government's to know? With technology that can capture all of this information routinely for private companies and governments, de facto mass surveillance becomes trivial. Today, it's almost impossible to hide from such data collection without essentially acting like a crazy person: ditching your phone, your car, and turning away from the modern world.

One of the most fundamental legal notions in the English legal system is encapsulated in the phrase *habeas corpus*. Roughly translated from medieval Latin, it means: "[We command] that you have the body [in court]." Basically, it is a brief judicial examination as to whether someone's detention was proper. The goal is to provide a check on the government's ability to arbitrarily arrest someone. The concept, which dates back centuries, is enshrined in the US Constitution: "The Privilege of the Writ of Habeas Corpus shall not be suspended unless when in Cases of Rebellion or Invasion the public Safety may require it."

In the latter half of the twentieth century, largely inspired by German efforts, emerged the concept of *habeas data*. Like a writ of *habeas corpus*, a writ of *habeas data* allows an individual to obtain data from corporations or government agencies for the purpose of verifying it, modifying it, or perhaps even deleting it. In the wake of the authoritarian regimes of the 1980s, the Philippines and numerous Latin American countries codified this concept into law. *Habeas data* does not really exist in the same way in the United States. In America, we have public records laws both at the state and federal level, but there is no affirmative right to receive such information from corporations. Oftentimes, filing a lawsuit is required to obtain the best results from public agencies. Or, put another way, there is no inherent right to privacy in the United States, and often there's little way to know exactly what technologies law enforcement, from the FBI down to the county sheriff, is using.

However, there is a historical skepticism of government power that we, as Americans, generally continue to hold. Our entire founding story revolves around violently overthrowing the reign of a distant monarch who exercised arbitrary power. A notable portion of the Declaration of Independence is essentially a laundry list of grievances: "He has refused his Assent to Laws, the most wholesome and necessary for the public good."

In a world that can be and is so easily monitored and recorded by government authorities, we as a society have abrogated our responsibility. Here, I mean *habeas data* beyond the literal legal meaning: we ought to reveal the government's vast stores of data to the public eye so that it can be scrutinized. After all, for nearly 250 years, our primary shield against government overreach has been ourselves.

"If men were angels, no government would be necessary," James Madison wrote in February 1788. "If angels were to govern men, neither external nor internal controls on government would be necessary. In framing a government which is to be administered by men over men, the great difficulty lies in this: you must first enable the government to control the governed; and in the next place oblige it to control itself. A dependence on the people is, no doubt, the primary control on the government; but experience has taught mankind the necessity of auxiliary precautions."

Now in the early twenty-first century, we are left with some lingering questions: Can the government force a company to act on its behalf—creating entirely new security-breaking software—simply by citing an obscure eighteenth-century law? Do we really relinquish all rights to data that we must give up to a cell phone provider, with cell phones a near-necessity in the modern world? Can law enforcement use a machine capable of tracking coarse or precise location data indefinitely without showing probable cause of a crime? Without a warrant, can police use an extrasensory machine to peer into the four walls of a home to learn about what is going on inside? What kinds of protections can and should we have over something as basic as e-mail? Should police use an invasive device that tricks our cell phones without adequate regulation or oversight from the public? Can cops search our phones without a warrant, potentially reaching into the most intimate of modern devices? Can or should they break the encryption on our phones?

This is a struggle that is happening all over the country, from the highest echelons of federal law enforcement, to the most local of police. Today, small towns across America already have LPRs and inexpensive drone units. Tomorrow, they will have standard facial recognition on all body-worn cameras, and perhaps even specialized hacking units—near-future digital SWAT teams. Unless we demand more from those who are sworn to uphold the law and protect us from the worst of our fellow citizens, this problem will only get worse.

Rather than wait years or decades for another *Carpenter*-like case to arrive at the Supreme Court, some communities—notably Oakland, California—have decided to take matters into their own hands. It is possible for city officials, activists, and even the police to talk about the realities of modern law enforcement and come up with a way for all sides to agree.

HABEAS DATA

CHAPTER ONE

Telephones: How a Fateful Call
in 1965 from a Los Angeles Pay Phone
Still Rings Out Today

If a statute were to authorize placing a policeman in every home or office where it was shown that there was probable cause to believe that evidence of crime would be obtained, there is little doubt that it would be struck down as a bald invasion of privacy, far worse than the general warrants prohibited by the Fourth Amendment. I can see no difference between such a statute and one authorizing electronic surveillance, which, in effect, places an invisible policeman in the home. If anything, the latter is more offensive because the homeowner is completely unaware of the invasion of privacy.

—JUSTICE WILLIAM DOUGLAS
CONCURRENCE, *BERGER V. NEW YORK* (1967)

October 16, 1967
Washington, DC

As the door slammed shut in his Washington, DC, hotel room, Harvey Schneider sat alone with his thoughts for the first time that day.

His boss, Burton Marks, had just gone out for the evening to visit his in-laws in nearby Virginia. Although Marks, 37, wasn't that much older than Schneider, he gave the impression that he was. Marks had an established law practice on Wilshire Boulevard in Beverly Hills. He wore well-pressed suits. He commanded courtrooms all over Los Angeles. Still, to save money, the two men shared a hotel room.

Marks, one of the top criminal defense lawyers in Southern California, seemed relatively unconcerned about the fact that the two of them were about to appear the next day before the Supreme Court of the United States. Nor, seemingly, was Marks worried about letting his young, recently-out-of-law-school protégé make the opening arguments to the court. After all, it was Schneider who had come up with a new legal theory that would challenge conventional privacy law and surveillance practices of the era.

Just one day earlier, Schneider had been formally admitted to the Bar of the Supreme Court. Marks, who had appeared before the court a year before (*Douglas v. California* [1966]), had to go through the perfunctory procedure to get his younger colleague admitted.

Schneider stared down at his notes, strewn across his makeshift desk. It was like preparing for an exam, only the stakes were higher. And unlike most, if not all, modern-day Supreme Court oral argument preparations, Schneider and Marks had not engaged in moot court, or a mock hearing, involving other lawyers playing the part of the justices.

Thus, Schneider would have been shocked at the time to know that their case, *Katz v. United States*, was to become, decades later, a landmark decision in the history of American surveillance and privacy law. It established a key phrase—"reasonable expectation of privacy," which has now served as the legal underpinning of a substantial portion of Fourth Amendment law for the last 50 years. In essence, it is shorthand for determining whether something is considered to be a search under the Fourth Amendment. After all, the Constitution does not prohibit all searches, but simply unreasonable ones. What exactly is considered a search has been a matter of debate since the founding of the Republic. Whether a particular surveillance technology or technique is permitted often hinges on this question, and others that derive from *Katz*.

Marks returned around midnight, fumbled about, and promptly collapsed in an exhausted heap on one of the beds. Schneider looked up, but didn't say a word. He went back to his notes.

Eventually, Schneider got himself to bed, but he barely caught a few hours sleep. This wasn't like a championship basketball game—years earlier, he'd been a guard on various youth teams. Appearing before the Supreme Court was every lawyer's dream, especially younger ones.

The next morning was Tuesday, October 17, 1967. Marks and Schneider suited up and walked over to the Supreme Court. It was a warm, clear day in the nation's capital.

Schneider was confident, but a little nervous. As the two lawyers walked into the imposing column-fronted building, they passed under the inscription "Equal Justice Under Law." They made their way to the main courtroom. As the pair began to get set up for the 10:00 AM oral argument, a marshal of the court approached.

"If you're caught in the middle of oral arguments, would you like to have lunch?" the marshal asked the two lawyers. They agreed—having lunch at the Supreme Court sounded stupendous. (This turned out to be much less grandiose than they had imagined: during the lunch break, Marks and Schneider were treated to "two little turkey sandwiches" at the end of a large dining table, with the only other person nearby being the marshal standing guard outside the room.)

The courtroom filled up, and the court was called to order. In walked eight justices—Thurgood Marshall, who had left the Office of the Solicitor General to join the Supreme Court just two weeks earlier, had recused himself from hearing the case as he represented the government's side in earlier filings. They took their places on the raised podium behind a desk, flanked by American flags on either side. The justices sat down, one by one.

Suddenly, the marshal called out:

> *The Honorable, the Chief Justice and the Associate Justices of the Supreme Court of the United States. Oyez! Oyez! Oyez! All persons having business before the Honorable, the Supreme Court of the United States, are admonished to draw near and give their attention, for the Court is now sitting. God save the United States and this Honorable Court!*

Chief Justice Earl Warren, a native Californian, presided over the court. By then, Warren was nearing the end of his influential 16-year tenure as the head of the nation's highest court. As chief justice, he had led the liberal majority in landmark cases like *Brown v. Board of Education* (1954), which eliminated racial segregation in schools nationwide. Before that, Warren had been governor of California, after being the state's attorney general. Before that, he served as district attorney of Alameda County and began his legal career as deputy city attorney of Oakland.

"Number 35, Charles Katz, Petitioner versus United States," Warren intoned flatly, in his tinny, high-pitched voice.

He paused for a few seconds and waited for Schneider to begin.

"Mr. Schneider?"

Schneider approached the lectern, and quickly glanced at the justices who sat several feet away, and saw giants: Warren, Hugo Black, William Douglas, John Harlan, Byron White, William Brennan, Potter Stewart, and Abe Fortas. They were all more than twice as old as he was.

"Mr. Chief Justice, and may it please the Court," Schneider began. His voice did not waver. He looked straight ahead at the justices.

> *The facts of this case that is now before the Court are really quite simple. The law applicable is something else again. But the facts are as follows. Mr. Katz was surveilled by agents of the Federal Bureau of Investigation for a period of approximately six days. During that period of time, the surveillance was conducted by the use of a microphone being taped on top of a public telephone booth or a bank booth, so it was actually three booths.*

"One booth had been placed out of order by the telephone company and with the telephone company's cooperation, the other two booths were used by Mr. Katz," he continued, building a rhythm.

The courtroom was silent.

"Sometimes he used one booth, sometimes he used another," Schneider read from his notes.

> *The tape was placed on top of the booth or the microphone was placed on top by a tape. The FBI Agents had undoubtedly read their homework and had not physically penetrated into the area of the telephone booth. Subsequently after about six days of surveillance, Mr. Katz was arrested. He was then taken to his apartment building where his room was searched under a search warrant and numerous items were seized from Mr. Katz's apartment. The issues before the Court are fairly clear. One, whether or not, the search and seizure or one of the interceptions of the telephone communications was proscribed by the Fourth Amendment; and two, whether or not, the warrant that was used to search his apartment building is constitutionally proper or constitutionally defective.*

After a few minutes of back-and-forth with Stewart and Warren, Schneider drove right to the heart of the matter.

Surprisingly, Schneider largely abandoned the entire question that the court was being asked to consider: Was a telephone booth a constitutionally protected area? If so, does the government necessarily need to physically trespass into it in order to violate the Constitution?

Avoiding this was a highly unusual move. No doubt the justices were a little bit surprised at the sharp left turn.

"We think and respectfully submit to the Court that whether or not, a telephone booth or any area is constitutionally protected, is the wrong initial inquiry," Schneider declared.

Schneider proposed a way to evaluate such a situation.

"It's an objective test which stresses the rule of reason, we think," he continued. "The test really asks or poses the question: 'Would a reasonable person objectively looking at the communication setting, the situation and location of a communicator and communicatee—would he reasonably believe that that communication was intended to be confidential?'"

Or put another way, could that "reasonable person" have a reasonable expectation of privacy?

The 1789 Bill of Rights enshrines a number of rights to individuals: freedom of speech, freedom of religion, the right to bear arms, and so forth. The Fourth Amendment protects against unreasonable searches and seizures. However, nowhere in the Bill of Rights, or in the Constitution, is the word "privacy" mentioned. But scholars, lawyers, judges, and others have intuited, or extrapolated, something resembling a privacy right from both documents.

Government overreach was certainly on the minds of the Framers of the Constitution. In the 1760s, American colonists were very much aware of the invasiveness of British authorities. At that time, a writ of assistance was issued by British courts as a way to combat smuggling. Unlike a modern warrant, these writs, also known as general warrants, allowed nearly anywhere to be searched. Worse still, they lasted for the lifetime of the King under which they were issued, and nearly always, in practice, could not be challenged.

In 1761, a 36-year-old lawyer, James Otis, Jr., represented dozens of Boston merchants, who argued that their rights had been violated by Charles Paxton, a British customs agent who had used writs of assistance against them.

In a famous five-hour argument, Otis argued before the Superior Court of Massachusetts that "every one with this writ may be a tyrant."

He continued:

> Now, one of the most essential branches of English liberty is the freedom of one's house. A man's house is his castle; and whilst he is quiet, he is as well guarded as a prince in his castle. This writ, if it should be declared legal, would totally annihilate this privilege. Custom-house officers may enter our houses when they please; we are commanded to permit their entry. Their menial servants may enter, may break locks, bars, and everything in their way; and whether they break through malice or revenge, no man, no court can inquire. Bare suspicion without oath is sufficient.

While Otis lost the case, his oratory made a lasting impression on a young John Adams, then 26, who observed in the courtroom. The 1776 Declaration of Independence itself refers briefly to this practice, in its laundry list of grievances against King George III: "He has erected a multitude of New Offices, and sent hither swarms of Officers to harass our people, and eat out their substance."

Fifteen years later, the Framers, and in particular James Madison, were so put off by the idea that anyone's home or business could suddenly be searched by a government agent that such protections were distilled into the single—albeit lengthy—Fourth Amendment, which was ratified in 1791:

> The right of the People to be secure in their persons, houses, papers and effects, against unreasonable searches and seizures, shall not be violated, and no warrants shall issue, but upon probable cause supported by oath or affirmation, and particularly describing the place to be searched, and the persons or things to be seized.

For well over a century, the Fourth Amendment right largely turned on the notion of a physical trespass. The idea, simply, was that it was the physical act of invading someone's private space that was so offensive to the Framers. It is still fundamental to our reading of the Fourth Amendment—the police cannot kick in your door without a warrant absent exigent circumstances.

But in the nineteenth century, new notions of what constituted an invasion of privacy began to develop—for example, the idea of invading someone's privacy through the telegraph line was patently offensive. Thus, in 1862, California became the first state in the union to formally outlaw the tapping of telegraph lines.

And in 1928, the Supreme Court considered its first telephone wiretapping case, the case of *Olmstead v. United States*. Roy Olmstead was a Seattle police officer turned bootlegger whose phone had been tapped, leading to his arrest. No warrant had been issued for the tap. (In an interesting side note, Mabel Walker Willebrandt, who served as assistant attorney general from 1921 until 1929 and served as the lead prosecutor at nearly all Prohibition-related cases, refused to represent the government at the Supreme Court because she opposed the use of the wiretap evidence.)

Ultimately, the court found that it didn't matter if federal authorities had wiretapped Olmstead's phone without a warrant. Writing for the majority opinion in a 5–4 decision, Chief Justice William Howard Taft concluded that the government had not violated Olmstead's Fourth Amendment rights, essentially, because there was no physical trespass on his private property. This focus on the physical infringement rather than moral trespass—honoring the letter, if not the spirit of the Founders, one might say—would haunt privacy cases in the county for nearly a century.

"The [Fourth] Amendment does not forbid what was done here," Taft wrote, noting that by that point, the telephone was 50 years old. "There was no searching. There was no seizure. The evidence was secured by the use of the sense of hearing, and that only. There was no entry of the houses or offices of the defendants."

In essence, the Supreme Court did not want to impose a new law where it felt Congress or the Constitution had not specifically authorized them to. (This is a common reasoning of many conservative judicial opinions, that the courts should not have an expansive view of the law. Rather, they should simply stick to what the law actually says. By contrast, liberal judges generally view the Constitution as a "living document"—its meaning can be reinterpreted over time to accommodate modern realities.) But by the 1920s, both telephones and wiretaps were decades-old technology. The law, then as now, often struggled to keep up with the common realities of the day.

Presciently, that was exactly the point made by Justice Louis Brandeis, then roughly midway through his fabled tenure on the court, in a dissent in which he referenced Otis' famous speech.

"The progress of science in furnishing the Government with means of espionage is not likely to stop with wiretapping," Brandeis wrote. "Ways may someday be developed by which the Government, without removing papers from secret drawers, can reproduce them in court, and by which it will be enabled to expose to a jury the most intimate occurrences of the home."

He continued, citing the Framers, asserting that they "sought to protect Americans in their beliefs, their thoughts, their emotions and their sensations."

Decades later, when Schneider told the 1967 Supreme Court, in the opening minutes of his argument in the *Katz* case, "The FBI Agents had undoubtedly read their homework and had not physically penetrated into the area of the telephone booth," he was largely referring to the *Olmstead* precedent. The government in the 1960s, as it had in the 1920s and decades earlier, relied solely on the physical trespass of the space.

In *Katz*, that meant that the FBI did not invade Katz' possibly private space—a telephone booth—but they went physically right up to the edge of it.

◇

The *Katz* case originated in October 1964, when FBI agents in Los Angeles were tipped-off to a local betting man. By February 1965, the FBI had determined that this person was 53-year-old Charles Katz, and that he lived at Sunset Towers West, 8400 Sunset Boulevard, Room 122.

Nearly every day, agents watched the dapper middle-aged man leave his apartment on Sunset Boulevard, and walk just a few blocks down to a bank of three telephone booths at 8210 Sunset Boulevard, across the street from the Chateau Marmont hotel. To anyone who might have seen Katz, he simply looked like a businessman. He wore suits, button-up shirts, and long ties, according to Joseph Gunn, a Los Angeles Police Department (LAPD) officer who testified at Katz' two-day bench trial.

"Some of these telephone calls," Benjamin Farber, a federal prosecutor, said during an April 5, 1965 court hearing, "were being placed to a telephone number in Massachusetts which was listed to an individual whose reputation was well known to the Federal Bureau of Investigation as that of a gambler."

Katz, it turned out, was a handicapper, someone who studies the outcomes of sporting events and places large bets on them. He'd been doing it for 30 years in Los Angeles, he told agents later, and claimed he made $60 a week (or $470 in 2017 dollars). After establishing a pattern of behavior, on February 19, FBI agents placed a microphone on top of two of the phone booths that were part of the bank of three that Katz liked to use. Likely as a way to make their jobs easier, law enforcement disabled one of the booths—with the phone company's permission—simply by putting a sign on the third one saying, "OUT OF ORDER." This tactic encouraged Katz to choose between the centermost and easternmost booths.

The FBI and the LAPD assigned several people to the Katz investigation. The FBI went as far as to rent the room next to Katz' in the Sunset Towers West—Room 123. Katz sometimes called East Coast bookies from his room and he could plainly be heard in the hallway outside his room. At the time, both federal and local law enforcement were particularly interested in vice cases, not only because they were illegal, but because controlling gambling was a powerful check on police corruption.

"We felt in LA that there wasn't any corruption as far as cops taking bribes, so one of the ways you make sure that there aren't takes like that is to get involved," Gunn, who retired from the LAPD in 1983 after 20 years on the force, told me. "You make sure that they don't get a major foothold and that they're not trying to pay off cops for protection."

Gunn was well-aware of the potential of his fellow officers to be corrupted. In fact, just one year earlier, in 1964, Gunn learned that his partner, Henry De Maddalena, a veteran vice officer, was accepting bribes from another bookmaking ring. At the behest of Police Chief William H. Parker, Gunn went undercover and helped dismantle one of the city's largest gambling rings. In the end, two LAPD officers, including De Maddalena, and four other men were found guilty of illegal betting and bribery.

The recording operation of Katz began on February 19, 1965. One team of agents would watch Katz at home, and then would radio to another agent closer to the phone booths. The two microphones and recording apparatus only took about a minute or so to set up—one person had to scramble up to the top of the booth and turn it on before Katz arrived. (Amazingly, during the six days that Katz was under surveillance, only one other person came to use the phone booth around the same time as he.) Then, once Katz left, the agents would turn the microphones off. In addition, agents also created a false surface on the counter of the phone booths, with carbon paper secretly placed underneath, so that it would capture anything that Katz wrote.

After recording Katz' calls for nearly a week, and in combination with the observations near his apartment, they moved in and arrested him on February 25 at the phone booth. Armed with a warrant, the LAPD and the FBI searched his apartment and recovered 148 written pages of betting notes, various sports magazines, and two $10 rolls of quarters, among other items. When he was arrested, Katz was polite and did not resist.

It was during Katz' two-day bench trial at the federal district court (the lowest level of federal court) in May of 1965 that Harvey Schneider's boss, Burton Marks, laid out the beginnings of his argument about the expectation of privacy.

"I think that *Olmstead* is a dead letter," he told US District Judge Jesse Curtis. "It hasn't been specifically overruled, but either by this case or some other case it is going to be in the very near future . . . The right to privacy doesn't just extend to a person's home, it extends to his office, and I believe it extends to any place in which there is intended to be privacy."

The judge was unconvinced; Katz was convicted and sentenced to a $300 fine (approximately $2,300 in 2017 dollars). Marks appealed to the 9th Circuit US Court of Appeals, where again, he reprised his arguments. Marks was denied, and the stage was set for a writ of *certiorari* petition— that is, the appeal to the Supreme Court.

◇

Burton Marks didn't argue against *Olmstead* due to mere bluster. Rather, the choice was tactical.

Just as general writs were an anathema to the values of Colonial Americans, so too was the entire concept that a person's telephone calls could be easily invaded without warning to modern Americans. Although the Supreme Court had not formally taken up the issue until the 1920s, other lower federal courts and even some local courts had, albeit sometimes in roundabout ways.

For example, on December 1, 1907, the *New York Times* reported on a curious local case where a Tenth District Municipal Court judge had ruled that "a protesting tenant has rights of privacy in the telephone that connects his apartment with the outside world."

The case involved a rental dispute and a tenant who was being eavesdropped upon by his landlord's wife on the common telephone line for the entire building. Judge Wauhope Lynn noted that the telephone had "passed the period of experiment and is now a real living part of ourselves." He went on, "where it is installed as a part of an apartment house and made an inducing cause for the rental of such apartment, then its presence must be regarded as a sacred part of the home, entering into its privacies and secrets and giving communion with those we love and cherish."

Of course, this case was a civil and not a criminal matter, and it was only relevant to the local court, but it is illustrative of at least some of the typical judicial thinking of the era. In the nineteenth century and well into the twentieth, sensitive telegrams often had the protection of some type of encryption. The telephone, by contrast, typically did not. Most people did not speak in code, and they usually didn't write letters in code, either. Judges were responding to the obviousness of this to people of the time.

In 1931, no less an authority than the head of the FBI, J. Edgar Hoover—certainly no wilting flower when it came to aggressive law enforcement—declared during a Senate hearing that he thought wiretapping was "unethical." (Hoover rather dramatically changed his tune on this later on.)

In 1932, a federal judge in Boston, during a bootlegging trial, denounced federal agents' wiretapping as a "contemptible, vile practice."

Two years later, Congress passed the Communications Act of 1934, which, among other things, established the Federal Communications Commission. Notably, the act specifically forbade wiretapping under Section 605. (However, federal agencies routinely ignored the law and conducted wiretaps, although they were forbidden from introducing the evidence at trial.)

In short, by the time of *Katz*, there was a growing consensus that wiretapping—or even warrantless eavesdropping, as was the case in *Katz*—was improper.

◇

Three Supreme Court cases in particular had a significant influence on Marks and Schneider's view that *Olmstead* was "dead letter"—one from the 1940s, one from 1961, and another decided in June 1967, just after *Katz'* cert petition had been submitted. Taken together, these three cases offered a distinct roadmap for how the young Los Angeles lawyers might convince the Warren Court in the fall of 1967.

The first of those cases, *Goldman v. United States* (1942), involved men who had been indicted for conspiracy to violate federal bankruptcy laws. The defendants had been eavesdropped upon by federal agents who rigged up a "listening apparatus in a small aperture in the partition wall with a wire to be attached to earphones extending into the adjoining office." Using this system, authorities were able to overhear and ultimately transcribe crucial moments of the conspiracy, which proved to be grounds for their indictment.

The men attempted to challenge the collection of this evidence, on the grounds that it violated both the Fourth Amendment and Section 605 of the Communications Act. Denied by lower courts, they challenged it up to the Supreme Court, which upheld the ruling.

The Supreme Court ultimately found (5–3) that the surveillance system was "no more the interception of a wire communication within the meaning of the Act than would have been the overhearing of the conversation by one sitting in the same room."

As in *Olmstead*, the case largely turned on whether a trespass had occurred, and it had not. However, again, the more liberal members of the court dissented, largely reiterating what Brandeis had argued decades earlier.

"The conditions of modern life have greatly expanded the range and character of those activities which require protection from intrusive action by Government officials if men and women are to enjoy the full benefit of that privacy which the Fourth Amendment was intended to provide," Justice Frank Murphy wrote in his dissent in *Goldman*. "It is our duty to see that this historic provision receives a construction sufficiently liberal and elastic to make it serve the needs and manners of each succeeding generation."

Nearly two decades later, in *Silverman v. United States* (1961), the Supreme Court again found itself faced with an eavesdropping case involving gamblers in a Washington, DC, house. In this instance, however, federal agents camped out in a house next door to the suspects and used a rather advanced listening apparatus, specifically, a spike mike. The microphone was effectively plugged into the target home's heating system, which enabled the agents to hear everything going on next door. Again, the defendants challenged the use of the listening apparatus under the Fourth Amendment and Section 605 of the Communications Act.

In a unanimous decision, the Supreme Court ruled that while the agents had violated the Fourth Amendment, it wasn't because they had trespassed (even slightly) into the home without a warrant. "But decision here does not turn upon the technicality of a trespass upon a party wall as a matter of local law," the court found. "It is based upon the reality of an actual intrusion into a constitutionally protected area."

This notion was rather strange, in light of *Goldman*.

"Our concern should not be with the trivialities of the local law of trespass, as the opinion of the Court indicates," wrote Justice William Douglas, in a concurring opinion in *Silverman*. "But neither should the command of the Fourth Amendment be limited by nice distinctions turning on the kind of electronic equipment employed. Rather, our sole concern should be with whether the privacy of the home was invaded."

While it seems somewhat quaint now, the late 1950s into the mid 1960s were a time when there was still a great deal of intense debate as to the ethics and legality of wiretapping and eavesdropping. Many, including the American Civil Liberties Union, argued that the practice should be banned outright. Others felt that it should be allowed in very narrow circumstances (such as situations pertaining to national security), while others felt that it should be allowed simply with a judge's approval. One of the most ardent pro-wiretap advocates of that era was Attorney General Robert F. Kennedy. In a June 1962 op-ed in the *New York Times*, he argued that properly crafted legislation could strike the necessary balance between privacy interest and the needs of law enforcement.

"Wiretapping should be prohibited except under clearly defined circumstances and conditions involving certain crimes," Kennedy wrote. "Because wiretapping potentially involves greater interference with privacy than ordinary search and seizure, it is proper to limit it narrowly and permit it only where honestly and urgently needed."

By January 1967, President Lyndon Johnson even mentioned the issue in his State of the Union address:

> We should protect what Justice Brandeis called the "right most valued by civilized men"—the right to privacy. We should outlaw all wiretapping—public and private—wherever and whenever it occurs, except when the security of this Nation itself is at stake—and only then with the strictest governmental safeguards. And we should exercise the full reach of our constitutional powers to outlaw electronic "bugging" and "snooping."

Months before Schneider and Marks arrived to argue their case, the Supreme Court had just decided on the legality of a New York state law that authorized specific eavesdropping, or bugging, under the approval of any high-ranking police officer, district attorney, or the state attorney general, if there is "reasonable ground to believe that evidence of a crime may be thus obtained."

At the time, nine states prohibited wiretapping—listening to a voice communication transmitted over a wire—in all circumstances. New York was just one of seven states that specifically forbade bugging, or eavesdropping, but of those seven, six (including New York and California) allowed it under certain circumstances. The 1967 case, *Berger v. New York*, was a case involving bribery of the chairman of the New York State Liquor Authority. There, a miniature recording device was used to capture voices in an attorney's office, with the approval of a judge of the state's supreme court.

In June 1967, the US Supreme Court decided 6–3 that the New York law was too broad, and was too close to the general warrants that were abhorred by the Framers.

"I can see no difference between such a statute and one authorizing electronic surveillance, which, in effect, places an invisible policeman in the home," wrote Justice William Douglas in his concurring opinion. "If anything, the latter is more offensive because the homeowner is completely unaware of the invasion of privacy."

◎

By the time the *Katz* case fell in the lap of a young Harvey Schneider, it was early 1967.

Marks and Schneider occupied a small office in Beverly Hills—just the two of them and a pair of secretaries. Marks at heart was really a skilled litigator and orator. The elder lawyer wasn't known for his creative legal writing. Marks likely thought that Schneider could persuade the Supreme Court to not only agree to hear the case, but to rule in Katz' favor.

Schneider spent long hours in the law library, ensconced in legal texts. He dove deep into the analysis and scholarship of *Goldman* and *Silverman* and he came to a quick conclusion about the federal prosecutors on the other side.

"They thought they had a *Goldman* case and not a *Silverman* case," he told me. "So I couldn't argue trespass because that was the going theory and so I argued whether a telephone booth was a constitutionally protected area."

Schneider learned there were other cases that had also taken place, showing that the court had found spaces that weren't private homes to be protected under the Constitution—these included hotel rooms and taxicabs.

"I argued that in the language the court had been using," Schneider continued. "The court never really articulated a two-step analysis, but I think there was one. The first inquiry was whether they were dealing with a constitutionally protected area, if not, then there was no second step. So the first step was protected area, if they found one, then the next issue was trespass, that was the old analysis. They never articulated [it,] but I think if you read the cases, that's what you glean from reading the cases."

This was the crux of the petition to the Supreme Court, which was formally accepted in early 1967. That summer, while the rest of the country was embroiled in the Summer of Love alongside riots over racial discrimination and police abuse broke out in several cities across America, Schneider began to formulate his arguments before the court.

One day, Schneider realized that there was another, better way that he might be able to convince the court, and it involved arguments that (highly unusually) were not mentioned in his petition briefs to the court.

Arguing the question of trespass was surely to fail, because, again, the microphones were on top of, and not in, the phone booth. Plus, asking the court to consider that a public phone booth was a constitutionally protected area was a dicier proposition. After all, unlike taxis and hotel rooms, phone booths are wholly transparent to the outside world. Whether the court, even the liberal-leaning Warren Court, would find this to be private nonetheless, was not a slam dunk.

Schneider thought that the justices might have an easier time adopting a new test of sorts: whether a person in a telephone booth would reasonably expect to have privacy inside of a phone booth. Immediately after this epiphany, Schneider rushed over to Marks' office.

◇

During the oral argument at the Supreme Court on October 17, 1967, Schneider quickly floated this idea of a reasonable expectation of privacy.

"The test really asks or poses the question, 'Would a reasonable person objectively looking at the communication setting, the situation and location of a communicator and communicatee—would he reasonably believe that that communication was intended to be confidential?' We think that in applying this test there are several criteria that can be used."

Justice Brennan, an influential liberal justice, jumped right in: "So that parabolic mic on the two people conversing in the field a mile away might—" (Brennan's comment appeared to reference a combination of two cases: *Hester v. United States* [1924] and *Silverman*. In *Hester*, the Supreme Court found that the Fourth Amendment does not apply to open fields, even when that land is within a person's private property. In *Silverman*, the Supreme Court had referred to the parabolic microphone as one type of "frightening paraphernalia" that could be used to conduct ever-more-invasive types of surveillance at a distance.)

Schneider didn't miss a beat.

"Absolutely," he said. "And I think that *Hester*, the *Hester* case which is cited on the Government's brief, we think that *Hester* is wrong."

Schneider's voice slowed down and rose towards the end of the sentence, as if to be gentle with the notion that he wanted the Supreme Court to upend *Hester*. (Ultimately, the court would decline to overturn it in its *Katz* decision.)

"We think that if a confidential communication was intended and all the other aspects of confidentiality are present, then it makes no difference whether you're in an open field or in the privacy of your own home," Schneider continued. "We would submit to the Court that there are factors present which would tend to give the Courts, the trial courts, and ultimately this Court, some guidelines as to whether or not, objectively speaking, the communication was intended to be private."

Part of the analysis, Schneider went on to argue, should be determined on various factors, such as the location of the conversation—was it surrounded by other people, or not? Was the person speaking in an unusually loud tone of voice?

And then Schneider really drove home his argument.

> *And again, I—we—feel that the emphasis on whether or not*
> *you have a constitutionally protected area may be placing*
> *the emphasis on the wrong place. We feel that the Fourth*
> *Amendment and at the Court's decisions recently for a long*
> *time, I believe, have indicated that the right to privacy is*

what's protected by the Fourth Amendment. We feel that the
right to privacy follows the individual.

This was the crux of Schneider's stunning point: that an affirmative right
to privacy is not necessarily contingent on where a person is—here, the
question of trespass was irrelevant.

◉

Then, it was the government's turn to present its arguments. That duty fell
to John S. Martin, Jr., 32, newly appointed assistant to the Office of the Solicitor General of the United States.

Martin called Schneider's arguments a "radical change in the concept to
the Fourth Amendment," and argued that under the *Goldman* standard—no
penetration of the phone booth itself—that eavesdropping was wholly justified.
Law enforcement did not need to get a warrant, he explained, and so the agents
didn't even attempt to. In the government's eyes, the case was that simple.

Martin got into an extended discussion with Chief Justice Warren about
the specific design of phone booths, pointing out that, after all, phone
booths are not soundproof.

Warren foiled his assertion: "Well, not many homes are soundproof."

To which Martin replied that in a phone booth, people don't "expect" to
be "protected in that area as you are in your home."

"Perhaps not as much but you certainly expect it to be private and you
don't talk to the world, when you talk on the telephone there, do you?"
Warren said.

"No, of course, you don't," Martin continued, explaining that anyone
passing by a phone booth might overhear a conversation. In other words,
Martin argued, the law should not recognize the same level of core, innate
protection, as is the case when someone is at home.

The justices seemed generally skeptical of the government's view. Chief
Justice Warren asked Martin to speculate as to why, in some places, there
were specific booths as opposed to just banks of phones. In the end, Burton
Marks himself had the final minutes for rebuttal—and he closed on the
question of the phone booth glass.

"I submit that if the Court wants to make a test, go and sit in some phone booth, the one at the Sunset Boulevard, it's the ordinary type with a little glass door," Marks said.

"Just sit in it and listen next door and see if you can hear a person and determine what he is saying in an ordinary conversational voice. I submit that you cannot so hear and that there was intended to be privacy and this right of privacy of the individual should be respected."

The case was submitted. As the justices went into conference, it wasn't necessarily obvious to Schneider and Marks how it was going to turn out. Justice Fortas, for example, who was a secret advisor to President Lyndon Johnson, thought that there shouldn't be any restraining of the government's power when it came to national security.

"[Fortas] didn't draw any distinction between informers who were wired for sound and electronic devices that were planted in someone's property," Laurence Tribe told me in an interview. Tribe, now a well-known Harvard Law professor, had been a clerk for Justice Potter Stewart at the time. "He thought that if you don't physically invade something it shouldn't require a warrant and it was not because of his analytical view of the Fourth Amendment—it was his practical sense of law enforcement."

At first blush, without Justice Marshall participating, the case seemed likely to split 4–4, which would have meant that the 9th US Circuit ruling—against Katz—would have stood. The *Olmstead* standard, based on physical trespass, would essentially remain intact. Justice Douglas was perturbed by the fact that such warrantless eavesdropping was essentially like a general warrant—it lacked specificity. Chief Justice Warren, by contrast, having served as a local prosecutor and also as California's attorney general, was mindful of the needs of law enforcement and the necessity for tools like this.

In Tribe's telling, the mood was indeed rather tense. Justice Stewart, a centrist Republican jurist, was prepared to affirm the 9th Circuit's ruling. The court was simply not prepared to overturn the *Olmstead* and *Goldman* precedents.

At the age of 26, Tribe was one of the younger clerks. He had just started that fall, fresh off of another clerkship at the California Supreme Court, which he'd taken on immediately after completing Harvard Law School.

Tribe hadn't attended oral arguments during *Katz*, but he was familiar with the crux of both sides' arguments. He had read their filings, the transcript of the oral arguments, and studied the case law. His job was to help Justice Stewart formulate and draft his opinion, which would be circulated amongst the other justices for review.

During the period of "conference" where the justices discuss privately how they might rule, Tribe approached Justice Stewart. The young lawyer wanted to change his boss's mind. But by that point, Justice Stewart had been on the court for nearly a decade and was set in his ways. Plus, it was Justice Stewart who had famously dissented in 1965 in *Griswold v. Connecticut*, where he wrote that he did not believe that the Bill of Rights, nor the Constitution, nor "any case ever before decided by this Court" afforded a "general right of privacy." Still, Tribe was undeterred.

"I had a little bit more spunk at the time than I did in years since," Tribe recalled. "Even though I was wet behind the ears, I had the tenacity or the chutzpah to say: 'Mr. Justice, it would be terrible if the case were affirmed by an equally divided court—the law is in a chaotic condition.'"

But Stewart wouldn't have it.

"I don't need a lecture from one of my law clerks on this," he said. Stewart and the other justices had made up their minds. The case was about to split, along predictable lines. "This case is going to be decided on Monday, without opinion. Get over it."

Tribe was undeterred. He stayed late one night and prepared a draft opinion. Stewart was incensed, and almost threatened to fire the young lawyer.

"Larry, you're new here," Stewart told him. "The Dragon Lady has made her decision."

"Dragon Lady" was the nickname the justices had given Margaret McHugh, Earl Warren's secretary. What Stewart meant was that she had already officially recorded the justices' votes. The circuit court's ruling on *Katz* was going to be upheld.

"This is a great opportunity to overrule *Olmstead* and rip the Fourth Amendment from its no longer plausible moorings in ancient property concepts," Tribe recalled feeling. "And so I said 'Would you give me a chance over the weekend to see if I can come up with a draft of something that could persuade people on both sides?'"

"Don't make a nuisance of yourself," Stewart retorted. Still, he gave Tribe until Monday. If this new opinion didn't impress Stewart, then the original plan—a 4–4 split—would stand.

On Monday, Stewart read Tribe's draft. After a few beats, he told Tribe: "Let me think about this. Actually, it's conceivable."

As Tribe explained years later, his "idea had to do with actually recognizing that something is a search when [there are] justifiable intrusions of privacy needn't mean that it would automatically be impermissible. It was a blueprint for the kinds of electronic surveillance warrants that would be required. We [didn't] have to decide [then] where there might be exceptions for national security concerns. It was designed to deal with the concerns of White, Fortas, and maybe Douglas."

This argument largely tracked with Schneider's arguments, but was designed to appease the concerns of the conservative wing of the court.

A few days later, Tribe got his own memo from Stewart: "Larry, the indication is AF [Abe Fortas] will join our Katz opinion, excepting only with reservations as to how we say that there is no constitutional right of privacy." This note currently hangs in Tribe's office at Harvard Law School.

Even Chief Justice Warren wrote in a one-sentence memo to Stewart: "I am happy to join your opinion, and I believe that it will be a milestone decision."

What Tribe presented was largely what ended up being the majority opinion in *Katz*.

"For the Fourth Amendment protects people, not places," the 7–1 opinion from December 18, 1967, states, echoing some of the language that Schneider had laid out. "What a person knowingly exposes to the public, even in his own home or office, is not a subject of Fourth Amendment protection. But what he seeks to preserve as private, even in an area accessible to the public, may be constitutionally protected."

Justice Harlan, in a concurrence, outlined a specific two-part test:

> My understanding of the rule that has emerged from prior decisions is that there is a twofold requirement, first that a person have exhibited an actual (subjective) expectation of privacy and, second, that the expectation be one that society is prepared to recognize as "reasonable." Thus, a man's home is, for most purposes, a place where he expects privacy, but objects, activities, or statements that he exposes to the "plain view" of outsiders are not "protected," because no intention to keep them to himself has been exhibited.

Indeed, since then, the question has been, What does it mean for society to recognize something as reasonable? Some legal scholars have even tried to conduct empirical research, using surveys, to better understand where ordinary people feel the limits are, or at least, ought to be. For now, such scholarship is largely limited to the academic realm, and has not yet made a substantive impact on what many courts, much less the Supreme Court, considers to be reasonable.

Katz' impact was immediately felt on both a local and national level: the LAPD quickly issued a notice to all personnel clarifying what officers could and could not do with respect to physical surveillance.

At a federal level, however, during the Johnson administration, months before *Katz* had been considered at the Supreme Court, Attorney General Nicholas Katzenbach spearheaded a commission to examine the state of criminal justice in America. In February 1967, the body produced a voluminous report: "The Challenge of Crime in a Free Society," which noted that the patchwork of laws pertaining to wiretapping and "electronic eavesdropping . . . is so thoroughly confused that no policeman, except in States that forbid both practices totally, can be sure about what he is allowed to do."

Congress largely incorporated much of the commission's recommendations, and passed the Omnibus Crime Control and Safe Streets Act of 1968. The law also included a provision, known as Title III, that would formally allow real-time wiretaps to exist, but only as part of a super-warrant, whereby, not only does a law enforcement agent have to establish probable cause of a crime, but the request must come from senior department officials, rather than any federal prosecutor. Further, the federal judge must also determine that any other investigative technique has failed, would fail, or would be too dangerous to undertake. Today, this law is a crucial foundation for most modern surveillance of suspected criminals.

But even at the time, Title III was not without its critics. While President Johnson signed the Safe Streets Act into law in June 1968, he specifically called out his unhappiness with that part of the bill:

> *If we are not very careful and cautious in our planning, these legislative provisions could result in producing a nation of snoopers bending through the keyholes of the homes and offices in America, spying on our neighbors. No conversation in the sanctity of the bedroom or relayed over a copper telephone wire would be free of eavesdropping by those who say they want to ferret out crime.*
>
> *Thus, I believe this action goes far beyond the effective and legitimate needs of law enforcement. The right of privacy is a valued right. But in a technologically advanced society, it is a vulnerable right. That is why we must strive to protect it all the more against erosion.*

Since *Katz*, the notion of a "reasonable expectation of privacy" is one that regularly comes up in court cases at all levels. But as Justice Harlan noted, the crucial question of whether that expectation is one that society is prepared to accept as reasonable remains open.

There are some more recent cases that have obvious outcomes. For example, does one have a reasonable expectation of privacy in the trash you leave curbside to be picked up? No, the Supreme Court ruled in 1988. Taken one step further, does a person have a reasonable expectation of privacy in documents that have been shredded and thrown out? No, the 1st Circuit US Court of Appeals concluded in 1992. Does a criminal have a reasonable expectation of privacy in a computer that was obtained fraudulently? No, the 9th Circuit US Court of Appeals decided in 2005. Does a burglar who abandons his cell phone at the scene of a crime have a reasonable expectation of privacy in the phone? No, a Sacramento federal judge ruled in 2016.

More recently, a federal judge in Seattle ruled in 2016 that users of the online anonymity tool Tor do not have a "reasonable expectation of privacy in their IP [Internet Protocol] addresses while using the Tor network." Therefore, a man who the government believed was running an online drug website (Silk Road 2.0) and obscuring his online tracks by using Tor was not searched when the government in effect hacked his Tor Browser to locate him.

Katz, in short, has become the bedrock of modern surveillance jurisprudence. It has benefited all of us by expanding our rights against some forms of warrantless government intrusion beyond the four walls of our homes. Thanks to Title III, the government must now clear extraordinary hurdles if it wants to listen in on our voice calls. But of course, in the early twenty-first century, investigators have many more tools at their disposal beyond mere wiretaps. The promise of *Katz*, and of the intent of Harlan's concurrence, has somewhat been lost in the intervening decades. Is it reasonable to accept video cameras everywhere? What about drones? What about mandatory DNA collection? Is it reasonable for individuals to carry digital devices that are difficult for the government to access?

After all, there's not always an obvious, immutable, bedrock expectation of privacy. That's a lesson well understood even today by Harlan's law clerk Louis Cohen, who wrote the first draft of Harlan's *Katz* opinion and is now an established Washington, DC–based lawyer.

"The rule that we are creating is not solely governed by the preexisting expectations of privacy, they are also determinative of what expectations are reasonable," Cohen said. "By writing rules about who can make what use of data, we are determining society's expectation. So that the next time there is a constitutional case and the question is: is this something that society is prepared to accept as reasonable? Well, maybe society has been influenced by developments on the ground."

CHAPTER TWO

How the Government Cracked an
iPhone—Without Apple's Help

From the beginning of our Nation's history, we have sought to prevent the accretion of arbitrary police powers in the federal courts; that accretion is no less dangerous and unprecedented because the first step appears to be only minimally intrusive.

—JUSTICE JOHN PAUL STEVENS DISSENT
UNITED STATES V. NEW YORK TELEPHONE CO. (1977)

February 13, 2016
Los Angeles, California

It was something of a chilly Saturday in Southern California, high 50s with a slight haze lingering over the western side of the city, just a few miles inland from the beach. Ted Boutrous was relaxing at his stately home in the hills of West Los Angeles, perched high above the constantly packed 405 freeway, when his phone buzzed.

He was expecting a call from Noreen Krall, one of Apple's top lawyers. She wanted to speak with him about a "potentially significant matter that would be on a fast track," but she didn't explain precisely what it was about.

When Krall called, she was all business.

"I need to talk to you about something," she said urgently.

Apple had a new problem, and it was with the federal government. Apple had complied with government access before—handing over data when presented with a court order. Apple could even extract data held on phones, and quietly did so for years. But in the wake of National Security Agency (NSA) whistleblower Edward Snowden in 2013, Apple reengineered its software (starting with iOS 8), making it impossible for even it to access data held locally on an iPhone. After a horrific and tragic terrorist attack, the government wanted Apple to break its own security to help the government.

The whole debacle turned on two seemingly distant pieces of law: the 1789 All Writs Act, and the more recent but no less outdated 1977 case known as *United States v. New York Telephone*. And they all centered on one big question: How far can strong encryption go?

Krall joined Apple in March 2010 as a new set of attorneys led the charge in what then CEO Steve Jobs dubbed the company's "thermonuclear war" (better known as patent lawsuits) against Google's Android smartphone and Android manufacturers, most notably Samsung. The lawyer who started her career as an electrical engineer and had been hired away from Sun Microsystems was now one of the top legal arrows in Apple's quiver.

Krall and Boutrous, both top-flight lawyers, had worked together previously on Apple's e-books case, where prosecutors had come after the company, alleging collusion with publishers over e-book pricing. Boutrous had gotten to know both Krall and her boss, Bruce Sewell, Apple's general counsel. (Weeks later, the Supreme Court would decline to hear the e-books case, which meant that the settlement that had been approved by a lower court would stand, and Apple was on the hook for a $450 million settlement.) Boutrous also had a reputation as a constitutional lawyer, and so Apple thought he could help again.

Krall explained that Apple was trying to talk the government—specifically US Attorney Eileen Decker—out of going ahead with an aggressive legal strategy. Decker had given Krall a helpful, but ominous, piece of information. Oftentimes, as a courtesy before pursuing a lawsuit or any other kind of legal action, one lawyer will let another know what's coming. This frequently takes the form of a demand letter, where one party wants another to do something, and if they don't, a lawsuit or other legal action will be filed. But the fact that this was coming from the federal government, and not another white-collar attorney, was unusual, and much more serious.

Yet this wasn't exactly a lawsuit. Instead, federal prosecutors planned to compel Apple to assist in an ongoing terrorism investigation. Specifically, US Attorney Decker planned to go to a magistrate—the lowest-ranked federal judge—and ask her to sign off on a court order. This order would force Apple to help the FBI in their investigation of Syed Rizwan Farook, one of two terrorists who died during the December 2015 shooting in San Bernardino, California.

As part of the investigation, authorities recovered an iPhone 5c that was used by Farook. The phone technically belonged to the San Bernardino County Department of Public Health, where Farook worked. It wasn't even his personal phone. And yet the information on it could potentially help with the government's ongoing investigation into an act of terrorism.

However, there was just one problem with this phone. It was passcode-protected.

This problem couldn't be solved by a visit to the Genius Bar of an Apple Store. Instead, what the government prosecutors wanted was to force Apple to reengineer its software so that the FBI could try an unlimited number of passcodes on the phone until it opened. As it stood, they were concerned that the phone might erase itself after ten wrong tries. But if Apple reprogrammed the phone to eliminate the passcode-entry limit, it would only be a matter of time before the FBI could brute force its way in.

Perhaps the FBI expected Apple to go along quietly, especially because of the ongoing investigation into a terrorist attack. But, as Krall warned Boutrous, if the court order comes, "Apple is going to have to fight it."

Boutrous immediately went into battle mode, calling, texting, and e-mailing colleagues at his own law firm, and other legal allies that he would need. He began reading up on the relevant case law, and tried to anticipate what the government would argue in its filings. By Monday morning, Boutrous and his colleagues had set up a call with Assistant US Attorney Tracy Wilkinson—to whom Krall had reached out earlier, hoping for a courtesy conversation through back channels—for Tuesday afternoon.

But with no advance notice, the government filed its opening salvo on Tuesday morning. Rather than a few warning shots, the Department of Justice (DOJ) went in with its heavy artillery. In a 40-page court filing faxed to Apple and later e-mailed to Boutrous, the government claimed as its legal authority the All Writs Act, a semi-obscure law dating back to the late eighteenth century. The last time the All Writs Act had come before the Supreme Court was in 1977, in a case known as *United States v. New York Telephone Co.*

On that Tuesday, February 16, 2016, DOJ prosecutors wrote in their filing with a federal court in Riverside, California (the nearest federal court to San Bernardino, the site of the terrorist attack):

> *In* New York Telephone Co., *the Supreme Court considered three factors in concluding that the issuance of the All Writs Act order to the phone company was appropriate. First, it found that the phone company was not "so far removed from the underlying controversy that its assistance could not be permissibly compelled." Id; at 174. Second, it concluded that the order did not place an undue burden on the phone com-*

pany. See id. at 175. Third, it determined that the assistance of the company was necessary to achieve the purpose of the warrant. see id; Each of these factors supports issuance of the order directed to Apple in this case.

US Magistrate Judge Sheri Pym signed off on it promptly, at 11:00 AM PT.

Boutrous had dealt with the All Writs Act before, but not like this. As far as he knew, this little law was mostly used for courts to obtain procedural results—transporting a prisoner from one place to another, for example—but not to order a company to provide sophisticated technical assistance beyond what it would normally do during its course of business.

"It was extraordinary and unheard of, the kind of order they had obtained," he told me, calling the order "offensive" to Apple.

"We never said the company couldn't do it and didn't have the ability or the resources to do it, that wasn't the hardship. It was the threats that it would cause and it was an anathema to the company and the consumers."

Wilkinson and her DOJ colleagues were cordial, but aggressive. They indicated that they were going to come back to the judge days later and file a motion to compel—yet another court order to enforce the first one.

"We indicated that we thought that made no sense," Boutrous said. "We did think that motion to compel was a publicity stunt." Despite the fact that the government ultimately didn't proceed (more on that shortly), Boutrous notes that "it will be interesting to see if the federal government tries again for this kind of radical order."

> *The key is: Will they try it again? Will they seek such an extraordinary order? I remain convinced that this legal theory under All Writs Act and* New York Telephone, *it's just not going to work. The leap from* New York Telephone *to the arguments that were being made in the Apple case are so gargantuan, it seems highly unlikely that the courts would ever accept that argument.*

While the court battle was ultimately called off, the legal theory sits like a Chekhovian gun, waiting to go off. There's a good chance that the government could try again to push its luck in court as a way to defeat encryption that it can't bust through on its own. In fact, prosecutors may have already done so, under seal, partially as a way to avoid public scrutiny.

◎

Ted Boutrous is a powerhouse attorney with Gibson Dunn, a major corporate law firm. He has a plum corner office on the fifty-fourth floor of 333 South Grand Avenue in downtown Los Angeles, along the northeastern corner of the building. If he spins around in his desk chair he directly overlooks Frank Gehry's Walt Disney Concert Hall, the brushed metal home of the Los Angeles Philharmonic.

Although he was born in Los Angeles, the silver-haired Boutrous was raised in Bismarck, North Dakota, his mother's hometown. As he grew up he decided he wanted to abandon the frozen plains for blistering deserts. That meant transferring out of college in North Dakota and into Arizona State University. He didn't initially set out to be a lawyer, despite the fact that his father was a lawyer. He signed up to take the LSAT, the national law school exam, on the last day of late registration. At first, he attended Colorado State University for law school, but later transferred to the University of San Diego. According to a 2007 profile of him in the *Los Angeles Times*, Boutrous "graduated No. 1 in his class and was editor in chief of the *San Diego Law Review*."

He decided that constitutional law was the route for him: that way, he could be involved in politics. As an undergraduate, he had majored in political science.

"Being able to have both a job that pays money but also lets you participate in these broader issues in society, that's what hooked me," he told an interviewer in March 2017.

After graduating, Boutrous decided not to clerk for a judge, and instead jumped right into corporate law. This was a highly unusual step. Most ambitious law students will go clerk for a judge for a time before entering the workforce, both as a way to gain experience from a judge's perspective, and also to make professional connections.

"I didn't want to clerk because I had taken a couple of extra years to get through law school," Boutrous said.

After graduation and being admitted to the bar in December 1987, he landed an interview with Gibson Dunn, a well-known Los Angeles–based law firm with a notable presence in Washington, DC. This was practically a dream come true. Noted conservative attorney Ted Olson interviewed Boutrous for the job at Gibson Dunn. (Olson is perhaps best-known in recent years for being one of the top attorneys who successfully argued in 2013 before the Supreme Court in favor of same-sex marriage.) The two men could not have differed more, politically speaking. The elder is a lifelong conservative, and the younger a liberal Democrat. But they bonded over their mutual love for the law.

When Boutrous arrived at Gibson Dunn in Washington, DC, one of his first assignments was to work with Olson, who then served as outside counsel to President Reagan during the Iran-Contra hearings. A few years later, Boutrous really began his career as a constitutional, corporate, and media lawyer. As a young lawyer, he represented *Newsday* and its reporter Tim Phelps in defending and quashing a subpoena from the US Senate over leaks regarding prospective associate justice Clarence Thomas and Anita Hill. In fact, a number of his early cases involved media outlets.

By the mid-1990s, Boutrous was invited to help expand Gibson Dunn's appellate practice in Los Angeles, and he jumped at the opportunity. Later, he represented other media outlets in their efforts to get documents unsealed as part of the Bill Clinton and Monica Lewinsky scandal. Boutrous reprised his efforts in 2004 as part of the Michael Jackson trial.

Boutrous is probably most famous for representing Wal-Mart in its stunning reversal of an employment class action, *Wal-Mart Stores, Inc. v. Dukes* (2011). In that case, a Wal-Mart employee, Betty Dukes, alleged gender discrimination despite positive performance reviews over several years. She sued Wal-Mart in a proposed class action that would have involved 1.6 million women who worked or have worked for the retail giant. Dukes won at the 9th US Circuit Court of Appeals, a decision that was overturned at the Supreme Court in a 5–4 decision—the highest court found that her case should not be certified as a class, but disagreed as to the legal rationale.

More recently, Boutrous is representing Uber in its ongoing labor dispute with its drivers. The case, known as *O'Connor v. Uber*, represents a major landmark in a rising tide of legal decisions and ongoing litigation in the so-called sharing economy. The four drivers, who now represent a class (like the *Dukes* case) are seeking to push Uber to recognize the service's workers as employees rather than contractors.

This case, along with dozens of similar ongoing lawsuits filed against Uber and other tech firms, seeks to answer a simple question: Are the workers (here, the Uber drivers) adequately labeled contractors or should they be properly classified as employees? If they should be employees, then Uber and the other corporations would be on the hook for unemployment benefits, workers' compensation, and reimbursement for mileage and other expenses. In short, it would cost Uber tens of millions, or hundreds of millions, if not more.

◯

Within hours of the judge's order on February 16, 2016—even before Apple was given a chance to respond in a court of law—the US Attorney's Office in Los Angeles released a statement to the court of public opinion.

"We have made a solemn commitment to the victims and their families that we will leave no stone unturned as we gather as much information and evidence as possible," Eileen Decker, the US attorney, wrote. "These victims and families deserve nothing less. The application filed today in federal court is another step—a potentially important step—in the process of learning everything we possibly can about the attack in San Bernardino."

On Twitter, Decker's office didn't put out anything in particular on the San Bernardino case (not even their own public statement), but they did retweet a local *NBC News* story: "Judge Forces Apple to Help Unlock San Bernardino Shooter iPhone."

In short, Boutrous and Apple were caught almost flat-footed. They knew that the government would probably go to a judge and try to get the order, but they didn't realize it would come this fast. Krall, Boutrous, and what had swelled to a team of over a dozen lawyers got on the phone again to plot their next move.

The case was starting to pick up steam in the press—in some ways, it was a legal case that everyone could understand. After all, most people have an opinion about terrorism and what the government should do about it. Moreover, 77 percent of Americans now own a smartphone. Most people feel their privacy being invaded more viscerally when the government wants access to a device that is within arm's reach at all times.

When the NSA's Section 215 metadata program was revealed by Edward Snowden there was some pushback in the press and popular culture (and some modest legislative reform), but to a lot of people the country's spookiest spy agency felt very far away. Section 215, which ran from 2001 until 2015, captured the incoming and outgoing calls of everyone in the United States. The government was not listening in to the calls, but rather was capturing the dates, times, durations, and phone numbers used—in other words, just the non-content metadata. (The program ended in 2015, but continues in a modified form where the government no longer holds this metadata directly, but rather is able to access it from private companies under court order.)

Still, for many people, metadata is a hard concept to grasp—its potential for revealing private information isn't immediately obvious. But the idea of the government being able to bust into a seized phone, and demand that a smartphone maker help, is concerning.

There was a two-prong strategy that needed to unfold, a legal one and a public one. Boutrous, Krall, and the other attorneys quickly got on the phone with the judge and a lawyer from the US Attorney's Office to figure out a briefing schedule, essentially an itinerary of what would come when. Unlike a usual civil case, which typically takes months to even have an initial hearing before a judge, the case was moving with unprecedented speed.

"They were taking this very aggressive position, and they viewed it as being in their interest in playing hardball and publicly and in their briefs and in the timing of their filings," Boutrous said.

When the clock struck midnight that evening in California, Apple CEO Tim Cook put out a lengthy public statement, saying that the company would resist what the government was demanding.

"We have great respect for the professionals at the FBI, and we believe their intentions are good. Up to this point, we have done everything that is both within our power and within the law to help them," he wrote. "But now the U.S. government has asked us for something we simply do not have, and something we consider too dangerous to create. They have asked us to build a backdoor to the iPhone."

The statement continued:

> *The implications of the government's demands are chilling. If the government can use the All Writs Act to make it easier to unlock your iPhone, it would have the power to reach into anyone's device to capture their data. The government could extend this breach of privacy and demand that Apple build surveillance software to intercept your messages, access your health records or financial data, track your location, or even access your phone's microphone or camera without your knowledge.*

Opposing this order is not something we take lightly. We feel we must speak up in the face of what we see as an overreach by the U.S. government.

We are challenging the FBI's demands with the deepest respect for American democracy and a love of our country. We believe it would be in the best interest of everyone to step back and consider the implications.

While we believe the FBI's intentions are good, it would be wrong for the government to force us to build a backdoor into our products. And ultimately, we fear that this demand would undermine the very freedoms and liberty our government is meant to protect.

Seventy-two hours later, the government made good on its promise to force Apple into court, and filed its motion to compel. Among other rebuttals, the government hit back against one of Apple's clearest arguments: that what the government was asking was unprecedented.

"The use of the All Writs Act to facilitate a warrant is therefore not unprecedented; Apple itself has recognized it for years," they wrote. However, this was a rather narrow reading of what Apple was claiming. It wasn't that use of the All Writs Act was new, but rather, claiming that law as the authority to force Apple to write entirely new software that it had never written before.

The judge allowed Apple an extension to file its reply on February 26. The government was then given a deadline of March 10 to reply, with oral arguments scheduled before Judge Pym in Riverside on March 22. The pace was extraordinarily fast.

◇

Antecedents of the All Writs Act date back to English common law, and before that, to Roman law. In essence, the concept is to empower judges to order that something be done, even if the legislative body (here, Congress) hasn't officially said that it should be so.

The entire text of the law, in its current incarnation, is rather short: "(a) The Supreme Court and all courts established by Act of Congress may issue all writs necessary or appropriate in aid of their respective jurisdictions and agreeable to the usages and principles of law. (b) An alternative writ or rule nisi may be issued by a justice or judge of a court which has jurisdiction."

The two-sentence law seems reasonable enough on its face. "AWA [All Writs Act] injunctions are rarely issued and are subject to judicial discretion," wrote Dimitri Portnoi, now a Los Angeles lawyer, back when he was a law student in 2007. In 1995, it was used to compel a handwriting sample. In 2005, it was invoked as an authority to halt frivolous litigation. In 2012, it was used by a federal judge in Colorado to order a woman accused of bank fraud to decrypt her laptop.

But, as lawyers note, the All Writs Act does not bestow upon the government power it would not otherwise have. Absent a law telling the government otherwise, investigators have and will continue to push the limits and test how far they can go.

As Jonathan Mayer, then a legal fellow at Stanford Law School (he now works for Senator Kamala Harris [D-California]), who holds both a doctorate in computer science and a law degree, said in an online video in November 2014: "With a warrant and writ, could the government require . . . pushing a backdoored software update to enable government access to a device? Or could the government require disclosing a vendor's private key, so the government can push its own update? What about decrypting data held on a smartphone? The answer is maybe."

The most prominent and recent Supreme Court precedent on the All Writs Act is *New York Telephone*, which was argued on October 3, 1977. The case involved the use of "pen registers," mechanical monitoring devices used at the telephone company's facility that records outgoing calls. Decades ago, companies routinely used them to monitor call quality and maintain proper billing records. Although the 1970s-era telecommunications system bears little resemblance to our early twenty-first-century all-digital system, the case law has remained valid.

In March 1976, US District Judge Charles Tenney of the Southern District of New York ordered that the local telephone company (New York Telephone) help the FBI in an investigation of a local gambling ring.

New York Telephone was required to provide "technical assistance necessary" in the form of a pen register. Specifically, the government needed to know what two numbers were called from 220 East 14th Street in Manhattan. The phone company challenged, lost, and then appealed to the 2nd US Circuit Court of Appeals, which ruled in its favor. The government appealed further, to the Supreme Court. Supporting the government in a 6–3 decision, the justices found that Title III—the provision of the landmark 1968 Safe Streets Act that codified some of the privacy gains of the *Katz* decision discussed in the last chapter—does not govern the use of pen registers; what the law bans is narrowly defined "interception," and pen registers do not "'intercept' because they do not acquire the 'contents' of communications." This distinction sounds confusing, but translates neatly—if regrettably—into our own time.

What happened is that the Supreme Court affirmed one standard for "content" and another for "non-content." Content, such as a wiretap, requires a warrant, if not more. Non-content, such as dialing information—today, we call this metadata—doesn't require a showing of probable cause. In other words, pen registers are allowed with fewer restrictions than a warrant would require.

"These devices do not hear sound," Justice Byron White wrote in the majority opinion. "They disclose only the telephone numbers that have been dialed—a means of establishing communication. Neither the purport of any communication between the caller and the recipient of the call, their identities, nor whether the call was even completed is disclosed by pen registers."

However, he noted: "We agree that the power of federal courts to impose duties upon third parties is not without limits; unreasonable burdens may not be imposed. We conclude, however, that the order issued here against respondent was clearly authorized by the All Writs Act and was consistent with the intent of Congress." (The Pen Register Act of 1986, however, eliminated the government's need to use the All Writs Act to deploy the mechanical device.)

However, the liberal wing of the court, led by Justice John Paul Stevens, disagreed. In his dissent, he noted that Congress had granted no such power regarding pen registers.

"The Court's decision may be motivated by a belief that Congress would, if the question were presented to it, authorize both the pen register order and the order directed to the Telephone Company," he wrote. "But the history and consistent interpretation of the federal court's power to issue search warrants conclusively show that, in these areas, the Court's rush to achieve a logical result must await congressional deliberation. From the beginning of our Nation's history, we have sought to prevent the accretion of arbitrary police powers in the federal courts; that accretion is no less dangerous and unprecedented because the first step appears to be only minimally intrusive."

The majority outlined a three-part test, which incorporated the company's "remove" (e.g., distance) from the case, whether the government's request imposed an "undue burden," and whether the assistance was, indeed, "necessary."

In the 2016 San Bernardino case, Los Angeles federal prosecutors, led by Decker, argued that Apple was not removed, as it sold the iPhone and wrote the software contained on it. Building an entirely new firmware was not overly burdensome, as this was something that Apple normally did (create software) as part of its normal business operations. And finally, Decker underscored, Apple's assistance is entirely necessary.

> *In this case, the ability to perform the search ordered by the user warrant on the SUBJECT DEVICE is of particular importance. The user of the phone, Farook, is believed to have caused the mass murder of a large number of his coworkers and the shooting of many others, and to have built bombs and hoarded weapons for this purpose.*

But this case was far different from *New York Telephone*, as Apple had already sold the phone and could not control how it was used. And yes, while it was true that Apple did employ legions of software developers, creating new software for the purpose of defeating the iPhone's security was not something that was normally part of their job. Finally, was it really Apple's job to be conscripted to work on the government's behalf, even if they were going to compensate them at market rates?

◯

This entire question of modern cryptography—and who has (or should have) access to such encryption—turns out to be decades old. In the 1970s and 1980s, military and academic researchers in the United Kingdom and the United States worked on how to make digital encryption easier to use. Specifically, the Diffie-Hellman (D-H) key exchange (1976) made it significantly easier to keep data secret. Its crucial innovation was the entire notion of public key cryptography, the idea that data could be kept secret by using a shared secret, even one that is publicly available.

Prior to this innovation, two parties could only secure messages by having the encryption algorithm exchanged in advance. In other words, before you pass encrypted notes to a classmate, both people have to already know what the code is. (Or, to put it into high-stakes terms, the Nazi government distributed secret encoding paper lists that described how to use their Enigma encrypting machines, which for years confounded the Allies. This is known as the trusted courier model, where you entrust someone with delivering a physical key.) With public key cryptography, however, one element of the key (the public, as opposed to the private key) could by definition be made public, so there was no need to trust anyone. With this new type of key exchange, the floodgates were now open for a new form of digital security.

Others expounded upon this idea and developed it, most notably into the RSA algorithm, which put the D-H key exchange into practice, commercializing it in the late 1980s into a product called Mailsafe. This application, which quickly drew other competitors, made it possible to send secure messages quickly and easily. But with personal computers typically costing several thousand dollars, these tools were really only available to a relatively small portion of the population.

Around that same time, Phil Zimmerman, a programmer and anti-nuclear activist in his early thirties based in Boulder, Colorado, was inspired to create his own public key encryption program. The release of his program, dubbed Pretty Good Privacy (PGP), was accelerated in January 1991 when an anti-terrorism bill authored by Senator Joe Biden (D-Delaware) included language that required that the government be allowed "to obtain the plaintext contents of voice, data, and other communications when appropriately authorized by law."

By April 1991, when Zimmerman and other privacy activists first heard about the legislation, they kicked into high gear. Rather than wait for his work to be made illegal, Zimmerman took his just-finished PGP and gave a copy to Kelly Goen, a fellow crypto-enthusiast in the San Francisco Bay Area. Goen drove around the region and with his own laptop, an acoustic coupler (a device turning older telephones, including pay phones, into modems), and countless quarters, he managed to upload PGP onto various Usenet groups. In short, it was made freely available to anyone who wanted it.

Meanwhile, starting in 1989, and unbeknownst to Zimmerman, the NSA was busy working on its own way to counter a slow rise of ever-easier, ever-cheaper encryption. The idea was something known as key escrow.

Key escrow ran counter to public key cryptography. Here, the government would allow encrypted communications, but it would also hold the key. The concept was that the government would promise to only use that key when it had a judge's permission.

This notion ended up becoming what the NSA and the White House dubbed, on April 16, 1993, the Clipper chip.

As the White House wrote in a press release:

> The chip is an important step in addressing the problem of encryption's dual-edge sword: encryption helps to protect the privacy of individuals and industry, but it also can shield criminals and terrorists. We need the "Clipper Chip" and other approaches that can both provide law-abiding citizens with access to the encryption they need and prevent criminals from using it to hide their illegal activities.

Use of the Clipper chip would not be required of device makers, but rather would be voluntary—AT&T, for example, would agree to ship devices with the chip already built-in. If the government bought thousands of such devices, then it might help accelerate other companies to also make competitor devices with a standard built-in Clipper chip. Members of the Clinton White House regularly received briefings from people at the NSA, FBI, CIA, and DOJ, all weighing in on the question of digital privacy.

Many of them—notably FBI Assistant Director James Kallstrom—made largely the same point: unless the government has access, crimes will go unsolved, children will be kidnapped, awful dangers will continue, and people will die. (In 1995, Kallstrom, an "electronic eavesdropping expert," was named the head of the FBI's New York office, its single largest bureau. In 2016, after having left the Bureau, he became a very vocal supporter of presidential candidate Donald Trump.)

Over 1993 and 1994, privacy and legal activists began to mount a campaign in what was eventually dubbed the "Crypto Wars." On May 3, 1994, Whit Diffie—one of the two inventors of public key cryptography—testified before a Senate subcommittee against the Clipper chip system.

"From the viewpoint of a user, any key escrow system diminishes security," he said. "It puts potential for access to the user's communications in the hands of an escrow agent [whose] intentions, policies, security capabilities, and future cannot be entirely known."

Not a month later, a young AT&T researcher named Matthew Blaze discovered one of Clipper chip's critical flaws, which would enable someone to circumvent the surveillance aspect—essentially defeating the entire purpose of Clipper chip. By the summer, the White House had realized that it had lost the battle.

But at the same time the Clipper chip was gaining traction, the FBI began floating a new bill that, if enacted, would extend the 1968 wiretap law to newer digital phone lines. And in the end, the FBI's efforts were more successful. In 1994, President Bill Clinton signed the Communications Assistance for Law Enforcement Act (CALEA), which mandated that phone companies build into their increasingly digital (rather than analog) telephone networks a method for police to conduct a wiretap. The law primarily targeted phone companies, and not Internet providers (although that changed in 2003). Crucially, the law does not require that a telecommunications carrier decrypt a transmission unless the company itself initiated the encryption.

In late June 1996, when Clipper chip was in its death throes, Zimmerman—the inventor and activist behind PGP encryption—testified before another Senate subcommittee.

> Advances in technology will not permit the maintenance of the status quo, as far as privacy is concerned. The status quo is unstable. If we do nothing, new technologies will give the government new automatic surveillance capabilities that Stalin could never have dreamed of. The only way to hold the line on privacy in the information age is strong cryptography. Cryptography strong enough to keep out major governments.
>
> The government has a track record that does not inspire confidence that they will never abuse our civil liberties. The FBI's COINTELPRO program targeted groups that opposed government policies. They spied on the anti-war movement and the civil rights movement. They wiretapped Martin Luther King's phone. Nixon had his enemies list. And then there was the Watergate mess.
>
> And now Congress and the Clinton administration seem intent on passing laws curtailing our civil liberties on the Internet. At no time in the past century has public distrust of the government been so broadly distributed across the political spectrum, as it is today.

In the wake of *New York Telephone* and the 1990s-era expansion of government surveillance under CALEA (and the failed Clipper chip), there were inklings that the government wanted to use ever-expanding digital technologies to their own advantage.

In 2000, the public caught wind of an FBI capability known as Carnivore—a custom-built packet sniffer designed to go after the "meat" of a surveillance target. The application allowed federal agents to essentially sit on the wire between the suspect and his or her Internet Service Provider, snapping up nearly all of his or her unencrypted traffic, which could include everything from e-mails to chats to online shopping.

The FBI official overseeing this effort was Marcus Thomas, the chief of the Cyber Technology Section.

"This is an effort on the FBI's part to keep pace with changes in technology—to maintain our ability," he told the *Washington Post* in July 2000. "It's not an increase in our authority; it doesn't present a change of volume in what we do."

Years later, Thomas, who now works for a company called Subsentio, said that during his time at the Bureau, agents typically had neither the time nor the background legal knowledge to evaluate the precise legality of particular tools that they were given.

"Everything is digging very deeply into crimes, identifying conspiracies, understanding criminal organizations," he told me.

> *They're not really as concerned about how they go about it. They just don't sit around and think about how to take a new technique and how to apply it. We're really, really focused on that. When they need it, they call upon it and they don't think about how much time was spent. They're not paid to decide whether it works or not or whether it's legal or not. Then the lawyers step in. They decide how do we justify how we use it.*

One notable and creative technical and legal feat came in November 2001, when federal authorities in Nevada obtained a court order against ATX, a company that provides an in-car communication system in certain Mercedes-Benz models. (In 2017, a *Forbes* reporter dubbed this "cartapping.") ATX had to remotely activate its Tele Aid system (similar to OnStar) in a customer's car for a period of seven days. It complied. Then, the government went back to the judge and asked for a similar order (not a warrant), but this time for a period of 30 days. The company attempted to go to court to get the order quashed, but the judge denied it. Then, on January 10, 2002, ATX was served with a third order, again for 30 days, which it challenged in federal court.

In its court filing, the company argued that this went far beyond what was authorized under the Title III wiretap act, and its more modern update, the Electronic Communications Privacy Act of 1986. Among other concerns, ATX's lawyers cited *New York Telephone* as a reason why the government should not be allowed to go forward. Their response would lay the groundwork for Apple's own defense just a few years later.

"In order to comply with the Court's order, ATX must fundamentally restructure its business and change the manner in which it conducts business," Bennee Jones, ATX's lawyer wrote. "Courts do not have unfettered discretion to order assistance of private companies."

Eventually, the order was appealed up to the 9th US Circuit Court of Appeals in San Francisco. In a 2–1 decision, the court ruled in favor of ATX. However, the court found that ATX was covered by the language of the statute, and that it may be required to assist the government's investigation. But that wasn't the end of the story.

"The question remains whether the order goes too far in interfering with the service provided by the Company, by preventing the Company from supplying the System's services to its customers when a vehicle is under surveillance," Circuit Judge Marsha Berzon wrote in the majority opinion in November 2003. "We conclude that it does."

In short, the 9th Circuit ruled in 2003 that because the government's order to cartap the Mercedes activated the Tele Aid system—which made it impossible for the owner to actually turn it on of their own volition, thus effectively disabling the emergency roadside service call ability that it was designed for—it went too far.

"The FBI, however well-intentioned, is not in the business of providing emergency road services, and might well have better things to do when listening in than respond with such services to the electronic signal sent over the line," Berzon continued. "The result was that the Company could no longer supply any of the various services it had promised its customer, including assurance of response in an emergency."

Over a decade later, in his March 15, 2016, brief, Ted Boutrous reprised ATX's arguments, and cited the 9th Circuit ruling. In essence, Apple made the "if you give a mouse a cookie" argument.

> *The government nevertheless contends that because this*
> *Court issued a valid search warrant, it can order innocent*

third parties to provide any service the government deems "necessary" or "appropriate" to accomplish the search. Opp. 5. But that "broad" and "flexible" theory of the All Writs Act has no limiting principle . . .

Indeed, it is telling that the government fails even to confront the hypotheticals posed to it (e.g., compelling a pharmaceutical company to manufacture lethal injection drugs, Dkt. 16 ("Mot.") at 26), or explain how there is any conceivable daylight between GovtOS today, and Location-TrackingOS and EavesdropOS tomorrow.

In other words, if Apple agreed to provide a bespoke solution for the government now, there's no reason to think that it wouldn't be required to do so again in the future. If Apple can be forced to open a locked iPhone today, maybe it could be compelled to turn the iPhone into a tracking device or a bugging device tomorrow.

◇

The All Writs Act cropped up again in a surveillance case when US Magistrate Judge James Orenstein ruled in favor of privacy interests on August 25, 2005. The core facts of the case (not to mention the result) remain under seal, more than 12 years later.

The government's legal argument was essentially that it could combine a pen register order and a d-order (the same at issue in *Carpenter v. United States*) for business records to get a phone company to provide the ongoing cell-site location information of a suspect.

But the judge denied the prosecutor's efforts. In that landmark August 25 decision, the judge ruled that he would not let the government "effectively allow the installation of a tracking device without the showing of probable cause normally required for a warrant." He is believed to be the first magistrate to reject the government's argument for such a request under this hybrid theory—that is, a hybrid of pen register order and d-order, the worst of both worlds from a privacy standpoint.

In other words, Judge Orenstein was not willing to let the government turn someone's phone—even a criminal suspect's—into something that could be used to track them without the authority of a warrant with supporting probable cause. It's worth noting that this judge, who was appointed to the federal bench in 2004, served as a federal prosecutor in New York for 11 years, from the tail end of the George H. W. Bush administration, through both terms of the Clinton administration, all the way to the beginning of the George W. Bush administration. In short, he is quite sensitive to the needs of law enforcement.

The government was not pleased with his ruling, and formally asked him to reconsider.

A week later, an outside group asked to present adversarial arguments. This was very unusual. Normally, in an *ex parte* (one-sided), the judge only hears from the government. The Electronic Frontier Foundation (EFF), a digital privacy advocacy group based in San Francisco, wrote to the judge to ask to enter the case as an *amicus curiae*, or friend of the court. This only occurs when other companies, groups, or individuals wish to make their thoughts known to the court, usually in a novel legal issue. He granted it, and the EFF wrote that what the government was asking for was a "statutory chimera."

The dispute largely turned on one particular phrase within CALEA (47 USC 1002).

> *A telecommunications carrier shall ensure that its equipment . . . are capable of . . . expeditiously isolating and enabling the government, pursuant to a court order or other lawful authorization, to access call-identifying information that is reasonably available to the carrier . . . in a manner that allows it to be associated with the communication to which it pertains, except that, with regard to information acquired solely pursuant to the authority for pen registers and trap and trace devices (as defined in section 3127 of title 18), such call-identifying information shall not include any information that may disclose the physical location of the subscriber (except to the extent that the location may be determined from the telephone number).*

The government interpreted the way this law was written to mean that the location information can be obtained via court order when combined with a pen/trap order. However, the EFF didn't see it that way at all. The organization felt that the government was going far beyond what Congress intended: it felt that "determined from the telephone number" meant literally the number, including the area code itself, and not the actual location of the phone.

On October 11, 2005, the government responded, largely reiterating its earlier arguments, and adding a notable new and final one, citing the All Writs Act. Responding in his October 25 opinion, Judge Orenstein was not convinced.

"Thus, as far as I can tell, the government proposes that I use the All Writs Act in an entirely unprecedented way," he wrote. "To appreciate just how unprecedented the argument is, it is necessary to recognize that the government need only run this Hail Mary play if its arguments under the electronic surveillance and disclosure statutes fail."

In 2006, the FBI created its Science and Technology Branch, a distinct division within the agency, with the goal of staying "on top of technical innovation." Among other things, that included regional computer forensics labs.

"In today's digital world, crime scenes have become much more complex," said Kerry E. Haynes, executive assistant director of the FBI's Science and Technology Branch, at the opening of one such lab in Buffalo, New York.

"Digital technology is often more important than physical evidence. Cell phones, [personal digital assistants], computers—each and every one of these devices has its own unique story and can be tainted and destroyed, but we can also extract their evidence."

In January 2007, the iPhone was released. The iPhone, more so than the Treos, Blackberries, and flip phones that came before, had incredible capabilities. It could browse the Web, play music, e-mail, and far more. But as consumer technology was getting better, law enforcement was upping its game, too.

In fact, the same month that the iPhone was released, Marcus Thomas was promoted and named the assistant director of the Operational Technology Division. By at least early 2008, within the halls of government and the FBI itself, Haynes and Thomas began expounding on what they termed Going Dark. Essentially, the FBI was concerned that if newer tools, ranging from Skype to Xbox Live calls, began offering encryption enabled by default, that there would be no way for law enforcement to access such data. In other words, the FBI and other federal law enforcement agencies feared that their ability to surveil suspects and gather data as part of routine investigations was becoming more and more difficult.

What worried Haynes and Thomas above all else was that "the ability of the FBI to collect intelligence and conduct investigations through the use of technology is shrinking every day," according to an April 2008 document not released until over two years later as part of a Freedom of Information Act lawsuit.

In 2009, the FBI asked Congress for $9 million for the Going Dark program as part of its fiscal year (FY) 2010 budget. (By FY 2017, the budget for this program had ballooned to over $38 million.) In 2010, the FBI started pushing more formally, along with other federal agencies, to get Congress to do something—essentially a CALEA for the Internet. That is, a new legal framework that would adjudicate FBI surveillance, while providing funds, training, and initiative for expanding their technology capacity.

"We're talking about lawfully authorized intercepts," Valerie E. Caproni, the FBI's top lawyer, told the *New York Times* in September 2010. "We're not talking expanding authority. We're talking about preserving our ability to execute our existing authority in order to protect the public safety and national security."

Caproni's language nearly exactly mirrored Thomas' language of "not an increase in our ability" from a decade earlier. There remains a very real tension between the difficult job that law enforcement is tasked with—solving crimes—and the technological reality that they face. Investigators are understandably put in a bind, but there doesn't seem to be a good way to balance the technological realities of easy-to-use strong encryption with the government's ability to break into it when needed.

Months later, in February 2011, Mark Marshall, the head of the International Association of Chiefs of Police, also warned a House committee of the potential danger.

"Many agencies that need to be able to conduct electronic surveillance of real time communications are on the verge of 'Going Dark' because they are increasingly unable to access, intercept, collect, and process wire or electronic communications information when they are lawfully authorized to do so," he said. "This serious intercept capability gap often undercuts state, local, and tribal law enforcement agencies' efforts to investigate criminal activity such as organized crime, drug-related offenses, child abduction, child exploitation, prison escape, and other threats to public safety."

For the most part, mainstream companies were not as concerned about countermanding a nebulous FBI effort that was slowly being discussed in Congress. Indeed, the June 2011 federal wiretap report noted dryly: "In 2010, encryption was reported during six state wiretaps, but did not prevent officials from obtaining the plain text of the communications."

Even Apple—a company that particularly since the 2016 San Bernardino case has really pushed for increased security—for years prior didn't take all of the security steps that it could have taken in the design of iOS.

"The lock screen is merely a screen saver lock, which as most people know doesn't equate to real security anyway," wrote Jonathan Zdziarski, an iOS security expert who now works for Apple, in April 2013.

> Under certain conditions, this is one technique law enforcement forensic engineers are able to perform to unlock a device they've seized, if all other forensic techniques fail. Apple is also capable of doing this, however to my knowledge they do not. Under a subpoena, Apple will, however, copy off the same readable contents of the file system if given a warrant.

Google did not offer full-disk encryption on its Android devices either.

However, everyone's notion of security changed overnight when Edward Snowden became a household name in June 2013. Snowden, a young contractor for the NSA, leaked a trove of classified documents to two American reporters, Glenn Greenwald and Laura Poitras. (Greenwald famously almost missed the Snowden story as he found setting up encrypted e-mail too difficult.) They reported on a seemingly endless amount of materials from Snowden's cache, describing in detail how the NSA was conducting its espionage and by what legal means. The net result was that all of a sudden journalists, activists, and even average citizens began taking these issues more seriously than ever before.

Within months, companies began hardening their services: Google, Yahoo, and Microsoft began stepping up their game.

"Recent press stories have reported allegations of governmental interception and collection—without search warrants or legal subpoenas—of customer data as it travels between customers and servers or between company data centers in our industry," wrote Brad Smith, Microsoft's top lawyer in December 2013. "If true, these efforts threaten to seriously undermine confidence in the security and privacy of online communications. Indeed, government snooping potentially now constitutes an 'advanced persistent threat,' alongside sophisticated malware and cyber attacks."

◎

It wasn't just companies that were taking notice and starting to think about privacy in a new way. A handful of federal magistrate judges started to push back against the government's efforts in digital surveillance cases. Judge Orenstein's ruling from 2005, where he found that the government was going too far with its interpretation of the All Writs Act, was one of the earliest instances of what came to be known, post-Snowden, as the "Magistrates' Revolt."

The term came from an April 2014 article in the *Washington Post*, which described the effort as having "gained power amid mounting public anger about government surveillance capabilities revealed by former NSA contractor Edward Snowden." Historically, most magistrates generally grant the government a lot of leeway when it comes to search warrant applications. But now at least a few judges in Texas, DC, and New York were starting to publicly push back against routine prosecutorial requests.

The article focused on one DC-based magistrate, Judge John Facciola. In one March 2014 case, Facciola wanted government investigators, as part of an investigation into the manufacture of ricin on the campus of Georgetown University, to specify "whether the target devices would be imaged in full, for how long those images will be kept, and what will happen to data that is seized but is ultimately determined not to be within the scope of the warrant—or, more precisely, Attachment B—can only be addressed by a search protocol; after all, the imaging actually occurs as part of the search process."

In short, this ruling demonstrated a level of technical fluency not commonly seen across most federal courts. This was a clear instance of at least one judge starting to really sit up and take notice of the implications of broad—and largely unchecked—government power.

Six months later—that is, only a year before the San Bernardino incident—

Apple joined the security party: its latest version of the iPhone and iPad's operating system, iOS 8, was designed in such a way that Apple could no longer get into a locked phone.

"On devices running iOS 8, your personal data such as photos, messages (including attachments), email, contacts, call history, iTunes content, notes, and reminders is placed under the protection of your passcode," the company wrote on its website.

"Unlike our competitors, Apple cannot bypass your passcode and therefore cannot access this data. So it's not technically feasible for us to respond to government warrants for the extraction of this data from devices in their possession running iOS 8."

That same day, in an open letter Apple CEO Tim Cook took a direct swipe at Google, its primary mobile competitor. "Our business model is very straightforward: We sell great products. We don't build a profile based on your email content or web browsing habits to sell to advertisers," he wrote. "We don't 'monetize' the information you store on your iPhone or in iCloud. And we don't read your email or your messages to get information to market to you. Our software and services are designed to make our devices better. Plain and simple."

Google followed suit the next day.

◌

In short, Snowden had the effect of making more individuals and companies care about privacy. Easy-to-use apps and strong encryption by default became a major roadblock in the government's efforts to deal with its Going Dark problem.

Government officials were not going to take this lying down. Within days of Apple's announcement, in September 2014, FBI Director James Comey told reporters that he was concerned that "companies [are] marketing something expressly to allow people to place themselves beyond the law."

The following month, Attorney General Eric Holder expressed similar concerns. "It is fully possible to permit law enforcement to do its job while still adequately protecting personal privacy," Holder said during an October 2014 speech before the Global Alliance Against Child Sexual Abuse Online conference. "When a child is in danger, law enforcement needs to be able to take every legally available step to quickly find and protect the child and to stop those that abuse children. It is worrisome to see companies thwarting our ability to do so."

The next month, they took it one step further, and invited Apple officials to a conference room at the DOJ. There, Deputy Attorney General James Cole bluntly told the company that they were "marketing to criminals."

According to the *Wall Street Journal*, Cole laid out a chilling prediction: "At some future date, a child will die, and police will say they would have been able to rescue the child, or capture the killer, if only they could have looked inside a certain phone."

The assembled team from Apple, which included its top lawyer, Bruce Sewell, found this assertion to be inflammatory. Law enforcement had many other ways of gaining information about criminal suspects that didn't involve busting into a seized phone—they could grab the cell phone's location data, or seek other electronic records.

"We can't create a key that only the good guys can use," Sewell told DOJ officials, echoing the key escrow discussion from a decade earlier.

As 2014 drew to a close, there were at least a handful of publicly known instances where the government invoked the All Writs Act to compel Apple's assistance in unlocking an iPhone or iPad. Taken together, these cases offer a preliminary road map as to how the government and Apple came to the brink of a legal battle in 2016 after San Bernardino.

"This Court has the authority to order Apple, Inc., to use any capabilities it may have to unlock the iPhone," Garth Hire, an assistant US attorney, wrote to the court on October 31, 2014, citing the All Writs Act. "The government is aware, and can represent, that in other cases, courts have ordered the unlocking of an iPhone under this authority . . . Additionally, Apple has routinely complied with such orders."

"This court should issue the order because doing so would enable agents to comply with this Court's warrant commanding that the iPhone be examined for evidence identified by the warrant," he continued. "Examination of the iPhone without Apple's assistance, if it is possible at all, would require significant resources and may harm the iPhone. Moreover, the order is not likely to place any unreasonable burden on Apple."

In April 2015, a House committee heard testimony from law enforcement that Apple's hardened stance posed a grave threat to law enforcement, and that any notion of a key escrow system was impractical.

"Backdoors create unnecessary vulnerability to otherwise secure systems that can be exploited by bad actors," Rep. Ted Lieu (D), a congressman with a computer science degree who represents western Los Angeles County, told Ars Technica at the time.

> *Backdoors are also problematic because once one government asks for special treatment, then other governments with fewer civil liberties protections will start asking for special treatment. In addition, computer code is neutral and unthinking. It cannot tell if the person typing on a keyboard trying to access private data is the FBI Director, a hacker, or the leader of Hamas as long as that person has the cryptographic key or other unlocking code. The view that computer backdoors can only be used by "good guys" reflects a lack of understanding of basic computer technology.*

Echoing this lack of understanding, Cyrus Vance, Jr., the district attorney for Manhattan, even testified before Congress in 2015: "Criminal defendants across the nation are the principal beneficiaries of iOS 8, and the safety of all American communities is imperiled by it."

As 2016 rolled around, there were three failed state bills proposed in New York, California, and Louisiana that would have made strong encryption effectively illegal, but the proposals went nowhere.

◯

This lengthy back-and-forth between federal law enforcement and tech companies finally came to a head in February 2016, when Apple received that first court order requiring the company to build a custom-made operating system that would bypass the passcode lockout on Farook's iPhone.

As federal prosecutors pushed forward at a breakneck speed, Republican presidential candidate Donald Trump weighed in from the campaign trail, with a not-entirely-accurate description of what was going on.

"First of all, Apple ought to give [authorities] the security to that phone," Trump told the crowd at a South Carolina rally. "What I think you ought to do is boycott Apple until they give that security number. I just thought of that—boycott Apple."

Later that day, Trump told *Bloomberg* that he would somehow pressure CEO Tim Cook into complying: "I would come down so hard on him—you have no idea—his head would be spinning all of the way back to Silicon Valley."

As Apple lawyers and Boutrous poured over the motion to compel, they realized that the government admitted that it may have inadvertently screwed up by disabling auto iCloud backup on the iPhone. Once they realized the government's error, Apple officials and their attorneys invited reporters nationwide to a hastily announced conference call.

During the Friday call, an Apple executive who was granted anonymity said the company has been diligently working with the FBI to try to aid the terrorism investigation. After days of working with the FBI, Apple proposed one final attempt to recover roughly six weeks of data that was locked on the phone.

The idea was to force the iPhone 5c to auto-backup to Farook's iCloud account. With a court order, Apple can and does routinely turn over iCloud data. For some reason, Farook had not backed up the phone for roughly six weeks prior to the attack. The executive said Apple does not know whether the auto-backup was disabled or enabled, but he did say that the previous iCloud backups, which were handed over to investigators, were sporadic.

Apple suggested that the FBI take the iPhone 5c, plug it into a wall, connect it to a known Wi-Fi network, and leave it overnight. The FBI took the phone to the San Bernardino County Health Department, where Farook worked prior to the December 2, 2015, attack.

When that attempt did not work, Apple was mystified, but soon found out that the Apple ID account password had been changed shortly after the phone was in the custody of law enforcement, possibly by someone from the county health department. With no way to enter the new password on the locked phone, even attempting an auto-backup was impossible. Had this iCloud auto-backup method actually functioned, Apple would have been easily able to assist the FBI with its investigation.

Two days later, FBI Director James Comey weighed in, in a lengthy public statement.

"The particular legal issue is actually quite narrow," he wrote. "The relief we seek is limited and its value increasingly obsolete because the technology continues to evolve." Here, Comey used the Going Dark language so pervasive among law enforcement. His point was that even if Apple helped the DOJ for the San Bernardino case, Apple would soon outdo themselves with new kinds of security in new generations of iPhones.

"We simply want the chance, with a search warrant, to try to guess the terrorist's passcode without the phone essentially self-destructing and without it taking a decade to guess correctly," Comey said. "That's it."

The following day, February 22, Apple CEO Tim Cook wrote an e-mail to employees that was quickly released to the public, arguing that what the government was asking was a step too far.

"Yes, it is certainly possible to create an entirely new operating system to undermine our security features as the government wants," he sad. "But it's something we believe is too dangerous to do."

◎

While all of this was going on, there was another important ruling by one of the judges that comprised the Magistrates' Revolt.

On February 29, 2016, Judge Orenstein ruled that Apple did not have to unlock a seized iPhone 5s running iOS 7. This case didn't involve the creation of new software, but was merely a task that Apple could perform with little effort—it had done so numerous times previously. Prosecutors in New York, like in San Bernardino, had argued that the All Writs Act gave it such authority.

The New York case began back in October 2015, when Judge Orenstein invited Apple to tell the court why it believed the government could not compel it to unlock a seized phone. At the time, bringing Apple into a case like this was new.

Nine days later, defendant Jun Feng pleaded guilty to one count of conspiracy to distribute and possession with intent to distribute methamphetamine. Judge Orenstein then asked prosecutors why the issue of Apple's compliance was still relevant given the guilty plea. In the government's own filing, dated October 30, 2015, prosecutors said that the investigation was not over and that it still needed data from Feng's phone. (Later, a district court judge overruled Orenstein, but eventually authorities got the passcode from someone else.)

Orenstein's conclusion largely echoed what Apple's attorneys had argued. "Finally, given the government's boundless interpretation of the All Writs Act, it is hard to conceive of any limits on the orders the government could obtain in the future," he wrote. "For example, if Apple can be forced to write code in this case to bypass security features and create new accessibility, what is to stop the government from demanding that Apple write code to turn on the microphone in aid of government surveillance, activate the video camera, surreptitiously record conversations, or turn on location services to track the phone's user? Nothing."

Days later, on March 1, 2016, both Comey and Apple's top lawyer, Bruce Sewell, testified before Congress. This was, again, extremely unusual. On March 11, President Barack Obama weighed in as well, speaking at the South by Southwest tech conference in Austin, Texas. "I suspect the answer will come down to how can we make sure the encryption is as strong as possible, the key as strong as possible, it's accessible by the smallest number of people possible, for a subset of issues that we agree are important," Obama said. "How we design that is not something I have the expertise to do."

For Boutrous, in a lifelong legal career, the way this case was unfolding was unprecedented.

"I never had a case where I had the president, the attorney general, the director of the FBI, all weighing in," he said. "They were all participating in the debate about what the right results would be in an ongoing case that was unfolding so rapidly."

Meanwhile, Boutrous was shuttling between Cupertino and Los Angeles. He was participating in mock hearings and preparing his arguments.

On Thursday, March 17, prosecutors told Boutrous and Apple's lawyers that they wanted the upcoming hearing to not just be procedural, but rather an evidentiary hearing with in-person testimony. If that had happened, Apple's rank-and-file experts would not only have to discuss their abilities to obey the governments orders, but Apple would have the ability to question government officials, and find out how far they had or hadn't gone already.

"They want to call live witnesses, including our engineers," Boutrous said. "One of the core things we wanted to examine was: 'What did you really do to see if you could access this phone? Did you consult with NSA or intelligence agencies?'"

The ante was raised even further.

"Suddenly we're preparing for a mini trial," he added.

The days continued, and Apple had dominated his time like no other case of that period.

Finally, the day before the hearing arrived, March 21. Boutrous had been rehearsing his arguments yet again in a moot court with a phalanx of lawyers in a fifty-fourth floor conference room near his office. Every chair was taken. People had stacks of papers and laptops in front of them. They were neck-deep in the All Writs Act.

Boutrous decided to take a break and get something from his office. He walked past his secretary, Irma Guerra, but she caught his attention.

"Eileen Decker, the US attorney is on the phone," Guerra told him.

Again, this was strange—usually it wouldn't have been the top prosecutor in the nation's largest US Attorney's Office outside of Washington, DC, making such a call, but rather, his or her deputy.

Boutrous strolled over, glanced down at Disney Hall out his window, and took the call.

Decker was cordial, even-keeled, and somewhat apologetic.

"I would never do this unless it was absolutely necessary and this is in complete good faith, but we believe, we just received [information] that we may be able to access the information on our own," she said.

The veteran lawyer hung up the phone and didn't miss a beat. He walked confidently back into the conference room, where his colleagues were waiting, and announced with a grin: "I've got some news!"

He explained what had happened. His colleagues were stunned, but a few chuckled that the government had pushed so far, only to back away.

"If you start a war, you say: 'This is the most important thing!' and you push us to the brink, and then say: 'Well, maybe we don't need to do this,'" he said.

"I was so ready to get in there and make the argument, because I just felt in my bones, Apple is correct here. It's not something the courts are authorized to do, it's wrong and it could have terrible consequences for our world if this were to go forward."

About a month later, FBI Director James Comey was asked at a London conference how much the FBI paid for the technique that enabled the agency to get into Farook's iPhone.

"A lot. More than I will make in the remainder of this job, which is seven years and four months for sure," Comey said, according to Reuters. "But it was, in my view, worth it."

As of January 2015, Comey made $183,300 per year—and assuming no raises or bonuses, he was set to make $1.34 million during his remaining tenure. This suggests the agency paid more than $1.3 million to get inside.

For now, *New York Telephone* remains good law: the government can compel companies to provide assistance, so long as it is not overly burdensome. The question of where that line is remains unresolved. How far can the government go in forcing a person or a corporation to assist isn't clear at all. Still, the fact that the government was able to effectively buy its way into Farook's phone suggests that Apple's help wasn't necessary at all, undercutting its previous legal arguments. Plus, neither the DOJ nor the FBI has said what, if anything, was gleaned from the iPhone—presumably if any of Farook's data had been useful, authorities likely would have said something by now.

In November 2017, the issue came up again, in the wake of a mass shooting in Sutherland Springs, Texas. There, after a gunman killed 26 people, including himself, the FBI said that it was unable to get into an iPhone found near the shooter's body.

"I'm not going to describe what phone it is because I don't want to tell every bad guy out there what phone to buy, to harass our efforts on trying to find justice here," FBI Special Agent Christopher Combs said at a press conference at the time.

CHAPTER THREE

How One Mugger's Calls Helped Create the NSA's Post-9/11 Phone Metadata Surveillance Program

> By virtually ignoring data communications and the new computer technology, the statute makes it possible for law-enforcement agencies to treat this important form of information transfer as if it were nothing more than a telephone conversation.
>
> —ARTHUR MILLER
> *THE ASSAULT ON PRIVACY* (1970)

October 1, 2013
Baltimore, Maryland

It was just another quiet Tuesday at home when a startling call from a reporter arrived on Stephen Sachs' phone. The reporter was with an outlet that Sachs had never heard of—*Wired*—and he was asking about a Supreme Court case, *Smith v. Maryland*, from decades ago. The career lawyer had practically forgotten about it.

"Hey honey, you may remember the first case I argued at the Supreme Court?" he called to his wife from across the house.

Sachs explained to his wife that the reporter, David Kravets, knew what Sachs initially did not: that the Foreign Intelligence Surveillance Court (FISC) had been secretly relying on *Smith*, which began as a late-night robbery in Baltimore in 1975, to justify a massive surveillance program at the National Security Agency (NSA). While all legal theories build on case law, the idea that a local purse-snatcher and days' worth of his phone records should allow years' worth of every American's phone records to be collected is orders of magnitude beyond what most lawyers or judges could imagine at the time.

After having spent decades as a federal and state prosecutor, and an attorney in private practice, Sachs' recent years have been largely quiet. He spends most of his time attending to family life, following the Baltimore Orioles, planning vacations, and periodically working on his own memoirs of a lifetime of public service and legal work. His home is on a quiet, leafy cul-de-sac in the northern part of Baltimore.

Sachs served as an assistant US attorney from 1961 until 1964, US attorney for the District of Maryland from 1967 until 1970, and as attorney general from 1979 until 1987, when he lost a gubernatorial election. (His ground-floor bathroom is filled with political cartoons and framed memorabilia from the 1988 campaign.) After that, he entered private practice, until he retired in 1999. More recently, in 2008, he was named by Governor Martin O'Malley to head a statewide commission to examine the Maryland State Police's use of surveillance against local protestors and activists.

In the wake of Edward Snowden, the FISC—whose hearings, opinions, and even dockets had nearly always been secret—had unusually decided to release a judicial opinion justifying the NSA's Section 215 program. This program, which began in late 2001 and ended in 2015, allowed the NSA to routinely capture all telephone metadata—all incoming and outgoing calls—of all Americans for years on end. (The new version allows the metadata to simply be held by the telecoms and accessed by the government with a court order, a distinction that former NSA head General Michael Hayden found to be trivial.)

Sachs was surprised, to say the least.

The 1979 *Smith* decision "was a routine robbery case," he told Kravets. "The circumstances are radically different today. There wasn't anything remotely [like] a massive surveillance of citizens' phone calls or communications. To extend it to what we now know as massive surveillance, in my personal view, is a bridge too far. It certainly wasn't contemplated by those involved in *Smith*."

The veteran prosecutor learned that, specifically, *Smith* had become a critical lynchpin in the third-party doctrine.

Today, the third-party doctrine works like this: if Alice calls Bob using Verizon, the fact that this call went over Verizon's network means that a third party (Verizon) was brought into the mix. Under this logic, neither Alice nor Bob can claim a privacy interest over the fact that the call took place. So, Verizon can disclose this metadata (who called whom, when, and for how long) to the police with little difficulty. In short, the government claims (and the Supreme Court agreed in 1979), that there was no "reasonable expectation of privacy" in numbers disclosed to a phone company.

The legal reasoning of the third-party doctrine for Alice and Bob may seem troubling enough. But that was only the beginning of the FISC analysis. "Put another way, where one individual does not have a Fourth Amendment interest, grouping together a large number of similarly situated individuals cannot result in a Fourth Amendment interest springing into existence *ex nihilo* [out of nothing]," wrote FISC Judge Claire Eagan in FISC Docket Number BR 13-109.

Sachs was disturbed after he read Eagan's opinion.

"I do not believe that I am the one who opened the door to massive surveillance, that's not what I want to be remembered for," he told me.

In *Smith*, the Supreme Court found that a Baltimore robber, Michael Lee Smith, did not have a reasonable expectation of privacy in the numbers that he dialed—the third party here was the Chesapeake and Potomac Telephone Company. As such, the police did not need a warrant to obtain the numbers dialed through the use of a pen register. Therefore, when it was shown that he repeatedly called a woman that he had burglarized, law enforcement was able to obtain a warrant to search his apartment, and ultimately convict him. Smith, through his lawyer, Howard Cardin, unsuccessfully challenged the evidence that derived from the original use of the pen register. It was Sachs' victory over Cardin in *Smith* that laid the foundation of the FISC's legal opinion that massive warrantless wiretapping was acceptable to the law.

On the same day, October 1, 2013, Kravets had also contacted Cardin. Nearly 25 years after the case had been argued, Cardin was even more certain in his arguments, and was as baffled as Sachs that it could be used to wantonly justify something far greater than what the Supreme Court had been asked to decide in 1979.

Defense attorney Cardin, though now well into his 70s, doesn't seem to be slowing down anytime soon. He's got a full caseload and is constantly rushing from his downtown Baltimore office to court, just blocks away. His dusty and carpeted office, replete with an anteroom filled with dozens of magazines and living-room chairs, feels like it belongs in a Dick Tracy movie. It's decades away from many contemporary law firms, which tend to favor large windows to illuminate their clean—and often sterile—modern design. Appropriately, the law practice of Cardin and Gitomer still has no website.

Cardin was briefly a prosecutor for the first few years of his career, from 1966 until 1970, and then entered private practice—largely as a criminal defense attorney—in 1971. He's never looked back. Cardin is political and legal royalty in Maryland. His brother, Benjamin Cardin, currently serves as the state's senior US senator. Their father, Meyer Cardin, served in the Maryland General Assembly and was a judge on Baltimore's Supreme Bench, now called the Circuit Court. One of Cardin's sons, Jon Cardin, now works with him in the law firm—after having lost the 2014 election for Maryland attorney general, and after having served in the Maryland House of Delegates for nine years. Cardin's grandson, Zach Cardin, is currently attending law school at the University of California, Berkeley.

Stephen Sachs and Howard Cardin are forever linked, not only because as of 2017, their grandsons play on the same high school baseball team, but because they faced off against one another on March 28, 1979, at the Supreme Court.

"What they [had was] this nexus between the phones, [with] Smith on one end and the woman on the other," Cardin said. All the parties were known entities. The case was over whether the authorities could use surveillance to fill in the gap between fixed points.

"Whereas today, when you start taking all these phone numbers and putting them in a warehouse," Cardin explained, you're not using it to fill in the gaps. But, instead, "to gain information. Information that I submit would have some protection of . . . privacy. That's [the] difference between *Smith* and the extension of the doctrine today." For Cardin, the question seemed analogous to the Founder's distinction between general writs and specific reasonable warrants: Are you looking for something specific, as explained to a judge, or are you simply trawling for anything, anywhere, all the time?

Even Albert Lauber, now a judge on the US Tax Court, who was then a clerk for Justice Harry Blackmun (and drafted the majority opinion), was shocked to learn that *Smith* was the legal foundation for the NSA metadata program.

"Is that right?" he told me, further explaining that his former boss likely would have been surprised at that expansion as well.

"I think his instinct would be to have been suspicious of what became the huge NSA interception effort," Lauber added. "Blackmun, he wouldn't have been able to get his head around the scope of that. The pen register case seemed very simple in terms of technology."

As the 1960s drew to a close, there was an increasing awareness of the government's ability to surveil its own citizens—often without any real check. Or, put another way, how far does the *Katz* "reasonable expectation of privacy" go? While it may be easier to understand clear-cut situations like a home or telephone booth, does this idea also extend to data, or even physical characteristics? Such concern spurred some modest legislative change at both the federal and state level, which then culminated in a landmark Senate committee that fully exposed the width and breadth of the government's surveillance program as never before.

Even while *Katz* was working its way through lower courts, there was a proposal to build a national data bank using the state-of-the-art computer technology at the time. This prospect was so alarming that in 1966, Representative Cornelius Gallagher (D-New Jersey), who chaired the Special Subcommittee on Invasion of Privacy, said: "The presence of these records in Government files is frightening enough, but the thought of them neatly bundled together into one compact package is appalling. We cannot be certain that such dossiers would always be used by benevolent people for benevolent purposes."

The plan was ultimately killed after Gallagher's subcommittee issued a cautionary report against it. Still, the specter of immutable, computerized data for law enforcement purposes inevitably loomed. The *New York Times* warned in June 1970, "Federal Computers Amass Files on Suspect Citizens."

By the end of 1970, the public began to have a better understanding of how far this surveillance power could go in practice. In December 1970, a University of Michigan law professor published *The Assault on Privacy*, which was one of the first major books to warn of the potential privacy risks in the digital age.

The book's author, Arthur R. Miller (now a professor at New York University), warned that even the 1968 Omnibus act was "a technological anachronism," because it "ignores the realities of modern communications and computer science."

"By virtually ignoring data communications and the new computer technology, the statute makes it possible for law-enforcement agencies to treat this important form of information transfer as if it were nothing more than a telephone conversation," he wrote. "Congress's failure to differentiate between voice and data communications displays either a lack of awareness of recent technological developments in the communications field or a certain amount of disingenuousness."

Miller also concluded something that the NSA would figure out years later: metadata is incredibly valuable.

"Data transmissions also are more likely than telephone conversations to contain privileged data, which typically are a prime objective of wiretappers," he wrote.

One of the crucial elements of the *Katz* decision, and the 1968 Safe Streets Act, was the fact that there was an exception for national security interests. The result of which was that—based solely at the president's or his administration's discretion—the government's vast intelligence apparatus could be turned towards essentially anyone. Years later, the Church Committee, the 1975 Senate subcommittee tasked with a review of intelligence activities, noted dryly that "the Nixon administration used these criteria to justify a number of questionable wiretaps."

◯

Richard Nixon was voted into office in November 1968 by just half a million votes, just months after both Senator Robert Kennedy and Dr. Martin Luther King, Jr., were assassinated. When he entered the White House in January 1969, President Nixon was met by a nation that was bitterly divided and viscerally hurting. By that point, the Vietnam War had been raging for nearly four years, with no end in sight. America had been paying the price in both treasure and blood: nearly 30,000 American lives had been lost from 1967 to 1968.

The dawn of the Nixon administration marked one of the high-water marks of mass surveillance in America. Even before Nixon, intelligence services were carrying out domestic surveillance operations dating back to the mid-1950s as a way to monitor and mitigate potential influence of communism or communist sympathizers. The intelligence community actively disrupted various civil rights groups through the Counter Intelligence Program (COINTELPRO). Other snooping efforts with more colorful names, like Project Shamrock, were designed to indiscriminately capture postal mail and telegram traffic. Others, like Project Minaret, intercepted the electronic communications of thousands of Americans—initially it was limited to antiwar activists, but by the time Nixon entered the White House, the list had grown to include senators, journalists, and even Muhammad Ali.

Those lists—and the programs themselves—would expand tremendously under Nixon. On April 30, 1970, Nixon announced the Cambodian Campaign, a military effort to strengthen the position of the South Vietnamese and capture Viet Cong matériel. The following day, students began striking in protest of this new policy to ramp up the Vietnam War. On May 4, four students were killed by members of the Ohio National Guard while protesting at Kent State University. Suddenly, Nixon's interest in what the various surveillance programs of the intelligence agencies were—and how they could be expanded for his use—became all the more urgent.

Not three months later, in July 1970, Nixon signed off on the Huston Plan, which formalized and legalized covert mail opening and increased electronic surveillance, among other tactics. The president quickly rescinded his approval, but that didn't stop the intelligence agencies from continuing what they had already been doing.

One surveillance case that preceded Nixon, but was ultimately championed by his attorney general, involved the wiretapping of dissidents. In September 1968, just over three months after the Omnibus act was signed, a small bomb went off in the CIA recruitment office at 450 Main Street in Ann Arbor, Michigan. Overnight, someone had placed a few sticks of dynamite nearby, which blew a sizeable hole in the sidewalk and damaged furniture, but did little else. No one was injured. Eventually, three men affiliated with the White Panthers leftist group were arrested and prosecuted for the crime.

As the case moved ahead in 1969 and 1970, prosecutors disclosed during a hearing that a phone conversation involving one of the defendants and a California-based Black Panther had been captured over a warrantless wiretap. As a trial date approached, defense attorneys pushed the government to disclose any electronic surveillance that was used against their clients. In an affidavit, Attorney General John Mitchell (one of Nixon's most trusted colleagues) wrote that one of the suspects, Robert "Pun" Plamondon, was overheard on a wiretap that was "employed to gather intelligence information deemed necessary to protect the nation from attempts of domestic organizations to attack and subvert the existing structure of government."

In other words, while under normal circumstances law enforcement would have to present a super-warrant application for a judge to sign off on the wiretap, the attorney general claimed a power, under the presumed mandate of national security, to be able to wiretap anyone unilaterally based on the power that stemmed from the Title III law. Put another way, under this logic, if Charles Katz had been perceived as a threat to national security, the FBI could have wiretapped the phone booth's line directly rather than going through all the gymnastics of rigging up a microphone atop the phone booth.

The Ann Arbor case ran right into a buzz saw, which came in the form of then US District Judge Damon Keith. By the time he had been randomly assigned the case, Judge Keith had been a judge for only a few years. In fact, when he was tapped for a judgeship by President Lyndon Johnson, he was just one of a handful of federal African-American judges nationwide.

In January 1971, Judge Keith came out strongly against the government and Mitchell's entire legal theory.

"An idea which seems to permeate much of the Government's argument is that a dissident domestic organization is akin to an unfriendly foreign power that must be dealt with in the same fashion," Judge Keith wrote in his decision. "There is a great danger in an argument of this nature, for it strikes at the very constitutional privileges and immunities that are inherent in United States citizenship."

Reminding everyone of the language of the *Katz* decision, the judge recalled that "the Fourth Amendment protects a defendant from the evil of the uninvited ear."

The Department of Justice appealed the case to the 6th US Circuit Court of Appeals, which upheld Judge Keith's ruling. The appeals court famously found, in what came to be known as the *Keith* case (rather than its official and cumbersome name: *United States v. United States District Court*), that there was not "one written phrase" in the Constitution or statutes to support the Justice Department's view. The government appealed up to the Supreme Court, which again, denied the government's efforts.

"The price of lawful public dissent must not be a dread of subjection to an unchecked surveillance power," Justice Lewis Powell wrote in the unanimous 8–0 opinion. One would think that would have closed the book on such wiretapping. But as we'll see, the government continued to find innovative ways to circumvent the courts.

◐

Beyond legal rulings, there was some legislative action as well—even at the state level. On the other side of the country, a California state assembly member proposed a state constitutional amendment designed to extend privacy protections to state citizens beyond what the federal government allowed.

In 1971, Assemblymember Kenneth Cory of Orange County submitted twin bills. The first bill proposed modifying the state's constitution, while the other expanded greater individual control over data and information held by the government. While the bills didn't pass, eventually, under Proposition 11, which was approved by the voters directly, the net result was a two-word modification ("and privacy") to the very last line of Article I, Section 1, of the California Constitution:

> All people are by nature free and independent, and have certain inalienable rights, among which are those of enjoying and defending life and liberty; acquiring, possessing, and protecting property; and pursuing and obtaining safety, happiness, and privacy.

Today, California is just one of 10 states that specifically outline an affirmative right to privacy, a definition that goes beyond *Katz*.

California's state right to privacy proved critical in a California Supreme Court case known as *Burrows v. Superior Court* (1974), which unanimously found that an attorney accused of grand theft had a privacy interest in his bank records—police could not simply arrive at the bank and make copies of bank statements without a warrant or court order to do so.

"For all practical purposes, the disclosure by individuals or business firms of their financial affairs to a bank is not entirely volitional, since it is impossible to participate in the economic life of contemporary society without maintaining a bank account," California Chief Justice Stanley Mosk wrote for a unanimous court.

As he continued:

> Development of photocopying machines, electronic computers and other sophisticated instruments have accelerated the ability of government to intrude into areas which a person normally chooses to exclude from prying eyes and inquisitive minds. Consequently judicial interpretations of the reach of the constitutional protection of individual privacy must keep pace with the perils created by these new devices.

◌

The year 1971 was also a big one for exposing the intelligence and crime-fighting techniques that had gotten out of hand.

On March 8, 1971, the Citizens' Commission to Investigate the FBI broke into an FBI office in Media, Pennsylvania, outside Philadelphia. The eight-person group sought, among other objectives, to determine "the nature and extent of surveillance and intimidation carried on by this office of the FBI, particularly against groups and individuals working for a more just, humane and peaceful society."

The group, whose members were not revealed until 2014, managed to spirit away and publish around 1,000 documents, including detailed descriptions of COINTELPRO, among other secret government programs.

Their efforts, combined with FBI Director J. Edgar Hoover's death (1972) and Nixon's downfall as a result of the Watergate bugging scandal and cover-up (1974), resulted in the formation of the Select Committee to Study Governmental Operations with Respect to Intelligence Activities, better known as the Church Committee, which began its work in 1975. The group released a multivolume report, several hundred pages long, the following year. It provided incredibly detailed testimony as to how the intelligence community had gone so far astray. The study remains the most comprehensive effort to evaluate the intelligence community to date.

One of the most telling moments during the hearings was when Senator Walter Mondale (D-Minnesota) questioned then NSA deputy director Benson Buffham. Mondale asked if the NSA had considered whether the Huston Plan was legal at the time, to which Buffham replied: "That particular aspect didn't enter into the discussions." A moment, later, Mondale asked the same question of Roy Banner, the NSA's general counsel.

Banner replied: "I think it was legal in the context of the law at the time," and further explained that since the *Keith* ruling, the president could no longer order that a domestic target be wiretapped without a warrant.

◌

The story of *Smith v. Maryland* began when a woman named Patricia Mc-Donough had just returned to her Baltimore home. It was just after midnight on March 5, 1976, and fog had begun to roll across the city. She spotted a man changing a tire in her neighborhood, but thought nothing of it. As she approached her front door, the man grabbed her from behind, snatching her purse away from her, and fled the scene.

Soon after, McDonough told Baltimore police officer Kenneth Lucas what her assailant looked like, and described the green bottom and tan top 1975 Chevrolet Monte Carlo that she'd seen earlier. But the robber wasn't done with her—he began making a series of "threatening and obscene" phone calls to McDonough, and even told her that he was the one who had committed the crime against her. He kept it up.

At the time, anonymous and bothersome phone calls were something of a scourge on the nation. Making such calls was formally made a crime in New York State in 1960. In April 1965, *The Atlantic* reported on the phenomenon, describing that "menacing, bizarre, sometimes ludicrous, telephone terrorism is an underground part of the public life of America." Ordinary people routinely got calls where callers would simply breathe heavily into the receiver, or would proffer unwarranted sexual or hateful remarks. The same article noted that AT&T spokesmen said, "95 percent of the complaints that are received do not prove valid enough for serious investigation."

By 1966, the New York Telephone Company set up an Annoyance Call Bureau, as a way to help people (primarily women) deal with the problem. That same year, AT&T (at the time, it controlled 80 percent of the telephone market nationwide) received 586,000 complaints of "abusive or annoying" calls. One common way that telephone companies dealt with this situation was to employ a pen register, which monitors inbound calls, while a "trap and trace" device monitors outbound calls. Today, pen registers and trap and trace (PRTT, or simply pen/trap) devices are often used in combination, or are just referred to simply as a pen register for a singular device that can capture both incoming and outgoing calls. Antiquated as these pen registers are, they ended up playing an enormous role in surveillance law, with serious echoes into our own time.

In September 1970, William Claerhout, Northwestern Bell's top lawyer, who previously served as the Iowa attorney general, described the pen register in a law journal article as a mere "mechanical metering device" that was used for "proper customer billing and to maintain good service." Claerhout lauded the use of the pen register and specifically called out that the 1968 Omnibus act allowed its use. During the first six months of 1970, he indicated that it was helpful to shield Northwestern Bell customers from unwanted calls. After all, customers reported 5,688 complaints in Iowa alone—88 percent of which were classified as "obscene."

By 1971, the *New York Times* reported that nearly 10 million AT&T customers had paid for an unlisted phone number as a way to deal with unwanted calls.

As a result of McDonough's complaints, on March 13, 1976, the Baltimore Police Department (BPD) asked Chesapeake and Potomac Telephone Company to install a pen register on McDonough's line. It would record the phone numbers of all incoming calls.

The device showed that McDonough was frequently being called from pay phones in the neighborhood. In this way, investigators hoped, they would be able to better ascertain who was harassing her. They were in luck. On March 15, she received yet another call. A man asked her to step outside of her house so that he could observe her, and amazingly, she did so. She watched the Monte Carlo slowly drive past her home.

The following day, March 16, Officer Lucas was on the lookout for the green car in McDonough's neighborhood. Incredibly, the driver of that car stopped him, asking for help, as he had locked himself out. Lucas took down the plate number, and eventually determined that it belonged to one Michael Lee Smith. The next day, the BPD asked the phone company to install a pen register to record all calls emanating from Smith's home. Later that same day, Smith again called his victim.

With this new information, the BPD got a warrant to search Smith's car and his apartment. There, authorities found "a page in Smith's telephone book was turned down; it contained the name and number of the victim." She positively identified him at police headquarters as part of a lineup on March 19. His age (mid-20s) and appearance (blond hair, average build) matched her memory.

Smith was formally indicted for robbery on April 6, 1976. By November 1976, his attorney, Howard Cardin, tried to raise the pen register's legitimacy on a motion to suppress evidence (which was denied). After a brief bench trial, Smith was found guilty and sentenced to six years in prison on March 9, 1977.

Cardin knew that he had an uphill battle—his only real way to help his client was to challenge the evidence that the government had. After all, everyone agreed as to the basic facts. The remaining question was whether the government's use of the pen register was, in fact, a search. So, that was the basis of his appeal to the intermediate Maryland Court of Special Appeals, which was filed the next day, March 10. However, in an unusual move, the Maryland Court of Appeals, the state's highest court, ordered that it hear the case before it had a chance to be adjudicated by the state's middle court. (Curiously, by the time the court of appeals heard the case, Smith had died, which normally would invalidate a case—with no appellant, there would be no standing.)

In a 4–3 decision on July 14, 1978, the court of appeals found that because a pen register was not a device that "intercepts" a telephone call, it did not violate the state's wiretap law, and was not a search. This decision turned on a specific distinction between data and metadata, much as pre-*Katz* law depended on a narrow understanding of physical intrusion.

Judge Harry Cole, the first African-American to be elected to the Maryland Senate and to serve on the Maryland Court of Appeals, was one of the judges who dissented.

"Today no one perhaps notices because only a small, obscure criminal is the victim," he wrote, quoting a 1971 dissent by Justice William Douglas in *United States v. White*. "But every person is the victim, for the technology we exalt today is everyman's master."

Judge Cole further explained that his colleagues' understanding of what a search was remained far too narrow, in his view. It is not the fact that a particular location was examined, or even that a call was intercepted, or items taken. Rather, it is the "gathering of *information*," regardless of what form it comes in.

"Technologically, a distinction between verbal and digital transmissions is absurd," he continued. "There can be no doubt that the fact that Smith made certain calls from his home telephone is highly relevant information in a criminal prosecution for obscene or annoying phone calls."

Judge Cole also made a point of calling out the abuses of Watergate that had been seared in the collective consciousness in recent years, and correctly foresaw what the NSA would do many years later. "If pen register data were fed into a central computer on a widespread basis, patterns of acquaintances and dealings among a substantial group of people would be available to the government," he concluded.

But Cole's view, of course, remained in the minority.

Three months after the Maryland Court of Appeals' decision, the Foreign Intelligence Surveillance Act was signed into law on October 25, 1978. The new law was designed to strike a balance between the needs of the government to conduct secret surveillance, and providing adequate oversight by creating an entirely new court, FISC.

The FISC, unlike all others nationwide, would have not only secret proceedings, but also (until 2013, after the Snowden revelations) a secret docket. Nearly all of its decisions, opinions, and transcripts still remain hidden. Government lawyers would present their arguments *ex parte*, or one-sided, to the judges as to why they needed to conduct surveillance on certain targets without anyone presenting a countering viewpoint. (In 2015, as part of a series of modest post-Snowden reforms, there are now standing *amici curiae*—or friends of the court, who serve as outside advocates for the public interest, but again, due to the secret nature of the court, it is unknown what impact, if any, they have had.)

In his *cert* petition to the Supreme Court, Howard Cardin largely reprised many of the same arguments that he had made at the lower courts. On the prosecution side, the arguments fell to Stephen Sachs, who had just been elected as the Maryland attorney general, and was installed in his position in January 1979. Sachs only had months to familiarize himself with the case, and prepare for what was to become one of the highest-profile cases of his career.

On March 28, 1979, Sachs was driven directly to the Supreme Court by a Maryland state trooper. As the state's top law enforcement official, he was granted certain privileges—including being driven all the way into the subterranean parking garage, below the court.

He got out and gathered his things, found the elevator, and made a beeline for the law library on the fourth floor. It was early morning, and he found himself the only person in the entire room. The Supreme Court law library would feel familiar to anyone who has spent time in an academic library. It has warm wood paneling, vaulted ceilings, and ornate carved archways.

Sachs pulled a wooden chair out and nestled himself against the long, sleek table. He retrieved his handwritten notes and spread them out on the table. But all he could hear was the silent rhythms of the law. The prosecutor knew what he was there to do. The job was to present the arguments that he felt confident about. He was there to take a prominent role in what he called the "secular ritual of arguing before the highest court in the country."

Cardin, for his part, arrived by cab with his longtime legal partner, James Gitomer. They did not make a pit stop at the law library, but rather went straight to the counsel's table. Gitomer had served as Cardin's argument sparring partner. The defense attorney had invited his recently retired father, Judge Meyer Cardin, to attend the oral arguments—he sat nearby. The younger Cardin was ready. Sachs' parents, wife, and children were also in the packed courtroom.

"I may have started in [the] Circuit Court [for] Baltimore City . . . representing a client, but by the time I got to the Supreme Court, I was championing a cause," Cardin told me.

By the time Cardin stepped up to the lectern, he faced a stern Chief Justice Warren Burger, who had been the head of the court since 1969. Some of the justices from *Katz* remained, including justices William Brennan, Potter Stewart, and Byron White. Justice Thurgood Marshall, one of Baltimore's most famous sons, who had arrived on the Supreme Court right before *Katz* was argued, was a veteran.

Burger, a conservative constructionist judge, had been selected by Nixon to be an ideological counterweight to the liberal Warren Court. Under his tenure, the court oversaw *New York Times v. United States* (1971), which validated the publication of the Pentagon Papers. Three years later, Burger wrote an 8–0 decision in *United States v. Nixon* (1974), which struck down Nixon's claimed executive privilege in communications between the embattled president and his advisors. Nixon resigned his position weeks later.

The court also featured Justice William Rehnquist, who by that point had been on the court for seven years. Previously he had served as Nixon's assistant attorney general in the Office of Legal Counsel, from 1969 through 1971, until he was tapped to be a Supreme Court justice. In this position as AAG, in effect, Rehnquist served as the top lawyer for Attorney General John Mitchell. Rehnquist would go on to become chief justice from 1986 until 2005.

"Mr. Chief Justice and may it please the Court," Cardin began. "As modern technology brings to society an improved standard of living and new conveniences, it also presents a serious challenge to the personal rights of an individual. This was anticipated many years ago by this Court in dissent when, in *Olmstead*, it was stated that similar, and far more reaching means of invading privacy, have become available to the government."

He had barely gotten three sentences out when Rehnquist jumped in to ask: "Well, actually, your client will be a lot better off if we still had the system where the operator answered when you picked up the phone and said 'number please,' wouldn't it—wouldn't he?"

This turned into an extended exchange that ultimately led to Cardin agreeing with the notion that had Smith lived in an earlier period where he voluntarily gave up the numbers he was dialing to a human operator, then at least he would have known that he was doing it. Smith did not expect that the numbers he dialed, even if they were to make harassing phone calls, would be recorded.

Cardin forcefully argued that the local phone company installed the pen register at the behest of the police—without a court order or warrant of any kind—and captured his client's information without any legitimate authority.

"What we're saying here is to allow an officer on his own, we don't even know who the officer might be, whether he has investigative background, whether he is high or low within the police department, but to allow anyone just to go ahead and place the pen register would be wrong," he continued.

"That there should be some pinpointing of responsibility, and the only way we can do it is to require that there'd be a Court order. As such, there is an accountability, there is supervision. Without it, there is complete decentralization, and decentralization leads to abuse."

He also pointed out that modern pen registers could easily be converted to surreptitious wiretaps, simply by plugging in headsets. Without adequate judicial oversight, police could easily abuse their authority without any meaningful consequences.

The justices seemed skeptical. Then, it was Sachs' turn to make his arguments. In the audio recording, he seemed to exude confidence, and employed anaphora in his legal rhetoric. Sachs began by explaining to the justices what a pen register was not:

> It captures no words uttered into the mouthpiece, as this Court phrased it in Katz.
>
> It captures no content. It achieves no communication, other than the limited communication between the user and the phone company itself. It has been defined by Congress, indeed, by its exclusion from the requirements of Title III as not to be a communication. It doesn't disclose if the call is completed. It doesn't reveal who the caller is. It doesn't say if the number was busy. It doesn't say who the parties are and it doesn't tell the duration of the call.

Later on Sachs continued, "We suggest to the Court that the average telephone user probably ought not have a subjective expectation of privacy as to the number called but, in any case, it's not an expectation that will be recognized for purposes of the Fourth Amendment."

Again, he flowed into an anaphoric list of earlier Supreme Court decisions, explaining that like anyone, criminals always run the risk that their transactions, interactions, or conversations will be transmitted to the government in some way. When found out, those criminals always feel that their subjective expectation of privacy has been violated.

The Supreme Court published its decision less than three months later, on June 20, 1979. The court found, in a 5–3 decision, in favor of Sachs and the State of Maryland. In the majority opinion, which was authored by Justice Blackmun, the justices noted "our lodestar is *Katz.*"

He continued:

> In applying the Katz *analysis to this case, it is important to begin by specifying precisely the nature of the state activity that is challenged. The activity here took the form of installing and using a pen register. Since the pen register was installed on telephone company property at the telephone company's central offices, petitioner obviously cannot claim that his "property" was invaded or that police intruded into [a] "constitutionally protected area." Petitioner's claim, rather, is that, notwithstanding the absence of a trespass, the State, as did the Government in* Katz, *infringed a "legitimate expectation of privacy" that petitioner held. Yet a pen register differs significantly from the listening device employed in* Katz, *for pen registers do not acquire the contents of communications.*

In other words, the justices still viewed metadata and content as distinct, with differing legal protections. The decision then spent a little time discussing *New York Telephone*, and how that law specifically did not consider pen registers an interception.

Furthermore, the majority found, "we doubt that people in general entertain any actual expectation of privacy in the numbers they dial." After all, consumers must realize that the phone company has the ability to retain those records, as they receive bills for long-distance calls. But even if Smith did have an "expectation of privacy" in his numbers dialed, society as a whole—according to the two-part Justice Harlan test from *Katz*, and subsequent rulings—does not recognize a privacy interest in information that he turns over to third parties.

"This analysis dictates that petitioner can claim no legitimate expectation of privacy here," the decision continues. "When he used his phone, petitioner voluntarily conveyed numerical information to the telephone company and 'exposed' that information to its equipment in the ordinary course of business. In so doing, petitioner assumed the risk that the company would reveal to police the numbers he dialed."

Decades later this logic carried over to the NSA's metadata program— essentially that if the police could get three days of one person's phone records, then the NSA could obtain years' worth of everyone's phone records.

Justice Marshall dissented, explaining that even if people knew that the phone company has the ability to monitor calls for its own internal purposes, "it does not follow that they expect this information to be made available to the public in general or the government in particular."

As he continued: "Privacy is not a discrete commodity, possessed absolutely or not at all. Those who disclose certain facts to a bank or phone company for a limited business purpose need not assume that this information will be released to other persons for other purposes."

Moreover, it makes no sense, he argued, to discuss the assumption of risk in a phone call when "individuals have no realistic alternative." After all, in cases like *Hoffa v. United States*, where the criminal was done in by a confidant, that person had the choice of whom to trust with their information. Here, by contrast, someone who wants to make a phone call has only one option.

"In my view, whether privacy expectations are legitimate within the meaning of *Katz* depends not on the risks an individual can be presumed to accept when imparting information to third parties, but on the risks he should be forced to assume in a free and open society," he concluded.

◯

Just as, in the wake of *Katz*, Congress passed the 1968 Omnibus Crime Control Act, so too was there a desire to modernize federal law in the wake of *Smith* to expressly include electronic and voice communications. The Office of Technology Assessment, which existed from 1972 until 1995, came out with an 82-page report that examined "Electronic Surveillance and Civil Liberties."

"Telephones, credit cards, computers, and cameras did not exist. Although the principle of the fourth amendment is timeless, its application has not kept abreast of current technologies," the report states.

Congress largely adopted many of these proposed changes as part of the 1986 Electronic Communications Privacy Act (ECPA), which updated the Omnibus Act. One section of the law, known as the Stored Communications Act (added in 1986 and updated subsequently), requires that a "provider of an electronic communication service" hand over any non-content metadata that is "relevant and material to an ongoing criminal investigation."

Yet another portion mandates that pen registers can only be authorized via a court order that includes an affirmation from the prosecutor "that the information likely to be obtained by such installation and use is relevant to an ongoing criminal investigation." Both of these are less legal standards than probable cause, the standard for search warrants and tracking surveillance. (Wiretaps, again, require even more from the government—they require super-warrants.)

Still, actual pen registers are hardly the issue anymore. In contemporary society, the amount of data that one person generates online is vast. A person generates data through their Internet service provider, through the websites that they interact with, what they search for, what they buy, who they correspond with on social media, and, increasingly, where they do it from. After all, Internet Protocol addresses are geographic, and mobile devices contain GPS and location data that can easily be obtained by the company in question, and by extension, the government—often without our knowledge.

The advent of ever-increasing digital devices—devices that individuals personally interact with, which have the ability to retain more information—means that this issue is more pressing than ever.

The third-party doctrine says that *Katz* doesn't apply to metadata. It's almost a modern-day extension of the line from the *Olmstead* wiretapping case from the 1920s, when Chief Justice Taft wrote: "There was no searching. There was no seizure." His argument seems almost laughable to us today. Of course conducting a wiretap was a search—in the eyes of Justice Marshall, though it was not a search of a tangible object obtained by traversing someone's doorway, it was certainly a search of intangible information.

In the late twentieth and early twenty-first centuries, the notion that there is no recognized constitutional privacy interest over data that we are obliged to share with private companies seems equally silly. How, after all, are we supposed to go about conducting our modern lives using all kinds of services that require us to give up data?

Fundamentally, it seems quite odd that (technically speaking) traditional postal mail has more protections—law enforcement cannot open it in most circumstances without a warrant—than any other form of modern communication. (However, since *United States v. Warshak*, a case that will be addressed more fully in Chapter 6, there has been a de facto warrant requirement for the content of e-mail.) This problem has been remarked upon by legal scholars for decades now. In 1990, Lewis Katz, a professor at Case Western Reserve University, was one of the earliest to articulate some of the major flaws of the third-party doctrine.

"It poses an untenable choice," he wrote, echoing Marshall's dissent. "An individual can withdraw from all contact with others and with society by not dealing with people, by not venturing outside, by not using banks, telephones, mail, garbage collection and other services, and maintain the type of informational privacy available to his eighteenth century forbearer. But it is impossible to lead an eighteenth century life today."

There is a vast amount of legal scholarship that lambasts this seemingly anachronistic rule. As Orin Kerr, a law professor at the University of Southern California, and one of the nation's top digital privacy legal scholars, quipped in a February 2009 article, "A list of every article or book that has criticized the doctrine would make this the world's longest law review footnote."

Most privacy law scholars have reached the conclusion that the third-party doctrine can no longer be clearly applied in a modern society. But Kerr, by contrast, mostly remains a defender of the third-party doctrine. He's argued that the notion "ensures that the same basic level of constitutional protection applies regardless of technology."

As Kerr sees it, the fact that Smith used a telephone to call his victim—as opposed to say, shouting at her from the street—is immaterial. The police can view anyone in public doing anything. But in reality, that's not how police investigations work. Until technology enabled a mass collection of phone numbers, or license plates, or anything else, there was simply a physical and financial limit to what law enforcement could do: they were forced to expend resources on only the most important targets.

Kerr also notes that under his preferred definition of the third-party doctrine, it should only continue to exist to preserve the government's right to access metadata, or non-content information. He analogizes it to address information physically written on a package, which is then carried to the neighborhood post office.

However, a critical difference—as evidenced by the Section 215 program— is that in a purely analog world it would be physically impossible for a set of humans to capture the routing information of all packages being transmitted nationwide. In short, technology enables far more surveillance at far lower cost than any non-digital scenario ever could. Scholars and judges differ as to exactly how the third-party doctrine should be changed. Should it be dependent on how sensitive the data is? Should it be determined by whether a person "knowingly" or "voluntarily" gave up that data? The law remains unclear.

In 2012, in the case of *United States v. Jones*, Justice Sonia Sotomayor became the first member of the Supreme Court within the last decade to explicitly describe the third-party doctrine as "ill-suited to the digital age." (This case will be explored further in Chapter 9.) "I for one doubt that people would accept without complaint the warrantless disclosure to the Government of a list of every Web site they had visited in the last week, or month, or year," she continued.

◎

There is one case, still pending, that may force the antiquated third-party doctrine of *Smith* into the twenty-first century. In the fall of 2017, the Supreme Court heard *Carpenter v. United States* to determine whether cell-site location information (CSLI) should be treated as simple metadata, and therefore not require a warrant. Or, as the American Civil Liberties Union (ACLU) claims, does extensive location information provided by a cell phone—which was not initially contemplated by the Stored Communications Act or the Supreme Court in *Smith*—require a warrant?

This case, more than any other in recent history, is a contemporary analog to *Smith*. The Supreme Court is expected to issue a decision in 2018.

The case began in April 2011, when four men were arrested for armed robberies at RadioShacks and T-Mobile stores in Detroit and its environs. One of those men quickly confessed, and said that he had participated in robberies of nine stores in Michigan and Ohio between December 2010 and March 2011. The one who confessed gave the FBI his own phone number and the numbers of his fellow suspects.

The following month, the FBI applied for three court orders to obtain 127 days' worth of "transactional records" for 16 different phone numbers. Among the information the government wanted was the "cell site information for the target telephones," which they hoped would provide evidence that two of the suspects—Timothy Sanders and Timothy Carpenter—among others, were in the vicinity of the robberies at the time they occurred. Eventually, Carpenter and the others were charged.

Specifically, the government sought a d-order, named for the provision of the Stored Communications Act, 18 USC 2703(d). That law requires companies provide some telecommunications records—essentially, metadata—when "specific and articulable facts show" that the data sought is "relevant and material to an ongoing criminal investigation." Perhaps all this sounds acceptable. But it is far different (and far less precise) than the legal permission required in other kinds of searches: that is, of course, a warrant that requires a showing of probable cause.

This is not a trivial distinction. A d-order does not, as the Fourth Amendment mandates for warrants, require as much particularity. A warrant also mandates a signed and sworn affidavit ("on oath or affirmation") regarding the "places to be searched and the things to be seized" that a d-order application does not.

"That's important because judges give a lot more scrutiny to a warrant application than they do a d-order," Nathan Freed Wessler, Carpenter's ACLU attorney, told me.

Before trial, the defendants attempted to suppress the cell-site records on the grounds that those records required a warrant, but the district court denied them. They appealed up to the 6th US Circuit Court of Appeals, which ruled against them. Court filings authored by Wessler and other lawyers argue that 127 days of data is simply too vast, too potentially revelatory of a person's constitutionally protected behavior.

In short, the government should be required to get a warrant. Plus, just like in *Katz* and *Smith*, the government could have sought a warrant, but chose not to.

"Assuming that they could have shown probable cause, I think there's a strong argument that the data would be tied to the actual investigation," Wessler added.

> *They either would have had to limit the information that they wanted or they would have had to provide an explanation to the court of why that whole four-month date range, [was needed]. That particularity requirement is what keeps the government in check. If they get a warrant for my house,*

because they think I stole washing machines off of a truck, it means they're allowed to look at my closet big enough to hide a washing machine but not my sock drawer. Those limitations have a lot of historical importance limiting the government's power.

The appeals court relied extensively on *Smith*, saying that the CSLI—admittedly less precise than GPS data, but still potentially revelatory—is effectively the same thing as the Baltimore robber's call records that the government obtained decades ago.

The 6th Circuit called out the ACLU's arguments on appeals as having "considerable irony," given that in its view, post-*Smith*, Congress has already established a middle ground through the 1986 ECPA. As the three-judge panel wrote:

> *The Katz standard asks whether the defendants' asserted expectation of privacy "is 'one that society is prepared to recognize as reasonable[.]'" Smith, 442 U.S. at 740 (quoting Katz, 389 U.S. at 361). Here, one might say that society itself— in the form of its elected representatives in Congress—has already struck a balance that it thinks reasonable.*

And what does Sachs make of this case, now decades removed from *Smith v. Maryland*? How would he have ruled if he were sitting on the 6th Circuit ruling on *Carpenter*? His prosecutorial roots still shine through.

"I would have felt constrained by the logic of *Smith* from our highest court," he e-mailed, noting that he probably would have "reluctantly" joined the conservative majority currently on the 6th Circuit, and ruled in favor of the government.

> *But I also would have drawn comfort from the presence of a judicial order under the Stored Communications Act requiring a "reasonable showing" for believing the records to be "relevant and material to an ongoing investigation." I recognize that this is not a warrant based on probable cause; but it is a slice of judicial oversight that attempts to accommodate advanced technology in pursuit of crime on the one hand, with the constitutional right of privacy, on the other.*

> *Along with the* Smith *logic that I helped create (oblivious to its potential for mischief down the road) I would have gotten over the hump.*

In short, absent further guidance from the Supreme Court, he would defer to the older precedent. However, were Sachs hypothetically on the Supreme Court when *Carpenter* was to be decided, he would probably rule the other way: "*Katz* has outlived its usefulness as a constitutional tool," and he certainly wouldn't have allowed the NSA metadata program to rely on the *Smith* ruling.

"I believe *Katz* must be replaced with a test that balances the constitutional right to privacy with public safety in the context of twenty-first-century technology," he concluded. "And, good old *Smith* is no longer a legitimate precedent for the massive surveillance undertaken in FISC Docket Number BR 13-109. It never was."

Sachs, who attended oral arguments for *Carpenter*, e-mailed me the following day that he thought Wessler was "professional and persuasive."

"I think the Court will attempt to create a digital-age Fourth Amendment doctrine, but there is no certainty what shape it will take," he wrote.

CHAPTER FOUR

When Big Brother Rides in the Back Seat

The system was kind of kept confidential from everybody in the public. A lot of people do have a problem with the eye in the sky, the Big Brother, so in order to mitigate any of those kinds of complaints, we basically kept it pretty hush-hush.

—Sgt. Doug Iketani
Los Angeles Sheriff's Department (2014)

July 27, 2012
Las Vegas, Nevada

At one of the world's most well-known hacker conferences, DEF CON, Mike Katz-Lacabe didn't stand out, even if he did sit in the front row.

As a middle-aged man with a protruding belly, a formidable salt-and-pepper beard, and a friendly smile, Katz-Lacabe was seated wearing a black T-shirt (the de facto DEF CON uniform) amidst hundreds of fellow conference attendees. Like these other digital security professionals, he was there to learn about all the new scary ways that devices could be threatened, and how to fight back. He was a regular, having attended DEF CON for over a decade.

The 45-year-old was attending a talk given by two American Civil Liberties Union (ACLU) lawyers and two technologists: "Can You Track Me Now? Government and Corporate Surveillance of Mobile Geo-Location Data."

"We are in a constitutional moment for location tracking," ACLU lawyer Ben Wizner began the talk (less than a year later, Wizner became Edward Snowden's lawyer).

"This year, a unanimous Supreme Court held that when the police put a GPS device on a car and track a driver's location over a prolonged period—that's a search under the Fourth Amendment." That is, a search that must be validated with a warrant. "They had never held that before. But we all know that the police probably do that thousands of times per year."

Over the course of about 100 minutes, the four-person panel outlined the myriad ways that location information can be obtained through mobile phone tracking, and how law enforcement can legally access that data. But, the panel only briefly addressed other ways that someone's location could be tracked or monitored, such as the license plate on a car.

When the panel was over, and the room began to empty out, Katz-Lacabe made a beeline for Catherine Crump, one of the ACLU attorneys.

As an experienced ACLU attorney, she was used to people approaching her with cockamamie theories about government surveillance. She'd even stopped answering her phone at her Lower Manhattan office because she'd otherwise be tied up with people who had a "wild theory about the micro-chip implanted in their head."

But Katz-Lacabe was different.

"I know all about [license plate readers (LPR)] and in fact, I have this photograph [of me] in my driveway getting out of the car," he told her, explaining that he had gotten a whole cache via a public records request, and promised to send it to her later that day.

Standing immediately beside Katz-Lacabe was Jennifer Valentino-DeVries, then a reporter with the *Wall Street Journal*—she immediately asked him for an interview and he was happy to oblige.

"He struck me as an old-school California nerd," she told me, recalling the first time they met.

"It's a particular type of nerd, you don't necessarily find them all the time. He had this combination of a little bit of paranoia that comes from knowing what the technology can do, but he was not one of the hard-core DEF CON hackers. He's an old-school guy and he brought his daughter to DEF CON—he seemed like a sweet, reasonable person."

But what sold her on Katz-Lacabe was the fact that he had the where-withal to file a public records request about himself.

"He had actual evidence of this happening to him personally," she added.

What had happened to Katz-Lacabe was happening to millions of Americans nationwide, almost entirely without their knowing. The government was not only collecting data on who people were calling and when, but was also recording where people were driving—often for years on end.

So, what provides the legal authority for law enforcement to routinely collect so much data? Proponents argue that a 1983 Supreme Court decision, *United States v. Knotts*, which found that there was no reasonable expectation of privacy in public, means that it's OK for officers to observe a license plate in public. Even though this ruling was made at least a decade before LPR went mainstream, the practical effect is that everyone's license plate can be scanned and potentially retained forever. In some ways, it's just like how Judge Eagan ruled in 2013 in FISC Docket Number BR 13-109 that if the third-party doctrine in *Smith v. Maryland* applies to one person in one limited situation (a single robbery in Baltimore), then it also applies to everyone, everywhere, authorizing the National Security Agency's metadata program.

◯

Katz-Lacabe attended UC Berkeley in the late 1980s and early 1990s, where he studied environmental science. As a student, he became politically active, joining Amnesty International. Years later, he and his Argentine wife, Margarita Lacabe, founded Derechos Human Rights, one of the first online human rights organizations.

As that work evolved, he became knowledgeable about the mechanics of filing a Freedom of Information Act request with federal authorities, or a similar request under the California Public Records Act. During the 1990s, he was the webmaster for School of the Americas Watch, an activist group dedicated to shutting down what was then called the School of the Americas. (The facility, based in Ft. Benning, Georgia, is now known as the Western Hemisphere Institute for Security Cooperation, or WHINSEC.) In 1961, during the Kennedy administration, the school was directed to "thwart armed communist insurgencies." Katz-Lacabe filed for, received, and digitized records from the Department of Defense to obtain the names of Latin American soldiers who had received training at the infamous school. The facility included among its alumni dozens of men who went on to become infamous authoritarians (Manuel Noriega) and drug lords (the two founders of Los Zetas cartel), among others.

In 2000, Katz-Lacabe and his wife moved from nearby Richmond to San Leandro. There, he threw himself into civic life, attending many public meetings, and eventually won a seat on the school board in 2006. Over time, his desire to understand the minutiae of government became insatiable. While in office, he went to numerous city council meetings. That was around the first time he heard the term "license plate reader." By 2010, he'd filed a public records request.

"I wonder what information they have on me," he thought to himself, and without missing a beat, sent off a public records request to the San Leandro Police Department. A few months later, they sent him over 100 photos, shot all over town, with their LPR cameras. But the photos weren't just of his license plate. Half of the photos were wide shots, of Katz-Lacabe's car: one at a coffee shop, one at a friend's house, among other places.

"Seeing those images caused me to be a lot more curious and pay a lot more attention," he said. "How long [was] the data retained? How [were] the images . . . captured? All sorts of stuff! And so I found out that my police department had no policy, or rather, their policy was to keep indefinitely."

Back at DEF CON, Katz-Lacabe kept his word to send the photo to Crump and to Valentino-DeVries. Albeit slightly blurry, it showed Katz-Lacabe and his two daughters getting out of his car in his driveway on November 14, 2009.

A few months later, on September 29, 2012, Valentino-DeVries and her colleague Julia Angwin published a front-page story in the *Wall Street Journal*: "New Tracking Frontier: Your License Plates."

That article was the first time this photo of Katz-Lacabe and his daughters was published in a major media outlet. It was also the first time that anyone on the San Leandro City Council had ever heard of LPR, despite the fact that they had already been in use in the Bay Area town for nearly five years.

◎

Sometimes, LPR misreads can even lead to a situation that results in guns being drawn.

On March 30, 2009, a woman named Denise Green, a local bus driver, was driving her 1992 red Lexus southbound on Mission Street in San Francisco. She was headed home, just after having picked up her sister from the hospital and taking her to the nearby 24th St. BART station. It was just after 11 PM—having been roused from her bed, she was wearing a zip-up sweatshirt and a beanie.

As she crossed the intersection of Highland and Mission Street, a police car appeared in her rearview mirror. She dutifully pulled over to allow the car to pass, but it followed her. Unsure of what to expect, Green simply waited. After just a minute, the police officer barked at her.

"Put your hands up!"

She did so, and then was promptly ordered to keep her hands up, open her window, open the door from the outside, and get out of the car. She did that, too. Other officers' voices began to crescendo, and she saw guns drawn.

"Don't look at us!" one yelled. "Turn around!"

The first officer demanded that she get on her knees—she thought about how they were already sore from being in bad shape. But again, she complied.

Some of the men started searching her car, and one told her to stand up. She said she was too weak to stand, particularly while handcuffed. With the help of two officers, she eventually did stand up.

"It's not a seven? No, three five zero," Green overheard one of the officers tell another. While waiting for the San Francisco cops to sort out what was going on, various of her fellow city bus drivers passed her while she stood, stunned, in handcuffs. Some were even local transit supervisor trucks, and she turned her back to them so they wouldn't see her: she was mortified.

Finally, one of the men came over to explain that a San Francisco Police Department vehicle equipped with an LPR had misread her license plate. Once they confirmed that her Lexus was not, in fact, stolen. She was free to go.

Later, as part of her civil lawsuit, she and her attorneys determined that the LPR had misread her plate, reading 5SOW750—the stolen car—rather than 5SOW350, her actual plate. Some of San Francisco's finest, however, had failed to check that what the machine read was actually the car that they observed with their own eyes. She sued the city and the officers in June 2010. When city lawyers attempted to get the case dismissed, Green's claims were upheld on appeal in 2014, and the case eventually settled in November 2015.

Green's case is indicative of what can happen when law enforcement is too reliant on automated technology.

Fourteen years after the FBI first began testing the technology, LPRs are now in use nearly everywhere across America. These are essentially specialized cameras that can scan license plates incredibly fast—60 plates per second. When mounted on a police patrol car, they can scan in multiple directions, capturing cars driving in front or parked perpendicular. LPRs use the same optical character recognition technology as modern-day desktop scanners. The software can read license plates, which have a standard size and format, and compare them against a "hot list" of stolen or wanted cars.

If the LPR scans a "hot" car, the computer inside the police car will alert the officer, and she or he is typically supposed to verify that the scanned plate actually matches the wanted plate, and that it's attached to the right make and model of car.

The three largest vendors of LPR hardware and software are Elsag North America (a subsidiary of an Italian defense contractor), Xerox, and 3M (the LPR division was sold in June 2017 to a private equity firm). These companies routinely encourage local police agencies to apply for federal grants to make the purchase of these products more palatable to budget-constrained localities.

In 2014, for example, the Central Marin Police Authority, which governs portions of Marin County, north of San Francisco, successfully obtained a $132,000 federal grant to bolster its anti-terrorism efforts. However, there have never been any terrorist attacks in Marin County, nor have any terror-ism suspects been caught. This money went towards purchasing three LPRs on Sir Francis Drake Boulevard, a major county thoroughfare.

The result is that law enforcement agencies, ranging from small towns in Marin County to the FBI, are routinely scanning the license plates of ordinary citizens. Because local money is rarely used, there's been relatively little scrutiny paid to how the devices are used in practice, who has access to the data collected, and how long it is kept.

Depending on the retention policy of the agency, police might keep that data for minutes, days, weeks, months, or even years. In New Hampshire, LPRs were banned outright until the state passed a 2016 law restricting data collection to three minutes, unless it was part of an arrest, citation, or another such limited circumstance. By contrast, the California Highway Patrol retains the data for 60 days. There are just 14 states nationwide that have some sort of regulation on LPRs—the rest leave it up to local jurisdictions. Police in Oakland, California, had no retention policy until their absurdly small 80GB hard drive filled up with LPR data in 2015.

While many people might feel that they have nothing to hide, or that their lives are so boring that it doesn't matter if the police keep a record of their movements, press a little and that viewpoint becomes a bit harder to defend. After all, LPRs don't just record your drives to and from work, but they also may collect information about your activities that you may not want the government to keep a record of: where you slept last night, what gun stores you go to, what mosque you attend, what doctor you visit, what sex-toy shop you like, what marijuana dispensary you frequent, or what gay bar you prefer.

To be fair, the snapshot that an LPR collects is not the same as pervasive tracking that can be performed through GPS or cell phone surveillance, and law enforcement are typically well-aware of this distinction. Most people have no idea what an LPR camera even looks like, much less where they are mounted. Police typically place them on patrol cars, but sometimes—as is the case in Piedmont, California, a small wealthy enclave surrounded by Oakland; and Tiburon, California, a well-to-do small town north of San Francisco—cities sometimes mount them in a stationary location along the only roads in and out of the city as a way to know who is coming and going. (In Piedmont's case, its 30 readers generate between 1 and 1.4 million records a month, according to Katz-Lacabe.)

"The collection itself and the retention of that information is a violation of norms in a free society," Kade Crockford, an activist with the ACLU of Massachusetts who has studied LPRs for several years, told me. "The basic norm [is] that [if] you are not engaged in unlawful activity and the government has no reason to believe that you're engaged in unlawful activity, the police should not be monitoring what you're doing. It's none of the government's business."

LPR collection is undoubtedly useful: there are numerous stories, often touted by the agencies and equipment vendors themselves, that provide easy anecdotes of how LPRs help investigate crimes. On its website, Elsag touts the February 2017 story of a burglar who was stealing from churches and who was ultimately stopped because police in Leawood, Kansas, were notified when he turned up at a church. In 2015, in a higher-profile example, LPRs were used to find Vester Lee Flanagan, the man who shot two Virginia television reporters while on the air.

However, these success stories overwhelmingly remain the exception rather than the rule. Katz-Lacabe's own research has repeatedly shown that nearly all of the data collected by LPRs does not off-set the "hot plate" trigger. In fact, more than 99 percent of all plates scanned are of innocent, law-abiding people, according to 2013 research spearheaded by Catherine Crump.

◯

The *Knotts* case is reminiscent of the cast of characters in the hit television series *Breaking Bad*: a group of Minnesota men conspire to create amphetamine. There was Leroy "Tuffy" Knotts and Daryl Petschen, plus the group's chemist, a man named Tristan Armstrong.

According to court filings, Armstrong worked as a chemical technician for many years at 3M in St. Paul, and had an academic interest in the creation of the drug. Armstrong, who had previously served in the US Army, was financially in dire straits. Armstrong and Petschen first met each other through a mutual friend in April 1978.

Petschen took Armstrong to his small house on a leafy street near the campus of Macalester College, where they had scoped out a possible lab site in the basement. Petschen led the operation, and took charge of the distribution of their product.

"Leave it to me," Petschen told Armstrong, adding that Armstrong should watch his back for surveillance, and that if he were caught, he should say nothing and request a lawyer immediately.

By the summer though, the operation had moved 20 miles out of town to Stillwater, Minnesota, along the banks of the St. Croix River, which forms the border with Wisconsin. (Later, however, they moved again to a new location back in St. Paul.) Much of the equipment and the chemical precursor phenylacetone were stolen by Armstrong from 3M. When 3M finally caught wind of this in early 1979, the company promptly fired Armstrong.

Amazingly, upon questioning, Armstrong agreed to speak with agents from the Minnesota Bureau of Criminal Apprehension (BCA), a state law enforcement agency. But he lied to them, saying that he had sold the stolen chemicals to a fictitious person. When Petschen learned of Armstrong's unmasking, he halted production. However, the two men changed tactics—they created companies, including Tandem Chemical Company and Research Ombudsman, to legally buy the chemicals and related equipment outright.

Minnesota authorities were still suspicious of Armstrong after their interview with him, and they continued to monitor his behavior. By June 1979, Petschen and the others had pulled out of the third lab location on 1698 Leone Avenue in St. Paul. Later, investigators found "tubing, hosing, glassware, and other lab-related items" at the abandoned location.

As summer turned into fall and then winter, local law enforcement continued to monitor the men. They watched them pick up boxes and move them around the region. On February 28, 1980, knowing that Armstrong was set to retrieve an order from Hawkins chemical company in Roseville, Minnesota, the police, with permission from the company, installed a beeper on a chemical drum of chloroform that he'd ordered.

This beeper—a low-range FM radio transmitter about three inches long and weighing half a pound—allowed the police to follow Armstrong's movements electronically while they also followed him in person. Notably, the police did not have a warrant to install this tracking device on the drum.

Armstrong took the drum to Petschen's small two-bedroom house at 1498 Albany Avenue in St. Paul. The pair then took some boxes and the chloroform drum and moved them into Petschen's vehicle, and Petschen then took off for Shell Lake, Wisconsin, approximately 100 miles away. According to court records, police lost sight of Petschen twice—once on purpose, when the agent following him pulled back, afraid that Petschen was aware that he was being surveilled. Court records also show that the police lost "total contact" (including via the beeper) for "approximately one half to one hour."

But Petschen's loss of the police tail was short-lived. After bringing in a helicopter to track down the beeper's signal once again, the police determined that Petschen was at a remote and isolated cabin near Shell Lake, and they set up a team to watch the comings and goings. The following day, February 29, authorities saw Petschen leave the cabin with Knotts in his car.

Four days later, on March 3, 1980, at 5:30 AM, Wisconsin police executed a search warrant of the cabin, where they found evidence implicating the men in the drug operation: especially a "fully operable laboratory located behind some moveable paneling." Chemists from the Minnesota BCA and the Drug Enforcement Administration (DEA) both determined that with the gear found in the cabin, the men would have been nearly ready to make methamphetamine.

Quickly, all three men were arrested. Armstrong pleaded guilty and testified against his former partners. Petschen and Knotts were charged with conspiracy to manufacture controlled substances.

As Mark Peterson, who served as one of Knotts' lawyers, explained, beepers were still a relatively new technology.

"Back then the monitoring capabilities were nothing close to what they are now," he said.

Before trial, the defendants' lawyers attempted to suppress the evidence found in the cabin due to the warrantless use of the beeper.

"That was really the only issue," Peterson added. "There was no question that they were guilty of what they were accused of, the question was whether they had a Fourth Amendment issue that was viable."

The judge ruled against Petschen and Knotts. The men were found guilty after a jury trial concluded on July 23, 1980, and were sentenced to five years on September 26, 1980.

Less than two weeks later, on appeal to the 8th US Circuit Court of Appeals, defense lawyers pursued a strategy based entirely on the notion that without the use of the beeper, police would never have found the cabin.

"Resolution of this contention must commence with consideration of the seminal privacy-expectation case, *Katz v. United States*," Petschen and Knotts' attorneys wrote in their brief to the court.

The government, in its responding brief, immediately cited both *Katz* and *Smith*, saying that because the beeper was installed with the company's permission before Armstrong took possession of it, "there is no violation of Fourth Amendment rights." That is, the chemical company is here analogous to the phone company, with whom the defendants did not have a reasonable expectation of privacy.

Plus, Department of Justice lawyers added, the "appellants could not reasonably have expected to keep private the route that Petschen drove through Minnesota and Wisconsin," citing the Supreme Court's conclusion in *Katz* that "what a person knowingly exposes to the public is not a subject of Fourth Amendment protection." This notion would prove to be key upon further appeal to the Supreme Court, and would go on to power all manner of trouble for those monitored in their cars via LPRs.

In October 1981, the 8th Circuit ruled that while Petschen did not have a privacy interest while leading the police to a secret drug lab, Knotts—as it was his farmhouse—did. The court ruled against Petschen, but in favor of Knotts.

In short, the 8th Circuit indicated that while Petschen was known to authorities beforehand as a person of interest as part of the Armstrong investigation, the case against Knotts was entirely pursued as a result of the search of his farm.

As the court, in a 2–1 ruling, concluded:

> The difficulty in applying the test of "legitimate expectations
> of privacy" in electronic surveillance cases is that consider-
> ation of such expectations leads almost ineluctably to the
> "philosophical question" whether the constitutional protec-

*tions of privacy must or should diminish with technological
innovations in surveillance . . .*

    *Knotts, as the resident of the property, could certainly
have a reasonable, legitimate expectation of privacy in the
kind and location of objects out of public view on his land.
With Petschen, however, this is not so.*

The government, unsatisfied that Knotts might be allowed to go free, appealed the case up to the Supreme Court.

In the 1982 term, the court was nearly the same as it was during *Smith*, with the notable exception of Justice Sandra Day O'Connor—who had just joined the court months earlier. A Reagan-nominated conservative jurist, O'Connor was the first female justice ever on the Supreme Court.

At oral arguments, which were held on December 6, 1982, early questions for Deputy Solicitor General Andrew Frey turned to the specifics of the technology, whether someone else might be able to hear the signal emitted by the beeper.

But, Frey quickly drove home his point, again, echoing *Katz*.

> *This is not a search in the traditional sense. It is not the un-
> invited eye or uninvited ear that is seeing or hearing what
> is going on in private areas. In fact, all that is examined
> in this search is the airwaves around the receiver being
> operated by the officers. Now, of course, Katz teaches that
> even such activity may be considered a search regulated
> by the Fourth Amendment, but whether it is depends on
> whether what is disclosed by this kind of activity is private
> or non-private information.*

Frey drew the line from *Katz* to *Smith* and now, to *Knotts*.

> *Now, this question of whether this use of the beeper in this
> case was a search is quite similar to the issue the Court
> confronted in* Smith against Maryland, *which involved the
> monitoring by use of a pen register of phone numbers dialed
> from the suspect's home.*
>   *The Court held that it was not a search, in large part be-
> cause the information acquired was not private information.*

*Now, so here, the monitoring of the transmitter to follow the
co-defendant's car while it moved on the public highways
would not be a search, and indeed neither the court of appeals nor Respondent has suggested otherwise.*

As Frey continued, he reiterated to the court that not all police surveillance
activity is considered in breach of the Constitution.

"I would want to make the point that even perfectly innocent activity,
walking down the street to have lunch, is subject without being regulated by
the Fourth Amendment to visual surveillance, bloodhounds, radar, night
glasses, many—" he said, before Chief Justice Warren Burger interrupted.

"Don't try to tell Sam Ervin that," Burger intoned, invoking the name
of a retired conservative Democratic senator from North Carolina who
was well-known during the 1970s for leading the investigation of President
Richard Nixon. Ervin was a staunch advocate of civil liberties and privacy.

But it was Justice Thurgood Marshall who had the last word in his quiet
voice, stepping on the words of Burger: "Don't try any of them on me." He
repeated it again, clearly this time. "Don't try any of them on me."

The normally silent court erupted in laughter. While his colleagues may
not have fully appreciated it at the time, Justice Marshall was saying something beyond a mere quip. As the nation's first African-American Supreme
Court justice, he knew that minorities were often subjected to police surveillance more than their white counterparts. He also knew that nobody
likes to be followed around.

Then, it was Mark Peterson's turn. As Knotts' lawyer, he had to convince
the eight men and one woman that the lower court's ruling was the correct one.

"If this Court allows warrantless beeper monitoring in any situation,
which is in essence what the government is asking for here, that rule would
allow virtually unlimited monitoring of our private lives," he argued.

The justices hammered Peterson on questions of why the installation of
the beeper required a warrant. Put simply, the government's goal was to
track Petschen's location. After all, as Chief Justice Burger wondered, "On
what basis would a magistrate issue a warrant for a lawful, innocent drum
of chloroform in a warehouse?"

After a few more questions, Peterson responded definitively: "Our
contention here, Mr. Chief Justice, is that they should get a warrant and
the Constitution requires them to get a warrant if they are going to use
the beeper which has been installed either to determine the location of

non-contraband property at a person's residence or to monitor its continued presence at that location."

Burger quickly interrupted him again.

"Well, what if [it's] a beeper that is sought to be put on a plane by undercover agents down in Bogota, Colombia, because they know that a couple of million dollars worth of heroin or something is going to be transported on an airplane?" he said. "Any authority on a U.S. magistrate or any magistrate in the United States to put a beeper on an airplane down in Bogota, Colombia?"

Peterson paused for what seemed like lengthy beats, and then admitted: "I am not aware of any such authority, Your Honor."

This was a direct reference to a similar situation from just a few years earlier: *United States v. Bruneau*. That 1979 case, which also arose from Minnesota, and also from the 8th Circuit, was denied a hearing before the Supreme Court. While the case was not formally heard before the court, the justices were undoubtedly familiar with the issues that it brought up.

In *Bruneau*, a Minnesota man named William Lloyd David Cooper orchestrated an "extensive scheme to import large quantities of marijuana from Mexico into the United States." He organized numerous flights into Arizona, Texas, Minnesota, and even Alaska between May 1975 and May 1976. Later that month, prosecutors returned a 28-count indictment against 15 defendants, including Cooper. Amongst the other defendants were two men, Dale David Bruneau and Jeffrey Charles Kohner, who were found guilty, and appealed their convictions.

During the investigation, a DEA special agent asked a federal judge in Phoenix to put a beeper on a particular plane that was believed to aid crimes within the United States. With the permission of its then owner, agents put the beeper on the plane before it was sold to Cooper. As a result, they were easily able to monitor the plane's movements as it crossed in and out of the United States.

Bruneau and Kohner challenged their guilty verdicts before the 8th Circuit on the grounds that the beeper was a search under the Fourth Amendment, and therefore required a warrant. If the beeper was not a search, the DEA didn't even need a court order, even though it sought one. By the time *Bruneau* had reached the 8th Circuit, there were numerous cases that involved the use of beepers, often as part of investigations into drug trafficking.

The argument that beepers aren't searches is somewhat analogous to the pen register argument: it only "facilitates manual, visual surveillance," as the 8th Circuit wrote. Basically, a beeper, under this theory, is more like binoculars—no warrant is necessary. But beepers also allow for "continual observation over longs periods of time," and give up location when inside the boundaries of private property. In short, the 8th Circuit found itself in a legal quandary.

"The apparent struggle in the above cases to reach an acceptable approach to the use of beepers indicates the complexity of this issue," the court concluded. "At the root of the debate is the philosophical question of whether our sense of privacy, and the protection afforded it by the Constitution, does and should adjust to technological advances. With due respect for the complexity of this issue we limit our decision to the precise issue before us: whether the use of a transponder to track aircraft in public airspace constitutes a search within the Fourth Amendment."

So how did the 8th Circuit eventually come down on the issue in *Bruneau*? "Applying the *Katz* test, our inquiry becomes: what is one's reasonable, subjective expectation of privacy in the airborne location of an airplane? There can be but one answer: none."

In other words, the court explained that planes need to broadcast their location in the interests of safety, so there can be no such privacy interest. As part of its analysis, the 8th Circuit in *Bruneau* also cited a 1977 law review paper that reached a similar conclusion for ground vehicles.

"When the electronic beeper is used to track vehicles, the relevant individual interests are the location and movement of the tracked subject while traveling public highways," wrote Kara L. Cook, the paper's author. "These interests or information are not private since they are not germane to the intimacies of personal identity. Hence, use of the beeper to track automobiles should not be considered a search."

Cook's language was echoed in the 1983 unanimous ruling that the Supreme Court reached in *Knotts*.

"A person traveling in an automobile on public thoroughfares has no reasonable expectation of privacy in his movements," the justices wrote, overturning the 8th Circuit's ruling for the would-be meth dealer. Law enforcement agencies have seized on this line as their legal justification for LPRs.

In other words, like in *Smith*, this was focused on only a limited circumstance—the court said that even if 1980s-era beeper technology were to improve, that was for a future Supreme Court to worry about.

"If such dragnet-type law enforcement practices as respondent envisions should eventually occur, there will be time enough then to determine whether different constitutional principles may be applicable," they wrote. "Insofar as respondent's complaint appears to be simply that scientific devices such as the beeper enabled the police to be more effective in detecting crime, it simply has no constitutional foundation. We have never equated police efficiency with unconstitutionality, and we decline to do so now."

When interviewed about the result in 2017, Frey, who is now in private practice, said that the court reached the right decision.

"The invasion of privacy was minimal in our view," he told me. "The way I like to think about these cases was if you were a law-abiding citizen, would you find it to be an offensive invasion of privacy to have this done to you, when you're trying to balance the interests in privacy against the law enforcement interests."

In other words, it's one thing to track one person over a short period of time. But it's another thing entirely for an entire population's data to be recorded for an undetermined period of time.

In 1997, an officer with the Metropolitan Police Department in Washington, DC (who himself was in charge of investigating extortion) was indicted on federal charges of carrying out his own extortion scheme of gay men. According to an FBI affidavit, Lieutenant Jeffery Scott Stowe used the department's computer system to identify the person who owned a car parked near a gay bar in Southeast Washington—and attempted to extort $10,000 from the man. (Stowe, who took a plea deal, was eventually sentenced to 23 months in prison.)

While this case did not use LPR technology, it would have been made considerably easier if it had. Rather than one officer having to manually write down a license plate, all he or she would have to do would be to routinely drive by gay bars, and let a machine do the work.

But as LPRs became commonplace, they began to be used to conduct investigations and capture data on a scale that was previously not humanly possible.

Documents released by the DEA suggest that the Bureau of Alcohol, Tobacco and Firearms (ATF) used LPRs to monitor those attending gun shows in 2009. In 2012, the New York Police Department (NYPD) used LPRs mounted on unmarked police cars to routinely capture all license plates seen near particular mosques as a way to conduct broad surveillance of Muslims in the area.

The following year, the NYPD expanded the program to capture all cars coming in or out of the city. According to a June 2013 Reuters report, New

York City had "about 120 license plate readers" mounted on bridges, tunnels, and traffic lights, with plans to up that number to 200. Another 100 were on regular police patrol cars. At the time the article was published, the NYPD retained LPR information for up to five years—officers could easily call up a given vehicle's history at the touch of a button.

In September 2014, an enterprising reporter at the *Minneapolis Star Tribune* obtained the LPR records—including date, time, location—of Mayor R. T. Rybak.

In January 2015, through a public records request to the Oakland Police Department, the Electronic Frontier Foundation showed that "lower-income neighborhoods are disproportionately captured by LPR patrols, with police vehicles creating a grid of license plates in the city's poorest neighborhoods."

Meanwhile, in November 2015, a Los Angeles city council member even went so far as to propose that LPRs be used to automatically send a Dear John letter to any car seen in neighborhoods known to be frequented by prostitutes and men who seek them out.

Mike Katz-Lacabe, the San Leandro privacy activist, remains unconvinced that such a vast trove of data is worth the potential for abuse.

"I don't doubt that having an unlimited amount of this data will be useful or could be useful, but so would getting rid of the requirement of warrants," he said. "I don't have anything to hide in the bathroom, but that doesn't mean I want a camera in there either."

Meanwhile, Frey, who served as the government's lawyer in *Knotts*, when informed years later that the case has since been used to justify the expansion of LPR technology, said he remained unconcerned.

"I would feel safer and I wouldn't feel intruded upon . . . to live in a society where those pictures can be retrieved by the police," he told me. "That's my approach to it. Other people have different approaches. If you have an authoritarian state it could be used to track down resistance. But if you had an authoritarian state, talking about search warrants would be pointless."

Then he paused a moment and mused, "I understand that when you have Jeff Sessions as attorney general and Donald Trump as president, those concerns become heightened."

Many cities are deploying their own LPRs either as stationary (above roads, for example) or mobile (on police cars) devices to collect license plate data, which is then compared to a city, regional, state, or federal database. Sometimes cities also access privately held license plate databases as well.

Vigilant Solutions, a company based in Livermore, California—45 miles east of San Francisco—is believed to hold the largest such database, with billions of records collected from all over the country. Through its subsidiary, Digital Recognition Network (DRN), Vigilant sells camera kits to repossession companies nationwide, according to a 2014 court filing by DRN's founder.

"The camera affiliates place DRN's ALPR systems on tow trucks or other vehicles," founder Todd Hodnett said in an affidavit. "DRN's ALPR systems then take photographs that include nearby vehicles' license plates. When DRN's camera affiliates collect license-plate data using ALPR systems, DRN then disseminates the resulting license-plate data to its clients and partners, which use the data for purposes such as identifying cars that should be repossessed and locating cars that have been stolen or fraudulently reported as stolen. For example, DRN earns substantial revenue by selling license-plate data to automobile lenders and insurance companies."

In addition, the parent company—Vigilant Solutions—takes that data and makes it available to law enforcement, often at little or no cost. Vigilant uses the data to entice companies to buy hardware and other services.

Its website and press releases herald numerous "success stories" with quotes from law enforcement agencies nationwide. (Access to Vigilant's database, known as LEARN-NVLS, requires that officers agree to a non-disparagement clause contained within the company's terms of service.)

"Woman's Life Saved using Vigilant Solutions' License Plate Recognition (LPR) Data," one success story touts. Another proclaims: "Survey: License Plate Recognition Is a Valuable, Well-Regulated Technology," citing a poll of hundreds of law enforcement officers.

As a private company, Vigilant Solutions does not disclose financial data, but in 2013, a company official told the *San Francisco Business Times* that its "products and services are used by more than 2,000 government agencies with 30,000-plus officers, including about two dozen agencies in the Bay Area." (Curiously, the same article noted that CEO Shawn Smith not only declined an interview, but also declined to have his photo taken.)

Vigilant has made a considerable effort not only to sell to law enforcement, but also to convince lawmakers and the public of the benefits of the company's technology.

One notable example came in January 2014, when State Senator Jerry Hill (D-San Francisco) introduced a bill that would have put a damper on Vigilant's business model in the Golden State—if passed, it would have restricted the private sale of LPR data.

"Law enforcement will still be able to continue to use LPR technology to catch criminals," Hill said in a statement. "But Californians will have peace of mind that their personal information is safeguarded."

In April 2014, Vigilant commissioned a poll, which concluded, according to a press release, that the "majority of Californians agree that license plate reader (LPR) technology helps law enforcement solve crimes and any restrictions on who can photograph license plates would be unacceptable."

However, under scrutiny, the poll was revealed to not be particularly scientific. Amongst other flaws, the poll did not explain to the respondents what an LPR was, or even confirm whether people had a basic familiarity with the technology.

Some of the questions were oddly worded: "Do you agree or disagree that license plates reveal nothing about me. People who see my license plate cannot determine my name or where I live."

While 24 percent of respondents said they strongly agree, the question refers to "people who see my license plate," not machines. The questions also do not make clear that LPR data, when gathered by a private firm like Vigilant, is then routinely handed to the cops who can definitely determine your name and where you live.

The following month, May 2015, Senator Hill withdrew the bill.

Later that year, however, Vigilant Solutions encountered some small-time competition: a new piece of open-source software that allows anyone to roll-their-own LPR, known as OpenALPR.

It seems like only a matter of time before this technology becomes so common that anyone can set up a camera at their home, or point it at their local police station.

"I would love to have something to rein in the use of private LPRs, I don't know how likely that is given our country, it seems that with our current administration and Congress, that would be unlikely," Katz-Lacabe said.

The idea that Vigilant Solutions has this database of 3.2 billion records and there is no regulation about it, that just

*bothers me. It enables law enforcement to do something that
they wouldn't be able to do themselves. How can government
make decisions on behalf of its citizens when they can be so
readily bypassed?*

◯

However, LPRs—despite the fact that most Americans wouldn't know what
one looks like even if it was staring them in the face—are practically old
news. There are even more advanced technologies, including body-worn
cameras and large-scale aerial surveillance that take wanton data capture
to an entirely new level. All of these technologies, under the *Knotts* precedent, are predicated on the legal theory that there is no reasonable expectation of privacy when in public. These technologies are converging, and
there seems to be little to stop their inevitable ubiquity.

Body cameras are rapidly becoming the norm across America, in cities
big and small. In May 2014, in Katz-Lacabe's hometown, the San Leandro
City Council formally approved the purchase of body-worn cameras for the
San Leandro Police Department. They cost the city more than $440,000 over
five years for the cameras and data storage. That wasn't too much for the city
to bear: the annual police budget for 2015–2016 was over $30.9 million.

While it couldn't have known it at the time, San Leandro was about to
join hundreds, if not thousands of American law enforcement agencies that
would quickly be pushed into acquiring cameras and putting them on their
officers.

San Leandro, a small working-class city (population 85,000) to the im-
mediate southeast of Oakland, is one of the Bay Area cities that had restric-
tive covenants—a clause in a deed or lease that restricts what the owners can
do with their property, often used to restrict African-Americans from own-
ing or leasing property in a given area—for decades. In 1960, the city was
nearly entirely white, while Oakland, in comparison, had a large African-
American population. By 2010, Asian-Americans comprised roughly one-
third of San Leandro's population.

Less than three months after the San Leandro City Council approved
the purchase of body cameras, in August 2014, Michael Brown, an un-
armed black 18-year-old in Ferguson, Missouri, was shot and killed by a

local cop. Like most law enforcement agencies nationwide at the time, the Ferguson Police Department lacked body cameras. On December 1, 2014, the White House announced a three-year, $263 million grant program for local law enforcement body cameras. Many agencies, like the San Leandro Police Department (SLPD), were already in the process of obtaining body cameras, but Ferguson helped accelerate deployment in many cities.

"There's been a lot of talk about body cameras as a silver bullet or a solution," said President Barack Obama in March 2015. "I think the task force concluded that there is a role for technology to play in building additional trust and accountability, but it's not a panacea. It has to be embedded in a broader change in culture and a legal framework that ensures that people's privacy is respected and that not only police officers but the community themselves feel comfortable with how technologies are being used."

As body cameras have become more and more commonplace, it's become clear that many police reform activists and lots of rank-and-file officers want cameras, albeit for different reasons. The activists want them because they don't trust the police and want a way to keep tabs on them. Cops, by contrast, often feel that they are being wrongly accused by over-zealous citizens who have been fed a steady diet of police brutality videos, and may use lethal force to express that anger.

Cities like body cameras as they can help exonerate officers accused of misconduct, and protect against lawsuits, which can be costly to defend. After all, even in quiet San Leandro, the city has silently ended numerous cases in recent years rather than let a civil rights case go to trial.

In 2013, the city paid out $80,000 to settle claims brought by the family of a man who was high on methamphetamine and ended up dying after a struggle with police. In an even stranger incident, San Leandro settled with two men for $45,000 after the pair was accused of engaging in lewd conduct at a local marina restroom. In 2007, San Leandro paid a $395,000 settlement to the family of Jose Maravilla Perez, Jr., who died at the hands of the SLPD after he was repeatedly shocked with a Taser.

In more recent and higher-profile examples from other cities the list goes on: In 2015, Baltimore, Maryland, settled with the estate of Freddie Gray for $6.4 million. In 2017, St. Anthony, Minnesota, settled with the estate of Philando Castile for $3 million. Also in 2017, Ferguson, Missouri, settled with the estate of Michael Brown for $1 million. In short, cities nationwide are pushing for body cameras to make sure that both citizen and officer are on their best behavior.

But like LPRs, where data-retention policies are all over the map, so it is with body-worn cameras. In Pueblo, Colorado, some camera footage is kept indefinitely. In Minnesota, traffic stops are kept for a year. In Orlando, Florida, non-evidentiary body-camera videos are kept for 90 days, while in Oakland, California, those same videos are kept for two years.

Just like with other consumer technology, which is getting faster, cheaper, and smaller all the time, law enforcement surveillance technology is as well. Even now, a Silicon Valley startup, Visual Labs, is selling body-camera software that runs on existing Android phones—eliminating the need for another dedicated piece of hardware on an officer's body.

The small, central California town of Dos Palos (population 5,000) in Merced County is one of a handful of law enforcement agencies testing out this system, and is paying considerably less than it would with one of Visual Labs' larger competitors, like VIEVU or Axon (the company formerly known as Taser).

◌

For now, facial recognition works a lot better in theory than it does in practice, but it's rapidly improving. While the idea of scanning someone's face to establish their identity has been floating around science fiction for years, it has now quietly become the norm.

The technology works, in essence, as a more sophisticated version of LPRs, where software—rather than analyzing letters and numbers—is quickly measuring various physical characteristics, ranging from the distance between the pupils to the shape of one's jaw, among many others. Like LPR technology, facial recognition is most useful when there's a "hot list" of faces to compare an unknown face with. To the government's advantage, there already is such a list: photos are found in the Department of Motor Vehicles of all states, and the Department of State's passport photo database.

However, facial recognition doesn't work nearly as well when the captured image is of a person who is African-American, captured at a distance, turned at a non-straight angle, or wearing a hoodie or a head covering of some type. Even the 2013 Boston bombing suspects were not caught via facial recognition—it is far more effective when the photo is taken under controlled circumstances (like a mug shot) and compared to a database with similar-quality photos. (Although, algorithms to mitigate this hurdle are rapidly improving, as 2015 research by Facebook shows.)

In October 2016, Georgetown researchers released a massive report titled "The Perpetual Lineup," which found that half of all adults in the United States are already in a facial-recognition database. The report also found that in many cases, steps are not being taken to create meaningful policies and oversight for use of the technology. To take one example, there's nothing stopping law enforcement from capturing faces at large gatherings like sporting events (which took place during the Super Bowl as early as 2001) and political protests.

Georgetown professor Alvaro Bedoya, top FBI official Kimberly Del Greco, and a number of other activists and government officials were invited to speak before a House committee hearing in March 2017. Bedoya and others warned that facial-recognition technology had potential racial bias built in. They found that such systems often issue more false positives for African-Americans compared to other groups. Plus, the technology could potentially be used to suppress political speech.

"I think there's been an aggressive development of technology come to the forefront," Representative Stephen Lynch (D-Massachusetts) said during the hearing. "When you think about how this could change who we are as a nation, it's very, very troubling. This nation was founded on protest and is continually shaped by protest. It disturbs me greatly whether it was the death of Freddie Gray and those protests, or the women's protest recently that was all over the country, it disturbs me greatly that we're out there taking in this information."

Lawmakers acknowledged that as a society we all want criminal suspects to be investigated, apprehended, and brought to justice as appropriate. However, the idea of pervasive image capture by street cops as a way to routinely and automatically identify individuals is just as invasive as demanding that everyone show their papers at a moment's notice.

For now, the most prominent uses of facial recognition are relatively low-level: a man who fled federal custody 25 years ago was arrested in Nevada in July 2017 due to that state's facial-recognition technology finding out that he had already been issued a driver's license under a different name.

In June 2017, a Jacksonville, Florida, man—who told undercover policemen that his name was "Midnight" during a $50 crack cocaine buy—was sentenced to eight years in prison after he was identified via facial recognition. An Indiana man who was suspected of child molestation in 1999 was arrested in Oregon in January 2017 due to a facial-recognition search. A year earlier, in January 2016, New York State authorities said they had arrested 100 people over identity fraud stemming from an upgrade to an automatic scan of their Department of Motor Vehicles records. Like with LPRs, it's likely that the hit rate remains quite low.

While facial recognition is currently in use by local and federal law enforcement, it is only a matter of time before this technology is fully integrated into body-worn cameras, making it yet another tool in an officer's toolkit. In fact, both Axon executives and at least some police officers relish the notion.

In July 2016, Lieutenant Dan Zehnder, of the Las Vegas Police Department, who runs the agency's body-camera program, imagines a near-future tool where an officer on patrol on the Las Vegas Strip's camera routinely captures all faces and the scans are sent to be analyzed off-site.

"And there is real-time analysis, and then in my earpiece there is, 'Hey, that guy you just passed 20 feet ago has an outstanding warrant.' Wow," he told *Bloomberg Businessweek*.

No courts anywhere have addressed the question as to whether facial recognition should be treated like a pair of binoculars (no court order or warrant required), or if it is an invasive law enforcement technique, analogous to a wiretap, which requires a super-warrant standard.

◎

For now, LPRs, body-worn cameras, and facial-recognition technology are largely limited to terrestrial applications. They routinely capture particular types of data in a limited environment, the field of view of the camera. But what happens when that field of view is expanded to 10,000 feet in the air?

Persistent Surveillance Systems (PSS) does exactly that. For years, the company has been operating a TiVo-in-the-sky setup: a plane equipped with specialized cameras designed to capture all movement down below over long periods of time. It's designed to help law enforcement track suspect vehicles and people, proving that they were at the location of particular crime scenes. (Harris Corporation, the maker of the stingray, which will be covered later in the book, makes a similar product, known as the CorvusEye.)

The Dayton, Ohio, company is run by Ross McNutt, a former Air Force officer who wants domestic policing to be more like military intelligence. He's been working on this technology for over a decade, back when it first began as a military research project at the Air Force Institute of Technology.

"We have hundreds of politicians that say crime is their number one issue, and no it's not," McNutt told Ars Technica in July 2014. "If it was true, they wouldn't stand for 36,000 crimes a year (per city), worth a $1 billion a year. It shows up in lower housing prices and it shows in people not wanting to move there. If you could get rid of the crime stigma you would see house prices rise and businesses move there. I am frustrated that politicians don't have the leadership to do it."

For years, PSS has attempted to get cities to sign on as permanent customers, but it's run into roadblocks. In 2011, the company ran a trial in Compton, California, for nine days, but kept it quiet from local politicians, community members, and reporters. That trial was not revealed publicly until the Center for Investigative Reporting did a story on it in April 2014.

"The system was kind of kept confidential from everybody in the public," Los Angeles Sheriff's Department sergeant Doug Iketani said. "A lot of people do have a problem with the eye in the sky, the Big Brother, so in order to mitigate any of those kinds of complaints, we basically kept it pretty hush-hush."

In 2013, Dayton, Ohio—the hometown of PSS—wouldn't even sign a deal with the company after pushback from local activists, and an expense it could not pay.

In the summer of 2016, *Bloomberg Businessweek* did a blockbuster story about how the Baltimore Police Department hired PSS in early 2016 for a test that lasted several weeks. Funds came not from local taxpayers, but rather from Texas philanthropists who funneled money through a Baltimore police charity, where it was not subject to normal oversight rules. McNutt and his colleagues set up shop in a small office in a downtown parking garage, with a simple, but vague sign outside: "Community Support Program."

After the *Bloomberg Businessweek* story came out in August 2016, McNutt made an appearance at a press conference with Baltimore police officials, defending the program.

"We believe we contribute significantly to the safety and support of the citizens in Baltimore," he said. "We do have the legal analysis that covers the program. We are no different than any other law enforcement program. There are four Supreme Court precedents."

But again, like the previous cases discussed, including *Knotts* and *Smith*, there remains a huge gulf between the facts of those cases and the vast implications that they have created.

McNutt was likely referring to the 1989 Supreme Court decision in *Florida v. Riley*, which found that no warrant is needed if police conduct aerial surveillance. However, that case only involved one helicopter flying over one person's alleged marijuana grow in a greenhouse that had some roofing panels removed. In that case, the police helicopter pilot could simply see what was inside with his own two eyes—he didn't even use an infrared imaging device or anything more advanced.

In June 2017, Miami-Dade Police Department floated yet another PSS trial in South Florida—but after concerns by the American Civil Liberties Union, among others, the plan was scrapped within two weeks.

◎

Just like *Smith*, which inadvertently paved the way for phone records to be indiscriminately captured on a much larger scale by the National Security Agency, the combination of *Knotts* and *Riley* are creating a legal theory that allows for everything to be watched from the sky, for now.

Many of these technologies, including LPRs, body-worn cameras, wide-area aerial surveillance—not to mention others, like drones, cell-site simulators, and more—would have been covered as part of a proposed California law that Katz-Lacabe helped push.

The bill, known as Senate Bill 21, aimed to bring the use of these technologies into the light of day. It declared:

> *(a) While law enforcement agencies increasingly rely on surveillance technologies because those technologies may enhance community safety and aid in the investigation of crimes, those technologies are often used without any written rules or civilian oversight, and the ability of surveillance technology to enhance public safety should be balanced with reasonable safeguards for residents' civil liberties and privacy.*
> *(b) Promoting a safer community through the use of surveillance technology while preserving the protection of civil*

*liberties and privacy are not mutually exclusive goals, and
policymakers should be empowered to make informed decisions about what kind of surveillance technologies should be
used in their community.*

*(c) Decisions about whether to use surveillance technology
for data collection and how to use and store the information
collected should not be made by the agencies that would operate the technology, but by the elected bodies that are directly
accountable to the residents in their communities who should
also have opportunities to review the decision of whether or
not to use surveillance technologies.*

If passed as it was drafted, every law enforcement entity in the Golden State
would be required to create a Surveillance Use Policy, describing exactly
how particular technologies are going to be used. In addition to that, municipal and county agencies would be required to produce an annual Surveillance Technology Use Report, which, among other things, would list
the costs and benefits of surveillance technologies.

The bill would have been the first state law in the nation to bring the
acquisition, use, and evaluation of such technologies to the fore. But, as of
September 2017, the bill died in committee.

For now, LPRs have shown no sign of abating. Every month, more and
more law enforcement agencies are deploying them. As the cost of this
technology falls and the level of sophistication increases, it will only be a
matter of time before it becomes easy enough to run on a smartphone. Just
like LPRs enable police to see and capture data that no human ever could in
public, so too can other technology do so in private.

CHAPTER FIVE

Can the Police Use Extrasensory Technology to Look into Your House Without a Warrant?

The Fourth Amendment does not require that citizens take extreme measures to protect the privacy of what one cannot see, feel, hear, taste, or smell out of fear that the government might be able to employ new technologies that reveal what may be going on inside their homes.

—Kenneth Lerner
Brief for Petitioner, United States Supreme Court
Kyllo v. United States (2000)

January 24, 1992
Florence, Oregon

Around 6:30 AM, on a chilly winter morning in a small coastal town due west of Eugene, Oregon, Danny Kyllo, 27, was in the shower when he heard repeated banging at his front door.

His first thought was that it must be his girlfriend's ex-boyfriend—she had told Kyllo that her ex was "a bit crazy."

He threw a towel around his waist and walked towards the front door, but before he could open it, the door was kicked in. Nearly two-dozen law enforcement agents burst into his living room, with guns pointed right at him.

"Down on the ground, get down on the ground!" one yelled at him. Kyllo complied, and fell to the floor, with the towel slipping slightly off of his waist.

Eventually, the agents let him sit in a chair and began questioning him.

"We know through an informant that you're selling pot in Brookings," one said, referring to another small coastal town about three hours south, near the border with California.

But Kyllo knew his rights.

"No, I want to talk to my attorney," he told them.

While this interrogation was going on, a 27-year-old National Guard officer began walking through the small corner unit of the triplex on the corner of Rhododendron Drive and Hemlock Avenue.

Sergeant Dan Haas was there to confirm the thermal scans that he had done about a week earlier around 3:00 AM with a small, camcorder-sized device known as the Agema Thermovision 210, showing that various parts of Kyllo's apartment were reading hotter than others.

While infrared scans are somewhat routine now, these devices were not in common use by local law enforcement at the time. This one was on loan from the Oregon National Guard; the Lane County Sheriff's Department surely didn't have one. In fact, it very well might have been one of only a handful of such devices in use in Oregon at the time.

Thermal scanners display pixelated images with anything that gives off heat showing up in different shades of white; the brighter the shade, the more heat the object is giving off. When Haas looked through the imager's viewfinder on January 16, the hottest thing outside was a power line transformer; but Kyllo's apartment glowed like a Christmas tree.

Kyllo's home wasn't the only location in Florence that he was asked to do an imaging scan of that night. There were three others, analogous to a police lineup: one was the "target" location (Kyllo), while the others were effectively dummy locations. None of those other locations came anywhere close to outputting the level of energy that Kyllo's place was.

Haas didn't have a warrant to conduct the thermal scan—but as far as he knew, he didn't need one. The entire investigation was based on the fact that law enforcement, originally spearheaded by a Bureau of Land Management (BLM) agent, William Elliott, had managed to subpoena Kyllo's utility records. The government claimed that Kyllo was somehow drawing much more power than was normal for that area. Based on that, and an informant's tip that Kyllo was selling marijuana, Elliott was fairly certain that a thermal scan of Kyllo's home would reveal something.

"Our policy was pretty clear . . . that you [don't] go out and look for something that's hot and start an investigation," Haas told me. "This was to be used as the last coat of mortar on the wall after you had built your probable cause. This was to be used to confirm other information that you had. And that was what it was most often used for."

In the late 1980s and early 1990s, Haas served numerous times on counter-drug operations. He and his fellow guardsmen often provided perimeter security, in their battle-dress uniforms, to free up local police to conduct raids of various suspect drug locations.

"We just kept the public back and kept any bad guys from fleeing the scene," he told me.

But on that chilly January morning, Haas walked through Kyllo's place. With clothes and odds and ends strewn about, it reminded Haas of his college apartment.

"It didn't have a maid or Mom there cleaning up," Haas quipped.

The primary difference was that this small apartment was filled with grow lights and marijuana plants—the ceiling was full of halogen lights, each one blazing out at 1,000 watts, and each light had a dozen or so plants growing underneath. As he stepped around the growing plants, Haas made his way to the nearby garage, which featured a small nursery for growing new buds. All in all, it was over a hundred plants, perhaps even as high as 300.

The map that Haas had created of the property based entirely on heat imaging scans was now starting to match up with the walls, doors, glass, and other materials that he found in the small house. Eventually, Kyllo was allowed to get dressed before he was driven hours away to a local jail in Portland. He was charged with one count of growing marijuana, punishable by only a few years in prison.

However, it took a little extra time for Kyllo to get released on bail. After all, it was the same weekend as Super Bowl Sunday, where the Washington Redskins defeated the Buffalo Bills by a score of 37–24. On Monday, Kyllo's mother, sobbing, came to pick him up from jail—she found him with shackles on his wrists and ankles.

Soon after being released, Kyllo got a call from his court-appointed attorney, Ken Lerner, who'd noticed immediately that the government did not have a warrant to use the imager. Perhaps there was a way to challenge the search, and therefore get the fruits of the search (the drugs) suppressed.

◯

In the early 1990s, Robert Thomson was just beginning his career as a rank-and-file federal prosecutor, an assistant US attorney. Based in Portland, the US Attorney's Office was in charge of covering a vast swath of the state.

Originally a California lawyer, Thomson moved to Oregon in 1980, first to Eugene and later to Grants Pass, a town that proudly proclaims "It's the

Climate!" in a large banner that hangs above a downtown street. Thomson quickly figured out that he was in the heart of "Southern Oregon bud."

"They were referring to the climate for growing roses and pears, and it was a good climate for growing marijuana, too," Thomson told me. "I spent two years doing nothing but drug cases, and the vast majority was growing marijuana."

At the time, a lot of cannabis plants were being grown outdoors, often on federal land run by the BLM, a division of the Department of the Interior.

Prosecutors often work in tandem with various agents across different branches of law enforcement, together developing a nose to investigate cases that they're commonly interested in. As Thomson began working more and more marijuana cases, he began to develop a professional relationship with a BLM agent named William Elliott.

One day in 1991, Elliott came to Thomson and said that he suspected that a man named Danny Kyllo was growing marijuana in his house. He'd learned this, he explained, through investigating Kyllo's next-door neighbor, Tova Shook, who lived one unit over with Kyllo's sister, Lori Kyllo. Tova was the daughter of Sam Shook, the original target of Elliott's investigation.

As Elliott's investigation of Sam Shook evolved, he contacted state and local law enforcement, who told him that Danny Kyllo lived in a triplex unit next door to Tova Shook, and that a police informant unknown to Elliott had told local authorities that Danny Kyllo could supply the informant with marijuana. With this information, Elliott subpoenaed Portland General Electric for Danny Kyllo's electrical usage records. After looking them over, Elliott believed that Kyllo's were abnormally high.

So Elliott came to Thomson, seeking legal advice, asking if it would be OK for him to use a thermal imaging device and scan Kyllo's house from a public street to use in conjunction with the other information that they had, as a way to really solidify his case against Kyllo.

"There had been a number of attempts by defense counsel to challenge the use of thermal imagers, but none had succeeded," Thomson said. "But the state of the law was pretty clear, we thought. In our estimated opinion, it was not a search."

This legal opinion seemed to be well-founded. It was based on a combination of a number of legal precedents, including *Katz v. United States*, *Smith v. Maryland*, and others. Essentially, the argument boiled down to the notion that there was no reasonable expectation of privacy in the natural physical emissions (infrared light) from a home. So long as the scan was being conducted from a public road (as opposed to right up against Kyllo's door), it was well within the bounds of the law—or so the theory went.

In fact, less than two months later, by pure coincidence, the Office of Legal Counsel (OLC), the advisory body to the Department of Justice (DOJ), published an opinion for the general counsel of the Department of Defense (DOD). In essence, the OLC signed off on the DOD's use of a forward-looking infrared camera (FLIR) to assist local law enforcement.

During the previous couple of years, various military legal experts reached different results: with some finding that it was a search, and others saying that it was not. One notable DOD memo, known as the Smith Memorandum, concluded that the warrantless use of a thermal imager was a search, citing *United States v. Knotts*. This would have made such thermal scans illegal without a warrant.

But the OLC disagreed:

> *Courts generally have held that the relevant question for determining whether surveillance infringes upon a legitimate expectation of privacy is not merely how information is collected but what information is collected. If an object of government surveillance is recognized by society as enjoying a privacy interest of sufficient magnitude, the government's activity will constitute a "search." Technology that allows the government to view the interior of a home almost certainly implicates the Fourth Amendment. But we are not prepared to say, as the Smith Memorandum suggests, that any "extra-sensory" technological development that assists authorities in ferreting out crime is automatically one that society would deem unreasonably intrusive, no matter how minimal the intrusion on the privacy interests of the citizenry. The Supreme Court has "never equated police efficiency with unconstitutionality," Knotts, 460 U.S. at 284, and we fear that acceptance of the Smith Memorandum's analysis would come perilously close to doing so.*

As such, federal investigators went ahead with using the FLIR.

"But this was for all intents and purposes, we thought, a very routine case," Thomson added. "It was not something that I would have ever imagined would have ended up in the US Supreme Court."

But this was the first time that Kenneth Lerner, a silver-haired, soft-spoken veteran Portland-based defense attorney, stepped into the issue. By the time 1992 rolled around, Lerner had been working for the previous 18 years as a defense attorney, including a stint from 1981 through 1990 as the assistant defender at the Federal Public Defender's Office in Portland.

Lerner picked up on a potential avenue to challenge the government's case: the notable absence of a warrant.

"I was so happy that I got an attorney that brought this up," Kyllo said years later. "I wouldn't have thought this up. I didn't know what a thermal imager was at the time."

As the case moved ahead, Lerner filed a motion to suppress evidence on behalf of his client, arguing, essentially that law enforcement did need a warrant to use the thermal imager to scan inside someone's home.

Lerner also challenged the government's claim about the power usage in court.

"This was one of the major points of contention we raised in challenging the search warrant to begin with," he said. "We asserted that this claim was factually not true and [Elliott] knew it."

As Lerner tells it, Elliott altered a power utility chart that he'd received from the local electrical utility. In his affidavit, as part of the warrant application, Elliott indicated that Kyllo was using more electricity than he should have, when in fact he was well within a normal range. The judge agreed with Lerner that Elliott was in the wrong. But since the judge thought that the officer had been merely negligent—and not deliberately reckless—he allowed the warrant application to stand. Years later, Lerner called this result "galling."

"It was clear that Elliott manipulated the chart without any basis and without any effort to discuss his situation or verify his assessment with the people at [Portland General Electric] who created the chart," he continued. "A person's life can turn on whether a single judge makes a determination on whether that sort of failure, when swearing an oath to the truth of factual claims, is reckless disregard for the truth, or mere negligence."

The district court denied the motion in December 1992, which meant there was only one obvious legal strategy left: plead guilty and preserve the right to appeal. Kyllo did so in March 1993, and in June, the judge sentenced Kyllo to five years and three months in federal prison.

Nearly immediately after sentencing, the case was appealed up to the 9th US Circuit Court of Appeals, which ruled that the district court had to hold an evidentiary hearing to learn more about how exactly the Agema Thermovision 210 worked. The case continued on for years, bouncing between the district court and the 9th Circuit. During that time, numerous media outlets and legal scholars reported on the use of thermal imaging as "the government's most recent weapon in the war on drugs."

Eventually, after one of the appellate judges retired, and a new panel of judges had to be selected, the 9th Circuit finally reached a conclusion in September 1999.

After years of work, the 9th Circuit found that the use of the thermal imager was not a search, and so no warrant was required. Citing *Katz* and *Smith*, the judges concluded, echoing Justice Harlan's two-part test: "We evaluate whether the individual has made a showing of an actual subjective expectation of privacy and then ask whether this expectation is one that society recognizes as objectively reasonable."

Then, after citing other appellate courts that had not found that a Fourth Amendment search had taken place in similar cases, the 9th Circuit in *Kyllo* wouldn't either. Practically mocking the entire exercise, the court wrote, "Whatever the 'Star Wars' capabilities this technology may possess in the abstract, the thermal imaging device employed here intruded into nothing."

Worse still, as the 9th Circuit saw it, because Kyllo "made no attempt to conceal these emissions," he couldn't possibly say that he had a privacy interest in the infrared energy released from his marijuana grow operation. (How he was supposed to have done so, the 9th Circuit did not address.)

On November 13, 2000, Lerner filed an opening brief with the Supreme Court. The brief made note of thermal imaging's development since Kyllo's home was first scanned.

> *Thermal imaging is becoming ever more technologically advanced at an astounding pace, with virtually limitless application (JA 38-9, 42-3, 133, 160-1). It is now possible to obtain clear images of items no bigger than an inch or two from navigable airspace, and computers can provide for even greater enhancement. (JA 43) The military is the largest market for thermal image technology, and is taking an increasing role in domestic law enforcement (JA 152).*

Primarily, Lerner's argument relied on the notion that the warrantless use of a thermal imager was, in fact, a search. The brief made heavy reference to *Katz*, but noted that it did not apply: *Katz* concerned privacy interests outside the home, while Kyllo was firmly within the four walls of his own house.

"Even if *Katz* [was] the proper analytical method, Mr. Kyllo certainly had a subjective and reasonable expectation of privacy in the activities he conducted in his home," Lerner wrote. "He took normal precautions against observation by conducting his activities inside his home. The Fourth Amendment does not require that citizens take extreme measures to protect the privacy of what one cannot see, feel, hear, taste, or smell out of fear that the government might be able to employ new technologies that reveal what may be going on inside their homes."

In response, government attorneys countered that because the use of the thermal imager was not a search, law enforcement agents did not need a warrant. In its opening lines of its own brief, the DOJ echoed the decades-old reasoning in *Olmstead v. United States* ("There was no searching. There was no seizure."), which found that there was no search in a wiretap of a bootlegger's home.

"Technological developments hold a serious potential to encroach on privacy, and in no context is the use of technology to conduct observations more sensitive than [in] an individual's home," attorneys for the Office of the Solicitor General responded. "But thermal imagers do not literally or figuratively penetrate the home and reveal private activities within. Unlike a hypothetical sophisticated X-ray device or microphone that could perceive activity through solid walls—observations that would amount to searches—a thermal imaging device passively detects only heat gradients on exterior surfaces and displays the read-outs as amorphous white or light gray blotches."

In other words, because the thermal imager was so crude and could not really peer in a detailed fashion into someone's home, its use was more analogous to an officer watching a house with a pair of binoculars. Sure, the imager, like the binoculars, provided a small level of enhancement, but did not go too far.

Plus, the heat lost through the walls of the house was essentially similar to smoke emanating from a chimney, or snow melting on a roof. Sure, combined with other information, this may allow officers to develop inferences about what else is going on inside, but taken by itself, simply scanning infrared radiation was permissible.

The government also cited *Knotts* and *Smith* as evidence that technology that can enhance human abilities is permitted. In *Knotts*, an officer could have followed the chloroform barrel all the way to the Wisconsin cabin—the beeper simply made that process more efficient. Similarly, in *Smith*, an officer could have recorded all the incoming and outgoing calls, but the pen register automated that process.

But Lerner had a powerful counterargument.

"However, both *Knotts* and *Smith* were premised on the fact that the defendant had knowingly exposed certain conduct, which the beeper or pen register made easier to capture," he wrote. "These cases permit the use of technology that makes police work more efficient, but which do no more than what the human senses could have done. Neither case addresses whether invisible radiation is knowingly exposed, nor authorizes surveillance of infrared radiation as a mere technological enhancement."

With numerous circuit courts split on the issue, the time was ripe for the Supreme Court to take up the case in the 2000–2001 term.

More than 18 years after *Knotts*, the Supreme Court was at the tail end of the Rehnquist Court, but was firmly in the middle of eleven years of institutional stability (no justices would leave the court from 1994 until 2005). During the years that Chief Justice William Rehnquist presided over the court, seven of the nine justices were appointed by Republican presidents. Ideologically, they ranged from John Paul Stevens and Ruth Bader Ginsburg anchoring the liberal side, and Antonin Scalia and Clarence Thomas on the conservative side.

After months of preparation with the Federal Public Defender's Office in Portland, including numerous moot courts, the day finally arrived for Lerner to head to Washington, DC, and make his arguments before the Supreme Court.

The day before oral arguments, February 19, 2001, Lerner took his wife and children to the National Zoo. He thought it would be a good way to clear his mind before the big day. The following day, February 20, Lerner and his family piled into a black stretch limousine. This was highly unusual for Lerner, who had never gone to court in style like this before. A relative and fellow attorney had arranged for the whole lot of them to be picked up from their hotel and driven to the Supreme Court.

The defense attorney sat in the back against the window, looking out across downtown Washington, DC, as the rest of the family marveled at their high-class transportation. All of a sudden, the voice of Nina Totenberg, a longtime legal correspondent with National Public Radio, came over the car radio just as they passed the Capitol Building. Lerner grinned from ear to ear, pleased that his little case from Oregon had made national headlines.

When they arrived at the Supreme Court, Lerner's family wished him luck as he climbed up the court's unassuming lower-level side entrance, not the grand marble entrance. As he began to get ready for the oral arguments, he came back to a point that he had realized during his practice sessions: don't concede the core principle. A lot of the questioning from the justices is designed to throw the attorneys off-balance, to get them to concede a point, which can sometimes be fatal.

"You have to figure out what it is that you cannot concede and to defend it, and that's how I prepared," he said. "The home is sacrosanct."

And that's exactly what he did.

When he stepped up to the lectern, Lerner got straight to the point.

"Mr. Chief Justice, may it please the Court, this case is about thermal imaging of a home without a warrant, and whether that constitutes an impermissible search under the Fourth Amendment," he said.

> Our home is the basic refuge for all citizens. It's where we have our greatest expectations of privacy, where we are free to let down our guard, and where we should have our greatest feeling that we are free from government spying. Unreasonable and unwarranted searching of the home is the chief evil that the Fourth Amendment protects us against, and . . . the home itself has a specific mention in the Constitution, and as a bedrock principle, the home is a place where we have our most heightened expectations of privacy.

A few minutes later, Lerner summarized his thinking: "I think anytime that the Government is seeking to capture information from a private place like the home, and they cannot do it with their own unaided human senses, then they may not use technology to do the same thing."

Justice Scalia challenged this assertion with the argument that the government should not have its investigatory powers hampered—it should be able to use technology, ranging from flashlights to binoculars, all the way up to thermal imagers.

"I guess our position is that the burden really is improperly placed on the citizen to anticipate what type of technology the Government may come up with, and perhaps you're correct that if it's sufficiently sophisticated rather than something that's very common and ordinary, then it shouldn't be the burden of the citizen to anticipate what they can't particularly know or may not know, and then take safeguarding measures," Lerner countered.

By the time Lerner concluded his arguments after about 28 minutes, he felt a little deflated. Justice Scalia, a conservative who was known to take pro-privacy views, should have been on his side. It can sometimes be hard to read a justice's viewpoint from the questions they ask, Supreme Court or otherwise. Sometimes a question expresses their disagreement, but other times it can simply be a test of a lawyer's mettle.

Up next was Michael Dreeben, the deputy solicitor general and a veteran of the DOJ, having joined in 1988. (In June 2017, Dreeben was tapped to aid in Special Counsel Robert Mueller's investigation into Russia's efforts to sway the 2016 US presidential election. In November 2017, Dreeben also argued the government's side in *Carpenter*.) Dreeben, with his receding hairline and salt-and-pepper beard, argued that the thermal imager was not as invasive as Lerner was making it out to be.

"It does not penetrate the walls of the house, it does not reveal particular objects or activities inside of a house, and the record in this case and the findings that the district court made indicate that it is not capable of doing so through walls of a house," Dreeben said. In short, because the thermal imager was simply reading heat that had already emanated from the house, then there was no privacy concern.

However, Justice David Souter, a conservative justice who often voted with the liberal wing, wasn't having it.

"But, you know, all of that could have been said but for a change of senses about *Katz*," he said. "What the bug in *Katz* was measuring was the effective sound on the exterior wall of the phone booth."

In essence, Souter was saying that like in *Katz*, where the privacy violation was found despite a lack of trespass into the phone booth, the court should find in Kyllo's favor.

The two went back and forth on this point for some time.

"Justice Souter, I think that *Katz* is fundamentally different in the respect that what the bug picked up in *Katz* was sound waves, which is what we hear with, and it amplified them and exactly reproduced what Mr. Katz was saying inside the booth," Dreeben said.

"Yeah, but it was the wave after it got through the phone booth, just as what infrared is picking up is the wave after it gets through the roof or the window," Souter countered.

Finally, the argument reached a personal moment, when Justice Stephen Breyer said that there is a "reasonable expectation of privacy that what you're doing in your bathroom is not going to be picked up when you take a bath." Breyer further explained that he liked to use his in-home Finnish sauna for a few hours each day and that perhaps he didn't want the police (or anyone else) to know about it.

In the end, months later, it was Scalia who wrote the majority 5–4 opinion, with Souter, Thomas, Ginsburg, and Breyer joining. "The question we confront today is what limits there are upon this power of technology to shrink the realm of guaranteed privacy," he wrote, noting at the very end of the opinion: "Where, as here, the Government uses a device that is not in general public use, to explore details of the home that would previously have been unknowable without physical intrusion, the surveillance is a 'search' and is presumptively unreasonable without a warrant."

The Supreme Court rejected not only the government's arguments in *Kyllo*, but the arguments put forth in the earlier OLC memo and the Smith Memorandum.

"In our hearing in the district court challenging the use of thermal imaging, we learned that the [Smith Memorandum's] entire legal analysis was written up by a retired DEA agent (named Charles Stowell) who became the marketing director for Agema," Lerner said, referring to the company that manufactured the handheld infrared scanner.

> He used this slanted legal analysis to sell their thermal imagers to law enforcement agencies with a prepared legal argument to defend their use if they were ever challenged. Some of this bogus analysis made its way into the OLC analysis, but was rejected by the DOD . . . By the time the Kyllo case arose there was only one federal district court to have ruled on the issue, adopting the Stowell analysis, as did the judge in Kyllo's case. These both proved to be wrongly decided.

Several months later, Lerner found out that he had won the case only after a reporter called him.

"I had to go online and pull the opinion so I could read it," he said. "They're very poor about communicating with you from the Supreme Court."

Still, Lerner was "hooting and hollering most of the day, and was calling everybody I knew."

One of his first calls was to his client, Danny Kyllo, who was living at his parents' house.

Kyllo's father handed him the phone: "Your attorney is on the phone."

"Please be good news, I've had so much bad news," Kyllo thought to himself.

When Lerner told him what had happened a smile crept across his face—and why, yes, he would like to do an interview with Oregon Public Broadcasting.

Eventually the Supreme Court sent Lerner a formal copy (known as a slip opinion). By coincidence, months later, when Justice Scalia came to Oregon to speak at a local law school, Lerner happily attended the lecture and asked Scalia to oblige him with an autograph of the opinion afterwards.

"I remember that case," Scalia said with a smile as he handed back the paperwork.

So, as of 2001, using a thermal imager to peer into a home without a warrant was an unconstitutional search. In some ways, this ruling marked a return to the *Olmstead*-era trespass rule of decades earlier. Justice Scalia, a textualist conservative, highlighted the fact in *Kyllo* that there was a "not only firm but also bright" line that the Fourth Amendment draws at the property boundary.

So, using a thermal imager without a warrant at close range was unconstitutional. But what about something as old as a drug-sniffing dog—a "technology" commonly in use by law enforcement agencies nationwide. Would the use of such a dog be considered a Fourth Amendment search as well?

More than five years after *Kyllo* was decided, Detective William Pedraja of the Miami-Dade Police Department unwittingly stepped into that question. In November 2006, Pedraja received a tip that a local man named Joelis Jardines was growing marijuana in his home.

Roughly a month later, early one morning, local police and the DEA sent a joint team to Jardines' home, where they found no vehicles present, and no activity in or around the home that they could observe. Pedraja's colleague Detective Douglas Bartlet arrived with a drug-sniffing dog that was well-trained to detect numerous narcotics, including marijuana.

With no trouble at all, Franky, a chocolate Labrador, alerted his handler to the presence of some sort of illegal drug—sticking his head high, sniffing the air, and bracketing, or walking back and forth as a way to find the source of the odor. In this case, it was the front door of Jardines' house.

Bartlet said later that he had walked right up to the front door and could smell marijuana. He later prepared an affidavit as a means to obtain a search warrant—when a formal search was conducted, marijuana was found.

At trial, attorneys for Jardines asked the court to suppress the evidence seized based upon an illegal search—and the lowest state court did so. Prosecutors appealed the ruling up to an appeals court, known locally as a district court. That court found that the "officer had the right to go up to defendant's front door," even without a warrant.

Jardines' attorneys appealed this ruling up to the Florida Supreme Court.

In its ruling in favor of Jardines, the Florida Supreme Court noted that while the Supreme Court of the United States had addressed some sniff test cases, none of them specifically addressed the situation of using a narcotics dog at a home. The others were sniffs at locations where privacy interest is notably less than in a home: at the airport or on the outside of one's car at a traffic stop.

The Florida Supreme Court ruled that a dog sniff at a house, with several officers who created a perimeter around the scene and more standing backup, was hardly subtle, unlike the circumstances detailed in the other drug cases. In fact, the entire affair—beginning with the arrival of the drug dog team, the sniffing, the affidavit writing, the signing off on a warrant, and the actual bona fide search—took hours.

"The 'sniff test' apparently took place in plain view of the general public," the Florida Supreme Court ruled. "There was no anonymity for the resident."

In essence, the Florida Supreme Court concluded, the warrantless drug sniff was an "unreasonable government intrusion into the sanctity of the home and violated the Fourth Amendment."

Unsurprisingly, prosecutors appealed this case up to the Supreme Court of the United States, largely relying on the previous Supreme Court dog sniff precedents that had been found in the government's favor.

In a 5–4 decision authored by Justice Scalia on March 26, 2013, a majority of the court found in favor of Jardines. Scalia noted that typically if someone approaches a house the physical boundary of a property—

known as curtilage—they simply knock or ring the bell and "wait briefly to be received."

"Complying with the terms of that traditional invitation does not require fine-grained legal knowledge; it is generally managed without incident by the Nation's Girl Scouts and trick-or-treaters," Scalia wrote with a bit of snark.

But a police dog is "something else."

"The scope of a license—express or implied—is limited not only to a particular area but also to a specific purpose," he continued. "Consent at a traffic stop to an officer's checking out an anonymous tip that there is a body in the trunk does not permit the officer to rummage through the trunk for narcotics. Here, the background social norms that invite a visitor to the front door do not invite him there to conduct a search."

The court did not even need to reach the question of an "expectation of privacy under *Katz*. One virtue of the Fourth Amendment's property-rights baseline is that it keeps easy cases easy."

But, despite the fact that the decision in *Kyllo* addressed the newness of the technology, which was irrelevant in this case, the principle employed in *Riley* was essentially the same. Scalia and the court's majority found that it made no difference that the police had been using such dogs "for centuries . . . when the government uses a physical intrusion to explore details of the home (including its curtilage), the antiquity of the tools that they bring along is irrelevant."

◎

Nearly two decades after *Kyllo*, most non-lawyers might think that the issue of warrantless use of thermal imagers is decided. Scalia's famous sentence seems pretty clear: "Where, as here, the Government uses a device that is not in general public use, to explore details of the home that would previously have been unknowable without physical intrusion, the surveillance is a 'search' and is presumptively unreasonable without a warrant."

Combined with the fact that drug-sniffing dogs approaching someone's front door without a warrant is also on its face "unreasonable," it would seem that short-range scanning into someone's home without a warrant should halt entirely.

Of course, absent a department policy or state law specifically forbidding a particular practice or regulating a particular technology, law enforcement will always push the limits until they are told to stop. The job of the police, after all, is not to figure out where the lines are, but rather to be cognizant of those lines, and aggressively (à la Michael Hayden) go right up to them.

Just as was the case in *Kyllo* and *Jardines*, a particular technique was legitimized until some enterprising lawyer bothered to try to stop it. Even then, challenging a practice is difficult, particularly when a technology is so new that hardly anyone even knows that it exists, or how it compares to what had been in use previously.

On November 7, 2012, less than two weeks after the Supreme Court heard oral arguments in *Jardines*, the secretary of corrections for the Kansas Department of Corrections issued an absconder's warrant for the arrest of Steven Denson. It took months before state authorities were able to locate him in Wichita. On February 27, 2013, a team of five agents arrived at a duplex on Hillside Street to arrest him.

At about 8:30 AM on that cold winter morning, one of the agents physically surveilled the building for 20 minutes, and saw nothing. At some point, some of the agents, moved towards the back of the unit, their boots crunching in the snow, while others stayed towards the front. One man, identified in court documents as Special Enforcement Officer Brandon Bansemer, stood at the front door and knocked for a while. When no one answered, US Marshals deputy Joshua Moff decided to go back to his car and retrieve a Doppler device.

Nearly a year later, during a court hearing, Moff described the handheld device as something that emits a Doppler radar signal, and "when it comes back, it will tell you if it's picking up somebody's breathing. Then it will tell you if that person is moving or if they're stationary."

Despite the fact that the Doppler did indicate that a person was in the house, prosecutors took the painstaking step of pointing out in court filings that "the government is not using this information to form the requisite reasonable belief that the defendant or any other person was inside the house at the time that the officers entered the residence." Though admitting, essentially, that the use of the Doppler may have been improper, they justified the search of the home by the fact that the electrical meter was running rapidly and that there were fresh footprints leading to the house.

In any case, Bansemer and Moff knocked on the front door.

"Police! Come to the door!" they shouted as loudly as they could, their breath visible in the air.

Finally, they decided to bang even harder, which had the effect of knocking a small piece of wood off of the outer door—and still no one came to the door. They decided to reach in and unlock the door anyway, and let themselves inside. In short order, they discovered Denson in bed. The officers roused him, handcuffed him, and sat him down on the couch with Officer Bansemer standing guard while the other officers, who entered from the back, began to sweep the house.

Deputy Moff quickly found a 12-gauge shotgun and a .22 long rifle in a bedroom closet. Eventually, Denson was charged with unauthorized possession of a firearm while being a felon, in addition to absconding from his parole for a previous charge.

As the case progressed through the court system, Denson's attorneys attempted to suppress the search of the house, and the found guns, on the grounds that the entry of the house did not reach to the level of "reasonable suspicion." The judge did not find Denson's attorney's argument convincing and denied the motion to suppress.

Ultimately, the case was appealed up to the 10th US Circuit Court of Appeals, which did not rule on the issue of whether the use of the Doppler was improper or not. Instead, it found that the "totality" of the other circumstances (the footprints, that there was a utility account in his name, the whirring electrical meter, the fact that he had absconded, that he had no known source of income) in which Denson was found made it such that it did not even need to consider the use of the Doppler.

"Unlawful searches can give rise not only to civil claims but may require the suppression of evidence in criminal proceedings," then circuit judge Neil Gorsuch wrote for the 3–0 opinion.

"We have little doubt that the radar device deployed here will soon generate many questions for this court and others along both of these axes. At the same time, in a criminal proceeding like ours the government is free to rely on facts gleaned independently from any Fourth Amendment violation."

In other words, while there might be a case in the future that will deal with whether a Doppler radar device had been used properly—this wasn't it.

◯

That 10th Circuit opinion was issued December 30, 2014, at a time when most court watchers were on winter holidays. However, by the time that

Brad Heath, a *USA Today* investigative reporter, got back to work on Monday, January 5, 2015, at his suburban Washington, DC, office, he had noticed the court's opinion.

Roughly midway through his 20-year career as a journalist, Heath decided to pursue a part-time degree in law at Georgetown University. In 2011, he passed the Virginia bar exam, but has never practiced law. However, he continues to use his legal training as part of his journalism that focuses on criminal justice issues: he likes to listen to appellate oral arguments on his smartphone while folding laundry or doing other household chores.

Heath read the opinion and decided to take a closer look at this almost discarded section of the appellate ruling. After reporting for a couple of weeks, he concluded that "at least 50" federal law enforcement agencies, "including the FBI and the U.S. Marshals Service, began deploying the radar systems more than two years ago with little notice to the courts and no public disclosure of when or how they would be used. The technology raises legal and privacy issues because the U.S. Supreme Court has said officers generally cannot use high-tech sensors to tell them about the inside of a person's house without first obtaining a search warrant."

This was the first time that many civil liberties groups had even heard of these devices, despite the fact that they apparently had been first deployed in 2013, with seemingly little, if any, public discussion on their acquisition or use.

"The idea that the government can send signals through the wall of your house to figure out what's inside is problematic," Christopher Soghoian, then the American Civil Liberties Union's principal technologist, told *USA Today*. "Technologies that allow the police to look inside of a home are among the intrusive tools that police have." (As of January 2018, Soghoian was hired to be a senior technologist for the offices of Senator Ron Wyden, an Oregon Democrat.)

Unlike an infrared scanner, which reads the heat emitted by a person or object, a Doppler sends out an electromagnetic wave, which bounces off the target and is returned. By calculating how fast the signal comes back, the device can determine instantaneously how far away something is.

According to an October 2012 report prepared by the DOJ's National Institute of Justice, "through-the-wall-sensors allow for enhanced situational awareness during operations when knowledge of the presence of individuals behind opaque barriers would be of benefit, during law enforcement operations requiring forced entry, in hostage situations, in building sweeps by firefighters or when locating individuals in rubble during search-and-rescue operations."

These devices have been commercially available to domestic law enforcement since at least 2009, and to military units going back years before that. Like with so many surveillance technologies, something that starts out in the hands of the military will likely make its way to domestic law enforcement within just a few years. However, unlike American service members deployed overseas, local police are restrained by the US Constitution, in addition to state and local law.

According to Heath's reporting, in early 2015, L-3 Communications, the Orlando-based firm that made the Range-R device used in Wichita, had sold around 200 devices nationwide. The ubiquity of such technology means that they are likely in use on a daily basis. Few, if any of them, have been subject to substantial legal challenges.

If it hasn't happened already, these sensors will be attached to aerial and terrestrial drones for use without any short-range human interaction at all.

Recall, in the case of *Kyllo*, it took a smart lawyer around a decade before the case finally made its way up to the Supreme Court. In the meantime, thousands of people were likely subjected to ever-more-sophisticated thermal imaging devices. How are local legislative bodies supposed to make informed judgments about the appropriate use of such devices if they don't even know that they exist?

Waiting for the courts to adequately understand the ever-accelerating abilities of these kinds of sensors will take quite some time indeed.

◁◯▷

So, if using a thermal imager aimed at someone's house from close range without a warrant is a search, and bringing a drug-sniffing dog to someone's door without a warrant is also a search, what about something potentially even more physically invasive? Can DNA be collected from a criminal suspect and then analyzed against a DNA database?

This was the question facing the Supreme Court on February 26, 2013.

In 2003, a man broke into a woman's home in Salisbury, Maryland, and

raped her. Based on the information provided, local authorities were unable to arrest anyone in connection with the crime, but they were able to
gather a DNA sample for an unknown male assailant.

Six years later, Alonzo King was arrested in the same Maryland county
and charged with felony assault. As part of the booking process, the inside
of his cheek was swabbed to obtain a DNA sample, consistent with state law
at the time. However, the sample was not used to merely identify that the
person in state custody was, in fact, Alonzo King. Rather, the DNA sample
was run against a DNA database of unsolved crimes.

King's DNA matched that of the unknown assailant in the 2003 crime.
In *Maryland v. King*, King was charged, tried, and convicted for the Salisbury rape. King appealed, on the grounds that the DNA sample collected in
2009 was an "unreasonable search." The Maryland Court of Appeals found
that the parts of the Maryland DNA Collection Act that allowed routine
genetic sample collection were unconstitutional. The State of Maryland
then appealed to the Supreme Court, posing the question: Does the Fourth
Amendment allow the states to collect and analyze DNA from people arrested and charged with serious crimes?

Unlike a license plate number, or nearly any other numerical identifier, DNA is immutable—it can never be changed. The notion of having a
permanent record of one's genetic material, particularly when it might be
cross-referenced with location information, is potentially disturbing. It's
not difficult to imagine a near future where police capture all naturally
discarded hair (containing a person's DNA) and record its GPS location,
much in the same way license plate readers capture vehicular data today.

However, in this case, law enforcement was not employing a DNA dragnet.

In the end, the Supreme Court found that the answer was yes.

"A suspect's criminal history is a critical part of his identity that officers
should know when processing him for detention," Justice Anthony Kennedy wrote in the majority 5–4 opinion.

In other words, the fact that a suspect's DNA might already be in a state
database for an unrelated crime is relevant to establishing the broad identity of a person.

However, for a notable four-justice minority—led by Justice Scalia—this
case was leaning too far in the direction of a general warrant abhorred by
the Founders. Just as kicking in everyone's doors surely would turn up evidence of more crime, that is a line we do not want to cross in a democratic
society.

Scalia felt that the logical extension of the majority opinion was the inevitable expansion of DNA collection.

"Make no mistake about it: As an entirely predictable consequence of today's decision, your DNA can be taken and entered into a national DNA database if you are ever arrested, rightly or wrongly, and for whatever reason," Scalia wrote.

As he continued:

> Today's judgment will, to be sure, have the beneficial effect of solving more crimes; then again, so would the taking of DNA samples from anyone who flies on an airplane (surely the Transportation Security Administration needs to know the "identity" of the flying public), applies for a driver's license, or attends a public school. Perhaps the construction of such a genetic panopticon is wise. But I doubt that the proud men who wrote the charter of our liberties would have been so eager to open their mouths for royal inspection.

While the Supreme Court arrived at the correct result in *Kyllo*, Scalia's "not in general use" line may remain a pesky thorn. In the intervening years, the use of this technology has now become so common that FLIR Systems, one of the largest such thermal imaging companies, released a short-range iPhone add-on in 2014, available for $350. (As of this writing in late 2017, the newest version of that product costs just $200.) Does this mean that the police can simply buy an inexpensive add-on for their iPhones and use it, circumventing the *Kyllo* decision? The answer remains elusive.

CHAPTER SIX

Why (Amazingly) E-mail Providers Won't Give Up Messages Without a Warrant, Even Though the Supreme Court Has Never Ruled on the Issue

The ability to store everything makes storage the greater privacy threat.

—Professor Orin Kerr
"The Next Generation Communications Privacy Act"
University of Pennsylvania Law Review 162 (2013)

May 24, 2013
Dallas, Texas

Dressed in a tank top and shorts, 31-year-old Ladar Levison had one thing on his mind on this warm Friday evening: playing volleyball. It had been a long week. As he was getting ready to head out, there was a loud, repeated knock at his door. Levison silently fumed as he walked to open it.

Levison owned and operated a small e-mail business out of his fifth-floor apartment: Lavabit. Most weeks, he put in 70 or 80 hours to service his privacy-minded e-mail provider—over 370,000 people used it. Although he didn't know it at the time, one of his customers was Edward Snowden (edsnowden@lavabit.com), who was about to become a household name.

Looking through his peephole, Levison was surprised to see two men in suits at his door. Upon opening it, they identified themselves as special agents of the FBI, and showed their badges.

The current standard requiring law enforcement to get a warrant before Internet service providers (ISPs) turn over the contents of e-mail has come about as a result of an important appellate court decision, *Warshak v. United States*—effectively, because tech companies, armed with high-powered lawyers, were willing to say to the government that this was the standard, and they were willing to litigate it.

But Lavabit was no ordinary e-mail provider. Levison knew the law and took extraordinary steps to protect his users' privacy. But how far would he be willing to go once federal agents were literally at his doorstep?

Levison invited the FBI agents in to sit down. He introduced them to his tiny dog, Princess. The agents cordially explained that they were there to conduct a background check, and they needed to learn more about who he was and about what Lavabit was all about. In order to present him with a classified court order from the Foreign Intelligence Surveillance Court (FISC), he had to be given a clearance. The first step in obtaining a clearance is an in-person interview.

The special agents didn't even know who the target of the FISC order was—they were simply acting on behalf of their colleagues in Washington, DC.

Still in his volleyball outfit, Levison patiently explained how he had set up Lavabit, with digital security in mind. For a select group of paying customers (roughly 10,000 at the time), Levison offered an encrypted e-mail feature.

As an e-mail provider, Levison was primarily worried about being served with a national security letter (NSL), which would force him to act as a government agent and conduct secret surveillance of one of his users. Worse than that, Levison wouldn't be able to tell anyone—not his own lawyer, and certainly not the target of the investigation—about what was actually going on.

As he wrote on Lavabit's website in 2013:

> Lavabit believes that a civil society depends on the open, free and private flow of ideas. The type of monitoring promoted by the PATRIOT Act restricts that flow of ideas because it intimidates those afraid of retaliation. To counteract this chilling effect, Lavabit developed its secure e-mail platform. We feel e-mail has evolved into a critical channel for the communication of ideas in a healthy democracy. It's precisely because of e-mail's importance that we strive so hard to protect private e-mails from eavesdropping.

Levison further explained, both on his website and to the agents, that to protect stored e-mails, Lavabit used elliptical curve cryptography, a mechanism that enables public key and private key encryption. In essence, as applied to Lavabit's setup, this meant that incoming messages were encrypted before they were saved to the Lavabit servers. This was related to, but distinct from, Pretty Good Privacy (PGP) encryption. It would be as if the post office put each letter and package into a locked safe before delivering it to your front door.

In short, if the user had paid for the extra security features, even he, as Lavabit's owner, might not be able to access the e-mails.

Initially, Levison didn't think much of the agents' visit—he tried to answer the agents' questions during their two-hour chat. He didn't even think to get a lawyer.

On June 10, 2013, Levison received a d-order for a name that he initially read as "Snowman." A court in the Eastern District of Virginia ordered him to turn over subscriber information and send it back. He did, via First Class mail.

"They weren't paying me so I wasn't going to spend $30 to overnight it so I put a stamp on it and sent it," he told me.

The d-order required that Levison turn over the user information, including name, address, "records of session time and durations, and the temporarily assigned networks addresses," length of service, means of payment, and other data, on the paying customer: Edward Snowden.

But Levison hadn't put together that the user data that he had gathered together in a slapdash fashion, and whom he still thought was Snowman, was, in fact, the world's most-wanted man.

◯

The d-order Levison received was named for 18 United States Code § 2703(d), a portion of the 1986 Stored Communications Act (SCA), or Title II of the 1986 Electronic Privacy Communications Act (ECPA).

In 1986, technology and online services were very different than they are today. The Internet largely existed as a fringe academic and corporate experiment. Most Americans didn't have a computer, much less access to any kind of online service. The first Macintosh debuted in 1984, the first version of Microsoft Windows had been released in November 1985, and AOL's predecessor, known as Quantum Link, had launched in 1985.

In the 1980s, it wasn't clear how the Fourth Amendment applied to data and online communications. In a traditional physical search of a home, law enforcement goes to a judge asking for permission to conduct a search. The judge then signs off on the warrant, at which point, the agents or officers can conduct the search. It's immediately obvious to the person whose home has been ransacked that a search has actually taken place—the police almost always leave a paper copy of the warrant, providing proof that the search was legitimate and that it was executed.

However, in the digital world, things work a bit differently. Under the SCA, law enforcement sends a court order—which requires a lesser legal standard than a warrant—to a provider. Unless the request is overbroad or asks for irrelevant information, the provider is expected to comply. Also, unless the provider has a specific policy to notify users (absent being under a gag order), there's no way for the target to know that her or his data is being targeted. Or, put another way, in the case of Snowden's data at Lavabit, Levison couldn't tell him that the government wanted his data—but Snowden probably figured it out anyway.

While it was popularly understood at the time that the SCA required a warrant for e-mail, the SCA imposes a warrant requirement only for un-opened e-mail less than 180 days old.

This warrant requirement turned on the (outdated) question of storage: Starting with the creation of e-mail in the 1960s, messages were transmitted from one computer to another and stored locally. This was still true even into the 1980s. Given that digital storage was expensive, it was believed that there was little motivation to keep e-mails longer than necessary. So, 180 days seemed like an adequate length of time before a message was considered "abandoned"—ostensibly relinquishing the strongest of privacy interests.

The ECPA draws a distinction between "electronic computing services" (ECS) and "remote computing services" (RCS)—a line that makes no sense today. Under 18 USC 2703(d), however, "contents of any wire or electronic communication" held at an RCS are to be turned over if that data has been held for more than 180 days. At the time, it was presumed that e-mails would only be held for relatively short periods of time (days or weeks) before being transmitted to another point, hence the ECS moniker. Meanwhile, RCS, which provides remote "computer storage or processing services," is really more about an off-site location that is contracted to perform certain tasks (such as spreadsheet-based accounting), nearly all of which can be performed today on any smartphone. This is a reference to mainframe ter-minals, popular at the time.

In 1991, Senator Patrick Leahy (D-Vermont), one of ECPA's primary au-thors, convened a task force to examine whether the law was adequately pro-tecting e-mail. The group found that the law was working just fine. However, the technology behind e-mail hadn't changed much in the intervening five years.

Modern e-mail, however, works a bit differently. Since the advent of Rocket Mail (later, Yahoo Mail) and Hotmail in 1996—where e-mail messages were not downloaded to a local machine but more often viewed through a browser and messages could be kept more or less indefinitely on the remote service—and the release of Gmail in 2004 ("built on the idea that you should never have to delete mail"), the distinction between ECS and RCS has been out-of-date. The law has failed to catch up.

◌

Somehow, due to the slowness of the United States Postal Service and/or the lagging internal mail delivery procedures at the FBI, it took roughly another two weeks for the same FBI special agents to turn up at Levison's door again, this time with a pen/trap order, issued by the FISC.

With the pen/trap order, according to a government filing submitted in 2014, investigators could get all non-content information. That meant all the metadata (dates, times, duration of connection, to/from, and more) of a specific account.

However, Lavabit was built on the Elliptic Curve Integrated Encryption scheme, encrypting the entire message, including metadata. "Safeguards were incorporated into the system which prevented anyone, like myself, with access to the server from extracting any sensitive data from memory during processing," Levison told me years later.

While the government could install its pen/trap device on Lavabit's network, it would be functionally useless—all it would allow them to do would be to capture encrypted traffic. So, that's where the "reasonable steps" portion came into play.

Lavabit had a Transport Layer Security (TLS) private key that would be able to unlock all the encrypted traffic between customers and Lavabit.

"In other words, while the data [was] theoretically available, in practice I could not access it without modifying the software. The system was intended to prevent a system administrator, like myself, from surrendering a user's private data without their knowledge (or password). This design is what led the FBI to demand the Lavabit TLS private key."

But that key would not only allow the government to access Snowden's real-time traffic, but also that of all other Lavabit users. And that's where

Levison drew the line. Levison tried to explain to the agents that he wasn't sure that the law allowed for compelled decryption on such a vast scale.

He told them, "I'm uncomfortable turning over the encryption keys. I would have to consult with a lawyer before I did anything."

"I would say the conversation ended within 15 or 20 minutes because it had reached a dead end."

◯

As a child growing up in Inner Sunset, a neighborhood near Golden Gate Park, Ladar Levison spent a lot of time at the nearby California Academy of Sciences, so that he could use their fast Internet connection. Before he was 13, they even put him to work creating web pages for endangered species. He poured over *2600* magazine and even administered his own dial-up bulletin board system (BBS), a precursor to the modern chat room. In 1995, when Levison was just 14 years old, he left home without telling his parents, and boarded a bus for Las Vegas to attend the third-ever DEF CON, a well-known annual hacker convention.

On April 1, 2004, Google changed e-mail forever by offering one gigabyte of storage, far more than other competitors offered at the time. For two years, Levison had been sitting on a domain name—Nerdshack.com—that he was trying to find a creative outlet for.

When Gmail debuted, Levison, then a political science student at Southern Methodist University, was doing some contract work here and there, but he wanted to do his own thing. And from the beginning of Gmail, Levison was disturbed by the entire business model behind the free service. After all, there's an old adage about tech companies: "If you're not paying for the product, you are the product." In other words, while Gmail didn't charge users for the service, Google routinely scans all messages and sells ads against them as a way to make money.

So, Nerdshack (which would eventually change its name to Lavabit), was born.

"I didn't like the idea that Google was going to be profiling people's private messages for advertising," Levison said. "I was creating the type of service that I wanted to use myself. It was developed with the type of features that I would choose to use. You have to remember, I was involved in that information security community and I wanted to build the type of service that my friends couldn't break into."

Early on, Levison offered TLS support, and thought user-level encryption was a way to secure himself against NSLs.

"I knew about the PATRIOT Act, I remember thinking that it was slightly too aggressive, that the pendulum had swung too far," he said. "I didn't know what instruments were in it and how they would be applied. The idea that the FBI would come to me with one of these NSLs—I knew I would have to pick between violating the United States Code and jail. Knowing myself, I would pick jail rather than hand over user data."

However, Levison wasn't an absolute opponent to government surveillance. He just was opposed to indiscriminate surveillance with inadequate oversight. In other words, as a third-party e-mail provider, he didn't want to be in a position where he would have to give up data on his own customers, as the *Smith* decision would require.

"I wasn't trying to end surveillance—I was trying to remove the service provider from the surveillance equation," he said.

"In other words, I didn't want intelligence agencies and law enforcement to be coming to us in secret and forcing us to turn over large swaths of data without being able to tell users that they were being targeted. It felt wrong to take money from customers while you were spying on them. My grandfather was in retail, he ran a series of toy stores. He taught me 'the customer is always right.' How could the customer be right if you were spying on them for somebody else?"

E-mail works in multiple steps. The first step is you, the author of the e-mail, have to write a message. When you sit down at your computer (or tap at your smartphone), type out a message to someone, and press send, the first thing that has to happen is that your device has to establish a connection to your mail server (Gmail, Lavabit, or whatever). There are two primary types of security protocols that are used to encrypt e-mails.

The security protocol known as TLS (or as it was previously known, Secure Sockets Layer [SSL]) creates a cryptographically secure link to that server. It's a type of encryption that only protects messages in transit. The e-mail provider then has to figure out to what server to send the message. If you use Gmail and you're sending a message to Lavabit, then Gmail's servers have to talk to Lavabit's servers and deliver the message. However, as of June 2013, very few major e-mail providers were employing TLS.

PGP (Pretty Good Privacy), by contrast, uses a much more cumbersome method to encrypt messages from end to end, and doesn't rely on what the mail server is or isn't doing. It requires that both parties on either side have a PGP key and have previously exchanged them (or looked them up on a public key server). PGP is notoriously difficult to set up and use regularly, particularly on a mobile device. The overwhelming majority of e-mail users do not encrypt their messages this way. PGP protects messages from the moment that they are sent to the moment that they are received, both in transit and at rest.

By coincidence, prior to the FBI showing up at his door, Levison wrote to his customers that protecting their e-mail from the strongest of adversaries, the United States government, with TLS was difficult.

> We should note that this encryption process is only secure if you select a strong password. If your password is weak, an attacker would only need to brute force the password to crack our encryption. We should also note that this feature only protects messages on the Lavabit servers. Messages can always be intercepted before they reach Lavabit or between Lavabit's servers and your personal computer, if SSL is not used. Finally, messages can be retrieved from your local hard drive if encryption software isn't used on your computer to protect the files. These vulnerabilities are intentional. Our goal was to make invading a user's privacy difficult, by protecting messages at their most vulnerable point. That doesn't mean a dedicated attacker, like the United States government, couldn't intercept the message in transit or once it reaches your computer.

◐

When Levison refused to comply with the June 28, 2013, order that the FBI agents presented him with, he began looking for a lawyer. His first call was to the Electronic Frontier Foundation, who eventually referred him to

Marcia Hofmann, a well-known San Francisco attorney who specializes in computer crime law. Levison hired her as his attorney on July 8.

On July 9, Levison received a formal court summons to appear before US District Judge Claude Hilton on July 16, 2013, in Virginia, to explain why he had not complied with the June 28 order. As Hofmann was not admitted to the bar in Virginia, she could no longer represent him—she was only his counsel for two days.

With what he later described as a "limited budget of $10,000," Levison quickly set out to find Virginia lawyers who were familiar with this element of the law. But as his entire case remained under seal, he could not even publicly say that he was looking for such an attorney, much less why. After interviewing over a dozen attorneys, none of whom he found satisfactory, Levison was forced to appear *pro se*, or on his own behalf, which put him at a significant disadvantage.

Within days, Levison did find a Fairfax, Virginia, attorney, Jesse Binnall, who promptly asked the court to unseal the case and "quash" the warrant that required the installation of the pen/trap device and the furnishing of the SSL keys to make it usable, likening what the government was asking for to an eighteenth-century-style general warrant, which the Founders abhorred.

For its part, prosecutors countered that all the pen register order allowed it to do, and all it was going to do, was to obtain metadata for Snowden's account.

"It cannot be that a search warrant is 'general' merely because it gives the government a tool that, *if abused, contrary to law,* could constitute a general search," Neil MacBride, the US attorney for the Eastern District of Virginia, wrote in a filing to the court.

In other words, the government was authorized to take any and all lawful measures to meaningfully impose the pen/trap device on Lavabit's servers as a way to get access to Snowden's metadata—even if that meant capturing traffic on every other user. In a sense, it really boiled down to whether or not one felt that the government could be trusted with so much information that it promised not to examine.

Levison was skeptical of the government's behavior, and thought that what was being asked of him was a step too far—his fears would later be confirmed by the Edward Snowden documents. Meanwhile, the Department of Justice (DOJ) and FBI clearly felt that they were wholly trustworthy and would not overstep their bounds.

On August 1, 2013, Levison was ordered to provide his TLS keys to the FBI in Dallas by 5 PM CT on Friday, August 2. At 1:30 PM, Levison went to that office in person and handed over several keys: 11 pages of text in 4-point font, which prosecutors later described as "largely illegible."

"It seemed only natural to turn that over," he said. "I figured at that point, they had been coming after me for six weeks, the least they could do is spend the weekend typing in the encryption keys."

But really, it was a ruse to buy himself more time to shut down the entire service. Levison had made a quiet deal with himself that were he to be ordered to hand over the TLS keys, he would rather commit digital hara-kiri than compromise his users' privacy. During this whole period, he had ordered a slew of portable hard drives that could be used to backup the software that had powered the Lavabit system.

On Monday, August 5, prosecutors were livid about the format the encryption keys had been delivered in. They went back to court, and successfully got an *ex parte* court order demanding that Levison provide them in a usable, electronic format, by that same day at 12 PM CT, or he would face a contempt of court order and a fine of $5,000 per day.

After being served with the order the following day, Levison went to play volleyball, had a beer, and began contemplating the onerous task that lay ahead of him. He went home, took a shower, and then headed to his Dallas data center, and began moving all of Lavabit's data onto the portable drives. Working all night, his last action was to copy the SSL keys to a CD (as the FBI had requested) and then deleted everything on the Lavabit servers.

On August 7, he drove the five miles up the road to the FBI Field Office, handed over the CD, drove home, put up a brief announcement on his website that Lavabit had shut down—he still couldn't say why, as the case remained under seal—and went to sleep.

As he wrote:

> *I have been forced to make a difficult decision: to become complicit in crimes against the American people or walk away from nearly ten years of hard work by shutting down Lavabit. After significant soul searching, I have decided to suspend operations. I wish that I could legally share with you the events that led to my decision. I cannot. I feel you deserve to know what's going on—the first amendment is supposed to guarantee me the freedom to speak out in situations like this. Unfortunately, Congress has passed laws that say otherwise. As things currently stand, I cannot share my*

*experiences over the last six weeks, even though I have twice
made the appropriate requests.*

Days later, on August 13, appearing on *Democracy Now* with his lawyer at
his side, Levison was cagey. "I was faced with the choice of watching it suffer
or putting it to sleep quietly," he said, still staying quiet as to why.

The government could have attempted to collect the $10,000 for missing
the deadline by two days, but it didn't. Levison remained a free man, albeit
a man without a business.

Levison appealed up to the 4th US Circuit Court of Appeals, and ultimately lost in April 2014, largely on procedural grounds—the court didn't
even address the heart of Levison's argument, that the order to disclose the
SSL keys was overbroad.

"Even though I expected to get arrested, I was careful in my actions," Levison said later.

"I positioned myself legally and politically such that it would be difficult
for them to pursue me. They would have had to convince a jury that I have
an obligation to operate a service strictly for their surveillance needs. That
I don't have the right to shut down my own business."

◌

The story of Lavabit is in some ways a prelude to the "FBI v. Apple" showdown of 2016. It illustrates the lengths to which the government is willing
to go to obtain e-mail information, and how difficult e-mail is to protect—
even though, to most of us, it feels like one of the most private forms of
communication that we have.

During his appeal to the 4th US Circuit Court of Appeals, Levison's attorneys cited a 2010 appellate decision from a case known as *Warshak*, a
bizarre case involving a "nutraceutical" that purported to enhance penile
erections. That case has now become the de facto standard nationwide, requiring that the content of an e-mail only be turned over with a warrant.

In the early 2000s, late-night television across America was blanketed
with television advertisements featuring a man who came to be known as
"Smilin' Bob." Thanks to a male enhancement product known as Enzyte,
Bob got a "big boost of confidence," the narrator intoned, inviting customers to get a sample pack of the pills.

When Berkeley Nutraceuticals, a company founded by Cincinnati entrepreneur Steven Warshak, began in 2001, it only had 15 employees. After a flood of advertising—including in *Penthouse* and *Outside* magazines, among other ads that boasted a "double your money back" guarantee—business was booming. By 2004, the company had grown to include a 24-hour call center and 1,500 employees—that year, it raked in $250 million in revenue. However, according to prosecutors, the entire operation was built not on the sale of these questionable pills, but rather, an auto-ship program. Customers who thought they were simply getting a sample pack were, in fact, signing up for a subscription of regular pills that was nearly impossible to shake.

As complaints began to mount, Warshak and his colleagues were finally hit with Federal Trade Commission charges in February 2006 and a criminal indictment in September 2006 alleging numerous counts of fraud.

Eventually, the criminal case moved towards trial, where the government planned to put on numerous witnesses, including former employees. They also obtained 27,000 of Warshak's e-mails, including one written by his nephew, Jason Cossman.

In that message, Cossman explored an idea that could help Berkeley Nutraceuticals make even more money: after dissatisfied customers canceled, sales representatives should simply call back, purporting to be conducting a health survey. If the customer told the rep that he used to take a Berkeley pill, then the rep would simply promote a less-expensive product "that the hospital is promoting"—neglecting to mention that this was also a Berkeley product.

"The poor customer bites, thinking he's gettin a deal, even though he's actually getting taken by my company for the second time around!!!!!!" Cossman wrote. "The scheme is beautiful. dreamed it up after many a bong hit one night. these customers are fish in a barrel, man. you already spent the media dollars to get em in the barrel when you bought the enzyte spot. dont let em get away so easy. exploit the shit out of them."

Late one night in February 2005, Warshak sent this message to five other executives, appending to the subject line: "The student has become the teacher—our company was built on this kind of creative thinking . . . thanks for the wake-up call jason!"

However, Warshak's lawyers were stumped as to how government investigators managed to get their hands on so many e-mails, until they learned that his e-mail provider, NuVox Communications, had been sent a 2004 letter from government investigators, ordering them to keep all copies of his future messages under a provision of the SCA. Warshak didn't find out about this until May 2006.

In court proceedings, Warshak was primarily represented by Martin Weinberg, a veteran criminal defense lawyer based in Boston.

Weinberg was a good choice in a Fourth Amendment case: he had successfully argued before the Supreme Court back in 1977 in *United States v. Chadwick*. That case involved two men who boarded an Amtrak train in San Diego with a "double-locked footlocker" and got off in Boston. Upon their arrival, they were met by federal agents, who insisted on seizing their case and taking it to a government facility to search it—without a warrant. In it, the agents found "large quantities" of marijuana and the men were accordingly charged.

As the case progressed, courts consistently found in the men's favor, citing precedent that warrantless searches are *per se* unreasonable. In a 7–2 decision, the Supreme Court found Weinberg's arguments persuasive, and ruled in Chadwick's favor, citing *Katz*.

> *We do not agree that the Warrant Clause protects only dwellings and other specifically designated locales. As we have noted before, the Fourth Amendment "protects people, not places," Katz v. United States, 389 U. S. 347, 389 U. S. 351(1967); more particularly, it protects people from unreasonable government intrusions into their legitimate expectations of privacy.*

If the officers wanted to search the footlocker, particularly when there was no urgent need to do so, they could have taken the time to seek a warrant. However, they chose not to. Upon learning of what investigators had done in pursuit of Warshak, Weinberg immediately thought of the *Chadwick* case.

"We were alarmed to realize that no one had challenged a long-existing but not-well-known policy that the DOJ would use secret subpoenas and orders to gain access to people's e-mails not through searches of people's computers, but by going to the ISPs," he said in an interview, years later. "This was deeply upsetting to anybody's reasonable expectation of privacy."

When it was all said and done, in August 2008, Warshak was sentenced to 25 years in prison and was ordered to forfeit over $459 million to the government. He and his lawyers appealed, and argued that the government should not have been able to obtain his e-mails without a warrant. In his opening filing to the 6th Circuit, Weinberg also underscored that Berkeley

Nutraceuticals was an "exceptional company," adding that Warshak had "spent a fortune to self-correct any operational failures."

If the 6th Circuit agreed, Weinberg argued, Warshak's conviction and sentence should be set aside due to the "exclusionary rule," a procedural notion designed to punish the government for bad behavior.

However, there is a counterpoint: the "good faith exception to the exclusionary rule," which says that so long as the government did something in good faith, the evidence derived from that questionable behavior can stand.

That's exactly what the 6th Circuit ruled in December 2010, when citing the *Kyllo* case, that "the Fourth Amendment must keep pace with the inexorable march of technological progress, or its guarantees will wither and perish." (The appeals court also reduced Warshak's sentence to 10 years—he was released early, in 2016.)

However, Circuit Judge Damon Keith, whose privacy colors were shown way back in 1971 during the *Keith* case, popped up again in *Warshak*. Judge Keith took a skeptical view of the government's behavior. In his concurrence, he wrote that while the end result should stay the same, the government had gone too far.

> *Following NuVox's policy, the provider would have destroyed Warshak's old emails but for the government's request that they maintain all current and prospective emails for almost a year without Warshak's knowledge. In practice, the government used the statute as a means to monitor Warshak after the investigation started without his knowledge and without a warrant. Such a practice is no more than back-door wiretapping. I doubt that such actions, if contested directly in court, would withstand the muster of the Fourth Amendment.*

Judge Keith analogized e-mail to a telephone call—both allow two people to "communicate in private." So, just as the government can't wiretap someone without a significant showing, neither can the government turn e-mail into a wiretap of sorts. At least in *Warshak*, federal investigators did not heed the 2005 warning provided by the American Prosecutors Research Institute, that d-orders could not be used "prospectively"—in other words, to get e-mails ahead of time.

⬮

Even before the 6th Circuit published its *Warshak* ruling in December 2010, major companies in the tech industry and various political advocacy organizations partnered in what was called the Digital Due Process Initiative. Together, they began to lobby Congress to update the law. Their concerns aligned with Judge Keith's opinion that "the government cannot use e-mail collection as a means to monitor citizens without a warrant anymore than they can tap a telephone line to monitor citizens without a warrant."

Within months, the House of Representatives convened a subcommittee hearing to discuss how the ECPA should be reformed in light of cloud computing and modern e-mail. In 2011, neither chamber of Congress was able to produce a bill that advanced very far. In November 2012, the Senate Judiciary Committee proposed an ECPA reform bill, but again the legislative process came to a halt.

⬮

The 6th Circuit decision in *Warshak* remains binding only in that particular federal judicial zone, which covers Michigan, Ohio, Kentucky, and Tennessee. Technically, courts in the other 12 appellate federal districts across the country are not obligated to follow their lead. When differing circuits reach opposite legal conclusions, this constitutes a circuit split, and makes it even more likely that the Supreme Court will take up a future case to resolve the difference.

But rather than wait for courts in other parts of the country to reach what they considered to be a favorable result, a number of major firms, including Google, Facebook, Yahoo, and Microsoft began unilaterally imposing the *Warshak* standard shortly after the 6th Circuit ruling was handed down. However, Google's decision was not widely known until January 2013.

"In order to compel us to produce content in Gmail we require an ECPA search warrant," Chris Gaither, a Google spokesperson, told Ars Technica at the time. "If they come for registration information, that's one thing, but if they ask for content of e-mail, that's another thing."

A few months later, in March 2013, at yet another House subcommittee hearing, a top DOJ official made a quiet, but notable announcement.

"We agree, for example, that there is no principled basis to treat email less than 180 days old differently than email more than 180 days old," Acting Assistant Attorney General Elana Tyrangiel said.

> *Similarly, it makes sense that the statute not accord lesser protection to opened emails than it gives to emails that are unopened. Acknowledging that the so-called "180-day rule" and other distinctions in the SCA no longer make sense is an important first step. The harder question is how to update those outdated rules and the statute in light of new and changing technologies while maintaining protections for privacy and adequately providing for public safety and other law enforcement imperatives.*

This statement suggested that the government was no longer going to defend this portion of ECPA in court proceedings, and would simply seek a warrant, as most major providers would require them to do. It's hard to know exactly why the DOJ decided to make that policy change when it did.

"I assumed they just knew that line was indefensible, and that after three years of *Warshak* they realized a warrant requirement for content wasn't the end of the world," Orin Kerr, who testifed at the same hearing and is now a law professor at the University of Southern California, told me.

The 46-year-old professor is one of the most frequently cited tech legal experts of the modern era. This jazz aficionado trained as a mechanical engineer and graduated from Harvard Law School in the early days of the commercial Internet. After graduation, he clerked for an appellate judge before working as a federal prosecutor for three years. Soon after, he became a law professor, churning out influential legal journal articles on a regular basis.

Several months after he testified before the House subcommittee in March 2013, Kerr put forward what is likely one of the most well-thought-out ways to amend ECPA. He quickly identified one of the crucial problems between the way that computers were thought of in the 1980s when compared to the modern era.

"The plummeting costs of storage have flipped the default understanding of how surveillance threatens privacy," he wrote.

> *ECPA was drafted at a time when electronic storage was expensive and therefore relatively rare. ECPA treated real-time*

> *wiretapping as the chief privacy threat. Access to stored com-*
> *munications was treated as a lesser concern. The opposite is*
> *true today. Storage has become remarkably cheap and there-*
> *fore ubiquitous. Service providers now routinely store every-*
> *thing, and they can turn over everything to law enforcement.*
> *As a result of that technology change, access to stored records*
> *has become the greater privacy threat. The incredible growth*
> *of stored records makes ECPA's structure exactly backwards*
> *for the operation of modern computer networks.*

Or, as he concluded: "The ability to store everything makes storage the greater privacy threat."

So, what is the appropriate remedy? Get a warrant.

While ECPA reform was still languishing in Congress, California began earnestly taking Kerr's advice to heart. In February 2015, a coalition of tech companies (Apple, Google, Facebook, among others) and organizations led by the American Civil Liberties Union (ACLU) of Northern California announced the California Electronic Communications Privacy Act (CalECPA).

"Californians shouldn't be forced to choose between using smartphones, email, social networks or any new technology and keeping their personal lives private," Nicole Ozer, one of the ACLU of California's top lawyers, said in a statement at the time. "Especially after revelations of warrantless mass surveillance by the NSA [National Security Agency], it is time for California to catch up with other states across the nation, including Texas and Maine, which have already updated their privacy laws for the modern digital world."

Ozer, an ACLU veteran, spearheaded this coalition.

"I became focused in California where we were well-positioned to enact not just a piece but a really holistic response to what really needed to happen," she said, noting that she postponed her own necessary back surgery to push forward with the legislation campaign. "When we drafted CalECPA, we . . . [wrote] the law in a way that makes sense for now—it's a clean slate, we were going to go for it."

The law, which was signed by Governor Jerry Brown eight months later, was dubbed by *Wired* magazine the "nation's best digital privacy law."

CalECPA goes further than any other similar law at the federal or state level. It forbids any law enforcement or other investigative entity from forcing a business to hand over not only e-mail content, but any metadata or digital communications of any kind whatsoever without a warrant. That means e-mails, texts, documents, chats, documents stored online, anything. Beyond that, the law also requires a warrant to track the physical location of any electronic device and to perform a search of those devices.

◎

Faced with increased pressure from tech firms and privacy advocates, the House of Representatives moved again towards real ECPA reform. They passed the reforms unanimously in 2016, under the name Email Privacy Act. The bill did away with the 180-day rule and also provided mandatory disclosure of the target, unless the government has made a showing that such notification needs to be delayed.

However, when it moved to the Senate, which happened in the wake of the "FBI v. Apple" case of March 2016, a few senators proposed amendments that ultimately torpedoed the bill. Among others, then senator Jeff Sessions (R-Alabama) filed one that would have required user data to be disclosed to law enforcement in the event of an emergency, while another amendment, pushed by the Obama White House, would have expanded the use of controversial NSLs.

In 2017, the House again took up the bill, and again passed it unanimously. As of this writing in late 2017, the Senate has yet to take up a companion bill. President Donald Trump has not yet publicly indicated whether he would sign it, should it pass the Senate.

One of the biggest problems with SCA orders is that they often come with a built-in gag order, with no end date. The only person who can lift that gag order is the same judge who issued it—barring extenuating circumstances, other judges will not do so. Again, unlike with a physical search, someone who has had their data handed over may never find out about it. And with such orders remaining sealed, journalists and activists can never find out that they even exist, let alone challenge their legitimacy in court.

So, as part of a larger legal strategy that evolved in the wake of the Snowden revelations in 2013, Microsoft announced that it would be "committed to notifying business and government customers if we receive legal orders related to their data." In 2016, the company took this notion one step further, and sued the DOJ, asking a court to allow it to speak to customers who were affected by data handovers, citing the company's First Amendment right to freedom of speech and its Fourth Amendment right to protect against unreasonable searches and seizures.

Specifically, it wanted the federal court in Seattle to declare unconstitutional the specific portion of federal law that deals with delayed notice, known as 18 USC 2705(b).

"We believe that with rare exceptions consumers and businesses have a right to know when the government accesses their emails or records," wrote Brad Smith, Microsoft's top lawyer, in a public blog post in April 2016. "Yet it's becoming routine for the U.S. government to issue orders that require email providers to keep these types of legal demands secret. We believe that this goes too far and we are asking the courts to address the situation."

Smith further explained that between October 2014 and April 2016, the DOJ

> has required that we maintain secrecy regarding 2,576 legal demands, effectively silencing Microsoft from speaking to customers about warrants or other legal process seeking their data. Notably and even surprisingly, 1,752 of these secrecy orders, or 68 percent of the total, contained no fixed end date at all. This means that we effectively are prohibited forever from telling our customers that the government has obtained their data.

For its part, the government asked the judge to dismiss the entire case, largely on the grounds that Microsoft lacked standing—it could not prove that it was harmed by the fact that it could not discuss the SCA orders with its customers. In February 2017, the judge dropped the Fourth Amendment question, but allowed the First Amendment claim to stand. However, in October 2017, the DOJ changed its policy, allowing companies to notify customers of such a data handover in most cases; Microsoft dropped the case.

◉

Meanwhile, the day after Levison killed Lavabit in August 2013, another secure e-mail provider, Silent Circle, shut down preemptively.

"We see the writing [on] the wall, and we have decided that it is best for us to shut down Silent Mail now," co-founder Jon Callas wrote on the company's website. "We have not received subpoenas, warrants, security letters, or anything else by any government, and this is why we are acting now."

Silent Circle went so far as to physically destroy its servers, a move that the *New York Times* likened to "the digital equivalent of a library setting fire to its membership records to keep the government from knowing who checked out what books."

Two companies committing corporate *seppuku* within days of one another sent chills throughout the industry. Levison himself began giving various media interviews and saying ominously cryptic things like: "I'm taking a break from e-mail. If you knew what I know about e-mail, you might not use it either."

He was still required under a court order not to say exactly what the government had demanded of him. The specifics of what the government sought in the Lavabit case were not unsealed until October 2, 2013. After the case was unsealed, Levison wrote publicly on Facebook about it: "Lavabit maintains that the government had no legal basis for demanding its confidential information, namely passwords, encryption keys and source code."

Not long after his case was unsealed, the entrepreneur started speaking publicly about the need to make e-mail not only more secure, but easier to use.

On October 30, 2013, Levison appeared at a Silicon Valley e-mail conference with Callas and Silent Circle's other co-founder, Mike Janke, announcing what they called the Dark Mail Alliance.

The idea was to create a non-profit organization that would take the responsibility for developing an entirely new e-mail protocol. This was a daunting task. After all, the current underpinning of e-mail, formally known as SMTP (Simple Mail Transfer Protocol), dates back to 1982. Getting rid of SMTP would be just as dramatic as swapping out all roads designed for cars with magnetic levitation railroad tracks.

"This is just another transport—what we're getting rid of is SMTP," Callas said at the time. "We like to laugh at it, but there are reasons why it was a good system. We're replacing the transport with a new transport. E-mail was designed 40 years ago when everybody on the Internet knew each other and were friends."

Levison added that he hoped that Dark Mail would be "easy enough that Grandma can use it. Our hope is that someday in the near future that anybody who uses e-mail today can use a Dark Mail client tomorrow."

The vibe in the room was a heady mix of bewilderment and fear. Here were some of the industry's most privacy-minded and tech-savvy people saying that e-mail as everyone knew and loved it needed to be entirely overhauled. But how would it happen?

More than four years later, though, the Alliance has had some setbacks—there are now only two team members: Levison and his trusty dog, Princess. Silent Circle, or any other company of any size, is nowhere to be found. And without other partners, the Dark Mail idea cannot grow, at least for now.

But Levison isn't giving up. On January 20, 2017, he relaunched Lavabit. He figured that under a new White House—regardless of who won the election—DOJ lawyers might take a different view the second time around.

Unlike the last time, where most accounts were free, this time all accounts are paid, and they all use the Dark Internet Mail Environment standard. (So far, Lavabit is the only company that supports it, making it a standard of one.) Levison charges $30 for "standard" (5GB of storage) or $60 a year for "premier" (20GB).

"We have 60,000 customers and about 40,000 to 50,000 are returning users, but I look at it as I['ve] only taken the first steps down a very long road," he said.

"The way I look at it [is that when] . . . I built Lavabit in 2004, I was about 10 years ahead of the curve, the way I look at it now is that again I'm 10 years ahead of the curve, so it's going to take me another 10 years to get all the pieces deployed."

It's now clear that in the aftermath of Edward Snowden, companies ranging from Lavabit to Microsoft are willing to stand up to the government like never before. In some ways, however, protecting e-mail is becoming increasingly less important as both Silicon Valley and consumers have moved on to easier-to-use ephemeral encrypted messaging (like Signal), which can quickly be set up on any smartphone. When messages can be set to be deleted automatically within minutes, it is even more difficult for authorities to gain access.

CHAPTER SEVEN

Why the Eighteenth-Century Constitution Protects Against Twenty-First-Century Satellite-Based Tracking

Prolonged surveillance reveals types of information not revealed by short-term surveillance, such as what a person does repeatedly, what he does not do, and what he does ensemble. These types of information can each reveal more about a person than does any individual trip viewed in isolation. Repeated visits to a church, a gym, a bar, or a bookie tell a story not told by any single visit, as does one's not visiting any of these places over the course of a month. The sequence of a person's movements can reveal still more; a single trip to a gynecologist's office tells little about a woman, but that trip followed a few weeks later by a visit to a baby supply store tells a different story.

—*United States v. Maynard*
US District Court for the District of Columbia Circuit opinion
August 6, 2010

Late June 2008
Washington, DC

The District of Columbia Central Detention Facility has a much catchier name to locals, lawyers, and inmates alike: the DC Jail. The multi-story earthen-brown-colored structure looms over the surrounds—with the sole exception of RFK Stadium just a few blocks away—and is one of the largest structures in the neighborhood. It overlooks the Congressional Cemetery, which serves as the final resting place for various DC types, ranging from John Phillips Sousa to J. Edgar Hoover.

On a sticky summer evening in 2008, Stephen Leckar went to the brutalist 1970s-era structure. He's an attorney who specializes in commercial litigation and occasionally white-collar criminal law, so it's not every day that he has to go to the DC Jail. His area of expertise is in financial and securities law, and he usually doesn't defend those accused of major drug crimes.

Leckar didn't know much about his client, Antoine "Toine" Jones, whose case, by that point, was already nearly three years old. The veteran attorney had only been assigned the case in May 2008, less than one month earlier, by the US Court of Appeals for the District of Columbia Circuit, shortly after Jones had filed his formal appeal of his conviction of conspiracy to distribute five or more kilograms of cocaine.

Jones and eight others had been arrested in the early morning hours of October 24, 2005, on drug conspiracy charges. FBI agents and the Metropolitan Police Department seized "nearly 220 pounds of cocaine and more than $900,000 in cash during raids in the District and Maryland," reported the *Washington Post*, citing a Department of Justice (DOJ) press release.

According to US Attorney Kenneth L. Wainstein, the men "had risen to the top of the drug world." Jones, a 45-year-old man from Waldorf, Maryland, a DC suburb, was the owner of the Levels Nite Club, a DC venue that a nightclub directory described as a "hybrid of both trendy-club and swank-lounge," which had been searched.

The case took years to unfold. The FBI and Immigration and Customs Enforcement (ICE) began investigating Jones and his crew in 2004. The authorities spoke with informants, obtained pen registers, and even installed a pole camera near Levels. Amazingly, Levels was across the street from the DC police's auto garage, known by local cops as the "Northeast Shop." Numerous marked police cars are easily visible from the street.

By August 2005, investigators got a warrant to seize and search text messages from suspected phones. The following month, authorities sought and received permission from a District of Columbia federal judge to secretly place a GPS tracking device on Jones' champagne-colored Jeep Grand Cherokee. However, for some bizarre reason, the tracker was not installed until a day after the warrant had expired, and it was installed in Maryland, rather than DC. Effectively, this meant that there was no warrant governing its use. On top of it all, within weeks, the GPS tracker broke down, and authorities had to sneak in again and replace its battery.

At that point, GPS was still a relatively novel technology as far as law enforcement was concerned. One of the most prominent GPS cases that had been litigated previously was *United States v. Garcia*, where the 7th US Circuit Court of Appeals ruled on February 2, 2007, in the government's favor that a warrantless installation of a similar GPS tracker on a suspect's car was not a search.

"Of course the amendment cannot sensibly be read to mean that police shall be no more efficient in the twenty-first century than they were in the eighteenth," Circuit Judge Richard Posner wrote in the unanimous opinion. "There is a tradeoff between security and privacy, and often it favors security."

A year after Jones' original October 2005 arrest, there was a trial, where all the other co-defendants were acquitted on all counts except one, which was eventually dismissed. However, while Jones was acquitted, the jury was unable to reach a verdict on the conspiracy charge—the judge declared a mistrial.

In March 2007, prosecutors filed a superseding indictment on a single count of conspiracy to distribute. That document describes an elaborate scheme that began in 2003 to acquire large quantities of cocaine from Mexico and then resell it in DC and elsewhere in the region. Jones and one of his co-conspirators who was added later, Lawrence Maynard (the manager of Levels), the government alleged, would sell their cocaine in various places.

These points of sale included not only the Levels nightclub, but also Sam's Car Wash in Temple Hills, Maryland, and a county sports facility in Landover, Maryland, among other locales. Jones and Maynard were eventually found guilty at trial in January 2008. Jones and his cohorts often used sports-related code words to facilitate their drug deals. The amounts of cocaine that they were selling were referred to as "little tickets," "big tickets," and "VIP tickets."

On May 2, 2008, Jones was sentenced to life in prison—his attorneys asked that he be assigned to a prison as close to Washington, DC, as possible so as to be closer to his wife and son. That same day, Jones and his first attorney, Eduardo Balarezo, appealed. Leckar was appointed by the court to be Jones' appellate attorney on May 22, 2008.

Leckar wasn't able to go see Jones until June, but fortunately it was before he'd been transferred to a federal prison.

After clearing the reception desk and the security checkpoint, the grey-haired attorney first laid eyes on Jones in an unventilated, concrete meeting room. In contrast to his attorney, Jones was the size of a football player: 6'2" at about 220 pounds. But unexpectedly, the accused drug kingpin walked in with a stack of papers and file folders from his crotch to his chin.

"I thought he was stark raving mad," Leckar said, marveling at how obsessed with his own case Jones had become. Jones had all kinds of theories as to what the government was up to and how he wasn't actually guilty of the vast drug conspiracy that prosecutors claimed.

For hours, the two men—one in a suit, the other in a prison jumpsuit—painstakingly went over Jones' notes, page by page and file by file, trying to figure out the best way to challenge the jury's verdict. Jones had a few ideas: one included challenging the necessity of the wiretaps conducted against him. Wiretaps, since the 1968 Omnibus act, required a super-warrant, a showing that all other conventional means of surveillance have already been tried and failed or would fail.

Leckar wasn't convinced that strategy would be a winning one. But among the slew of papers that Jones practically shoved at Leckar was one that stood out: a sealed September 2015 affidavit filed by an FBI agent, asking for a judge's permission to place a tracking device on Jones' Jeep.

"To have somebody subject to such intrusiveness, I thought to myself that there was something here," Leckar recalled.

By the end of their initial meeting, which ended around midnight, the lawyer finally had a road to go down: whether the warrantless physical tracking of Jones' Jeep was constitutional.

Over the next six months, Leckar and Jones began corresponding weekly, largely by letter, as a way to hash out their final arguments for the DC appellate court. Leckar knew that he had an uphill legal battle.

Eventually, everything was distilled into a February 18, 2009, brief that challenged the jury verdict on behalf of both Jones and Maynard.

The appellants' brief raised a number of procedural questions for the court to consider, nearly all of them applied to both Jones and Maynard. But the only issue that was raised solely on Jones' behalf was the question of the legality of the GPS.

"The GPS logged all of Jones's movements, including trips to and from a suspected 'stash house,'" Leckar argued in the brief. "Its 3,106 pages of movement-location data proved a critical piece of evidence. Should its revelations have been suppressed?"

In the government's reply brief, Peter S. Smith, assistant US attorney, countered by formulating the question before the DC Circuit in a different fashion.

"Whether the Fourth Amendment permitted the government's warrantless installation and monitoring of a Global Positioning System tracking device on appellant Jones's Jeep, where agents installed the device on the vehicle's exterior when the Jeep was located in a public place," he wrote.

"The evidence used at trial involved only the Jeep's movements on public streets; and the installation of the GPS tracking device and the use of data from that device were supported by probable cause to believe that Jones was engaged in a conspiracy to distribute narcotics."

Essentially, Leckar pushed the court to consider the fact that a surreptitiously installed GPS device, which emits a signal of its precise location every 10 seconds, was far beyond simply sensory-enhancing. Leckar, in fact, likened the technology to "a thousand police officers standing and monitoring you as you drive by."

He also took a notable approach, and made sure to highlight the conservative property-based factor as part of the privacy analysis.

"Jones had a reasonable expectation of privacy that was violated when the agents physically installed and when they reactivated the GPS on his vehicle without a warrant," he argued. "The Government covertly took dominion over a portion of his car and used it to acquire information about his location."

In other words, because the GPS tracker was physically installed on Jones' Jeep (while the car was parked at a public lot in Maryland), it was actually both a seizure and a search within the meaning of the Fourth Amendment. Leckar even likened the GPS install to *Silverman v. United States* (where a spike mike plugged into an adjacent ducting tube, without a warrant, was a search) that a young Harvey Schneider raised in *Katz v. United States* in 1967. Law enforcement's actions to force a constant disclosure of location information was a search, and therefore, he argued, required a warrant.

Citing a 2003 opinion by the Washington Supreme Court, Leckar noted a GPS device "can provide a detailed record of travel to doctors' offices, banks, gambling casinos . . . the strip club, the opera, the baseball game, the 'wrong' side of town, the family planning clinic, the labor rally."

In short, this is precisely the type of intimate information that the Fourth Amendment is designed to protect.

Meanwhile, when the government responded with its own filing, it relied heavily on *United States v. Knotts*, and argued that like in that case, there was no "reasonable expectation of privacy" in one's location on a public road. Prosecutors even cited a line from *Katz*, noting, "What a person knowingly exposes to the public, even in his own home or office, is not a subject of Fourth Amendment protection." So, if one officer can record one person's location in public, then a machine that can record orders of magnitude more information for far longer, is also legitimate, under this argument.

So, as the DOJ argued, because Jones' Jeep was exposed to the public, including the undercarriage, where the tracker could be installed, there was no issue. Plus, prosecutors continued, the GPS installation was not a seizure as it did not disrupt in any way the operation of the vehicle.

"The record does not indicate that there was any intrusion into the interior of the Jeep, nor did agents open or disturb any enclosed areas of the Jeep or in any way damage the Jeep," Smith, the prosecutor wrote. "Accordingly, as in *Garcia*, the GPS tracker had no effect on Jones's dominion or control over the Jeep."

On November 17, 2009, the US Court of Appeals for the District of Columbia Circuit heard oral arguments in the case. Unusually, it took until August 6, 2010, for a ruling to come down. Normally the court only takes a few months. Such a lengthy wait suggested that the judges may have struggled with this case.

After many pages explaining why the court was denying all the other portions of the appeal—including the portion that applied to Maynard, thereby allowing the verdict against him to stand—the court finally arrived at the GPS question on Jones' car at the end of page 15.

Unequivocally, the DC Circuit unanimously found that "*Knotts* is not controlling," meaning that the government's claims on this point were not valid. The three-judge panel cited a line from the *Knotts* Supreme Court decision that projected into the future, where the justices noted that "if such dragnet-type law enforcement practices as respondent envisions should eventually occur, there will be time enough then to determine whether different constitutional principles may be applicable."

The DC Circuit, in 2010, found that this was the right time to examine that question. The court concluded that just because Jones' car was exposed to the public for a series of discrete moments doesn't mean that the cumulative location information was exposed in the same way.

"Two considerations persuade us the information the police discovered in this case—the totality of Jones's movements over the course of a month—was not exposed to the public," the judges wrote. "First, unlike one's movements during a single journey, the whole of one's movements over the course of a month is not actually exposed to the public because the likelihood anyone will observe all those movements is effectively nil. Second, the whole of one's movements is not exposed constructively even though each individual movement is exposed, because that whole reveals more—sometimes a great deal more—than does the sum of its parts."

On appeal at any federal circuit court, three judges are randomly selected from the full panel of sitting appellate judges. (The DC Circuit has
11 judges.) In the case of *Jones*, the three judges selected were Circuit Judge
David Tatel, Circuit Judge Thomas Griffith, and Circuit Judge Douglas
Ginsburg.

Years later, Leckar called this particular grouping of judges a "dream
panel," comprised of a Democrat (Tatel), a "principled conservative" (Griffith), and a libertarian who was once considered for the Supreme Court
(Ginsburg). The latter judge also had the distinction of helping create an
early computerized dating service (Operation Match) in the 1960s. These
judges ascribed to, and gave a full-throated endorsement of, the notion of
the mosaic theory. This idea stipulates that a long-term historic collection
of data points can establish a definitive pattern of behavior whose value
exceeds the sum of its parts.

"Prolonged surveillance reveals types of information not revealed by
short-term surveillance, such as what a person does repeatedly, what he
does not do, and what he does ensemble," the judges wrote.

> *These types of information can each reveal more about a
> person than does any individual trip viewed in isolation.
> Repeated visits to a church, a gym, a bar, or a bookie tell a
> story not told by any single visit, as does one's not visiting
> any of these places over the course of a month. The sequence
> of a person's movements can reveal still more; a single trip
> to a gynecologist's office tells little about a woman, but that
> trip followed a few weeks later by a visit to a baby supply
> store tells a different story.*

The government lost at the DC Circuit.

◯

If a losing side wishes to appeal, it can take a few half measures before the
cert petition to the Supreme Court. An appellant can ask the circuit court
to simply reconsider (this often doesn't work), or seek an *en banc* review of
the case, where the case is heard before all the appellate judges that sit on

that court. The court itself can decide whether to grant either of those petitions—unlike appeals, they are not automatic.

So that's exactly what the DOJ did. In its *en banc* petition, the government reiterated many of its views that hadn't held water with the original
three-judge panel—prosecutors dismissed the mosaic theory as "novel."

"The panel's conclusion that Jones had a reasonable expectation of privacy in the public movements of his Jeep rested on the premise that an
individual has a reasonable expectation of privacy in the totality of his
or her movements in public places," Assistant US Attorney Smith wrote.
"Although 'prolonged monitoring' may capture more information than
discrete instances of surveillance, the type of information collected is the
same regardless of the duration of the collection."

On November 19, 2010, the vote to hear the case *en banc* was voted down
6–3, setting the stage for a *cert* petition to the Supreme Court. With the
ruling at the 7th Circuit in *Garcia* going one way, and the ruling in the DC
Circuit going another, the conditions were ripe for the Supreme Court to
hear the case. Nearly a year later, on November 8, 2011, the Supreme Court
convened to hear Case 10-1259, *United States v. Jones*.

The composition of the Supreme Court had changed somewhat since
Kyllo in 2001. First, it was led by Chief Justice John Roberts, a conservative who formerly served as a clerk for Chief Justice Rehnquist. (Roberts
has held this position since September 2005.) But the 2012 Supreme Court
had five notable holdovers from 2001, including Antonin Scalia, Anthony
Kennedy, Ruth Bader Ginsburg, Stephen Breyer, and Clarence Thomas.
Rounding out the court was Justice Samuel Alito (a conservative), along
with Sonia Sotomayor and Elena Kagan (two liberals).

Representing the government again was Michael Dreeben, who argued
for the government in *Kyllo* more than a decade earlier, as deputy solicitor
general. As the petitioner, the government spoke first.

"Mr. Chief Justice, and may it please the Court," Dreeben's somewhat
high and reedy voice intoned.

> Since this Court's decision in Katz v. United States, *the*
> *Court has recognized a basic dichotomy under the Fourth*
> *Amendment. What a person seeks to preserve as private in*
> *the enclave of his own home or in a private letter or inside of*
> *his vehicle when he is traveling is a subject of Fourth Amend-*
> *ment protection. But what he reveals to the world, such as his*
> *movements in a car on a public roadway, is not. In* Knotts v.

United States, *this Court applied that principle to hold that*
visual and beeper surveillance of a vehicle traveling on the
public roadways infringed no Fourth Amendment expecta-
tion of privacy.

Chief Justice Roberts jumped right in.

"*Knotts*, though, seems to me much more like traditional surveillance,"
he said. "You're following the car and the beeper just helps you follow it
from a—from a slightly greater distance. That was 30 years ago. The technology is very different and you get a lot more information from the GPS
surveillance than you do from following a beeper."

Dreeben acknowledged that while the technology was different, in
Knotts, police lost track of the car as it was driving from Minnesota to Wisconsin for a full hour.

"They only were able to discover it by having a beeper receiver in a helicopter that detected the beeps from the radio transmitter in the can of
chloroform," he replied.

"But that's a good example of the change in technology," Roberts retorted.

> *That's a lot of work to follow the car. They've got to listen to*
> *the beeper. When they lose it they have got to call in the heli-*
> *copter. Here they just sit back in the station and they—they*
> *push a button whenever they want to find out where the car*
> *is. They look at data from a month and find out everywhere*
> *it's been in the past month. That—that seems to me dramat-*
> *ically different.*

Eventually, Justice Scalia chimed in—noting his displeasure with the entire
Katz reasonable expectation of privacy notion—and focused on the phys-
ical trespass of the GPS device on Jones' car. Not long after, Chief Justice
Roberts stunned the court with a key question.

"You think there would also not be a search if you put a GPS device on
all of our cars, monitored our movements for a month?" he asked Dreeben.
"You think you're entitled to do that under your theory?"

"The justices of this Court?" the deputy solicitor general asked.

"Yes."

"Under our theory and under this Court's cases, the justices of this Court
when driving on public roadways have no greater expectation—"

"So your answer is yes, you could tomorrow decide that you [want to] put a GPS device on every one of our cars, follow us for a month; no problem under the Constitution?"

"Well, equally, Mr. Chief Justice, if the FBI wanted to it could put its team of surveillance agents around the clock on any individual and follow that individual's movements as they went around on the public streets and they would thereby gather—"

Leckar, sitting at the other counsel table, was stunned. He said to himself: "That's it, we've won."

After some more repartee, Justice Sotomayor stepped in with this inquiry to Dreeben: "Tell me what the difference is between this and a general warrant?"

She continued: "What motivated the Fourth Amendment historically was the disapproval, the outrage, that our Founding Fathers experienced with general warrants that permitted police indiscriminately to investigate just on the basis of suspicion, not probable cause and to invade every possession that the individual had in search of a crime. How is this different?"

Dreeben didn't have much of an answer, other than to say that the observations of movements in public did not constitute a search.

When it was Leckar's turn, he initially focused not only on the search question, but on the seizure—that Jones' car was temporarily "seized" in order to place the GPS device on it. By focusing on the physical trespass, he was directly addressing Justice Scalia, and perhaps Justices Thomas and Alito as well.

After some back-and-forth between Leckar, Alito, Roberts, and Scalia, the outspoken conservative justice finally cut through the chatter: "You do not give anybody permission to have your car carry a tracking device."

Leckar was, by his own admission, a bit nervous—until he regained his footing when Scalia asked why using the GPS tracker was unreasonable, if a police department could unquestionably post dozens of officers along Jones' route.

This was the moment where Leckar really drove to the heart of the matter, that a GPS tracker was a "complete robotic substitute" for human law enforcement.

"A GPS in your car is, or anybody's car, is like—without a warrant, is like having an—it makes you unable to get rid of an uninvited stranger," he said.

Scalia pushed him, asking him how a GPS was different than a traditional police tail, where a human officer was following along in another car.

"A tail—if they can—if they want to tail, if they want to commit the resources, that's fine. But what a GPS does, it involves—it allows the government to engage in unlimited surveillance through a machine, through a machine robotically," Leckar concluded, almost rushing through the words. "Nobody is even involved monitoring it. The record in this case showed that many times the police officers just let—let the machine go on."

Some minutes later, Alito seemed to articulate a split between the Scalia wing—which focused on the physical trespass onto Jones' car—and the broader point that warrantless surveillance of this magnitude was unconstitutional.

"So what you're concerned about is not this little thing that's put on your car," Justice Alito said. "It's not this invasion of your property interest. It's the monitoring that takes place."

"The monitoring makes it meaningful," Leckar replied. "Putting it on enables them to—"

"But to ask Justice Alito's question in a different way," Justice Kagan jumped in. "Suppose that the police could do this without ever committing the trespass. Suppose that in the future all cars are going to have GPS tracking systems and the police could essentially hack into such a system without committing the trespass. Would the constitutional issue we face be any different?"

In the end, Leckar's proposed rule for law enforcement was simple: "If you want to use GPS devices, get a warrant, absent exigent circumstances or another recognized exception to the Fourth Amendment, because of their capacity for—to collect data that you couldn't realistically get; because of the vanishingly low cost, because of their pervasive nature, that you should get a warrant any time—you must get a warrant any time you're going to attach a GPS to a citizen's effect or to a citizen's person."

Dreeben got a few more moments at the end of the hour-long oral argument, and the case was submitted.

◉

On January 23, 2012, the Supreme Court ruled unanimously in favor of Leckar and his client, Antoine Jones. However, the justices were split on exactly why the installation of the GPS tracker was, in fact, an unconstitutional search.

Justice Scalia wrote the opinion that four other justices signed onto, largely relying on the question of the physical trespass onto Jones' Jeep. In fact, because there was the trespass onto the Jeep, that was basically the beginning and the end of the legal analysis: no questions of *Katz* or a reasonable expectation of privacy even needed to be considered.

By contrast, Justice Alito, writing for the remaining four justices, criticized Scalia's opinion as being "unwise" and "highly artificial," as it was too reliant on eighteenth-century notions of trespass. Rather, Alito continued, he would "analyze the question presented in this case by asking whether respondent's reasonable expectations of privacy were violated by the long-term monitoring of the movements of the vehicle he drove."

Plus, Alito continued, twenty-first-century snooping was entirely different. After all, it was impossible to track someone's movement so discretely—recording a precise location every 10 seconds for a month straight—centuries ago.

> But it is almost impossible to think of late 18th-century situations that are analogous to what took place in this case. (Is it possible to imagine a case in which a constable secreted himself somewhere in a coach and remained there for a period of time in order to monitor the movements of the coach's owner?).

In any case, the Alito wing pointed out that in the pre-computer age, there was an inherent mechanism that made such broad surveillance untenable: economics.

"Traditional surveillance for any extended period of time was difficult and costly and therefore rarely undertaken," Alito continued.

> The surveillance at issue in this case—constant monitoring of the location of a vehicle for four weeks—would have required a large team of agents, multiple vehicles, and perhaps aerial assistance. Only an investigation of unusual importance could have justified such an expenditure of law enforcement resources. Devices like the one used in the present case, however, make long-term monitoring relatively easy and cheap.

Most curiously, Justice Sotomayor, who signed onto the Scalia opinion, wrote her own concurrence as well, taking the question presented by *Jones* one step further. She suggested that most people would not consider that a vast aggregation of one's movements by the government would be reasonable. Sotomayor also noted that it may be worthwhile for the court, in a future case, to entirely reevaluate the notion of the third-party doctrine (as solidified by *Smith v. Maryland*), which allows the government to obtain vast quantities of data without a warrant.

"This approach is ill-suited to the digital age, in which people reveal a great deal of information about themselves to third parties in the course of carrying out mundane tasks," she concluded.

In the end, Sotomayor noted that these further questions need not be reached as part of *Jones*, as she found herself joining on to the trespass analysis.

◇

The *Jones* decision sent shockwaves throughout the privacy and legal world.

"Law enforcement is now on notice," Walter Dellinger, another one of Jones' attorneys, told the *New York Times*, "that almost any use of GPS electronic surveillance of a citizen's movement will be legally questionable unless a warrant is obtained in advance."

The FBI put out a guidance to all special agents that effectively said: "turn off all your GPS," and another that instructed agents as to how to go retrieve devices that had already been deployed. That single agency alone had over 3,000 GPS trackers out in the field at the time, according to then FBI general counsel Andrew Weissmann, who spoke at a law school conference in San Francisco roughly a month after the Supreme Court's 2012 ruling.

During that panel discussion, Weissmann spoke about two memos that the FBI was currently drafting: one focused on the use of GPS tracking on forms of transportation beyond cars, the other speaking on how *Jones* applies to tracking methods outside of GPS (presumably like cell phone ping data).

"Is it going to apply to boats, is it going to apply to airplanes?" Weissmann asked. "Is it going to apply at the border? What's it mean for the consent that's given by an owner? What does it mean if consent is given by a possessor? And this is all about GPS, by the way, without getting into other types of techniques."

Within several months of Weissmann's talk, activist attorneys from the American Civil Liberties Union (ACLU) and the Electronic Frontier Foundation sued the FBI to obtain the new memos that Weissmann discussed as a way to better glean what the agency was doing.

"We still have no idea what the FBI is doing in terms of tracking, post-*Jones*," Catherine Crump, then an ACLU attorney, told Ars Technica at the time. "If all *Jones* means is that law enforcement agents have to track you through your phone instead of your car, it's not going to mean much in the end."

That's still true today. More than five years later, the ACLU has yet to receive any meaningful documents responsive to its original public records request. The FBI did release over 100 pages, but they were almost entirely redacted. The ACLU chose not to pursue further litigation.

Neither the Supreme Court nor the DOJ have come up with a precise definition of what kinds of surveillance should be restricted, or even prohibited. In *Garcia*, Circuit Judge Posner, who ultimately ruled that the installation of the GPS device was not a search under the Fourth Amendment, nevertheless was aware of the potential for broad invasiveness.

"Technological progress poses a threat to privacy by enabling an extent of surveillance that in earlier times would have been prohibitively expensive," Posner wrote. "Whether and what kind of restrictions should, in the name of the Constitution, be placed on such surveillance when used in routine criminal enforcement are momentous issues that fortunately we need not try to resolve in this case."

In the wake of *Jones*, various lawyers and judges have tried to come up with a qualitative definition as to why using newer and potentially invasive technology in place of what could have been accomplished by older gear is problematic. In other words, if society accepts that in most circumstances, the police can follow a suspect on foot or in a car, then why is it problematic for the police to use a GPS, an infrared scanner, or a drone? The answer may lie in how far beyond the human capacity for observation a particular technology can go. GPS, after all, can retain indefinite volumes of information in ways that a fully mobilized police department cannot.

Amongst Fourth Amendment scholars, there's something of a split as to whether the Supreme Court's reliance on the mosaic theory even makes practical sense.

Orin Kerr, for example, a noted law professor at the University of Southern California, argued in a paper published just weeks after the *Jones* decision that adopting the mosaic theory "implicates fundamental questions" about the Fourth Amendment. Notably, he argued, the Supreme Court casts aside the traditional sequential analysis as to whether particular actions constitute a search. Traditionally, a search has occurred when law enforcement is able to take something that was hidden and make it visible—whether that object or information is contained within a home, a bag, a car, or a computer.

By contrast, the mosaic theory is predicated on the notion that a series of discrete "non-searches" (observing Jones' location in public, for example), over a great enough (and unspecified) period of time, becomes a Fourth Amendment search.

"In the past, however, this was considered good police work rather than cause for alarm," he wrote. "The repeated use of nonsearch techniques has been considered an essential way to create probable cause that justifies searches rather than an unlawful search itself."

Worse still, Kerr concluded, it's impossible for law enforcement, legislators, and judges alike to know precisely where the mosaic line has been crossed. What marks the magical moment when a Fourth Amendment search is triggered? Does it apply equally to all technologies?

Kerr also explained how under the sequential approach courts typically have two options when it comes to adjudicating police practice. Judges can say that a particular conduct is never a Fourth Amendment search but that legislative bodies can erect new laws regulating the state's behavior. The California Electronic Communication Privacy Act, the California state law that generally requires the use of a warrant to obtain various types of electronic information, is one example of this. It sets a higher bar over the existing federal law, which doesn't consider the acquisition of certain types of non-content data to be a search.

Alternatively, they can say that some conduct is always a Fourth Amendment search (for example, using an infrared imaging device without a warrant, like in *Kyllo*).

"The mosaic theory offers a vague middle ground as a third option," Kerr concluded. "The theory allows courts to say that techniques are sometimes a search. They are not searches when grouped in some ways (when no mosaic exists) but become searches when grouped in other ways (when the mosaic line is crossed)."

In fact, in the wake of the *Jones* ruling, hundreds of law professors and legal experts who convene annually at the Privacy Law Scholars Conference (held every June) invited attendees to a casual competition to see who could come up with a brief (under 1,000 words) workable rule under *Jones*.

One law professor, Christopher Slobogin, of Vanderbilt University, in response to Kerr, did so decisively. His proposal was eventually enhanced and turned into yet another legal journal article, where he attempted to actually codify what a mosaic theory–based statute might look like. In essence, it prescribes firm time limits as to what kind of data can be collected, for how long, and what legal authority is required. It also, unusually, upends the legalistic definition of a search, and attempts to put it in closer alignment with what most non-lawyer laypersons might understand.

Slobogin presents clear and easy-to-understand rules like this:

> *(a) A targeted public search that lasts longer than 48 hours in aggregate requires probable cause, and a warrant unless exigent circumstances exist.*
> *(b) A targeted public search that lasts longer than 20 minutes in aggregate but no longer than 48 hours in aggregate requires reasonable suspicion, and a court order unless exigent circumstances exist.*
> *(c) A targeted public search that does not last longer than 20 minutes in aggregate may occur at a law enforcement officer's discretion whenever the officer believes in good faith that the search can accomplish a legitimate law enforcement objective.*

◁▷

While Kerr argued that the validation of the mosaic theory in light of *Jones* is unworkable, and Slobogin (among other law professors) have attempted to articulate a clear set of laws that might address a post-*Jones* landscape, one of the most creative and persuasive ways to understand surveillance is in economic terms. In either case, for now this debate remains largely academic as neither Congress nor the Supreme Court seem interested in providing a clear answer.

In another 2016 legal academic paper by Kevin Bankston (a former ACLU lawyer now with the New America Foundation) and Ashkan Soltani (not a lawyer, but a prominent independent technologist and privacy researcher), yet another way to understand what kinds of newer surveillance tools should be questioned relative to older ones was proposed. They put forth a simple rule: "If the new tracking technique is an order of magnitude less expensive than the previous technique, the technique violates expectations of privacy and runs afoul of the Fourth Amendment."

Using essentially back-of-the-envelope calculations, Bankston and Soltani conclude that a five-person FBI team conducting in-person surveillance of a target on foot costs roughly $250 per hour. When a single agent moves her surveillance to a car, that cost drops to about $105 per hour. A squad of five cars goes up to $275 per hour, while putting in a short-range *Knotts*-style beeper costs just over $100 per hour. The modern equivalent, the cell-site simulator, costs roughly the same.

However, when it comes to GPS tracking, a single-day use costs about $10 per hour, but when spread out over 28 days, the cost plummets further, to about $0.36 per hour. Using a d-order and getting cell-site location information—the very data at issue in *Carpenter v. United States*—not quite as precise as GPS, but still very usable, the cost for 30 days of surveillance crashes even further, from $4 to as low as $0.04 per hour, depending on what the carrier charges.

Bankston and Soltani concluded by noting the fact that in his law school talk, the FBI's Weissmann said that the agency had to shut off 3,000 GPS trackers in the wake of the *Jones* decision. This suggests that as of 2012, the FBI had the capacity to track at least 3,000 people simultaneously.

"Without that technology, it would require 15,000 agents to covertly follow the same number of targets (assuming five agents for each target)," they wrote.

> *Therefore, even if the FBI were to instruct all of its 13,785 special agents to ignore all other duties and remain active for every hour of every day (an assignment that is humanly impossible), it would still be 1,215 agents short of being able to follow that many suspects. These figures dramatically illustrate how mass surveillance that was impossible prior to the introduction of new technologies like GPS is now firmly within the government's grasp. When such surveillance would have required ludicrous expenditures of time and treasure, there was no need for the Fourth Amendment to protect against it. However, now that the structural constraints against that surveillance have disappeared and the absolutely impossible has become easily possible, Fourth Amendment protection is desperately necessary.*

◯

In the *Jones* decision, Justice Scalia cited a 1986 Supreme Court case known as *California v. Ciraolo*, as one of the cases that affirmed the "reasonable expectation of privacy." *Ciraolo* asked the question as to whether a naked-eye observation of backyard marijuana plants constituted an unconstitutional search. In a 5–4 decision, the court ruled that it did not. In 1989, in a similar case, *Florida v. Riley*, that limit was lowered further to naked-eye observations at 400 feet in yet another 5–4 decision.

In that case, Justice Sandra Day O'Connor described in a dissenting opinion what she foresaw coming soon: "a helicopter capable of hovering just above an enclosed courtyard or patio without generating any noise, wind, or dust at all." That "miraculous tool" now exists. We call it a drone. Indeed, the low cost of government surveillance tools is the driving factor of local law enforcement's recent expansion of drones.

As of April 2017, at least 347 local law enforcement, fire, and first-responder agencies have acquired drones. By comparison, as of July 2009, only roughly one in five large law enforcement entities (defined as having 100 or more sworn officers) had conventional aircraft, or 201 air units. A September 2016 study from the National Institutes of Justice (a division of the DOJ) noted that helicopters typically cost around $250 per hour to operate, and found that cost was the largest factor as to why more police departments don't have air units.

Case in point: in August 2017, Spring Hill, Tennessee, a town with under 35,000 people, acquired a drone when a helicopter would have been otherwise prohibitively expensive. As of 2017, a fully equipped police drone costs just several thousand dollars each to acquire, and has a pretty low operational cost of around $28 per hour (the median police officer's wage), making it proximate to the Bankston and Soltani order of magnitude rule.

The Scalia wing of the 2012 *Jones* court predicated their analysis on what's known as a property-based analysis. For them, the case was really about the specific fact that the GPS tracker was placed on Jones' Jeep Grand Cherokee. For those justices, had the police used a different means to record his detailed movements that didn't involve touching his car at all, it would be a different case.

(This is one of the Alito wing's criticisms: "The Court's reliance on the law of trespass will present particularly vexing problems in cases involving surveillance that is carried out by making electronic, as opposed to physical, contact with the item to be tracked.")

There are other ways to conceptualize what the Fourth Amendment protects against, and when something is considered to be a search. There's the "reasonable expectation of privacy" standard, which flows from *Katz*. (But for Scalia and other similarly minded conservatives, this test makes no sense either: How can justices or society fully understand what, in fact, is or should be considered reasonable? In his view, the reasonable expectation proxy was too "circular.")

Within the scholarly legal landscape, there's also another notion that privacy is increasingly becoming unmoored in the twenty-first century. Modern technology makes many aspects of privacy—at least, as it would have been understood in the eighteenth or nineteenth centuries—nearly obsolete. After all, nearly all of us routinely share information about ourselves with each other online, ranging from the mundane (Instagram photos of yesterday's sushi lunch) to the life-altering (baby pictures for days). The fact that the unsolicited publication of someone's private documents and information online (doxing) has become a twenty-first-century weapon is also illustrative of this fact.

Given new communications technologies, perhaps it's better to understand the Fourth Amendment in terms of power, and more specifically, limiting what the government is able to do. After all, it is the government, and not Google, that has the monopoly on violence and incarceration.

Read as a whole, the Bill of Rights clearly articulates limits on the government's own power. The First Amendment's first five words are "Congress shall make no law." The final words of the Second Amendment are "shall not be infringed." The Third Amendment: "No soldier shall, in time of peace." And the Fourth Amendment describes limits to how "searches and seizures" should be performed: "but upon probable cause, supported by oath or affirmation." In other words, the law is meant to check the power of the state.

In short, this analysis argues, each amendment should be read in the context of limiting the government's power against the individual. One of the most prominent proponents of this theory is Paul Ohm, an affable forty-five-year-old tech-minded laid-back California-born lawyer, who is now a law professor at Georgetown University. He's a rare legal mind that knows how to write perl and python code, and continues to do so regularly.

Ohm came to legal scholarship in something of a roundabout way. He did his undergraduate work at Yale University, earning dual degrees in computer science and electrical engineering, before going on to be a programmer and network administrator at the RAND Corporation for several years. Then, he decided to go to law school, and was accepted at nearby UCLA.

Upon graduating from law school in 1999, Ohm had two clerkships with two different federal judges in California, and finally, by 2001, he served as a DOJ trial attorney, specializing in computer crime and intellectual property. He then became a professor at the University of Colorado for nearly a decade before being hired at Georgetown in 2015.

"What the Framers wanted was distance between you and your government," he said in a May 2017 interview in his office, replete with law books and computer books alike. "They didn't want general warrants and writs of assistance."

Or, put another way, he argued that for centuries, "it was a quirk of physics that this lined up with privacy pretty well."

In the eighteenth century, trespass, privacy, and imposing restraints on the government's power were more or less coterminous. To execute a search upon someone's home required physical force, trespassing into someone's home, and projecting the government's ability to manifest its will upon a citizen. Even by the mid-nineteenth century and well into the twentieth century, obtaining vast amounts of information about someone required extensive, long-term investigation. However, as technology improves, invasive power can be projected from ever-increasing distances, ranging from a Prohibition-era wiretap, to a *Kyllo*-era thermal scan, to a forthcoming pervasive drone.

Unless one wishes to be a total hermit, it's almost impossible to lead a fully private life in the twenty-first century. Since just after the *Jones* decision, Ohm has written in both academic and popular forums that in recent decades, privacy has often been lost as part of the transactional cost of doing business. If I want to use a cell phone, for instance, I have to give up my location information at all times. If I want to use a service like Uber or Lyft, I have to tell them where I want to go at specific times, and they are effectively allowed to retain that information forever. Under the third-party doctrine, that data can be accessed by the government relatively easily.

But the Fourth Amendment does not regulate the power of private companies, it regulates government. In America, we have a tradition, going all the way back to the Constitution, of a general skepticism of government's power, and more of a broad willingness to allow corporate power. Partially, this may be because there are often corporate alternatives. If you don't like Google, there are other search engines to use. But, there is only one entity that can legally take away your liberty: the state.

If we assume that the Fourth Amendment is really about power, and not about privacy, what is the proper remedy? For Raymond Shih Ray Ku, a law professor at Case Western Reserve University, the answer is fairly straightforward: let them be regulated by the legislative process.

"Requiring the use of surveillance technologies to be authorized by statute recognizes that the people should determine just how much power government should wield," he wrote in a 2002 paper.

> *Popular control over government's power to search was the driving force behind the adoption of the Fourth Amendment. Moreover, requiring statutory authorization for law enforcement's power to search—even if it is not used to determine reasonableness—would bring search and seizure law in line with the doctrine of separation of powers governing executive power in general. Outside the Fourth Amendment, the Supreme Court is highly skeptical of the executive branch defining its own powers.*

Just as Moore's law has described the phenomenon of computing power doubling every 18 months, so too is there an analogous effect in the government's ability to track location data through physical GPS trackers. However, in some sense, the technology described in *Jones* is already obsolete, less than a decade after the Supreme Court ruled on it. After all, we all already carry tracking devices with us, constantly: they're called smartphones.

CHAPTER EIGHT

How Your Phone Can Lead the Authorities Right to Your Door

We determine that cell phone users have an objectively reasonable expectation that their cell phones will not be used as real-time tracking devices through the direct and active interference of law enforcement.

—State of Maryland v. Andrews
Court of Special Appeals of Maryland opinion (2016)

August 3, 2008
Santa Clara, California

On a warm summer's day, police spotted a man walking outside his apartment in Santa Clara, California, one of the many bedroom communities spread across Silicon Valley.

Law enforcement—undercover FBI officers—saw him outside the building and began following him on foot, radioing to their colleagues nearby. The man saw the agents, and so he began to walk quickly. They followed suit.

After months of tracking him via sting bank accounts and confidential informants, the officers had their man. They didn't even know his name: after watching his activities at a distance, they called him simply the "Hacker." Between 2005 and 2008, federal investigators believed that the Hacker and two other men filed over 1,900 fake tax returns online, yielding $4 million sent to over 170 bank accounts.

The Hacker was found out through the warrantless use of a secretive surveillance technology known as a stingray, which snoops on cell phones. Stingrays, or cell-site simulators, act as false cell phone towers that trick phones into giving up their location. They have become yet another tool in many agencies' toolbox, and their use has expanded with little oversight. While they are used in felony and fugitive investigations, stingrays have also been used to go after 911 hang-ups and other low-level offenses. In 2016, a Capital News Service report described one occasion when the Annapolis (Maryland) Police Department used its stingray to go after someone accused of stealing $56 worth of chicken wings. In short, a tool originally developed for military use overseas was now being used to go after petty takeout thieves.

◎

The Domicilio apartment complex, a set of six-story high-rise buildings surrounding an internal courtyard with a swimming pool, sits adjacent to a local baseball field and soccer pitch. The Santa Clara Caltrain station—where thousands of local commuters board trains daily northbound for Palo Alto, San Mateo, and San Francisco—is just a few blocks away. The Hacker had told the apartment complex's manager that he was Steven Travis Brawner, software engineer: a profile that fit right in with many other tenants in the area.

The Hacker began breathing more heavily. He may have thought about heading towards the train station, which would take him out of town, or perhaps towards the San Jose International Airport, just three miles away. The Hacker couldn't be sure if there were cops following him, or if he was just being paranoid. But as soon as he saw the marked Santa Clara Police Department cars, he knew the truth, and he started running.

But the Hacker didn't get far. He was quickly surrounded, arrested, and searched. The police found the key to the Hacker's apartment. Once they had a warrant to search his apartment, they began to tear it apart. Authorities found there a folding chair and a folding table that served as a desk. There was no other furniture—his bed was a cot. Law enforcement also found his Verizon Wireless mobile Internet AirCard, and false driver's licenses with the names "Steven Travis Brawner," "Patrick Stout," and more.

A 2010 FBI press release later stated that the agency also "seized a laptop and multiple hard drives, $116,340 in cash, over $208,000 in gold coins, approximately $10,000 in silver coins, false identification documents, false identification manufacturing equipment, and surveillance equipment."

Investigators identified the Hacker, via his fingerprints, as Daniel Rigmaiden, previously convicted of state-level misdemeanors.

According to an Internal Revenue Service (IRS) special agent's search warrant, Rigmaiden's computer also included "email regarding leaving the United States for the country of Dominica . . . [and] documents regarding obtaining citizenship in other countries; emails regarding paying off Dominican officials to get Dominican birth certificates and passports; and a Belize residency guide."

Rigmaiden's case dates back several years. In 2007 and early 2008, the IRS identified a bank account at Compass Bank in Phoenix that was receiving fraudulent tax refunds under the name Carter Tax & Accounting, LLC. Authorities identified Carter as being involved in the possible scheme. In early 2008, undercover operatives identified another man they dubbed the Hacker, as well as another as-yet-unnamed co-conspirator, who served higher up than Carter. Those law enforcement agents, with the assistance of a bank, then opened an account for the Hacker, who unknowingly deposited some fraudulently obtained tax refunds electronically into that account. That way, investigators could monitor his banking activities more easily.

In April 2008, the second co-conspirator was arrested in Utah, and that case remains under seal. This suspect and the Hacker were deemed to be above Carter in the tax-fraud ring. From April to August 2008, federal investigators tracked the Hacker via his Arizona bank account, and via packages sent to FedEx Kinko's locations across Northern California. Rigmaiden's indictment was initially sealed, pending cooperation with a federal investigation. But from the start, Rigmaiden declined to cooperate, and moved to represent himself (after firing three attorneys) and the case was subsequently unsealed.

"Representing myself was the only way I was able to force the case to proceed," Rigmaiden later recalled.

As the case moved through the legal system over the following years, it became increasingly clear as to how the FBI was able to locate Rigmaiden and pinpoint his exact physical location. In a February 2011 afternoon court hearing, during a back-and-forth between Rigmaiden and Frederick A. Battista, assistant US attorney, the suspect told the judge:

> One key point that Mr. Battista leaves out is that they've actually already identified what the device [to determine my location] is. Postal Inspector Wilson identified it as a StingRay and he indicated FBI used the device to locate the air card [the mobile Internet device], and I suspect those so-called generic terms he's talking about they redacted out of all these documents, I'm willing to bet that most of these terms actually read "StingRay."

> *And I know from research that has been done by the*
> *defense is [sic] that the StingRay's made by Harris Wireless*
> *Products Group and it's a trademark term. There's only one*
> *StingRay in existence, it's not generic, and that's the device.*
>   *So for them to sit there and say they didn't know that,*
> *that's hard to believe. And I don't think that it's really sen-*
> *sitive. Especially when I have pictures of a StingRay here,*
> *and other Harris products that they manufacture. There's a*
> *StingRay, StingRay 2, the KingFish and the AmberJack. And*
> *these are pretty much the devices the government uses—the*
> *FBI used—to locate cell phones.*

While StingRay is a trademark, as Rigmaiden told the judge, *stingray* has since become so ubiquitous in law enforcement and national security circles as to also often act as the catch-all generic term—like Kleenex or Xerox.

A stingray acts as a fake cell tower and forces cell phones and other mobile devices using a cell network (like Rigmaiden's AirCard, which provided his laptop with Internet access) to communicate with it rather than with a bona fide mobile network. Stingrays are big boxes—roughly the size of a laser printer—like something out of a 1950s-era switchboard, with all kinds of knobs and dials and readouts. Stingrays can easily be hidden inside a police surveillance van or another nearby location. But like everything else in the tech world, they're getting cheaper, smaller, and better all the time.

The Harris Corporation, a longstanding American military contractor, won't say exactly how its stingrays work, or exactly who it's selling to, but it's safe to say that it's selling to lots of federal agencies and, by extension, local law enforcement. A 2008 price list shows that its StingRays, KingFish, and related devices sell for tens to hundreds of thousands of dollars.

The company's 2017 annual financial report filed with the Securities and Exchange Commission shows that in recent years Harris has increased its sales of surveillance equipment and related tactical radio systems. It works with not only the US military and law enforcement, but also Canada, Australia, Poland, and Brazil, among other countries. The company has profited over $1.8 billion from fiscal year 2013 through 2017.

◎

All of our cell phones rely on a network of towers and antennas that relay our signal back to the network and then connect us to the person that we're communicating with. As we move across a city, mobile networks seamlessly hand off our call from one tower to the next, usually providing an uninterrupted call. But in order for the system to work, the mobile phone provider needs to know where the phone actually is so that it can direct a signal to it.

It does so by sending a short message to the phone nearly constantly—in industry terminology this is known as a ping. The message basically is asking the phone: "Are you there?" And your phone responds: "Yes, I'm here." (Think of it as roughly the mobile phone version of the children's swimming pool game Marco Polo.) If your phone cannot receive a ping, it cannot receive service. The bottom line is, if your phone can receive service, then the mobile provider (and possibly the cops, too) know where you are.

In short, our mobile phones can really easily be turned into tracking devices. Today, stingrays cost thousands of dollars, and aren't typically deployed everywhere as a matter of course. But it wouldn't be hard to do so, particularly as the technology gets more efficient.

This tracking technology is even more invasive than law enforcement presenting a d-order to a mobile phone provider. Rather than have the government provide a court order for a company to hand over data, the stingray simply eliminates the middleman. The government, armed with its own stingray, can simply pluck the phone's location (and possibly the contents of calls, text messages, or any other unencrypted data being transmitted at the time, depending on the configuration) directly out of the air.

Stingrays come in two basic types: passive and active. Passive stingrays fool all phones in a certain area into thinking they're the nearest or strongest cell tower. A passive stingray simply waits for a phone to connect, at which point the phone will automatically transmit its unique International Mobile Subscriber Identity (IMSI) number. For this reason, stingrays are often also called IMSI catchers. The IMSI number is tied to a service account, and can be a strong identifier for a person. (Another number, known as the International Mobile Equipment Identity [IMEI] number, analogous to a unique serial number, identifies the particular mobile phone that a person is using, irrespective of the carrier or customer.) Once the IMSI has been collected, the stingray tells the phone to disconnect and use another tower. This entire process takes mere moments to occur and nearly always happens without the phone's owner realizing it.

The technique that most stingrays use was first patented back in 1993.

IMSIs reside directly on a phone's SIM card, the small digital chip found in GSM phones around the world. (In the United States, that's all AT&T or T-Mobile users. Sprint or Verizon users also have IMSI numbers, but they work slightly differently.)

In normal use, when a mobile phone is turned on, the phone broadcasts its IMSI to the closest cell phone tower. Every phone will always default to the strongest (usually nearest) mobile phone tower—and stingrays take advantage of an inherent quality that exists even in bona fide cell towers: phones are designed to accept all commands issued from them. That also means that a stingray can tell the phone to not communicate in an encrypted manner—it doesn't require any advanced software or hardware. Spoofing the tower means that the tower can simply tell the phone to transmit unencrypted data, and that phone will do so with no problem, and without alerting the user in any way. In fact, it's extremely difficult to know if a stingray is being used. (In 2011, German mobile security researcher Karsten Nohl released Catcher Catcher, a piece of software that analyzes network traffic to determine if a stingray is in use.)

With a basic passive stingray, law enforcement doesn't know that a given IMSI number is linked with a particular person. That link can be positively identified later by compelling the mobile provider with a subpoena or other legal procedure to connect a given IMSI number with a subscriber.

But it's a useful tool for establishing which IMSI numbers were at a particular location at a specific moment in time. Those IMSI numbers could then also be kept and scanned for again at a later date. For example, does this IMSI number show up at a train station, airport, international border, or another location where a positive identification document has to be presented with a physical person? In other words, can a given IMSI number be positively linked with a particular person, even without contacting the mobile carrier? Stingrays could easily filter out any non-target IMSI numbers—and only alert the stingray operator if a certain IMSI number is observed.

While it does take time for a stingray to force a particular mobile phone to switch off of a real network and onto the fake network, there are many other methods that can be used to speed up this process. That includes frequently rotating the Location Area Code (LAC) that the stingray transmits. Ordinary towers broadcast an LAC, letting other towers know where they are. When a phone detects new LACs, it begins the process of handing off a call without interruption. In this case, that means that the target phone has more traps to fall into. Another technique commonly used since 2008 to speed up this process is to block all 3G (third-generation) signals—which are much better encrypted than an earlier protocol, 2G—by using radio frequency noise. (3G is designed to drop down to 2G when a 3G signal isn't available. While that may be a good feature to increase the reliability of mobile phone service, it's also highly insecure.) This forces the target phone to employ 2G, making it much easier to track.

According to testimony in the Rigmaiden case by Assistant US Attorney Battista, authorities were able to locate their suspect through the Internet Protocol (IP) address that he was using to file the fraudulent tax returns. IP addresses are unique strings of numbers that identify any device on the Internet at any given moment—but they can be obscured. Under normal use, it can be fairly easy, in collaboration with the Internet service provider (ISP), to connect a given IP address to a user account. The FBI was able to determine that the IP address their suspect was using was connected to a Verizon Wireless account.

"They had identified one of the IP addresses I was using, or a couple I had been assigned by Verizon over a short period of time," Rigmaiden said later.

"I was always using proxies, but at some point one of the proxies forwarded my real IP address, or my proxy software otherwise failed and my computer connected directly to the e-file website. I'm not really sure what happened. I was using thousands of proxies in an automated fashion over many months. But it wasn't as simple as, 'oh, let's just look up his IP we have logged.' Law enforcement sent out hundreds of subpoenas to ISPs for physical addresses tied to IP addresses I was using. The Verizon account was just one out of many they had identified. It took months for them to do more cross-referencing before making an educated guess that the Verizon account was tied to my actual IP address."

When the FBI contacted Verizon, the company provided records (likely including the IMSI number connected to the historical IP addresses) showing that the suspect's AirCard was transmitting through certain cell towers in a certain part of Santa Clara, California. Likely by using a stingray, the FBI was then able to determine that a device matching that IMSI number was transmitting "from an area the size of approximately three to four apartment units within an apartment complex," according to Battista's testimony from February 2011. (However, according to Rigmaiden, "this claim was debunked and the judge agreed with me. The government was forced to concede, but never factually admit, that the StingRay identified my exact apartment. With this concession, they also had to concede that the Stingray device had conducted a Fourth Amendment search and seizure.") In essence, like in *Kyllo*, the stingray penetrated the four walls of his apartment and determined Rigmaiden's precise location.

Battista continued:

> So in a sense, what had happened was by using the false identity to obtain the apartment, in a sense unknowingly Mr. Rigmaiden, we believe, in a sense painted a bull's eye on the door to that particular unit. Because we were looking for a person—the air card had been obtained using a false identity. The apartment had been obtained using a false identity. So it was—we were able then to, using these different classic investigative techniques, zero in on this one particular apartment.

But part of the problem is that stingrays aren't targeted devices—they don't just go after one device at a time. In the Rigmaiden case, while the FBI probably knew which IMSI number they were interested in, they were also capturing data (other IMSI numbers) from any other mobile device that happened to be in the area at the time. And that's one of the biggest problems: like many other dragnet data-collection programs, there is a lot of incidental data collection of a huge number of people just to go after one or a few targeted suspects.

While passive stingrays can simply track and log IMSI numbers, active stingrays are far more sophisticated.

"Some make requests to phones, route traffic through the device, break the [encrypted] A5/1 cipher stream, and can listen to the calls, and ones with text message [capabilities], there are ones that swap words out for messages being sent," Eric King, then of Privacy International, an advocacy group based in London, told me in a 2015 interview.

King has been at the forefront of trying to understand where, when, and how stingrays are being used. He's repeatedly gone to law enforcement and military technology industry conventions around the world (which are normally closed to outsiders), and has come away with documents showing the rapid and unchecked growth of these types of technologies. In December 2011, Privacy International, WikiLeaks, and several media organizations worldwide partnered to publish *The Spy Files*.

King added that he's taken photographs of stingrays "that are not much bigger than a BlackBerry." In 2013, Ars Technica reported on possible stingrays being deployed in the Moscow Metro system, and worse still, a body-worn stingray vest.

"The unit is optimized for short-range covert operation, designed to allow users to get close to Target(s) to maximize the chances of only catching the Target(s') identities and minimal unwanted collateral," boasts one of the marketing pamphlets from a company called Cobham. "The solution can be used as a standalone device or integrated into wider data-gathering and geo-tracking systems."

In a dense urban area, stingrays are sometimes only effective within a radius of about 50 meters, whereas in a rural area they can be effective up to five kilometers, given that there is less physical interference due to the lack of buildings and other structures. Stingrays can also be reprogrammed to work for nearly any carrier in nearly any country.

As stingrays become cheaper and smaller, they will undoubtedly be used not just by large organizations like the FBI, but also by small-town police forces, or worse, organized crime. In 2010, Kristin Paget (then known as Chris Paget) demonstrated to an audience at the hacker conference DEF CON how he built a rudimentary, but functional, stingray for about $1,500 in parts. In that talk, he controlled ("pwned") around 30 audience members' phones with his homebrew device.

Like many other enforcement tools, the federal government has used grants to encourage local law enforcement to acquire this hardware in the name of fighting terrorism. But, as the Rigmaiden case shows, over time, particularly as these tools become cheaper and more commonplace—they're used to bust criminal suspects like him.

The Los Angeles Police Department (LAPD), for example, first purchased stingrays back in 2006 with a grant from the Department of Homeland Security for the purpose of "regional terrorism investigations." However, they're also being used for burglary, drug, and murder cases, too.

Already, national security and federal law enforcement agencies are putting stingrays on drones, and are likely flying them over locations (like political protests) to ascertain who is present. What happens when a stingray is small enough to be innocuously worn on an article of clothing, or hidden in someone's eyeglasses? What happens when a local police force has the capability to locate and capture voice traffic at any time, essentially for any reason? What happens when a criminal group captures data on men's phones and uses it to extort money from those men cheating on their wives?

The Czech police are already concerned that stingrays have fallen into the hands of local criminals. "It's been a known fact for a few years now that some companies do sell these devices," Andor Šándor, the former head of the Czech Military Intelligence Agency, told Radio Prague in 2012. "But if their use will not be in any way regulated, and access to these devices will not be in any way controlled, then a regular citizen can do absolutely nothing. The only way people can safeguard themselves is if they reveal only the necessary information during their mobile communication. But, obviously that goes against normal behavior of free persons."

And this is one of the biggest problems: purchase and use of such devices is unregulated. Law enforcement agencies worldwide claim the right to use them, but such evidence has rarely been challenged in court by either a criminal suspect or by unwitting bystanders, whose data has been captured (and likely kept) by the cops.

"The question is what's the law that governs its use?" King said, who was trained as a law student in the United Kingdom. "The use of IMSI catchers is completely unclear. We know that the police have them and we know that the police use them, not that they've ever admitted it, and have done so for 10 years. They refuse to engage, they refuse to say that they bought them. We need a public debate around this sort of stuff."

That debate is very slowly starting to happen. And that is due, in large part, to Rigmaiden's unlikely exposure of the stingray.

Rigmaiden grew up in Seaside, California, a small, working-class town about 70 miles south of San Jose. His father was (and remains) a civilian employee for the Navy, working primarily on space systems at the Naval Postgraduate School in nearby Monterey. In his off hours, the elder Rigmaiden serves as a local Boy Scout leader. Today, Daniel's brother co-owns a local bicycle shop in Monterey.

Growing up, Rigmaiden had a Commodore 64, a popular mid-1980s computer. His parents more or less left him alone as he explored the machine.

"I had the Commodore 64 from age five to about age nine," Rigmaiden told me. "I used to program on it starting at age five, but became discouraged and gave up because it had no floppy disk drive to save my work. Imagine if it had a disk drive? I'd probably be a lot more skilled at computers and technology than I am currently."

In elementary school and moving into middle school, Rigmaiden considered himself something of a rebel. He didn't feel like he fit in with society "as the adults were currently running it." This point was driven home when he was 12, and participated at school in a mock 1992 presidential election, between Bill Clinton, George H. W. Bush, and Ross Perot.

"I remember thinking that it wasn't fair—how I didn't get the whole two-party system," he said.

> They were attacking Perot a lot and weren't giving him a fair
> shot. I felt like there was some problem there. I was confused
> as to why anyone couldn't just be president. They always tell
> you that, but it doesn't pan out that way. That's when I real-
> ized there were problems with the political system. I guess I
> have to choose between the Republicans and the Democrats,
> and I don't really fit in with either of these.

The nascent World Wide Web arrived at the Rigmaiden household in 1996, when Daniel was 16. Mostly, his parents left him to his own devices, and allowed him to explore online as he saw fit.

"They understood what I could get into, but they didn't think I would get into anything," he said.

Still not feeling like he fit in anywhere politically or socially, Rigmaiden decided he wasn't going to lead a conventional life. He was going to try to "beat the system in some way that involves breaking all the rules that I didn't agree with."

In the mid and late 1990s, Rigmaiden spent some time on various Internet Relay Chat (IRC) rooms—a now-waning form of text-based chat.

"I think I was first in IRC chat rooms and there was some fake ID chat rooms," he said. "I started making IDs in high school, they were crappy but they seemed to work at certain liquor stores. I had a laminator from Staples—I didn't even have a color printer."

His parents never caught wind of his activities, but they knew that he didn't seem to be on a predictable path towards university or an obvious job. Rigmaiden's father told him that he had to leave the house when he turned 18, and so he did. With no other source of income in the late 1990s, Rigmaiden hit the road as a semi-nomadic salesman, plying the one trade that he knew: making and selling fake IDs.

His website was called FakeID.tv, and at least as of 2003, it purported to sell "replica driver license identification cards available for movie productions only." Rigmaiden initially charged $150, which was eventually upped to $250 and $500 for rush jobs.

"I did it based on supply and demand," he said. "They would take a long time to make."

Rigmaiden was precise and methodical. Unlike his competition at the time, he said, his fakes were the correct thickness and weight—30 millimeters thick and 3.4 grams. He advertised on ShadowCrew, a notorious online criminal message board that operated from 2002 until 2004, and also on Counterfeit Library, a British-hosted website. He's pretty sure that Max Vision (aka Max Butler, aka Iceman), a convicted hacker scheduled for release from federal prison in 2019, bought one. Rigmaiden specialized in California driver's licenses and made nothing else.

"I think I had the best quality," he said. "I wasn't the most 'out there,' I think there were other people and they would say I was a scammer."

Here's how his operations would work: Rigmaiden would first set up shop in a city, oftentimes using college towns as a plausible cover where he could easily pass as a local student, and tell people that he was a programmer. This took him as far north as Humboldt County and as far south as Santa Barbara County. He'd stay in each place for a few months, or maybe a year at the most, often in small motels, sometimes a single room occupancy (SRO) hotel.

Moving from place to place required transporting a pair of bulky 25-gallon containers—with snap-on tops—that contained all of his equipment, including a die cutter, an inkjet printer, a hologram printer, a laminator, and more.

Rigmaiden was detail oriented and he worked hard to make sure that his own physical and digital protocols were followed to a t. (In military parlance, this is what's known as good OPSEC, or operational security.) By keeping his operation small, nimble, and constantly moving, it was easy for him to stay ahead of local authorities. He only accepted payment in e-gold, an early electronic payment system that was not particularly scrupulous as to who could open accounts. Money orders and Western Union would have been too risky. He required that all customer interactions occur over encrypted e-mail, and provided customers with a computer program that guided them through the process. For shipping, he would buy prepaid priority mail envelopes, and was careful to not do more than one order at a time. He only shipped out from public mailboxes, never from post offices.

"I was definitely overly paranoid," he told me. "I never got caught for the IDs, I got caught for the tax stuff."

This assertion is not entirely accurate: In 1999, Rigmaiden was sentenced to probation and 180 days in Monterey County jail for four counts of "acquisition of access card information." He failed to appear at a probation hearing, and a warrant remained outstanding for his arrest until 2014. (The warrant issue was partly why he never left California.)

In the mid-2000s, Rigmaiden decided to move on to something bigger. His fake ID business, while stable, wasn't making tons of money. Mostly he was just breaking even (thanks to constantly moving around), and paying in cash for nearly everything was becoming exhausting.

"I wanted to make a bunch of money so I wouldn't have to worry about money," he said. "I didn't want to make fake IDs forever."

But while he sought profit, there were limits. He wasn't going to use violence, or expose himself. Mostly, he didn't want to get caught.

Rigmaiden eventually found out about fraudulent tax return schemes. He quickly figured out that tax returns are largely voluntary. The IRS simply doesn't have enough agents and auditors to do a thorough check of everyone. Most IRS personnel do the best they can, but a few slip through the cracks. This meant that Rigmaiden could file a fake tax return for someone who had died, and pocket the refund. He would file dozens at a time, sometimes more, before one would come back with money. His first successful one netted $9,000.

"I was going to make a million and then I was going to stop," he said. (He told WNYC's *Note to Self* in 2015 that he was planning on leaving the country altogether.)

Rigmaiden spent weeks at a time camping in the Los Padres National Forest, a large swath of land that stretches from near his childhood home in Monterey, down the coast hundreds of miles to Ventura, California, one county north of Los Angeles. He'd only pop back up in cities when he needed to use the Internet or withdraw cash.

In late 2007, Rigmaiden moved to Santa Clara. The city, then as now, is home to students and lots of tech workers. He had a comfortable life in an urban area, and lived near a train station and airport should he need to make a quick getaway.

"I didn't want to go through the stress of moving again," he thought to himself, as he considered perhaps staying there long term. But he knew that the longer he stayed in one place, the more exposed to law enforcement he would be.

Unbeknownst to the fraudster, federal prosecutors in Arizona—one of the places where he had stashed his money—filed a sealed indictment against Rigmaiden on July 23, 2008.

By August 2008, his lease was nearly ending, and so he packed up all of his things into the blue plastic bins. Doing tax fraud entirely electronically, after all, didn't require nearly as much equipment. But he hadn't actually moved yet.

By the time he was arrested, Rigmaiden had made about $500,000.

After Rigmaiden was arrested in California, he was quickly transported to the Florence Correctional Center, about 65 miles southeast of Phoenix. Despite being incarcerated, Rigmaiden could not sit still. He knew that he had been careful. He had used multiple fake identities, with fake documents, and paid in cash. How could law enforcement have not only found him out, but found him in his own apartment, where hardly anyone knew he lived?

Rigmaiden thought there might be something that the government wasn't telling him—there might be some secret surveillance tool afoot. He tried pressing his federal public defenders to listen, but they wouldn't. Within two months, he'd fired one of his lawyers, and then another. In essence, he didn't feel that they were technically sophisticated enough to be able to help him get the answers he needed. Eventually, the accused fraudster got permission to represent himself (*pro se*), a legally risky move.

Once he was representing himself, he was allowed to use the law library for five hours a day (up from the usual three hours a week). It became a full-time job, immersing himself in legal procedures—but it was likely the most productive way to spend his time behind bars. Fortunately, at the beginning, a fellow inmate and disbarred attorney helped him out with some of the basics, including general court procedure, how to draft a motion, and correct legal citation. By October 2009, Rigmaiden had received boxes and boxes (over 14,000 pages in total) of criminal discovery that would help him understand how the government planned to prosecute its case. In the penultimate box, he saw the word "stingray" in a set of notes.

As a prisoner, he wasn't allowed Internet access, but sometimes a "case manager," a sort of guidance counselor, could be convinced to run online searches for inmates who were pursuing legal research. Though this process, Rigmaiden located a Harris Corporation brochure with the StingRay name. Bingo. The device advertised various types of cellular interception. Soon enough, he found evidence that this same device was being acquired by law enforcement nationwide, including in Maricopa County, just one county over from where he was being held in Pinal County. Eventually, he was able to get patent filings and other records to better understand what, exactly, the StingRay was, how it worked, and who had them.

Although Rigmaiden was *pro se*, he had a shadow counsel, or a lawyer who was ready to step in if the *pro se* defendant wished to take on formal counsel. That lawyer had a paralegal, a man named Dan Colmerauer. Rigmaiden could call Colmerauer from a jailhouse pay phone and ask him to run Google searches for him, and tell him the results by phone. Then Colmerauer would print those Web pages, and put them in the mail to Rigmaiden, who in turn would have to make handwritten notes about which links to follow and mail that back to Colmerauer.

As 2010 rolled around, Rigmaiden decided that he needed allies. He began sending his case details and research file out to various privacy and civil liberties organizations, including the American Civil Liberties Union (ACLU) and the Electronic Frontier Foundation (EFF). There were likely two major red flags that led to him being ignored—he was representing himself without the benefit of counsel, and believed that the government had used some secret surveillance tool against him. They likely thought he was totally nuts—despite the fact that there was already some evidence that the police were using phones as tracking devices. None of the organizations ever responded.

One of the people Rigmaiden sent his file to was Christopher Soghoian, a bearded and ambitious privacy researcher. At the time, Soghoian was a computer science doctoral student always looking for another way to push the envelope, as well as discover how surveillance was actually being conducted in the real world.

Years earlier, as a first-year doctoral student at the University of Indiana, Soghoian figured out by futzing around with Facebook which of his classmates likely moonlighted at local strip clubs. The next month, October

2006, however, he caused something of a stir when he created a website titled "The Northwest Airlines Boarding Pass Generator. Or the TSA Emperor Has No Clothes." The website allowed anyone to create a boarding pass, with the click of a button, that would let them through an airport TSA checkpoint. The net result was that Soghoian was subject to an FBI raid, and a sitting congressman called for his arrest.

In 2009 and 2010, Soghoian worked at the Federal Trade Commission (FTC), and at one point used his government ID to get into a security industry trade show and made a surreptitious recording of Sprint executives bragging about how they'd handed over customers' GPS information to law enforcement eight million times in a single year. In short, Soghoian was the perfect match for Rigmaiden.

On Monday April 11, 2011, while visiting the offices of the EFF in San Francisco, Soghoian received this unsolicited e-mail from Colmerauer.

From: Dan Colmerauer <screenwriter2@earthlink.net>

Date: Mon, Apr 11, 2011, at 7:28 PM
Subject: Cell Phone Tracking and Locating re: United States of America v. Daniel Rigmaiden
To: chris@soghoian.net
Dear Mr. Sohoian[sic],
Daniel Rigmaiden instructed me to e-mail you the attached Memorandum. This is in regard to cell phone tracking and locating. He thinks it may be of interest to you but you may have to read past the introduction before understanding why. If you want the exhibits please e-mail Dan Colmerauer at screenwriter2@earthlink.net and make said request.
Dictated but not read.
Daniel Rigmaiden

Soghoian tried to get other lawyers that he knew interested, but they saw the extensive *pro se* filings as a huge red flag. Lots of people think they're being surveilled by the government with secret technology, but hardly anyone can prove it. Soghoian didn't dismiss it out of hand.

"My reaction wasn't, 'what is this strange device,'" Soghoian told The Verge in 2016. "It was, 'oh I read about this in graduate school.' But I read about it as a thing that was possible, not a thing that the police . . . were using."

But the grad student was skeptical. Still, Soghoian asked Colmerauer to send what he had. What Soghoian received back was a 200-page "meticulously researched" document that had been originally handwritten in a jailhouse library.

Soghoian understood how to get lawmakers' attention—through the media and advocacy organizations. He eventually sent it on to a friendly reporter, Jennifer Valentino-DeVries, as she was boarding a plane bound for Las Vegas, where she was going to attend the 2011 DEF CON. (This was the same reporter who would later break the story about Mike Katz-Lacabe's experiences with license plate readers.)

On September 22, 2011, Valentino-DeVries' story hit the *Wall Street Journal*: "'Stingray' Phone Tracker Fuels Constitutional Clash." (It was her first front-page story for the *Journal*.)

This was also the first time that a major American media outlet had reported on the issue, and likely how many lawmakers first heard about the device that had already been in use for years. In the same article, Sherry Sabol, a veteran FBI attorney, sent the *Journal* a statement about stingrays, noting that the technology is "considered Law Enforcement Sensitive, since its public release could harm law enforcement efforts by compromising future use of the equipment."

In short, Rigmaiden unveiled a new chapter in the story of sophisticated surveillance to the public—citizens, journalists, lawyers, judges—that law enforcement had already known for years, mostly without telling anyone.

◌

After Rigmaiden and Soghoian began corresponding, the doctoral student was introduced to Stephanie Pell, a former veteran federal prosecutor, who was then serving as counsel to the House Judiciary Committee. Notably, Pell had been one of four Miami-based lead prosecutors on the José Padilla case, who was implicated in the so-called dirty bomb plot. That case dominated her professional life from 2002 until 2007—the case didn't end until 2014, when Padilla was sentenced to 21 years on appeal.

Starting with her work on Capitol Hill, Pell was tasked with working on the reauthorization of the PATRIOT Act, and then worked on Electronic Communications Privacy Act (ECPA) reform, which came before the House Judiciary Committee in the spring of 2011 (see Chapter 6). It was one of those strictly professional opposites attract moments: Soghoian was wary but intrigued by a former high-level prosecutor. Pell, for her part, wanted to know what this technologist hired by the FTC could teach her.

Months later, sitting on the steps of a frozen yogurt shop in Washington, DC's Dupont Circle neighborhood, Soghoian told Pell about what he had learned about stingrays from Rigmaiden. Even as someone who had served as an assistant US attorney in a prominent terrorism case, Pell was entirely unfamiliar with stingrays.

Stingrays aside, the two had a lot to talk about. They quickly put together a research paper ("Can You See Me Now? Toward Reasonable Standards for Law Enforcement Access to Location Data That Congress Could Enact") that they presented at the 2011 Privacy Law Scholars Conference, an annual three-day gathering of some of the world's top legal minds in privacy law.

As the two began collaborating and discussing their mutual interest in government power and surveillance, Pell began to understand that stingrays were an entirely new class of surveillance tools that few in government knew about. Over time, the two of them began to accept what Rigmaiden already knew: that a new class of technology was being used without a clear explanation to judges as to what was going on.

"If courts don't know what they are authorizing, then information doesn't flow through that channel and it puts a whole lot of unsupervised power in law enforcement's hands," Pell said.

By the end of 2011 and into early 2012, Soghoian began filing his own Freedom of Information Act (FOIA) requests to learn more about stingrays. (At one point, Harris Corporation, the makers of the StingRay, offered him a job!) Primarily, he wanted to know how they worked and who had them. Soon, a picture began to emerge. Immigration and Customs Enforcement (ICE) was buying them. Agencies all over the country, ranging from Houston, Texas, to Alexandria, Virginia, were using them. There was even something called an Airborne Kit, allowing stingrays to be mounted on aircraft.

The tenacious privacy researcher even teamed up with others (including Eric King) to try to submit an *amicus* brief detailing their research into stingrays and other new information about surveillance in technology in *United States v. Rigmaiden*—published in the December 2011 *Spy Files* on WikiLeaks—but the request was denied by the judge. (These friend of the court filings, written by outside parties, which can either be accepted or denied by the judge, are often meant to help provide more context in rapidly evolving areas of the law.)

As 2012 rolled in, Soghoian and Rigmaiden worked in parallel. Rigmaiden continued to be consumed by his own case and worked it as best as he could from prison, largely by himself. He became frustrated with the bureaucracy, and the slowness of the legal system. In May 2012, he handwrote a highly unorthodox filing: "MOTION Requesting Court to Order Defendant's Private Investigator to Do His Job or In the Alternative, MOTION to Dismiss the Case With Prejudice." (The filing didn't amount to much.)

In February, the Electronic Privacy Information Center (EPIC) filed an FOIA request, which resulted in a lawsuit. Its efforts definitively showed that government law enforcement agencies have not been completely upfront about using stingrays when they asked federal magistrate judges for permission to conduct electronic surveillance. In fact, search warrants have generally not been used at all.

In the summer of 2012, Soghoian arranged to provide a demonstration to a handful of congressional staffers of how easy it was to build and use a homebrew stingray. They gathered in a small room on Capitol Hill, handed out a few clean phones operating on a temporary cell network created by Kurtis Heimerl using OpenBTS software—the same software used by Paget at DEF CON back in 2010. After the staffers used the phones to make a few calls and send a few texts, Heimerl easily showed them that all of their calls and text messages were being intercepted—content and metadata alike. The goal was to clearly illustrate the power of stingrays and to goad Congress into doing something about it. But no meaningful legislation happened.

Soghoian, meanwhile, kept at it as his doctoral program wound down. His August 2012 dissertation, titled "The Spies We Trust: Third-Party Service Providers and Law Enforcement Surveillance," was published nearly four years to the day after Rigmaiden's arrest.

Other journalists began taking notice of the *Rigmaiden* case and asking whether their local law enforcement agencies were acquiring or using stingrays. In September 2012, *LA Weekly*, a local alternative newspaper, published a story, "LAPD Spy Device Taps Your Cell Phone," describing the ongoing Arizona case. It also noted that the LAPD, the nation's third-largest police force, "refuses to say whether its detectives are required . . . to obtain a search warrant."

According to public records, the LAPD had purchased two stingrays "around 2006," with little notification or public discussion, for the purposes of "regional, terrorist-related investigations." Four years later, in April 2010, the Los Angeles City Council approved the acquisition of StingRay II gear, funded by the Los Angeles Police Foundation, an outside charity.

Without knowing what gear the LAPD had acquired years earlier, of course, it was impossible for there to be a meaningful civic discussion as to what, if any, limits there should be on stingrays.

"We can't have a public debate on what kinds of location-monitoring technologies are appropriate, and when they're justified," Peter Bibring, of the ACLU of Southern California, told LA Weekly.

The Rigmaiden story in the Journal hadn't only grabbed the attention of journalists, but also the attention of lawyers. One lawyer, Linda Lye of the ACLU of Northern California, took particular notice. Lye was new to the ACLU, having largely focused on labor and civil rights issues in her previous decade as an attorney.

Quickly, Lye pushed the federal court in San Francisco to unseal the court orders that had authorized the initial use of the stingray against Rigmaiden, as it was unclear from the Arizona case (where the prosecution against Rigmaiden was unfolding) what the order specifically authorized the government to do.

"What on Earth was this technology?" she said. "It seemed that there would be all kinds of novel and troubling issues. What sort of court authorization was being obtained? How widespread was it? It was also just a very unlikely story."

Initially what drew her in wasn't the technology itself, but the fact that the government was keeping "novel surveillance orders" a secret.

In October 2012, Lye and other ACLU and EFF attorneys decided that they would formally jump into the case, not as Rigmaiden's lawyer, but rather as amici. They wrote to the court, noting that this case would "likely result in the first decision to address the constitutional implications" of stingrays.

Months later, Lye was allowed to argue her points formally in front of US District Judge David Campbell, a judge who clerked previously for Chief Justice William Rehnquist.

On March 28, 2013, Lye arrived in the Phoenix federal courthouse and met Rigmaiden for the first time shortly before the hearing on his motion to suppress the stingray evidence and everything that derived from it. This was an important day. After all, without the stingray, the government's case would be lost.

Lye was dressed for court in a dark suit. Rigmaiden, still a prisoner, sat next to her in an orange jumpsuit. Department of Justice (DOJ) attorneys, nearly all men, were seated at the opposing counsel's table—an army of suits. After Rigmaiden was allowed to present his arguments, it was Lye's turn.

"This case raises highly consequential issues in our current technological era about the government's duty, its obligations to the Court to be explicit, to be candid and forthright when it is using forms of technology with which courts are not familiar," she said during the hearing.

Judge Campbell was not easy on the prosecutors. At multiple points, he pushed them, pointing out where they could have been more forthcoming with the magistrate judge who originally signed off on Rigmaiden's surveillance.

"I was shaking with the incredible implications of this," Lye told me in 2017. "I was cautiously optimistic. What the domino effect was going to be? There must be hundreds maybe thousands of investigations across the country where the government didn't disclose the stingray. It would have called into question unknown numbers of criminal prosecutions."

Ultimately, however, in early May 2013, the judge ruled in the government's favor, finding that Rigmaiden lacked a "reasonable expectation of privacy" while shrouded under multiple false identities—after all, his air card, his apartment, and postboxes that he paid for were all done under assumed names.

At the end of the year, there was another big media push about stingrays, this time in *USA Today*. The national newspaper partnered with dozens of reporters around the country, requesting public records from local and state police law enforcement agencies. The months-long investigation resulted in one of the most comprehensive examinations of stingrays to date.

The newspaper concluded that "at least 25 police departments" have a stingray, and noted that in some states "the devices are available to any local police department via state surveillance units. The federal government funds most of the purchases, via anti-terror grants."

Slowly but surely, lawmakers, activists, and journalists were learning more about the details of the device. This newfound attention undoubtedly made life harder for federal authorities as pressure mounted. Rigmaiden wasn't backing down. By late January 2014, Rigmaiden and federal prosecutors reached a plea deal: he'd plead guilty and prosecutors would recommend that he be given a sentence of time served. The agreement was signed on April 9, 2014.

Assistant US Attorney Battista, who had been Rigmaiden's adversary since the beginning, tipped his hat to the fraudster.

The "defendant challenged virtually every aspect of the United States' investigation, hoping to dismiss the case or suppress the incriminating evidence," Battista wrote. "He did so on his own, after requesting the removal of a series of attorneys and electing to represent himself. Although he was ultimately unsuccessful in dismissing the charges or suppressing evidence, he mounted an impressive defense, especially considering that his only formal education is a high school diploma."

While the *Rigmaiden* case wound down, Soghoian (who had joined the ACLU as its chief technologist) and his colleagues were just getting started. The ACLU, along with other privacy groups, including EPIC and the EFF, spearheaded efforts to speak publicly, file record requests, sue, and campaign for meaningful legislative reform.

Soghoian continued to talk to whoever would listen about stingrays, at one point speaking before Michigan state legislators. On May 16, 2014, the young activist appeared with Brian Owsley, a law professor and former magistrate judge from southern Texas, before an Oversight Committee hearing organized by then representative Tom McMillin.

The Republican from Rochester Hills had a difficult time getting forthcoming answers from the Oakland County Sheriff's Department, so he invited Soghoian and Owsley.

"I've been told to 'just trust us,' but I think if law enforcement is saying they're doing nothing wrong, they should welcome oversight," McMillin said during the hearing.

Sheriff Michael Bouchard denied that his agency's stingrays were being used on innocent people. "Unfortunately, because of people like Tom that inflame completely false information, they're building animosity against law enforcement," he said, assuring the committee. "Let me be real clear— the technology that we have does not do surveillance, it does not data mine, does not capture anyone's personal information and it does not listen in on any phone conversation of any kind."

Of course, this kind of response is predicated on the common notion often held by federal agencies and local law enforcement that "surveillance" is not how most people understand the term.

As Jennifer Granick, now an ACLU lawyer, noted in her 2017 book, *American Spies*, in many government circles, the word "surveillance" is defined in a very particular way: it specifically means electronic surveillance (ELSUR) as governed by the Foreign Intelligence Surveillance Act. So what might a government agency call the use of stingrays? Perhaps "data collection," or maybe even just good police work. After all, in their view, the unreasonable search threshold has not been crossed.

In an interview years later, McMillin, who now serves on the state board of education, told me that as a libertarian, he felt that the "Fourth Amendment is on the line and I'm not a fan of Big Brother," adding that "once they're using it, it's hard to pull it back."

He said he was pleasantly surprised that this was an area where libertarians and supporters of the ACLU could "work together."

Upon his release from prison, as part of his plea deal, Rigmaiden was assigned to do community service. At first, he volunteered at a food bank, but his talents were better put to use at the ACLU as a researcher. He helped Lye put together a comprehensive guide about stingrays for criminal defense attorneys. After all, defense attorneys would likely be the ones encountering stingrays in their cases.

The guide was blunt, noting that few attorneys were even aware of what a stingray was or how it was used. "This is entirely understandable because the federal government has a policy of not disclosing information about this device," Lye wrote.

> *The government appears to be withholding information from criminal defendants. It even appears to be providing misleading information and making material omissions to judicial officers when it seeks purported court authorization to use this device—inaccurately referring to it as a "confidential source" or calling it a different kind of device (like a pen register), and failing to alert courts to constitutionally material facts about the technology, such as the full breadth of information it obtains from a suspect and its impact on third parties. As a result, courts are probably not aware that they are authorizing use of this device and have not had an opportunity to rule on its legality, except in very rare instances.*

Another ACLU attorney based in New York, Nathan Freed Wessler, began giving regular talks to criminal defense attorneys, alerting them to the paper. (Recall that in November 2017, Wessler argued *Carpenter* at the Supreme Court.) Meanwhile, also in California, an EFF attorney who specialized in criminal law (and is named in the ACLU guide), Hanni Fakhoury, went on to become a federal public defender based in Oakland. The seeds had been planted nationwide, and would soon bear fruit.

Meanwhile, an enterprising reporter based in Tacoma, Washington, did what other good journalists were doing: looking at how stingrays were being used in their own backyards. However, Kate Martin took it one step further: she was able to speak to the ranking judge in the county (frequently, sitting judges are reluctant to speak to the press on the record).

Judge Ronald Culpepper, then the presiding judge of the Pierce County Superior Court, was taken aback when presented with information about how stingrays were being used in his corner of Washington State.

"If they use it wisely and within limits, that's one thing," he told the *Tacoma News Tribune* on August 26, 2014. "I would certainly personally have some concerns about just sweeping up information from non-involved and innocent parties—and to do it with a whole neighborhood? That's concerning."

The local police chief, Don Ramsdell, through a spokeswoman, declined to speak with the paper, citing a non-disclosure agreement (NDA) with the FBI. Through public records, Martin learned that Tacoma acquired stingrays at least as early as 2008, seemingly without anyone outside of the police department knowing about it.

"I've got to find out what I voted on before I comment," Councilman David Boe said at the time. "This is new information."

Other lawmakers, including the mayor, seemed to be unbothered, indicating essentially that they had full confidence in the police's ability to apprehend bad guys and wanted them to have the appropriate tools to do it.

In its 2013 grant application to acquire an upgraded version of the stingray, the Tacoma Police Department cited its need to combat the threat of improvised explosive devices (IED). However, Tacoma has never been subjected to a major IED attack.

"Chances are the city of Tacoma is not using it to find IEDs," Soghoian told the paper. "They're using it to get drug dealers."

Martin's reporting quickly had a major impact on Pierce County. By November 2014, local county judges banded together to require new language in law enforcement applications to use stingrays: law enforcement had to explicitly articulate what device they were using, and it had to also affirmatively swear that the agency would immediately delete non-target data captured incidentally.

◯

Several months later, in April 2015, the New York Civil Liberties Union (the New York State chapter of the ACLU) managed to do what no one else could: successfully sue to obtain an unredacted copy of the NDA that the FBI had law enforcement agencies sign when they acquired stingrays.

In essence, the document explained that due to the authorization granted by the Federal Communications Commission to the Harris Corporation, the law enforcement agency had to sign an NDA with the FBI. The six-page letter essentially said that agencies that acquired stingrays could not talk about them "in any manner including but not limited to: press releases, in court documents, during judicial hearings, or during other public forums or proceedings."

In short, keeping courts, lawyers, and lawmakers in the dark about exactly what stingrays were and how they worked was entirely deliberate. When Ars Technica asked the FBI for comment, the news outlet was told that without this secret tool, bad guys would basically go free.

"This knowledge could easily lead to the development and employment of countermeasures to FBI tools and investigative techniques by subjects of investigations and completely disarm law enforcement's ability to obtain technology-based surveillance data in criminal investigations," Bradley Morrison, chief of the Tracking Technology Unit at the FBI, said in an April 2014 affidavit.

However, government secrecy in law enforcement is anathema to American democracy. Wiretaps have been regulated for 50 years now, and yet they continue to be effective. Most people, having learned about them in television shows like *The Wire*, are fully aware of this element of law enforcement. However, no one has ever argued—nor was it argued at the time—that the existence of wiretaps should be kept entirely secret from judges and the public.

In May 2015, the FBI issued a bizarre public statement saying that despite the NDA's language to the contrary, it "should not be construed to prevent a law enforcement officer from disclosing to the court or a prosecutor the fact that this technology was used in a particular case."

Later that same month, Washington governor Jay Inslee signed a bill that passed both houses of the state legislature specifically requiring that law enforcement seek a warrant before using a stingray. Rigmaiden worked on the drafting of this bill with Jared Friend of the ACLU of Washington. (Before its passage, Soghoian even testified in support of the bill.)

While Washington was not the first state to impose such a law, it had passed one of the most comprehensive—the law codified extra requirements requiring that police fully describe the technology and its impact in detail to judges—presumably despite any NDA that those agencies may have with the FBI and the dominant manufacturer of the devices, Harris Corporation. Months later, California followed suit, with its comprehensive California Electronic Communications Privacy Act (covered in Chapter 6), which, among other things, also required a warrant for stingray use.

But the most prominent change regarding stingrays came in September 2015, when the DOJ said it would require a warrant in most situations.

The policy, which took effect the day it was announced (September 3, 2015), applied to numerous agencies, including the FBI; the Bureau of Alcohol, Tobacco and Firearms; the Drug Enforcement Administration; and the US Marshals Service, among others.

"Cell-site simulator technology has been instrumental in aiding law enforcement in a broad array of investigations, including kidnappings, fugitive investigations and complicated narcotics cases," Deputy Attorney General Sally Quillian Yates said in a statement. "This new policy ensures our protocols for this technology are consistent, well-managed and respectful of individuals' privacy and civil liberties."

The Department of Homeland Security followed suit the next month.

The new state laws and federal policies came as a result of dogged activism by the ACLU and other privacy groups, which all stemmed from *Rigmaiden*. After all, it was Rigmaiden who had initially reached out to Soghoian and presented him with a 200-page memo on a technology that few outside the government had known about.

"It was the most well-researched memo I'd ever seen on this technology," Soghoian later told WNYC. "Written by a guy rotting in jail."

Now that lawyers know what to look for and how to challenge them, some of those efforts have been successful. Notably, in March 2016 a state appellate court in Maryland took local law enforcement to task, and ruled unequivocally: "We determine that cell phone users have an objectively reasonable expectation that their cell phones will not be used as real-time tracking devices through the direct and active interference of law enforcement."

The three-judge panel in the *State of Maryland v. Andrews* case also blasted law enforcement's blanket use of NDAs for stingray acquisition, noting that they were "inimical to the constitutional principles we revere."

In June 2016, Santa Clara County, California, in the heart of Silicon Valley—where Rigmaiden was arrested—became the first county in the United States to vote in a new law that requires "continued oversight and regular evaluation" of law enforcement agencies prior to the acquisition of surveillance technology. The ordinance, which was unanimously approved by the Santa Clara County Board of Supervisors, requires that the county sheriff and district attorney's offices seek board approval before those agencies even begin the process of obtaining new snooping gear. The agencies are not required to immediately notify the board in exigent circumstances, but they must do so within 90 days.

Agencies must also submit a usage policy to the county government and, notably, an annual surveillance report, which should describe what data the device captures, how the agency deals with information collected about people not suspected of any wrongdoing, and whether the gear has been effective, among other requirements.

"The ordinance doesn't prohibit the acquisition of any surveillance technology," Supervisor Joe Simitian, a longstanding local privacy advocate and former state senator, told me. "It says if you're going to acquire any surveillance technology, let's talk about privacy and due process rights. The issue is not the technology. The question is whether or not we have the wisdom to use the technology appropriately."

Although Rigmaiden has since moved from Arizona to Florida to work as a freelance Web developer, his name continues to occasionally ring out in legal filings and courtrooms nationwide in regard to stingray cases.

In August 2016, his case was cited in a formal legal complaint by Laura Moy, a Georgetown law professor, to the FCC. Moy argued on behalf of her clients, a handful of advocacy organizations, that because stingrays act as fake cell towers, law enforcement agencies are, in effect, broadcasting without the proper spectrum licenses. Worse still, when deployed, legitimate cell service, including 911 calls, are disrupted in the area. (As of late 2017, this case remains pending before the FCC.)

Just three months later, in November 2016, years after stingrays were first used by law enforcement, their use finally reached a federal appeals court. In *United States v. Patrick*, the 7th US Circuit Court of Appeals ruled that law enforcement's warrantless use of a stingray against a man wanted on a probation violation was allowed—but the court dodged the larger question as to whether stingray use required a warrant in all cases.

Rigmaiden's name was also invoked in an August 2017 ruling in an attempted murder case in Oakland, California. In the 39-page ruling, US District Judge Phyllis Hamilton notably found that the January 2013 use of a stingray to find a suspect named Purvis Ellis was a search under the Fourth Amendment. So, law enforcement should have gotten a warrant. However, in this particular case, exigent circumstances (one of the crucial exceptions to the warrant requirement) dictated that the police did not need one and the search was allowed.

"Cell phone users have an expectation of privacy in their cell phone location in real time and . . . society is prepared to recognize that expectation as reasonable," Judge Hamilton wrote, citing *Katz v. United States*.

In September 2017, the District of Columbia Court of Appeals, the functional equivalent of a state supreme court for the nation's capital region, agreed. "A person's awareness that the government can locate and track him or her using his or her cellphone likewise should not be sufficient to negate the person's otherwise legitimate expectation of privacy," the majority concluded.

In other words, judges seem to be resoundingly echoing the 1967-era language of *Katz*, finding that the use of a stingray—a technology kept hidden for years—did require a warrant. Those judges have found that there is a "reasonable expectation of privacy" in one's location. But as of this writing, no cases challenging the use of stingrays have reached the Supreme Court, so this legal theory hasn't been cemented just yet.

What these judges have realized is that there is now a turning point with respect to smartphones: we carry them with us and they hold all of our secrets. No wonder the police find them valuable during an investigation. But should the police need to get a warrant to get into our phones?

CHAPTER NINE

Can Police Search Your Phone When You're Arrested?

We refuse to authorize government intrusion into the most private and personal details of an arrestee's life without a search warrant simply because the cellular phone device which stores that information is small enough to be carried on one's person.

—*SMALLWOOD V. FLORIDA*
SUPREME COURT OF FLORIDA OPINION
MAY 2, 2013

August 22, 2009
San Diego, California

The intersection of Euclid and Imperial avenues is fairly unremarkable. It's comprised of wide Southern California streets, with at least two lanes of traffic (more if you include the left-turn lanes) in each quadrant. On one corner is an Arco gas station, just in front of St. Rita's Catholic Church. On the northeast corner is Greene Cat Liquors, a strip mall liquor store, adjacent to Jaquin Mexican Food, which advertises $1 tacos ("w/ ONION AND CILANTRO ONLY"). Along the southwest corner is El Real Mexican Food, a single-story green-and-white building with a small balcony. Its sandwich board advertises "5 rolled tacos—$4.25."

This was where David Leon Riley, 19, was driving very early in the morning before being pulled over by San Diego police officer Charles Dunnigan. The cop told Riley that he'd pulled him over for having expired registration tags. Dunnigan asked for Riley's driver's license, but it was expired. Dunnigan then asked Riley to step out of the car. The young man complied and started to reach for his right pocket—Dunnigan barked at him to stop. Riley tried to explain that he was merely trying to grab his cell phone (which was later found in the car), and admitted to the cop that he had been arrested previously on weapons charges. Dunnigan frisked Riley, and found no weapons.

However, he did find a green bandana and two miniature Converse sneakers on his keychain—one red and one green.

By this point, one of Dunnigan's colleagues, Officer Matthew Ruggiero, had arrived. The two cops made a crucial determination based on the colors found on Riley's person. They believed that these were the colors commonly used to identify membership in the Lincoln Park Bloods. The gang claims turf in this particular neighborhood of southeastern San Diego, squarely a historic African-American neighborhood that had been subjected to redlining decades earlier.

Dunnigan decided to arrest Riley, suspecting him of being a gang member. Then, the officers began to impound the Lexus, citing department policy. With Dunnigan standing next to Riley, Ruggiero began performing an inventory search on the car. This is a standard search where officers are allowed to conduct a cursory check as to the particular items found in the car—the list can be relied upon later after an impounded vehicle is returned. However, in this case, the inventory search unusually happened on the spot, and the Lexus was never towed.

Ruggiero began looking through the inside of the car. The officer opened the hood—a highly unusual move—where he found two handguns tucked inside socks. At that point, things started to escalate. Dunnigan grabbed Riley's phone, a Samsung SPH-M800, an early smartphone designed to compete with the first iPhone. As Dunnigan scrolled through the phone, the officer could see that all contacts in the phonebook starting with the letter "k" had a letter "c" in front of them. This, the police believed, confirmed their suspicion that Riley was a gang member: "ck" is common gang slang for "Crip Killer."

The officers took Riley downtown for booking. The two officers invited Detective Duane Malinowski, who was off-duty that day, to have a look at this new suspect. Malinowski was investigating a shooting incident that took place on August 2, 2009, near Riley's traffic stop.

But after being read his Miranda rights, Riley refused to speak. Malinowski then got ahold of Riley's phone, where he found "a lot of stuff" on the candy bar–shaped phone, including videos of street fights, and what he thought was Riley's voice encouraging the fighters ("Get brackin' Blood!") and more.

A search incident to arrest is one of the well-understood exceptions to the usual warrant requirement. The idea for this is straightforward: officers taking a suspect into custody want to make sure that he or she is not going to destroy evidence, or have a weapon that could be harmful to the officer.

When Riley went to trial, prosecutors introduced evidence taken from the phone searches that day. There were photos of Riley flashing what police believed to be gang signs. The government argued that this showed Riley's connection to the earlier shooting: he was charged with attempted murder, assault with a semi-automatic weapon, and more. Plus, ballistics tests of the guns found in the socks matched shell casings found at the scene of the August 2 shooting.

Riley's first trial resulted in a hung jury. And it would take nearly five years after Riley's arrest for the Supreme Court to weigh in on whether the warrantless searches of Riley's phone were unconstitutional. Along with *United States v. Jones*, *Riley* would become one of the most important Fourth Amendment Supreme Court decisions in recent years.

◌

In January 2011, the San Diego officers' practice was enshrined by the California Supreme Court. In *People v. Diaz*, the Golden State's highest court found that such searches of phones incident to arrest were authorized as an exception to the warrant rule. The case dated back to 2007, when a man, Gregory Diaz, in Ventura County, California, was observed by sheriff's deputies as buying ecstasy from a police informant who was wearing a wire. Diaz' phone was later seized, and police began reading his text messages without even trying to get a warrant. He and his attorneys challenged the search, but in 2011, the California Supreme Court eventually ruled in favor of law enforcement. That ruling came over the objection of a single member of the high court, Justice Kathryn Werdegar, a Republican appointee.

"In my view, electronic communication and data storage devices carried on the person—cellular phones, smartphones and handheld computer—are not sufficiently analogous to the clothing considered in [*United States v.*] *Edwards* or the crumpled cigarette package in [*United States v.*] *Robinson* to justify a blanket exception to the Fourth Amendment's warrant requirement," she wrote, referring to decades-old Supreme Court precedents.

Justice Werdegar was referring to the 5–4 decision in *Edwards*, a 1974 Supreme Court case involving the clothing of a suspected burglar that was seized and warrantlessly searched. In that case, the suspect was arrested late one night while trying to break into a post office in Lebanon, Ohio.

The next day, 10 hours after he was taken into custody, he was ordered to surrender his clothing in exchange for new clothes purchased by the jail. The clothes that he had been wearing during the burglary were taken and eventually found to contain the same type of paint chips that were found on the post office's busted window.

The Supreme Court ruled that this warrantless search was entirely appropriate even if it took 10 hours to give Edwards new clothes.

"The intrusion here was hardly a shocking one, and it cannot be said that the police acted in bad faith," Justice Potter Stewart wrote in the dissenting opinion. "The Fourth Amendment, however, was not designed to apply only to situations where the intrusion is massive and the violation of privacy shockingly flagrant."

Justice Stewart, of course, was the same justice that a young Larry Tribe had persuaded to rule in Katz' favor seven years earlier.

Robinson, a 1973 decision, revolved around a Washington, DC, man who was arrested for driving with a suspended license. During that traffic stop, which led to his arrest, Willie Robinson was patted down by a Metropolitan Police Department officer. The cop found a crumpled package of cigarettes on Robinson's person, and when the police officer opened it up, he found heroin inside—and Robinson was prosecuted accordingly. Ultimately the Supreme Court ruled in a 6–3 decision that it was, in fact, a reasonable search.

◯

In the summer of 2011, just a few months after the *Diaz* ruling had come down, Riley was tried again. He was convicted and sentenced to 15 years to life. But before being sent off to a state prison to serve his sentence, Riley made a decisive phone call from the San Diego Central Jail.

The man who picked up the phone was Pat Ford. A silver-haired veteran defense lawyer based in downtown San Diego, he specialized in criminal appeals. Ford works almost entirely on cases in Southern California. Sometimes he's selected as a court-appointed attorney, but, as he told me, more often gets paid by clients "whose families make great sacrifices to hire a private lawyer."

Ford is perhaps best known in the legal community for the *California*

Criminal Law Reporter. Since 1983, he has summarized every published opinion in the state and provided these digests as a paid service to attorneys. As of September 2017, Ford charges $225 per year.

Riley wanted to hire Ford as his appeals attorney. After Riley explained the case, Ford headed to the jail to meet his prospective client—less than a mile south of his office. Within just a few minutes of meeting Riley, Ford agreed to take the case.

"He's a charming and likeable guy," Ford told me. "He's a person that came from a tough neighborhood, but he wasn't a thug—there was a sense of mistrust and hopelessness in his eyes."

Ford came to understand that Riley grew up in rough circumstances and was trying to better himself, but struggled. When he was arrested, Riley had been enrolled as a community college student.

"If he had been in a different circumstance he would have been living a different life," Ford added.

As the attorney and his client went forward, the searches of the cell phone weren't where they were focusing their appeal. As is the case with many appeals, there are multiple avenues upon which to challenge the lower court's ruling, often in order of importance, starting with the best argument. In Riley's December 27, 2011, appeal to the Court of Appeal for the State of California, Fourth Appellate District, the cell phone search appeared second in a list of four lines of argument.

Ford knew that the cell phone search incident to arrest question was probably something of a dead end given the *Diaz* case. But, like any thorough lawyer, he left it in.

"I included his search issue in the event and it's such an unbelievable long shot to have the Supreme Court take a case, but you include it on the odd chance that it might," he said.

The first challenge in the list of four arguments was the inventory search that eventually yielded the guns. Ford wrote that the San Diego Police Department's policy at the time was in conflict with the Constitution—officers were conducting an improper search without a warrant. The second issue was the delayed search of the phone itself. Unlike in some other precedents, Riley's phone was taken from inside the car, not from the pockets of his clothing.

Even then, however, Ford's argument was a little more circumspect.

"Appellant does not seek to overturn *Diaz*, although that may well happen in the near future," the lawyer wrote. "Instead, appellant argues that its ruling does not apply in the situation where the phone was not on the suspect's person at the time of the arrest. Under the reasoning of *Diaz*, the search cannot be found to be valid as incident to arrest under the present circumstances."

◎

As 2012 continued, Ford moved ahead with the case, and the California Attorney General's Office prepared its replies. By February 2013, the state appellate court made its ruling against Riley. Not only was the inventory search proper, but the entire issue of the cell phone search was dictated by *Diaz*. It appeared to be a dead end.

Ford prepped his appeal to the California Supreme Court—like the highest court in the land, the San Francisco–based court only agrees to hear a tiny percentage of cases that are submitted. On May 1, 2013, the California Supreme Court denied the petition to review *Riley*. That left Ford and Riley nearly out of options, except for an appeal to the Supreme Court of the United States.

The next day, May 2, 2013, on the other side of the country, in Tallahassee, Florida, the Florida Supreme Court reached the opposite conclusion than the California Supreme Court had arrived at in *Diaz*. There, the Florida high court was asked in *Smallwood v. Florida* to evaluate whether the *Robinson* precedent extended to a warrantless search of a cell phone. The court, in a 5–2 opinion, concluded that it did not. In short, phones were entirely different.

"In our view, allowing law enforcement to search an arrestee's cell phone without a warrant is akin to providing law enforcement with a key to access the home of the arrestee," the majority ruled.

> *Physically entering the arrestee's home office without a search warrant to look in his file cabinets or desk, or remotely accessing his bank accounts and medical records without a search warrant through an electronic cell phone, is essentially the same for many people in today's technologically advanced society. We refuse to authorize government intrusion into the most private and personal details of an*

> *arrestee's life without a search warrant simply because the*
> *cellular phone device which stores that information is small*
> *enough to be carried on one's person.*

Weeks later, back in California, Professor Jeffrey Fisher was tapping away
at his computer at his ground-floor office at Stanford Law School, when
he read *Smallwood*. Since 2006, Fisher has co-directed the Supreme Court
Litigation Clinic, the first clinic in the country to focus solely on Supreme
Court work.

Law clinics are common at law schools around the country—they provide legal services, pro bono, for clients who cannot afford them as a way to
conduct activism for causes that they believe in. It is also a crucial opportunity for lawyers-in-training to garner real-world experience, under the
tutelage of experienced counsel. However, clinics that specialize exclusively
on Supreme Court cases are relatively few and far between. Even more rare
is a law school clinic with such a high-caliber attorney at its head.

By May 2013, Fisher had argued and won at the Supreme Court 9 of 21
times. Fisher had extensive experience at the high court, beginning with
his clerkship for Justice John Paul Stevens during the 1998–1999 term—a
framed picture of Stevens remains on Fisher's office wall. (According to
a December 2014 report by Reuters, Fisher is one of the most frequent
non-government attorneys to appear before the court.)

As the head of Stanford's clinic, he's constantly looking for issues and
cases that he could work on with his students. Back in 2011, when *Diaz*
was first decided in the California Supreme Court, Fisher had worked on
it as a moot court case for his law students to practice on, and he'd even
reached out to the lawyer involved to possibly explore it as a case for the
clinic. (Diaz' attorney declined Fisher's request.)

Due to another case dropping off the clinic's docket, Fisher and his assembled team of students were looking for one more case to round out their
term. Knowing that the Florida Supreme Court had reached a different
conclusion than the California Supreme Court, Fisher thought, perhaps the
time was right to bring a challenge.

So, he did what any good lawyer would do: he searched on Westlaw, a
commercial legal database, for pending cases in California that applied the
Diaz standard. Fisher found three such cases, including *Riley*. After discussing it with his students, they all agreed, *Riley* had the potential to be a
great petition to the Supreme Court.

Fisher called Ford out of the blue, introduced himself, and asked if they could work together on the *cert* petition to the Supreme Court. He explained the recent ruling from the Florida Supreme Court, and illustrated how this might make for a good candidate to be granted *cert*. Ford knew of Fisher's work, but didn't know him personally. It was a *deus ex machina* moment—unexpected, high-level help that appeared out of nowhere. In his 30 years as an attorney, Ford had only filed a handful of petitions to the Supreme Court, but none of them were ever successful.

"Is this a trick question?" Ford thought to himself when Fisher asked him if he'd let him take the case. "Who would say no to that?"

Ford not only had Fisher as an ally, he had a team of four crackerjack law students devoted to his client, effectively full time, for free.

The team got to work immediately on a *cert* petition. After Riley was incarcerated in Kern Valley State Prison, in Delano, California, about 240 miles southeast of Stanford, Fisher and his students drove down to meet him.

"As a lawyer you're representing a person who has a criminal conviction who is challenging his conviction and you have to bear that in mind from start to finish," he said, saying that this was a rare opportunity for himself and his students to meet a client face-to-face. After all, Fisher and his students could drive to Delano and back to Stanford in a day.

During the summer of 2013, Ford flew up to the Bay Area a few times to help in person, but otherwise contributed by phone and e-mail. While the team was preparing their *cert* petition, they became aware of a decision from the 1st US Circuit Court of Appeals in Boston—*United States v. Wurie*. In this case, like *Smallwood* in Florida, a federal appellate court found that a criminal suspect's phone could not be searched without a warrant during an arrest. For Fisher, this solidified his opinion that they had hit on the perfect moment after the issue had adequately percolated throughout the system of lower courts before the Supreme Court should adjudicate it.

Cert was granted on January 14, 2014. The Supreme Court heard *Riley* and *Wurie* as essentially one case, and ruled accordingly. The stage was set for oral arguments on April 29, 2014.

During the three months leading up to the big day, Fisher and his students conducted moot courts at Stanford Law, UCLA Law, and then George-town Law, with its famous detailed-oriented replica of the Supreme Court chambers. When in DC, Fisher spent a lot of time rereading notes and cases at the local offices of his old law firm, Davis Wright Tremaine. Finally, one or two days before the oral argument, Fisher took a three- to four-hour walk around the National Mall "to get my eyes off the written word."

Essentially, the crux of their argument was "digital is different"—data held on a phone is totally unlike any level of physical information that someone could conceivably keep on their person. An analogy that he and his students came up with was that saying "a phone is just another con-tainer . . . [is] like saying that a ride on a 747 is no different than a bicycle."

On April 29, Ford sat with Fisher at the counsel's table. They had agreed that Fisher, as the Supreme Court veteran, would be arguing on behalf of Riley. Before they got down to the case at hand, Ford asked the court to admit his sister, also an attorney, to the bar of the Supreme Court. This was something of a formality and a small honor. Chief Justice Roberts granted Ford's motion.

As Ford re-took his seat, he looked at Fisher and grinned: "I just kicked ass, I don't know how you're going to do." Fisher smiled back, and collected his thoughts before it was time to begin.

In the two years since the 2012 *Jones* case of GPS tracking, the panel of nine justices remained the same.

"Mr. Chief Justice, and may it please the Court," Fisher intoned.

> *This case involves applying the core protection of the Fourth Amendment to a new factual circumstance. It has always been the case that an occasion of an arrest did not give the police officers authority to search through the private papers and the drawers and bureaus and cabinets of somebody's house, and that protection should not evaporate more than 200 years after the founding because we have the technologi-cal development of smartphones that have resulted in people carrying that information in their pockets.*

After some interplay with Justice Anthony Kennedy over the *Robinson* case, Justice Samuel Alito cut to the chase.

"What is the difference between looking at hardcopy photos in a billfold and looking at photos that are saved in the memory of a cell phone?" he asked, seemingly leaning towards the government's position.

"The difference is digital information versus physical items," Fisher responded. "Physical items at the scene can pose a safety threat and have destruction possibilities that aren't present with digital evidence. What is more, once you get into the digital world, you have the framers' concern of general warrants and the—the writs of assistance."

In other words, having a device that could contain vast quantities of data and wholly different types of information far beyond what people used to carry even as recently as decades ago—small slips of paper and photos—is an entirely different equation.

Fisher was peppered with questions and presented with numerous hypotheticals. In the end, his position was clear: digital is different, so the police need to get a warrant.

Arguing for the State of California was Edward DuMont, the state's solicitor general—an unusual choice for Supreme Court cases. DuMont, who had been nominated by President Barack Obama in 2010 for a federal judgeship, was tasked with trying to convince the justices that the *Robinson* rule should indeed apply to cell phones.

"Thank you, Mr. Chief Justice, and may it please the Court," he said.

"As Mr. Fisher has said, if Mr. Riley had been carrying physical photographs in his pocket at the time of his arrest, there's no dispute that arresting officers could have looked at those photographs to see whether they contained evidence of crime. Now, what would have been reasonable in that situation does not become constitutionally unreasonable simply because Mr. Riley instead carried his photographs in digital form on a smartphone. The shifted digital format does not make the photographs any less his papers or effects—"

That's when Justice Sonya Sotomayor jumped in, pointing out that a lot had changed since the *Robinson* era.

> Counsel, in one of our Court decisions in the past, a series of justices asked—or noted that many of our rules were based on practical considerations. Practically speaking, a person can only carry so much on their person. That is different because carrying a billfold of photographs is a billfold of photographs. It's, you know, anywhere from one to five generally and not much more. But now we're talking about potentially thousands, because with digital cameras people take endless photos and it spans their entire life. You don't see a difference

> *between the two things? What has now become impractical.*
> *A GPS can follow people in a way that prior following by*
> *police officers in cars didn't permit.*

Sotomayor, of course, was referring to the *Jones* decision from just two years earlier.

Essentially, what DuMont argued, along the lines of what the government had said in earlier briefs, was that Riley actually didn't have his entire life on his phone.

"This cell phone had a handful of contacts," he said. "I don't think it's in the record, but what we understand is there were 250 some-odd contacts, there were about 59 photos and there were perhaps 42 videos that ranged from 30 to 45 seconds."

In other words, perhaps there would be other situations that could have been more revelatory, but this wasn't it.

Michael Dreeben, the deputy solicitor general of the United States, gave a brief statement, and Fisher gave a brief rebuttal, and the case was submitted.

Roughly two months later, the Supreme Court came back with a rare, 9–0 opinion in both *Riley* and *Wurie*. In the unanimous opinion Chief Justice John Roberts lambasted the government's claim that searching a cell phone was "materially indistinguishable" from simply searching someone's pockets.

"That is like saying a ride on horseback is materially indistinguishable from a flight to the moon," he famously wrote.

> *Both are ways of getting from point A to point B, but little*
> *else justifies lumping them together. Modern cell phones,*
> *as a category, implicate privacy concerns far beyond those*
> *implicated by the search of a cigarette pack, a wallet, or a*
> *purse. A conclusion that inspecting the contents of an ar-*
> *restee's pockets works no substantial additional intrusion on*
> *privacy beyond the arrest itself may make sense as applied to*
> *physical items, but any extension of that reasoning to digital*
> *data has to rest on its own bottom.*

Roberts went further: "Our answer to the question of what police must do before searching a cell phone seized incident to an arrest is accordingly simple—get a warrant."

At home in Palo Alto, Fisher had set his alarm for 7 AM PT, or 10 AM ET, when Supreme Court opinions are expected to be posted. When he read the opinion online, he was thrilled. Coming out of the argument, he'd thought he had the liberal wing, but wasn't sure if he'd have five, much less nine votes. Even better, Justice Roberts had encapsulated the analogy that he and his students had thought of ("ride on a 747").

"It was somehow a true mind meld," he recalled during a 2017 interview at his office, where his desk had neatly organized stacks of paper, and a red bicycle helmet perched near his window. "The court wrote back what you wanted to say, but even better."

◇

Riley was a huge decision. Like *Jones*, it wasn't at all obvious that the court was going to rule this way. But as is the case so often, as the case worked its way through the courts, the technology raced ahead. By the time the Supreme Court ruled on *Riley* and *Wurie*, the phones in question were hopelessly out of date. Riley had an early model of smartphone, which didn't even run a modern operating system, while Brima Wurie had a flip phone. In neither case, as they made their way through the court system, was encryption an issue.

In September 2013, Apple introduced Touch ID, a fingerprint scanner embedded into the home button of iPhones. The idea was that rather than have users memorize ever-longer and ever-more-complex passcodes, they could use something physical (a fingerprint) as a key to unlock the device.

But while the *Riley* case implicated Fourth Amendment concerns, allowing a fingerprint to open an iPhone could potentially touch on Fifth Amendment issues. The crucial portion of the Fifth Amendment precludes testifying against oneself.

By adding this technology, while undoubtedly intended to make digital security easier, Apple may have unintentionally created legal problems. As Marcia Hofmann—the San Francisco lawyer who was briefly Ladar Levison's lawyer—noted in a 2013 *Wired* op-ed, that Fifth Amendment privilege only applies when there is a testimonial statement. Or, put another way, the Fifth Amendment protects what you know (a passcode, in your mind), but not what you are (a biometric fingerprint.)

"We can't invoke the privilege against self-incrimination to prevent the government from collecting biometrics like fingerprints, DNA samples, or voice exemplars," Hofmann wrote. "Why? Because the courts have decided that this evidence doesn't reveal anything you know. It's not testimonial."

In the *Riley* decision, the Supreme Court quaintly noted that encryption was essentially not an issue. But just three months after the ruling, in September 2014, Apple released iOS 8 (as discussed in Chapter 2), which was reengineered to have full-disk encryption on by default.

"On devices running iOS 8, your personal data such as photos, messages (including attachments), email, contacts, call history, iTunes content, notes, and reminders is placed under the protection of your passcode," the company wrote on its website.

"Unlike our competitors, Apple cannot bypass your passcode and therefore cannot access this data. So it's not technically feasible for us to respond to government warrants for the extraction of this data from devices in their possession running iOS 8."

Shortly thereafter, Google's latest update to Android enabled full-disk encryption as well.

In other words, within just a few months of the Supreme Court's decision in *Riley*, the technology itself had changed the game. Full-disk enabled encryption by default makes it notably harder for law enforcement to conduct searches of computers and smartphones. The prevalence of such encryption is what contributed to the late-2017 revival of the government's efforts to combat Going Dark.

In order to get around this level of encryption, and knowing that a fingerprint hasn't historically been considered by the Supreme Court to be testimonial, the Department of Justice (DOJ) has, at least in some instances, tried to get around the encryption with some unusual tactics. On at least three known occasions since the technology became available in 2013, federal prosecutors have gotten a judge to sign off on an order authorizing a compelled fingerprint depression in an attempt to unlock a seized iPhone.

As Ars Technica reported in February 2016, a woman in Glendale, California, just outside of Los Angeles, was ordered to depress her fingerprint on a seized iPhone. Months later, federal investigators, also in Los Angeles County, were successful in getting judicial approval for two highly unusual searches of seized smartphones at two different Southern California homes, one in Lancaster and one in West Covina, about 90 miles away. The signed warrants allowed the authorities to force a resident reasonably believed to

be a user to press their fingerprints on the phone to see if it would unlock. (Under both iOS and Android, fingerprints as passcodes only work
for 48 hours; after that timeframe, the regular passcode is required. Court
records show that the warrants were presumably executed within that 48-
hour window.)

It's still not clear whether this stratagem was legal: no challenge was ever
made.

◇

Riley also does not answer another pesky question that continues to linger:
Can someone be forced to provide a passcode to unlock an encrypted device, cell phone or otherwise, or can a suspect use the Fifth Amendment to
shield themselves from the government's demands?

It turns out that such cases involving compelled decryption are relatively
new and still somewhat rare—the first such case only goes back to 2007.
Courts have generally protected the Fifth Amendment rights of defendants
who refuse to hand over passwords that could decrypt a computer.

In 2012, the 11th US Circuit Court of Appeals ruled in favor of a Florida
man ("John Doe") who invoked his Fifth Amendment privilege in relation
to accusations that he had child pornography across numerous encrypted
external hard drives. For now, the Doe case (known formally as *In re:
Grand Jury Subpoena Duces Tecum Dates March 25, 2011*) remains the highest federal court to address the issue. In 2013, a federal judge in Milwaukee
allowed a child porn suspect to invoke a Fifth Amendment privilege, and
refused to force him to give up the passcode.

There is a crucial exception to this Fifth Amendment privilege: the "foregone conclusion." In other words, if, for example, the government already
knows that the target files exist on a particular computer, a suspect can't
simply use that part of the Constitution as an impenetrable shield. Indeed,
on the same day that the Supreme Court ruled in *Riley*, the Massachusetts
Supreme Judicial Court, the state's highest court, concluded in a 5–2 decision that a criminal suspect could be ordered to decrypt his seized computers. Why? Because the defendant had already admitted to the police that
they were his, and that he had the ability to decrypt them: in other words, it
was a foregone conclusion.

An extreme example of this is the case of Francis Rawls, who, as of September 30, 2017, has been held in jail for two years and counting for refusing to disclose the password to a seized laptop, drive, and iPhone that the government alleges contains child pornography. Rawls, a former Philadelphia police sergeant, has failed in his attempts to get his contempt order thrown out—again due to the foregone conclusion doctrine.

In early August 2017, the 3rd US Circuit Court of Appeals ruled that because, at his earlier contempt hearing, prosecutors had brought witnesses, including Rawls' sister, who testified that she had witnessed him enter the passwords and showed her some child pornography files. So, the magistrate judge ruled, and the appellate court agreed, that forcing him to give up the password would be a foregone conclusion and not violate the Fifth Amendement.

In July 2016, a Miami reality TV star, Hencha Voigt, and her friend Wesley Victor were charged with extortion of another South Florida woman: Julieanna Goddard, also known online as "YesJulz."

According to court records, which the *Miami Herald* provided to Ars Technica, Voigt contacted Goddard's assistant, Imani Simmons, on July 20, 2016. Voigt told Simmons that someone was trying to sell sex videos of Goddard and even provided examples to prove that she was telling the truth. (Other filings indicate that Voigt herself had "compromising pictures/videos" published online without her consent prior to this incident.)

Voigt warned Simmons that someone would be contacting Goddard from a trap phone (burner phone) and further warned: "Don't threaten them, be super nice." While Voigt was texting Simmons, she was also calling and texting Victor.

While Voigt only used an iPhone 6 (referred to as "Phone A"), complicating matters, Victor used three different phones, including an iPhone 6S ("Phone B"). The messages that the government wanted were the iMessages between Voigt and Victor, which, as the government explained, "do not appear in telephone service provider records as anything other than generic data usage. Therefore, the only practical way of determining whether iMessages were sent or received from a particular phone is to actually examine the contents of the phone." The government wanted these messages to further link Voigt and Victor.

Hours later, Victor asked Voigt for Goddard's number, which Voigt provided. Victor then allegedly provided further examples of the racy material he possessed. The next day, Goddard asked how she could get the images and videos back or prevent their release. Victor asked for $18,000 in cash. Minutes later, Victor and Voigt were "apprehended together" in a car parked in Miami Beach—according to police records, Voigt even tried to hide the phone by sitting on it.

Weeks later, the Miami Beach police obtained a warrant to search Voigt's iPhone and Victor's three phones. Authorities were stymied by the two iPhones, as they were both passcode-protected.

By May 2017, a Florida judge ruled against Voigt, likening the disclosure of the iPhone passcode to be analogous to handing over the key to a safe-deposit box—a non-testimonial act not protected by the Fifth Amendment. Two months later, after Voigt still refused to help authorities, the FBI stepped in and offered to cover the state's costs to get at the messages contained on the iPhone. The FBI paid the costs of doing so to Cellebrite, an Israeli digital forensics firm that frequently provides services to American law enforcement.

In the Voigt case, according to the *Miami Herald*, evidence from the newly unlocked iPhone "seem[s] to show Voigt and her then-boyfriend actively plotting to get $18,000 from a social-media celebrity known as Yes-Julz, in exchange for not releasing the video clips to the Internet. '*We on some Bonnie Clyde shit I couldn't have choose a Better partner* [*in*] *crime lol*,' reads one text sent from Victor's phone."

In another message, Voigt added in a warning to Victor: "Change all your passwords in your accs she doesn't try some slick shit to u."

This was highly unusual: the last time that the public knew that the FBI had paid for such a service was in the "FBI v. Apple" showdown of 2016 (and covered in Chapter 2). Here, this was not a terrorism case, nor was it even a federal crime. This was a relatively low-level extortion dispute involving small amounts of money, and very local Instagram celebrities.

As discussed earlier, the Fourth Amendment does not prohibit all searches, simply unreasonable ones. It has been long-settled law that a search when crossing the US border does not require a warrant. The border search exception is what authorizes customs searches that all travelers must be subjected to upon th in a dissenting opinion eir arrival in the United States.

The idea is that in maintaining sovereign boundaries, the government has a compelling interest in what comes into the country.

Despite the strong finding for privacy in *Riley*, the border search exception remains key. On September 28, 2015, Sergio Caballero was driving into the United States from Mexico, and tried to cross at the Calexico, California, border checkpoint. A drug dog alerted agents to the possible presence of narcotics—he was found to have 33 pounds of methamphetamine and 2.75 pounds of heroin inside the gas tank of his car. Agents also searched his phone, which contained some incriminating photos of large piles of cash.

Caballero's federal public defender, Nathan Feneis, tried to argue that *Riley* was the Supreme Court decision that should dictate the outcome. But the judge ruled in April 2016 that the border search exception superseded it.

"The question presented by this case is this: once a person is placed under arrest at the border, may officers conduct a cursory search of the arrestee's cell phone without a warrant?" US District Judge Roger Benitez wrote. "*Riley* says, 'No.' But, *Riley* does not address a search at the border. The border search exception says, 'Yes.' But, neither the Supreme Court, nor the Ninth Circuit, has decided a case involving the heightened privacy interests implicated by a cell phone search at the border after an arrest."

It turns out that between 2015 and 2016, during the tail end of the Obama administration, digital searches at the border increased five-fold, according to Customs and Border Patrol's (CBP) own figures. However, despite the large jump by percentage, federal authorities maintain that such searches are exceedingly rare.

"In [fiscal year 2016], CBP processed more than 390 million arrivals and performed 23,877 electronic media searches," a statement sent to Ars Technica by Robert Brisley, a CBP spokesman based in Atlanta, said. "This equates to CBP performing an electronic search on 0.0061% of arrivals. This is an increase over the FY15 numbers when 4,764 electronic media searches were conducted, accounting for .0012% of arrivals. CBP officers processed 383 million arrivals in [fiscal year 2015]."

Under the Trump administration, this figure has grown even more, with no discernible explanation as to why. In March 2017, NBC reported that 2017 was to be on pace to be a "blockbuster year" for border searches of electronic devices. According to the news outlet, 5,000 "devices were searched in February alone, more than in all of 2015."

In early 2017, there were a few high-profile examples of warrantless border searches of electronic devices, including one of a Jet Propulsion

Laboratory scientist and a California artist. In September 2017, those men, along with several others, sued CBP in federal court in Massachusetts. They are being represented by attorneys from the American Civil Liberties Union and the Electronic Frontier Foundation (EFF) in the case, known as *Alasaad v. Duke*.

"The border doctrine does not say that the Constitution doesn't exist at the border. What it does say is that the balance between privacy and security is drawn differently," Adam Schwartz, one of their EFF lawyers, told Ars Technica.

"What we say is that *Riley* redraws the equation. Your phone, it's not like your backpack, it's like every backpack and every desk and every movie theatre you ever walked into. It's profoundly different in quality and quantity than what people have historically carried over the border."

All the plaintiffs, during their interrogation at the border, decided to provide the passcodes to their phones. But what authority grants federal border agents this power?

The most recent public document to date on this topic appears to be an August 2009 Department of Homeland Security (DHS) paper titled "Privacy Impact Assessment for the Border Searches of Electronic Devices." That document states that "for CBP, the detention of devices ordinarily should not exceed five (5) days, unless extenuating circumstances exist."

The policy also states that CBP or Immigration and Customs Enforcement "may demand technical assistance, including translation or decryption," citing 19 US Code Section 507. The 2009 DHS document also says that "officers may seek such assistance with or without individualized suspicion." An individual refusing to comply with this statute is "guilty of a misdemeanor and subject to a fine of not more than $1,000."

But as Orin Kerr, the University of Southern California law professor, tweeted in February 2017: "Border agents say that this law requires people crossing border to disclose their password if asked. But does it say that? No cases."

As of this writing, in late 2017, it remains unclear as to whether the judge hearing *Alasaad* will find *Riley* controlling, or if, like Judge Benitez, they will hold that the border search exception doctrine wins the day.

◯

It turns out that digital is different in another way too: the act of investigation. Since at least 2002, federal authorities have created their own specialized software to go after technically sophisticated targets. This strategy has a specialized, almost-sanitized name, too: lawful hacking.

Just as a stingray can locate someone whose whereabouts are unknown in the physical world, a network investigative technique (NIT) can locate or describe someone online by forcing a computer or phone to give up its IP address.

A NIT is essentially a fancy government phrase for a piece of unauthorized software, often known as malware, that can infiltrate a target computer and reveal information about it. While NITs, and their precursors, known as Computer and Internet Protocol Address Verifiers (CIPAV), have been around for at least 15 years, it's only within recent years that more cases have come to the fore.

One of the best-known cases involving a NIT emerged in July 2012, after a deranged man shot and killed 12 people in a movie theater in Aurora, Colorado. The day after the shooting, a man who identified himself as "Andrew Ryan" called the Arapahoe Sheriff's Department and claimed to be a "friend" of the alleged killer, James Holmes. (In reality, the link between the two men is extremely unlikely.)

Ryan, who spoke with some sort of non-native English-speaking accent, demanded that Holmes be freed, and threatened to blow up a building if the authorities did not comply. The number he called from turned out to be facilitated via Google Voice, while a proxy server obscured his true Internet Protocol (IP) address. Ryan, who later told the Arapahoe deputy he regularly spoke with to call him "Mo," made over 12 similar threats to various hotels, universities, and airports. By September 2012, investigators got ahold of some identifying information from Google (via a warrant) indicating that Mo may, in fact, be in Iran.

Finally, in December 2012, a Denver police officer went to a judge, asking for a warrant to install a NIT on Mo's computer—in other words, authorities wanted to send a link to Mo and trick him into clicking it, which would surreptitiously install software on his computer, akin to what malevolent hackers do. It would collect various details, including Mo's operating system, IP address, media access control (MAC) address, time zone, and more.

The judge signed off on it, and the warrant was executed. Court records indicate that the NIT was only "partially successful." While the NIT itself did not run, the recipient of the e-mail did attempt to click the link from an

Iranian IP address. News of the NIT didn't become public for about a year, until the *Washington Post* reported on it.

A few months later, in April 2013, US Magistrate Judge Stephen Smith (one of the judges commonly identified with the privacy-minded group of judges known as the Magistrate's Revolt) in the Southern District of Texas, issued a ruling against a federal agency seeking to install a NIT against a certain target. Like many warrant applications, the entire case remained sealed until the judge's order.

As Judge Smith explained, sometime in early 2013, "unknown persons" gained access to a person's ("John Doe") e-mail account. Those scofflaws used this unauthorized access to then gain access to Doe's bank account. While the judge's order doesn't say how much money was transferred abroad, it must have been large enough to draw the ire of federal authorities. Either way, the magistrate was highly skeptical of what the government was asking for.

"The Government does not seek a garden-variety search warrant," he wrote. "Its application requests authorization to surreptitiously install data extraction software on the Target Computer. Once installed, the software has the capacity to search the computer's hard drive, random[ly] access memory, and other storage media; to activate the computer's built-in camera; to generate latitude and longitude coordinates for the computer's location; and to transmit the extracted data to FBI agents within this district."

Judge Smith rejected the government's warrant application for three major reasons: under Rule 41 of the Federal Rules of Criminal Procedure, magistrates were only allowed to sign off on warrants within their own district; the warrant didn't fulfill the particularity requirement; and the video element is subject to Title III super-warrant standards, which the affidavit does not fulfill.

It's worth noting that reporting on this type of novel surveillance order, even years after it was issued, remains sealed. The only public document on the entire docket that exists is the judge's order, likely because he wanted others to read it. It's impossible for anyone to know if this technique was attempted with a different judge, and if so, how successful it was. As such, it is difficult to evaluate these novel legal questions—the government will always have the upper hand, as only it knows the techniques that it is keeping a secret.

At the tail end of Judge Smith's ruling, he provided a caveat to watchful DOJ attorneys.

"The court finds that the Government's warrant request is not supported by the application presented," he wrote. "This is not to say that such a potent investigative technique could never be authorized under Rule 41. And there may well be a good reason to update the territorial limits of that rule in light of advancing computer search technology. But the extremely intrusive nature of such a search requires careful adherence to the strictures of Rule 41 as currently written, not to mention the binding Fourth Amendment precedent for video surveillance in this circuit."

At the time Judge Smith was writing, Rule 41 required that in nearly all cases, magistrates only sign off on warrants within their own judicial district. This territoriality requirement helped provide two important bulwarks against government overreach: that the search or seizure is adequately relevant to the court authorizing it and that it helps protect against forum shopping—law enforcement seeking a warrant from judges that they know will be favorable.

It was around this time that the DOJ heeded Judge Smith's advice, and began formal efforts to change this rule. In September 2013, Mythili Raman, the acting assistant attorney general, sent a letter to the judge who headed the rules committee at that time, setting off a three-year process. Raman cited Judge Smith's order.

"There is a substantial public interest in catching and prosecuting criminals who use anonymizing technologies, but locating them can be impossible for law enforcement absent the ability to conduct a remote search of the criminal's computer," Raman wrote. "Law enforcement may in some circumstances employ software that enables it through a remote search to determine the true IP address or other identifying information associated with the criminal's computer."

The DOJ had a real-world example of such a criminal enterprise in early 2015, when it seized a child porn website, Playpen. The site was only accessible through the Tor Browser, a specialized Web browser that uses a series of technical steps to anonymize one's footprints online. As such, anyone who accesses a Tor-hidden site (designated by a .onion URL) is very difficult to find out.

Playpen's founder, David Lynn Browning, of Kentucky, was identified in 2015, initially by a foreign law enforcement agency as part of an investigation into yet another child porn website. His IP address was exposed when those overseas cops provided him a "hyperlink to a streaming video" (or, a NIT) configured to go around his Tor browser, which then exposed his true IP address. After realizing it was an American IP address, the foreign agency handed it over to the FBI.

Eventually, the FBI located Browning in Kentucky, seized Playpen, and allowed it to continue operating for 13 days to further investigate the site's American users. While under the FBI's control, on Playpen's login screen, each user's computer was secretly hit with the NIT, which was designed to expose that person's true IP address. With a real IP address, unmasking individuals was trivial—a simple subpoena to the Internet service provider would suffice.

While most of the cases were successfully prosecuted or ended in plea deals, a handful of defendants succeeded in challenging their cases and getting the charges dropped. In all of the Playpen cases, a magistrate in Virginia authorized a NIT to be used against suspects not only across the United States, but across the world.

For future cases, the government now won't have to be as strict with the territoriality rule: the revision to Rule 41 went into effect on December 1, 2016. However, the government has generally done a poor job of publicly disclosing how many times NITs have been deployed, and what technical vulnerabilities they exploit. Unlike wiretaps, for example, which have to be disclosed in detail in annual reports, the DOJ has never disclosed how often NITs are sought or used. With little transparency in their use, it's impossible to even attempt to evaluate their effectiveness.

Just as was the case with stingrays, which began as a military tool, and then were brought home for law enforcement (largely in secret), it is only a matter of time before local police departments begin deploying NITs, if they haven't already.

CHAPTER TEN

Why Privacy Needs All of Us

We have to shape policies in case there is a Trump running every department.

—Raymundo Jacquez
Oakland Privacy Advisory Commission (2017)

There is one American city that is the furthest along in creating a workable solution to the current inadequacy of surveillance law: Oakland, California—which spawned rocky road ice cream, the mai tai cocktail, and the Black Panther Party. Oakland has now pushed pro-privacy public policy along an unprecedented path.

Today, Oakland's Privacy Advisory Commission (PAC) acts as a meaningful check on city agencies—most often, police—that want to acquire any kind of surveillance technology. It doesn't matter whether a single dollar of city money is being spent—if it's being used by a city agency, the PAC wants to know about it. The agency in question and the PAC then have to come up with a use policy for that technology and, importantly, report back at least once per year to evaluate its use.

The nine-member all-volunteer commission is headed by a charismatic, no-nonsense 40-year-old activist, Brian Hofer. During the PAC's 2017 summer recess, Hofer laid out his story over a few pints of beer. In the span of just a few years, he has become an unlikely crusader for privacy in the Bay Area.

◇

In 1998, when Hofer left his hometown, Weed, California, at the age of 21, he transferred into the University of California, Berkeley. As the third-largest city in Siskiyou County, the town at the farthest northern extremes of California boasts about 3,000 residents.

"There's no young people in between 18 and 40 in Weed, there's no jobs, there's no education," Hofer lamented to me.

Hofer's father is a Berean (an offshoot of mainstream Protestantism) reverend, and former official with the Siskiyou County Republican Central Committee. Growing up in the 1980s, Hofer remembered, there were two portraits side-by-side in the family's home: President Ronald Reagan and Jesus.

"I came from a place where the thing to do was to hang out at McDonald's because there was no humanity around," he said. "Half of our main street is abandoned, it's a ghost town."

Hofer's always followed politics—he's voted in every election he's been eligible for. "But I'm like every nine out of ten people, I just sat on the sidelines," he said.

After graduating with a BA in cconomics, Hofer bounced around, first getting a job as a paralegal in 2004, and eventually landing in law school at the University of San Francisco in 2008. By 2011, he'd graduated, and later joined one of the protest marches to the Port of Oakland as part of the broader Occupy movement. In June 2013, he read in horror about Edward Snowden and revelations of the National Security Agency's (NSA) overreach. He was trying to figure out how to best channel his nascent political identity—a mix of Bay Area progressivism with an undercurrent of his rural libertarian roots. Hofer once attended a Berkeley City Council meeting, but found it baffling. It was often more crazed grandstanding than actual meaningful discussion.

Then, in July 2013, when Snowden was still a fresh name, the City of Oakland formally accepted a federal grant to create something called the Domain Awareness Center (DAC). The idea was to provide a central hub for all of the city's surveillance tools, including license plate readers (LPR), closed circuit television (CCTV) cameras, gunshot detection microphones, and more—all in the name of protecting the Port of Oakland, the third largest on the West Coast.

Had the city council been presented with the perfunctory vote on the DAC even a month before Snowden, it likely would have breezed by without even a mention in the local newspaper. But because government snooping was on everyone's mind, including Hofer's, it became a controversial plan.

After reading a few back issues of the *East Bay Express* in January 2014,

Hofer decided to attend one of the early meetings of the Oakland Privacy Working Group, largely an outgrowth of Occupy and other activists opposed to the DAC. The meeting was held at Sudoroom—then a hackerspace hosted amidst a dusty collective of offices and meeting space in downtown Oakland.

Hofer, who didn't know anyone at the meeting, walked in at the same time as an Oakland Police Department (OPD) detective, who may have been monitoring the group, through the building's side door. Hofer sat down in the back and listened. There were various speakers and presentations, but nothing seemed to click.

"How are these guys going to combat this crazy surveillance project that I've just heard of?" Hofer wondered to himself.

The group was not organized. While well-intentioned, they had no clear plan as to how they were going to effectively provide political opposition to the DAC. At one point, Hofer piped up and asked the few who seemed to be running the meeting how many city council members they had met with. When they told him none, he stood up to go home.

Before walking out, Hofer was pulled aside by Eddan Katz, a local tech-minded attorney and one of the co-founders of Sudoroom, trying gently to stop Hofer from leaving. Hofer, frustrated, tried to point out that their street theater efforts were unlikely to result in meaningful change. Still, Katz asked Hofer a few basic questions: "Do you want to meet with the city council? How can you not, with the people voting on the project? What's your strategy?"

Katz impressed upon him the motto of Sudoroom and other hackerspaces like it: it's an anarchist collective, yes, but it's also a do-ocracy. If you want something done, do it. Hofer decided to take him up on the offer. Amazingly, it worked. Within weeks, Hofer, who had no political connections whatsoever, had meetings scheduled with city council members and other local organizations. By September 2014, Hofer was named as the chair of the Ad Hoc Privacy Committee. In January 2016, a city law formally incorporated that Ad Hoc Privacy Committee into the PAC—each city council member could appoint a member of their district as representatives. Hofer was its chair, representing District 3, in the northern section of the city. Hofer ended up creating the city's privacy watchdog, simply because he cared enough to do so.

◯

On the first Thursday of every month, the PAC meets in a small hearing room, on the ground floor of city hall. Although there are dozens of rows of theater-style folding seats, more often than not, there are more commissioners in attendance than citizens. While occasionally a few local reporters and concerned citizens are present, most of the time, the PAC plugs away quietly. Turns out, the most ambitious local privacy policy in America is slowly and quietly made amidst small printed name cards—tented in front of laptops—one agenda item at a time.

Its June 1, 2017, meeting was called to order by Hofer. He was flanked by seven fellow commissioners and two liaison positions, who do not vote. (At the time, the seat for the commissioner associated with District 2, in North Oakland, was vacant.)

The PAC was comprised of a wide variety of commissioners: a white law professor at the University of California, Berkeley; an African-American former OPD officer; a 25-year-old Muslim activist; an 85-year-old founder of a famed user group for the Unix operating system; a young Latino attorney; and an Iranian-American businessman and former mayoral candidate. (One commissioner, Clint M. Johnson, declined to be interviewed for this book.)

Professor Deirdre Mulligan, who as of September 2017 announced her intention to step down from the PAC pending a replacement, is probably the highest-profile member of the commission. She too was recruited by Eddan Katz—her former student—who initially was slated to serve on the PAC, but had to bow out. Mulligan is a veteran of the privacy law community: she was the founding director of the Samuelson Clinic, a Berkeley Law clinic that focuses on technology-related cases.

"The connection between race and surveillance and policing has become more evident to people," she told me. "It seemed like Oakland was in a good position to create some good examples. To think about how the introduction of technology would affect not just privacy, but equity and fairness issues."

For his part, Robert Oliver tends to sit back—his eyes toggling between his black laptop and whoever in the PAC happens to be speaking. As the only Oakland native in the group, an Army vet with a computer science degree from Grambling State University, and a former OPD cop, Oliver comes to the commission with a very unique perspective. When uniformed OPD officers come to speak before the PAC, Oliver doesn't underscore that he served among them from 1998 until 2006. But he understands what a difficult job police officers are tasked with, especially in a city like Oakland, where, in recent years, there have been around 80 murders annually.

"From a beat officer point of view, who doesn't have the life experience—and of course they're not walking around with the benefit of case law sloshing around in their heads—they're trying to make these decisions on the fly and still remain within the confines of the law while simultaneously trying not to get hurt or killed," he told me over beers.

The way he sees it, *Riley* is a "demarcation point"—the legal system is starting to figure out what the appropriate limits are. Indeed, the Supreme Court does seem to understand in a fundamental way that smartphones are substantively different from every other class of device that has come before.

Meanwhile, Reem Suleiman stands out, as she is both the youngest member of the PAC and the only Muslim. A Bakersfield, California, native, Suleiman has been cognizant of what it means to be Muslim and American nearly her entire life. Since September 11, shes known of many instances where the FBI or other law enforcement agencies would turn up at the homes or workplaces of people she knew.

"It felt like a prerequisite as a Muslim in America," she told me at a downtown Oakland coffee shop.

After leaving home, Suleiman went to the University of California, Los Angeles, to study, where she also became a board member of the Muslim Student Association. After graduation and moving to the Bay Area, she got a job as a community organizer with Asian Law Caucus, a local advocacy group. She quickly realized that a lot of people, including her own father, take the position that if law enforcement comes to your door, you should help out as much as possible, presuming that you have nothing to hide.

But what most people don't realize, Suleiman said, is that even though most law enforcement officers are "very friendly," it's still a "crime to lie" to them—even when it's unintentional.

"It's your word against theirs—you may misremember something," she said, recalling what she would tell people.

"Never speak with them without an attorney. Ask for their business card and say that your attorney will contact them. People didn't understand that they had a right to refuse and that they [weren't required] to let them enter without a warrant. It could be my father-in-law. It could be my dad, it was very personal."

This background was her foray into how government snooping could be used against Muslims like her.

"The surveillance implications aren't even in the back of anybody's heads," she said. "I feel like if the public really understood the scope of this they would be outraged."

In some ways, Lou Katz is the polar opposite of Suleiman: he's 85, Jewish, and male. But they share many of the same civil liberties concerns. In 1975, Katz founded USENIX, a well-known Unix users' group that continues today—he's the nerdy, lefty grandpa of the Oakland PAC. Throughout the Vietnam era, and into the post-9/11 timeframe, Katz has been concerned about government overreach.

"I was a kid in the Second World War," he told me over coffee. "When they formed the Department of Homeland Security [DHS], the bells and sirens went off. 'Wait a minute, this is the SS, this is the Gestapo!' They were using the same words. They were pulling the same crap that the Nazis had pulled."

Katz got involved as a way to potentially stop a local government program, right in his own backyard, before it got out of control.

"It's hard to imagine a technology whose actual existence should be kept secret," he continued. "Certainly not at the police level. I don't know about at the NSA or CIA level, that's a different thing. NSA's adversary is other nation states, the adversaries in Oakland are, at worst, organized crime."

Serving alongside Katz is Raymundo Jacquez, a 32-year-old attorney with the Centro Legal de la Raza, an immigrants' rights legal group centered in Fruitvale, a largely Latino neighborhood in East Oakland. Jacquez' Oakland-born parents raised him in nearby Hayward with an understanding of ongoing immigrant and minority struggles. It was this upbringing that eventually made him want to be a civil rights attorney.

"This committee has taken on a different feel post-Trump," he said. "You never known who is going to be in power and you never know what is going to happen with the data. We have to shape policies in case there is a Trump running every department."

Rounding out the group is Saied Karamooz, an Iranian-American entrepreneur who unsuccessfully ran for mayor in 2014. He said he first became aware of government surveillance issues in the wake of Snowden. In addition to wanting to help the city, Karamooz wanted to better understand how such issues are worked out at the grassroots level.

"It might be a lost cause—trying to fight the privacy battle," he said. "Because it's a slippery slope that is perpetuated by people who have a vested interest and are dedicated to their cause and their personal pursuits and aspirations, and the people who are trying to fend them off are volunteers and activists."

Karamooz, 53, who spent a career working as a top-level executive for CallidusCloud and Accenture, has now devoted himself to his and his wife's West Oakland beauty products company. He still has an eye towards public service and may run for mayor again.

◯

As the June 1, 2017, meeting was called to order, and no one in the audience wanted to speak, Hofer quipped, "We may see the second half of the Warriors tonight," referring to the underway Game 1 of the NBA Finals.

On this particular night, the PAC first discussed a proposed city law: Non-Cooperation with Identity-Based Registry Ordinance/Internment Ordinance. The bill addressed the city's efforts to not assist in "any government program that creates or compiles a List, Database, or Registry of individuals on the basis of religious affiliation, kinship, belief, or practice; national origin; or ethnicity."

There was a brief exchange between the commissioners about what immigration information the OPD keeps.

Timothy Birch, the non-voting police liaison to the PAC (and himself a former police officer in nearby Daly City), reminded his colleagues that he had initially told them that the OPD does not retain any immigration data. However, seated at one end of the U-shaped table in a suit and tie, Birch was now revising his statement, to elaborate that it did retain that information, but only in situations where people were reporting incidents of human trafficking and may have U or T visas. (Those federal immigration visas are reserved for victims of certain crimes who are helpful to law enforcement or are testifying against human traffickers, respectively.) But, he assured the commissioners, the data was only accessible to around 12 OPD employees.

"This is one of those times when I'm actually glad that OPD doesn't have the systems that people wish it had," he said. "It is literally inaccessible outside of a computer that we have."

Earlier that day, the OPD had published a new public policy on this exact topic.

"We are not the immigration police," Birch tried to reassure the commissioners.

Birch's city counterpart is Joe DeVries, a career city employee who began working as a city council legislative aide two decades earlier. DeVries, who was named as the city's first chief privacy officer in late 2017, is the non-voting liaison for the city government.

After some back-and-forth, the commission moved on to a discussion of how certain OPD databases are shared with various outside agencies and how that impacts Oakland's immigration stance. A printed packet circulated amongst the commissioners listed 20 such databases, ranging from LPR data to CRIMS and ARIES, a county-wide and regional criminal database, respectively.

The rest of the meeting revolved around Hofer's proposal to terminate an agreement between Immigration and Customs Enforcement (ICE) and OPD in the name of promoting Oakland's sanctuary city policy. As a committee, its recommendations must be formally adopted by the city council to take effect. Of course, the PAC can only influence what Oakland itself does. It has no control over the Alameda County Sheriff's Office, the California Highway Patrol, the FBI, ICE, Drug Enforcement Administration (DEA), DHS, or any other federal agency. The meeting adjourned until the following month. Most often, the affected city agencies are notified by Birch or DeVries, and sometimes are invited to speak directly before the PAC.

As of late 2017, the PAC's most comprehensive policy success has been its stingray policy. Since the passage of the California Electronic Communications Privacy Act (CalECPA), California law enforcement agencies must, in nearly all cases, obtain a warrant before using them. But the OPD must now go a few steps further: as of February 2017, stingrays can only be approved by the chief of police or the assistant chief of police. (In an emergency situation, a lieutenant or above must approve.) In either case, each use must be logged, with the name of the user, the reason, and results of each use. In addition, the OPD must provide an annual report that describes those uses, violations of policy (alleged or confirmed), and must describe the "effectiveness of the technology in assisting in investigations based on data collected."

CHAPTER ELEVEN

Who Watches the Watchers?

Quis custodiet ipsos custodes?

—JUVENAL

From *Katz v. United States* to *Riley v. California*, each of these cases has a common theme: law enforcement's actions would have been allowed if they had simply sought a warrant. Had FBI special agents tried to get a warrant to go after Charlie Katz in that Los Angeles phone booth in 1965, they probably would have gotten one. Decades later, had the Oregon National Guardsman worked with the federal prosecutor to seek a warrant, Danny Kyllo might—even now—be behind bars. It's rare that law enforcement is turned down by a judge when they are able to present probable cause of a crime. This is, after all, one of the workaday functions of federal magistrate judges, and of local county judges. In each of those cases, warrants were not sought, and yet law enforcement used its authority to make novel legal interpretations, and employ new surreptitious technologies, be they hidden microphones or infrared cameras.

For now, Fourth Amendment legal analysis primarily turns on two crucial words in the actual text of the Bill of Rights: "searches" and "unreasonable." For the last half century, there has been an entirely new understanding of what is and isn't a search. If there is no search, then generally the action is presumed to be legal. Law enforcement can wantonly drive police cars and indiscriminately scan license plates, as it's not considered a search. Same goes for allowing a "TiVo-in-the-sky" to capture days' worth of human activity down below.

Without a legislative body or a judge to step in, it seems inevitable that these actions will continue to expand through pervasive monitoring, advanced facial recognition, DNA, biochemical analysis, constant location capture via autonomous vehicles, and more.

Today, so long as the search remains "reasonable" and doesn't conflict with an "expectation" that "society is prepared to recognize as reasonable," then law enforcement behavior is permitted. Or, to put it in e-mail spam terms, Fourth Amendment law is basically a blacklist: police actions are generally permitted unless they run into conditions that tell them to stop, such as conducting a physical search of "persons, houses, papers, and effects," which requires a specific warrant.

From the writing of the Constitution up until the 1928 *Olmstead* decision, searches were largely limited to the physical property realm anyway. Then, by the time *Katz* came along, this nebulous notion of "privacy" began to be kicked around, which, according to Justice Antonin Scalia, added to the historic property analysis. But what if our understanding of the Fourth Amendment has been wrong for the last century? What if what the Fourth Amendment is really about isn't property, or even privacy: perhaps it's really about limiting the government's power.

In 1972, just five years after the *Katz* decision, a 36-year-old Stanford Law professor named Anthony Amsterdam convinced the Supreme Court in *Furman v. Georgia* (5–4), to strike down death penalty laws nationwide, and impose a moratorium on the death penalty. Four years later, in *Gregg v. Georgia*, Amsterdam was back at the Supreme Court again, but he was unsuccessful. In *Gregg*, the court ruled 7–2 that the modifications made to various state death penalty laws were sufficient, paving the way for future executions.

However, in between the two Supreme Court cases, in 1974, Amsterdam, then at the height of his celebrity in the legal community, was invited to give the Oliver Wendell Holmes Lecture—a notable talk given every three years by a well-known scholar. Amsterdam, whose celebrity has been likened to the late-1990s and early-2000s star pitcher Pedro Martínez, gave his talk a fairly dry title: "Perspectives on the Fourth Amendment."

At the time, violent crime in America was at one of its highest levels between 1960 and 2010. According to the FBI's Uniform Crime Reports as prepared by the National Archive of Criminal Justice Data, in 1974, there were 20,710 murders and nonnegligent manslaughters around the country, the first time that statistic had ever topped 20,000. In Chicago alone, 970 people were killed that year, a tragic single-year record that stands to this day.

Amsterdam spoke in the waning days of the Nixon administration—he referred to the police as the New Centurions, the title of a 1972 film, and mocked the president's predilection for referring to the police as "peace officers." Over the course of a landmark three-day lecture, the professor went through a comprehensive perspective on the history of the Fourth Amendment, and its modern-day interpretation.

In 1965, the Los Angeles Police Department (LAPD) only had three helicopters. By 1974, the LAPD was up to 15 helicopters. (Today it has 19, the country's largest such municipal unit.) But other than wiretaps and helicopters, police surveillance tactics hadn't advanced much since 1965, when Charlie Katz was strolling down Sunset Boulevard. While the first personal computer, the Xerox Alto, debuted in 1973, it was still largely an obscure research and commercial project, hidden away from most Americans. Mainstream PCs, like the Commodore PET or the Apple II didn't arrive until 1977. The standard kit for law enforcement in most cases didn't go beyond a sidearm and radio.

"An actual, subjective expectation of privacy obviously has no place in a statement of what *Katz* held or in a theory of what the fourth amendment protects," Amsterdam said. "It can neither add to, nor can its absence detract from, an individual's claim to fourth amendment protection. If it could, the government could diminish each person's subjective expectation of privacy merely by announcing half hourly on television that *1984* was being advanced by a decade and that we were all forthwith being placed under comprehensive electronic surveillance. I need hardly add that, for many of us, the announcement would be gratuitous."

He concluded with a pithy quasi-slogan: "Fortunately, neither *Katz* nor the fourth amendment asks what we expect of government. They tell us what we should demand of government."

By the end of his voluminous lecture, Amsterdam reached a clear answer: To stave off government overreach, rather than allow law enforcement to interpret the edges of the law on its own, its power should be exercised with an affirmative authorization to perform that function or use a particular technology. The legislature, or other executive rulemaking body, should outline specifically what is permitted. Any undefined action, such as an e-mail whitelist, would not be allowed by default.

"The fourth amendment is thought to tolerate that power only as the result of a fine balance between its recognized intrusion upon personal privacy and security and its justification by a specific police need," Amsterdam concluded.

While Amsterdam has since gone on to New York University and has devoted his life to death penalty cases, the mantle of his theory has been taken up by various legal scholars including Paul Ohm (Georgetown Law),

Raymond Shih Ray Ku (Case Western Reserve University), and Barry Friedman (New York University), among others.

"Right now, we kind of let the government buy the tech and engage in the search first and then we ask after if it violates [the] Fourth Amendment, as opposed to having accountability from the beginning" Shih told me.

He explained that traditional, conservative notions of law only allow the executive branch—be that a local police force or the FBI—to act when it has been given explicit authorization. However, in recent decades agencies have employed the Hayden-esque policy of playing to the edge rather than waiting for a deliberative, legislative body to grant authorization. In short, the problem isn't just that courts are slow and behind the times—they always will be.

"Technology, honestly, has rapidly advanced so much that the courts are in a quandary," former California Supreme Court justice Kathryn Werdegar told me.

As Friedman concluded in his 2017 book, *Unwarranted*, even small towns have regular, boring, stodgy democratic bodies that perform a variety of functions, including regulating liquor, historic properties, and library policy. There's no reason why cities can't and shouldn't do the same thing.

"Rather than simply telling the police to go forth and enforce the law as they choose, it is essential that we partner with them in determining how," he wrote.

At the federal level, with respect to digital privacy, Congress remains stuck in a sclerotic morass.

"Right now, I will tell you that the Congress does not really want to be asked hard questions about detentions and interrogations and surveillance," Michael Hayden, the former NSA and CIA director, told me. "The Congress is built to diffuse responsibility. They aren't in a position to have personal responsibility for these things. They get to complain when they're too scared, and then they get to complain when they're not scared again."

With partisanship driving the day, and the country divided on a profound level (even before Donald Trump's election to the presidency), a meaningful change to surveillance practices is unlikely anytime soon. After all, the House unanimously passed Electronic Communications Privacy Act reform in 2016 (an astonishing feat in its own right), only to see the Senate not move at all on the bill. For now, some states (notably, California) have stepped in, enhancing privacy protections. The Golden State, for example, under the California Electronic Communications Privacy Act, requires that law enforcement obtain a warrant to use a stingray, get location information, and access the content of e-mail, among other requirements. Since its passage, there has been no dramatic uptick in crime. The sky has not fallen.

While that particular law is broad, it does not adequately address what Amsterdam and his more contemporary disciples remain primarily concerned with: how to come up with policies and procedures that deal with the acquisition and use of surveillance technology in advance, and to have regular check-ups on whether they are being used properly. Numerous academic law articles have reached a similar conclusion—that the legislature, rather than the judiciary, is best suited to guide policy—and many judges (conservatives and liberals alike) have agreed with this answer.

At the federal level, the only body that is remotely close to Oakland's Privacy Advisory Commission (PAC) (besides Congress) is the Privacy and Civil Liberties Oversight Board (PCLOB). Like the PAC, the PCLOB is designed to serve as a check on the government's national security and surveillance policy. However, it has been fraught with problems. For starters, despite being created by statute in 2007, it was not fully staffed and operational until 2013. Since then, it has produced a handful of reports. Second, it is tasked only with conducting after-the-fact analysis, rather than creating policy ahead of time. Notably, in January 2014, a majority of PCLOB members went as far as to declare the NSA's Section 215 metadata program (which was disbanded months later anyway) "illegal." This conclusion came 13 years after Section 215 began.

Worse still, by the time Donald Trump was inaugurated, four of the five PCLOB members had either termed out or resigned, leaving the body without a quorum. One March 2017 article in *McClatchy* noted that the body "barely functions." The White House seems wholly uninterested in reviving it. But the law is on the books for any administration—Republican or Democrat— to bring it back. After all, doing something is better than doing nothing.

Back in Oakland, Saied Karamooz articulated what many legislators should take to heart: "Do you think people have the time to protect their privacy? They don't even know that they've been violated—doing nothing is admitting defeat."

NOTES

vii   **The fantastic advances:** *Lopez v. United States*, 373 U.S. 427 (1963).

vii   **I just hate Fourth:** Justice Antonin Scalia, interview with Susan Swain, C-SPAN, June 19, 2009. Available at: https://www.documentcloud.org/documents /3984805-AScalia.html#document/p13/a373041.

Introduction

xi   **I believe in big data:** Author's interview with Paul Rosenzweig, May 25, 2017.

xii   **"At issue in this case":** *Carpenter v. United States*, 484 U.S. 19-1987 (2017). Available at: https://www.documentcloud.org/documents/4312483-16-402-d102.html.

xiii   **"chalk dust on my cleats":** Michael Hayden, "CIA Director's Address at Duquesne University Commencement" May 4, 2007. Available at: https://www .cia.gov/news-information/speeches-testimony/2007/cia-directors-address -at-duquesne-universitycommencement.html.

xiii   **"order of magnitude":** Cyrus Farivar, "Grand Theft Auto Meets Robocop," *Wired*, June 17, 20015. Available at: https://www.wired.com/2005/06/grand -theft-auto-meets-robocop/

xiv   **Eventually, I found out that LPR:** Ibid.

xiv   **I learned that in the decades:** Convention for the Protection of Individuals with regard to Automatic Processing of Personal Data, Council of Europe (Strasbourg, January 28, 1981). Available at: https://www.coe.int/en/web/conventions /full-list/-/conventions/rms/0900001680078b37.

xiv   **One of Germany's most:** Federal Data Protection Act, Bundesministerium der Justiz and für Verbraucherschutz (January 14, 2003, amended August 13, 2009). Available at: http://www.gesetze-im-internet.de/englisch_bdsg/englisch _bdsg.html#p0013.

xv   **In the United States, no one:** Catherine Bolsover, "German Foreign Minister Joins Criticism of Google's Mapping Program," *Deutsche Welle*, August 14, 2010. Available at: http://www.dw.com/en/german-foreign-minister-joins-criticism -of-googles-mapping-program/a-5910738.

xv   **In the end, Google came up:** "Low Number of Objections: Germans Unfazed by Google Street View," *Der Spiegel International*, October 21, 2010. Available at: http: //www.spiegel.de/international/germany/low-number-of-objections-germans -unfazed-by-google-street-view-a-724369.html.

xv   **But Google gave up:** Matt McGee, "Google has stopped Street View Photography in Germany," Search Engine Land, April 10, 2011. Available at: https://search-engineland.com/google-has-stopped-street-view-photography-germany-72368

xvi   **"Where someone goes can reveal":** Cyrus Farivar, "We Know Where You've Been: Ars Acquires 4.6M License Plate Scans from the Cops," Ars Technica, March 24, 2015. Available at: https://arstechnica.com/tech-policy/2015/03/we-know -where-youve-been-ars-acquires-4-6m-license-plate-scans-from-the-cops/.

xvii **In the latter half of the twentieth century:** Luisa Parraguez Kobek and Erick Caldera, "Cyber Security and *Habeas Data*: The Latin American Response to Information Security and Data Protection," *Oasis* 24 (July–December 2016), pp. 109–128. Available at: http://revistas.uexternado.edu.co/index.php/oasis /article/view/4679/5673.

xvii **However, there is a historical skepticism:** Ellen M. Kirsh, David W. Phillips, and Donna E. McIntyre, "Recommendations for the Evolution of Cyberlaw," *Journal of Computer-Mediated Communication* 2 (September 1996). Available at: http://www.egov.ufsc.br:8080/portal/sites/default/files/anexos/2632-2626-1 -PB.html.

xvii **"If men were angels":** James Madison, *The Federalist* 10 and 51 (1787–1788). Available at: https://www.ourdocuments.gov/doc.php?flash=false&doc=10&page =transcript.

Chapter One

3   **His boss, Burton Marks:** Author's interview with Harvey Schneider, April 17, 2017.

5   **"If you're caught in the middle":** Ibid.

5   **Chief Justice Earl Warren:** "Earl Warren," Oyez. Available at: https://www.oyez .org/justices/earl_warren.

5   **"Number 35, Charles Katz":** *Katz v. United States*, 389 U.S. 347 (1967). Available at: https://supreme.justia.com/cases/federal/us/389/347/case.html.

6   **"The tape was placed":** Schneider told the author during a phone call on August 11, 2017, that during *Katz* oral arguments, rather than "read their homework," he meant to say "done their homework," and rather than "the area of the telephone booth," he meant to say the "airspace of the telephone booth."

7   **Government overreach was:** "Writ of Assistance," Wikipedia. Available at: https://en.wikipedia.org/wiki/Writ_of_assistance.

8   **"every one with this writ may be a tyrant":** James Otis, "Against Writs of Assistance," Superior Court of Massachussets, February 24, 1761. Available at: http://www.constitution.org/bor/otis_against_writs.htm.

9   **But in the nineteenth century:** H. Lee Van Boven, "Electronic Surveillance in California: A Study in State Legislative Control," *California Law Review* 57 (1969), pp. 1182. Available at: https://www.documentcloud.org/documents/3759963 -Electronic-Surveillance-in-California-a-Study-in.html#document/p9/a355569.

9   **And in 1928, the:** Richard F. Hamm, "*Olmstead v. United States*: The Constitutional Challenges of Prohibition Enforcement," *Federal Trials and Great Debates in US History* (Federal Judicial Center, Federal Judicial History Office, 2010). Available at: https://www.documentcloud.org/documents/3727803 -Olmstead.html#document/p13/a361375.

9   **Ultimately, the court found:** By that point, the telephone had been around for decades—but it wasn't until the following year, 1929, that President Herbert Hoover had one installed in the White House.

9   **Writing for the majority opinion:** Chief Justice Taft (1921–1930) had also
     served as president of the United States (1909–1913), the only person to ever
     hold both positions.

9   **"The [Fourth] Amendment":** *Olmstead v. United States*, 277 U.S. 438
     (1928). Available at: https://www.law.cornell.edu/supremecourt/text/277/438
     #writing-USSC_CR_0277_0438_ZO.

10   **The *Katz* case originated:** United States v. The Premises Known as Room 123-
     8400 Sunset Blvd, Sunset Towers West, Los Angeles, California, A. O. 98 Search
     Warrant, Doc. no. 42, Case no. 129 (S.D. Cal., 1965). Available at: https://www
     .documentcloud.org/documents/3475712-Katz-Search-Warrant-Unsigned
     .html#document/p2/a354479.

10   **Nearly every day, agents:** The *Olmstead* and Katz cases had another link, too:
     Mabel Walker Willebrandt's law partner, Fred Horowitz, funded the construc-
     tion of the Chateau Marmont, which opened in 1929.

10   **"Some of these telephone calls":** *United State v. Charles Katz*, No. 34715-CD
     (S.D. Cal., 1965). https://www.documentcloud.org/documents/3523334-34715
     -Transcripts.html#document/p10/a354463.

10   **Katz, it turned out:** Ibid. Available at: https://www.documentcloud.org
     /documents/3523334-34715-Transcripts.html#document/p38/a354466.

11   **He'd been doing it:** Ibid. Available at: https://www.documentcloud.org
     /documents/3523334-34715-Transcripts.html#document/p214/a354475.

11   **After establishing a pattern:** Ibid. Available at: https://www.documentcloud
     .org/documents/3523334-34715-Transcripts.html#document/p141/a354474.

11   **"OUT OF ORDER":** David Sklansky "Katz v. United States: The Limits of Apho-
     rism," *Criminal Procedure Stories* (Foundation Press, 2006) p. 225.

11   **The FBI and the LAPD:** *United State v. Charles Katz*, No. 34715-CD. Available at:
     https://www.documentcloud.org/documents/3523334-34715-Transcripts.html
     #document/p18/a354481.

11   **"We felt in LA":** Author's interview with Joseph Gunn, February 27, 2017.

11   **Gunn was well aware:** *People v. Canard*, No. 11448. (Cal. App. 2d, 1967). Avail-
     able at: https://law.justia.com/cases/california/court-of-appeal/2d/257/444.html.

12   **In the end, two LAPD officers:** Matt Lait, "Police Panel Selects Mayoral Aide,"
     Los Angeles Times, July 10, 1998. Available at: http://articles.latimes.com/1998/jul
     /10/local/me-2385.

11   **The two microphones:** *United State v. Charles Katz*, No. 34715-CD. Available at:
     https://www.documentcloud.org/documents/3523334-34715-Transcripts.html
     #document/p147/a354483.

11   **In addition, agents also:** Author's interview with Joseph Gunn, February 27,
     2017.

12   **After recording Katz':** "FBI Arrests Man Here for Betting on Cage Contests,"
     Los Angeles Times, Sept. 26, 1967 Available at: https://www.documentcloud.org
     /documents/3922216-155115244-1.html.

12   **Armed with a warrant:** *United States v. The Premises* (S.D. Cal., 1965). Available
     at: https://www.documentcloud.org/documents/3475712-Katz-Search-Warrant
     -Unsigned.html.

12   **It was during Katz' two-day:** *United State v. Charles Katz*, No. 34715-CD. Available at: https://www.documentcloud.org/documents/3523334-34715-Transcripts.html#document/p65/a345436.

12   **"I think that *Olmstead*":** Bob Egelko, "Retired Judge Jesse Curtis Jr. Dies at 102," *San Francisco Chronicle,* August 8, 2008.

12   **For example, on December 1, 1907:** "Rights of Privacy Includes Telephone," *The New York Times*, December 1, 1907. Available at: https://www.documentcloud.org/documents/3727732-106769814.html.

13   **In the nineteenth century:** Jason Fagone, *The Woman Who Smashed* Codes (Dey Street Books, 2017).

13   **Of course, this case:** Major J. Andrew White, *Military Signal Corp Manual* (Wireless Press, 1918).

13   **In 1931, no less:** William Grigg, "The Wire-Tapping Controversy: A Symptom of the Times," Duke Bar Journal 4, no. 2 (Summer 1954). Available at: https://www.documentcloud.org/documents/3727902-The-Wire-Tapping-Controversy-a-Symptom-of-the.html#document/p6/a354508.

13   **In 1932, a federal judge:** Associate Press, "Judge Denounces Tapping of Wires," *The New York Times*, December 3, 1932. Available at: https://www.documentcloud.org/documents/3727688-105891871.html.

13   **Two years later:** Communications Act of 1934, Pub.L. 73-416, 48 Stat. 1064. Available at: https://www.documentcloud.org/documents/3727664-41786769082578.html#document/p121/a354487.

13   **However, federal agencies:** Hearings Before the Select Committee to Study Governmental Operations with Respect to Intelligence Activities of the United States Senate, 94th Cong. 1, *Vol. 5: National Security Agency and Fourth Amendment Rights*, October 29 and November 6, 1975, p. 88. Available at: https://www.documentcloud.org/documents/3766735-94intelligence-Activities-V.html#document/p90/a356388.

14   **The first of those cases:** *Goldman v. United States*, 316 U.S. 129 (1942).

14   **Nearly two decades later:** *Silverman v. United States*, 365 U.S. 505 (1961).

15   **Many, including the American Civil Liberties Union:** Associated Press, "Wiretap Bill Hit as Freedom Peril," *The New York Times*, April 5, 1962. Available at: https://www.documentcloud.org/documents/3727648-96964864.html.

15   **In a June 1962:** Robert F. Kennedy, "Attorney General's Opinion on Wiretaps," *The New York Times*, June 3, 1962. Available at: https://www.documentcloud.org/documents/3727574-83495803.html.

15   **By January 1967:** Lyndon Johnson, "Annual Message to the Congress on the State of the Union," American Presidency Project, January 10, 1967. Available at: http://www.presidency.ucsb.edu/ws/index.php?pid=28338.

16   **At the time, nine states:** *Berger v. New York*, 388 U.S. 41 (1967). Available at: https://supreme.justia.com/cases/federal/us/388/41/case.html.

16   **"If anything, the latter":** Ibid.

16   **"They thought they had a *Goldman*":** Author's interview with Harvey Schneider, April 17, 2017.

18   **"The test really asks":** *Katz v. United States*, 389 U.S. 347 (1967).

18   **Brennan's comment:** *Hester v. United States*, 265 U.S. 57 (1924).

18   **"We think** *Hester* **is wrong":** *Katz v. United States*, 389 U.S. 347 (1967).

19   **Then, it was the:** "John S. Martin Jr." Wikipedia. Available at: https://en.wikipedia
        .org/wiki/John_S._Martin_Jr.

19   **Martin called Schneider's:** *Katz v. United States*, 389 U.S. 347 (1967).

20   **"[Fortas] didn't draw":** Author's interview with Laurence Tribe, May 11, 2017.

20   **At the age of 26:** Laurence H. Tribe, "The Constitution in Cyberspace," Key-
        note Address, First Conference on Computers, Freedom and Privacy, Burling-
        ham, CA, 1991. Available at: http://www.sjgames.com/SS/tribe.html.

21   **Plus, it was Justice Stewart:** *Griswold v. Connecticut*, 381 U.S. 479 (1965)

21   **"I had a little bit more spunk":** Author's interview with Laurence Tribe, May
        11, 2017.

21   **"Dragon Lady" was:** Graeme Zielinski, "Margaret McHugh Dies," *The Washing-
        ton Post*, April 4, 2002. Available at: https://www.washingtonpost.com/archive
        /local/2002/04/04/margaret-mchugh-dies/e3fb2813-3201-4e0a-8cb5
        -c770c6c7bb46/?utm_term=.de484ee4ab7e.

21   **"Don't make a nuisance":** Peter Winn, "*Katz* and the Origins of the Reasonable Ex-
        pectations of Privacy Test," *McGeorge Law Review* 40, Issue 1 (2016), p. 2. Available at:
        https://www.documentcloud.org/documents/3475720-05-Winn-Master1MLR40
        .html#document/p2/a355568.

22   **A few days later:** Abe Fortas to Potter Stewart, "Re: No. 35—Katz v. U.S.," *Bren-
        nan Papers*, November 30, 1967. Available at: https://www.documentcloud.org
        /documents/3761752-Ms-0858-s01-b057-f1179.html#document/p12/a355956.

22   **Even Chief Justice Warren:** Earl Warren to Stewart Potter, "Re: No. 35—Katz v.
        U.S.," *Brennan Papers*, November 20, 1967. Available at: https://www.document-
        cloud.org/documents/3761752-Ms-0858-s01-b057-f1179.html#document/p6
        /a355955.

22   **"For the Fourth Amendment":** *Katz v. United States*, 389 U.S. 347 (1967).

22   **Indeed, since then:** Christopher Slobogin and Joseph E. Schumacher, "Rea-
        sonable Expectations of Privacy and Autonomy in Fourth Amendment
        Cases: An Empirical Look at 'Understandings Recognized and Permitted by
        the Public,'" *Duke Law Journal* 42, no. 4 (February 1993). Available at: https:
        //www.documentcloud.org/documents/3759949-Reasonable-Expectations-of
        -Privacy-and-Autonomy.html.

23   *Katz*' **impact was immediately:** Gene Blake, "What Can and Can't Be Done:
        L.A. Police Get Directive on New 'Bugging' Rules," *Los Angeles Times*, Feb-
        ruary 1, 1968. Available at: https://www.documentcloud.org/documents
        /3922218-155831913-1.html#document/p1/a367718.

23   **At a federal level, however:** The President's Commission on Law Enforcement and
        Administration of Justice, *The Challenge of Crime in a Free Society* (Washington, DC:
        United States Government Printing Office, 1967), p. 106. Available at: https://www
        .documentcloud.org/documents/3728666-42.html#document/p106/a355595.

23   **Congress largely incorporated:** Pub.L. 90-351, 82 Stat. 197, enacted June 19,
        1968, codified at 34 U.S.C. § 10101 et seq. Available at: https://www.law.cornell
        .edu/topn/omnibus_crime_control_and_safe_streets_act_of_1968.

24   **The law also included:** Title III of The Omnibus Crime Control and Safe Streets Act of 1968, Pub. L. 90-351; 6/19/68, 18 U.S.C. §§ 2510-22. Available at: https://it.ojp.gov/PrivacyLiberty/authorities/statutes/1284.

24   **only as part of a super-warrant:** "Procedure for Interception of Wire, Oral, or Electronic Communications," 18 U.S. Code § 2518. Available at: https://www.law .cornell.edu/uscode/text/18/2518.

24   **Further, the federal judge:** "Title III Procedures: Attachment C," Office of the United States Attorney, US Department of Justice, December 2008. Available at: https://www.justice.gov/usam/criminal-resource-manual-92-title -iii-procedures-attachment-c.

24   **But even at the time:** Lyndon Johnson, "Statement by the President Upon Signing the Omnibus Crime Control and Safe Streets Act of 1968," American Presidency Project, June 19, 1968. Available at: http://www.presidency.ucsb.edu /ws/?pid=28939.

24   **There are some more:** *California v. Greenwood*, 486 U.S. 35 (1988).

24   **Taken one step further:** *United States v. Scott*, 975 F.2d 927 (1st Cir., 1992).

24   **Does a criminal have:** *United States v. Caymen*, 404 F.3d 1196 (9th Cir., 2005). Available at: http://www.leagle.com/decision/20051600404F3d1196_11483/U.S. v. CAYMEN.

24   **Does a burglar who:** Cyrus Farivar, "Crook Who Left His Phone at the Scene Has 'No Reasonable Expectation of Privacy,'" Ars Technica, June 23, 2016. Available at: https://arstechnica.com/tech-policy/2016/06/crook-who-left-his-phone -at-the-scene-has-no-reasonable-expectation-of-privacy/.

24   **More recently, a federal:** *United States v. Brian Farrell*, NO. CR15-029RAJ (W.D. Wash. 2016). Available at: https://www.documentcloud.org/documents /2719591-Farrell-Weds.html#document/p3/a279648.

24   **After all, there's not:** https://www.wilmerhale.com/louis_cohen/.

24   **"The rule that we are creating":** Author's interview with Louis Cohen, May 24, 2017.

Chapter Two

26   **From the beginning:** *United States v. New York Telephone Co.*, 434 U.S. 159 (1977).

26   **It was something of a chilly:** Author's interview with Ted Boutrous, May 2, 2017.

26   **He was expecting a call:** Apple did not make Krall, or any of its own lawyers, available for an interview.

26   **She wanted to speak with:** Author's interview with Ted Boutrous, May 2, 2017.

27   **Krall joined Apple in March:** Katie Marsal, "Apple's Chief Counsel Profiled as 'Field Marshal' in Fight Against Android," *Apple Insider*, September 10, 2012. Available at: http://appleinsider.com/articles/12/09/10/apples_chief_counsel _profiled_as_field_marshal_in_fight_against_android.

28   On that Tuesday, February 16, 2016: UNITED STATES V. IN THE MATTER OF THE SEARCH OF AN APPLE IPHONE, GOVERNMENT'S EX PARTE AP-

PLICATION, ED NO. 15-0451M, February 16, 2016. https://www.documentcloud
.org/documents/2714000-SB-Shooter-MOTION-Seeking-Asst-iPhone.html
#document/p14/a278095.

29   **US Magistrate Judge Sheri Pym:** UNITED STATES V. IN THE MATTER OF
THE SEARCH OF AN APPLE IPHONE, ORDER COMPELLING APPLE, ED
NO. 15-0451M, February 16, 2016. https://www.documentcloud.org/documents
/2714001-SB-Shooter-Order-Compelling-Apple-Asst-iPhone.html.

29   **"It was extraordinary and unheard of":** Author's interview with Ted Boutrous,
May 2, 2017.

29   **"We indicated that we thought":** Author's interview with Ted Boutrous, June
27, 2017.

30   **Although he was born in Los Angeles:** Josh Beser, "Ted Boutrous on the
Trump Admin, the First Amendment, And Why Now Is Such an Exciting Time
for Journalism," JDSupra, March 31, 2017. Available at: http://www.jdsupra
.com/legalnews/ted-boutros-on-the-trump-admin-the-26536/.

30   **According to a 2007 profile:** Abigail Goldman, "He's a Hired Gun of the Highest
Caliber," *Los Angeles Times*, June 24, 2007. Available at: http://articles.latimes
.com/2007/jun/24/business/fi-sunprofile24

30   **"Being able to have both a job":** Josh Beser, "Ted Boutrous on the Trump Admin, the First Amendment, And Why Now Is Such an Exciting Time for Journalism," JDSupra, March 31, 2017. Available at: http://www.jdsupra.com/legalnews
/ted-boutros-on-the-trump-admin-the-26536/.

30   **Noted conservative attorney:** https://www.gibsondunn.com/lawyer/olson
-theodore-b/.

31   **Boutrous is probably most famous:** *Wal-Mart v. Dukes*, 564 U.S. 338 (2011).

31   **Dukes won at the 9th US Circuit:** David Kravets, "Court Says Wal-Mart Must
Face Bias Trial," Associated Press, February 6, 2007. Available at: http://www
.chicagotribune.com/business/sns-ap-wal-mart-discrimination-story.html.

31   **More recently, Boutrous:** Cyrus Farivar, "Startup Workers Sue to Be Recognized As Employees, Not Mere Contractors," Ars Technica, March 26, 2013.
Availabe at: http://arstechnica.com/tech-policy/2015/03/startup-workers-sue
-to-be-recognized-as-employees-not-mere-contractors/.

31   **This case, along with dozens:** Cyrus Farivar, "Judge Expresses Notable Concerns over Proposed $100M Settlement in Uber Case," Ars Technica, June 2,
2016. Available at: https://arstechnica.com/tech-policy/2016/06/most-drivers-in
-uber-labor-case-would-get-under-25-so-some-protest-settlement/.

32   **Within hours of the judge's order:** Eileen Decker, "Statement of United States
Attorney Eileen M. Decker in Response to Court Order Directing Apple to Assist
FBI in Accessing iPhone Used by Syed Rizwan Farook," Department of Justice,
February 16, 2016. Available at: https://www.documentcloud.org/documents
/3863397-Sb-Shooter-Iphone-Access-Usa-Statement.html.

32   **"We have made a solemn commitment":** Decker did not respond to repeated
requests by the author for an interview.

32   **On Twitter, Decker's office:** Andrew Blankstein, "Judge Forces Apple to Help
Unlock San Bernardino Shooter iPhone," *NBC News*, February 16, 2016. Avail-

able at: http://www.nbcnews.com/storyline/san-bernardino-shooting/judge-forces-apple-help-unlock-san-bernardino-shooter-iphone-n519701.

32 **Moreover, 77 percent:** "Mobile Fact Sheet," Pew Research Center, January 12, 2017. Available at: http://www.pewinternet.org/fact-sheet/mobile/.

32 **When the NSA's Section 215:** Cyrus Farivar, "Secret Court Declassifies Opinion Providing Rationale for Metadata Sharing," Ars Technica, September 17, 2013. Available at: https://arstechnica.com/tech-policy/2013/09/secret-court-declassifies-opinion-providing-rationale-for-metadata-sharing/.

33 **"They were taking this very aggressive position"** : Author's interview with Ted Boutrous, May 2, 2017.

33 **When the clock struck midnight:** Sebastian Anthony, "Tim Cook Says Apple Will Fight US Gov't Over Court-Ordered iPhone Backdoor," Ars Technica, February 17, 2016. Available at: https://arstechnica.com/gadgets/2016/02/tim-cook-says-apple-will-fight-us-govt-over-court-ordered-iphone-backdoor/.

33 **"We have great respect":** Tim Cook, "A Message to our Customers," February 16, 2016. https://www.apple.com/customer-letter/.

34 **Seventy-two hours later:** UNITED STATES V. IN THE MATTER OF THE SEARCH OF AN APPLE IPHONE, GOVERNMENT'S MOTION TO COMPEL, February 19, 2016. https://www.documentcloud.org/documents/2715997-Apple-iPhone-Access-MOTION-to-COMPEL.html.

34 **The entire text of the law:** 28 U.S. Code § 1651. Available at: https://www.law.cornell.edu/uscode/text/28/1651.

35 **The two-sentence law:** Dimitri Portnoi, "RESORTING TO EXTRAORDINARY WRITS: HOW THE ALL WRITS ACT RISES TO FILL THE GAPS IN THE RIGHTS OF ENEMY COMBATANTS," New York University Law Review, December 10, 2007. Available at: https://www.documentcloud.org/documents/3863455-SSRN-id1009340.html#document/p11/a357561.

35 **In 1995, it was used:** US v. William Li, Nos. 94-2630, Reply Brief for Defendant (7th Cir. 1995). Available; at: https://www.documentcloud.org/documents/3863512-United-States-of-America.html#document/p40/a357643.

35 **In 2005, it was invoked:** Thomas F. Liotti, "Enjoining State Courts under the All Writs Act," The Nassau Lawyer, October 2010. Available at: https://www.nassaubar.org/Articles/Archive/Article345.aspx.

35 **In 2012, it was used:** Order Granting Application Under the All Writs Act, US v. Ramona Camelia Fricosu, 1:10-cr-00509-REB, USDC Colorado, 2012. Available at: https://www.documentcloud.org/documents/3863634-Decrypt.html.

35 **As Jonathan Mayer, then:** Jonathan Mayer, "Assistance for Current Surveillance," Stanford University, November 28, 2014. Available at: https://www.youtube.com/watch?v=PoNJvmB16bQ.

35 **In March 1976:** Preliminary Memorandum, *United States v. New York Telephone Co.*, 434 U.S. 159 (1977). https://www.documentcloud.org/documents/3727203-76-835-US-NewYorkTelephoneCo.html#document/p2/a396623.

36 **"These devices do not hear sound":** *United States v. New York Telephone Co.*, 434 U.S. 159 (1977). Available at: https://www.law.cornell.edu/supremecourt/text/434/159.

37   **This entire question of modern cryptography:** Whitfield Diffie and Martin
      E. Hellman, "New Directions in Cryptography," IEEE Transactions on In-
      formation Theory, Vol. IT 22, No 6, November 1976 Available at: https://www
      .documentcloud.org/documents/3866958-24.html.

38   **Others expounded upon:** Vin McLellan, "Data Network to Use Code to Insure
      Privacy," *The New York Times*, March 21, 1989. Available at: http://www.nytimes
      .com/1989/03/21/business/data-network-to-use-code-to-insure-privacy.html.

38   **Mailsafe:** Harold Joseph Highland, "Encryption packages offer business us-
      ers a choice," *Computerworld*, July 13, 1987. Available at: https://books.google
      .com/books?id=-_HA2pUErI8C&pg=PT94&dq=%22rsa+mailsafe%22&hl=en
      &sa=X&ved=oahUKEwjDrPHLhMPUAhWV8oMKHdVwBhoQ6AEIMTAC
      #v=onepage&q=%22rsa%20mailsafe%22&f=false.

38   **Around that same time, Phil Zimmerman:** Steven Levy, *Crypto* (Penguin
      Books, 2002), p. 191.

38   **Pretty Good Privacy:** John Markoff, "Move on Unscrambling Of Messages Is
      Assailed," *The New York Times*, April 17, 1991. Available at: http://www.nytimes
      .com/1991/04/17/business/move-on-unscrambling-of-messages-is-assailed.html.

38   **"to obtain the plaintext contents":** Joseph Biden, "All Information (Except
      Text) for S.266 - Comprehensive Counter-Terrorism Act of 1991," January 24,
      1991. https://www.congress.gov/bill/102nd-congress/senate-bill/266/all-info.

39   **This notion ended up becoming:** Office of the Press Secretary, "Statement
      by the Press Secretary," April 16, 1993. Available at: http://cd.textfiles.com
      /hackersencyc/PC/CRYPTO/CLIPPER.TXT.

39   **Clipper chip would not:** John Markoff, "Big Brother and the Computer Age,"
      The New York Times, May 6, 1993. Available at: http://www.nytimes.com
      /1993/05/06/business/big-brother-and-the-computer-age.html.

39   **Many of them—notably FBI:** Levy, p. 245.

39   **In 1995, Kallstrom:** James C. McKinley, Jr., "Wiretap Expert Named to Head
      New York City Office of F.B.I.," *The New York Times*, February 17, 1995. Avail-
      able at: http://www.nytimes.com/1995/02/17/nyregion/wiretap-expert-named
      -to-head-new-york-city-office-of-fbi.html.

39   **Over 1993 and 1994:** Testimony of Jerry J. Berman, Executive Director Elec-
      tronic Frontier Foundation before the Committee on Science, Space and Tech-
      nology Subcommittee on Technology, Environment and Aviation U.S. House
      of Representatives Hearing on Communications and Computer Surveillance,
      Privacy and Security, May 3, 1993. Available at: https://totseans.com/totse/en
      /zines/cud_a/cud644.html.

40   **Not a month later, a young AT&T:** John Markoff, "Flaw Discovered in Plan for Fed-
      eral Wiretapping," *The New York Times*, June 2, 1994. Available at: http://www.ny-
      times.com/1994/06/02/us/flaw-discovered-in-federal-plan-for-wiretapping.html.

40   **one of Clipper chip's critical flaws:** Matt Blaze's Clipper attack—details, sci.
      crypt, May 3, 1994. Available at: https://groups.google.com/d/msg/sci.crypt
      /J5QT1l6t8Vk/3howjM9tNxoJ.

40   **By the summer, the White House:** "White House Wants a Clipper Alterna-
      tive," *Washington Technology*, July 14, 1994. Available at: https://washington-

technology.com/articles/1994/07/14/white-house-wants-a-clipper-alternative
.aspx?m=.1

40 **But at the same time:** Anthony Ramirez, "FBI's Proposal on Wiretaps Criticized by Federal Agency," *The New York Times*, January 15, 1993. Available at: http://www.nytimes.com/1993/01/15/us/fbi-s-proposal-on-wiretaps-criticized-by-federal-agency.html

40 **And in the end, the FBI's efforts:** John Markoff, "Big Brother and the Computer Age," *The New York Times*, May 6, 1993. Available at: http://www.nytimes.com/1993/05/06/business/big-brother-and-the-computer-age.html.

40 **The law primarily targeted:** Nate Anderson, *The Internet Police* (W. W. Norton & Company, 2014). p. 107.

40 **Crucially, the law does:** 47 U.S. Code § 1002. Available at: https://www.law.cornell.edu/uscode/text/47/1002.

40 **In late June 1996:** Philip Zimmermann, "Testimony of Philip R. Zimmermann to the Subcommittee on Science, Technology, and Space of the US Senate Committee on Commerce, Science, and Transportation," June 26, 1996. Available at: http://www.philzimmermann.com/EN/testimony/index.html.

41 **In 2000, the public:** John Schwartz, "FBI's Internet Wiretaps Raises Privacy Concerns," *The Washington Post*, July 12, 2000. Available at: https://www.washingtonpost.com/archive/politics/2000/07/12/fbis-internet-wiretaps-raise-privacy-concerns/2bc839c0-d5f0-4d96-85b6-390d49e59fb2/?utm_term=.1a473bab125e.

41 **Years later, Thomas:** Subsentio, "Former FBI Official Takes Charge of Tech Development at U.S. Surveillance Industry's Leading Lawful Intercept Service Bureau," December 10, 2013. Available at: http://www.subsentio.com/ssio_pr/subsentio-names-marcus-thomas-chief-technology-officer/.

41 **"Everything is digging":** Author's interview with Marcus Thomas, August 2, 2017.

41 **One notable and creative:** Thomas Fox-Brewster, "Cartapping: How Feds Have Spied on Connected Cars for 15 Years," *Forbes*, January 15, 2017. Available at: https://www.forbes.com/sites/thomasbrewster/2017/01/15/police-spying-on-car-conversations-location-siriusxm-gm-chevrolet-toyota-privacy/.

41 **ATX had to remotely activate:** In the matter of the emergency application for an order compelling ATX Technologies to show cause, 2:01-cv-01495-LDG, USDC Nevada, December 19, 2001. Available at: https://www.documentcloud.org/documents/3868115-Show-Temp-55.html.

41 **The company attempted:** In the matter of the application of the United States for an order authorizing the roving interception, 2:01-cv-01495-LDG, USDC Nevada, December 21, 2001. Available at: https://www.documentcloud.org/documents/3868114-Show-Temp-56.html.

42 **Then, on January 10, 2002:** ATX motion to reconsider, In the matter of the application of the United States for an order authorizing the roving interception, 2:01-cv-01495-LDG, USDC Nevada, February 8, 2002. Available at https://www.documentcloud.org/documents/3868117-Show-Temp-57.html#document/p2/a358580.

42   **"In order to comply"**: Ibid. https://www.documentcloud.org/documents /3868117-Show-Temp-57.html#document/p7/a358607.

42   **"The question remains whether"**:. Opinion, The Company v. United States, No. 02-15635, DC No. CV-01-01495-LDG, November 18, 2003. Available at: https://www .documentcloud.org/documents/3868104-629.html#document/p22/a358610.

42   **"The FBI, however well-intentioned"**: Ibid. https://www.documentcloud.org/ documents/3868104-629.html#document/p25/a358612.

42   **Over a decade later:** Apple Inc's reply brief to government's opposition, In the Matter of the Search of an Apple iPhone, ED No. CM 16-10 (SP), USDC Central California, March 15, 2016. https://www.documentcloud.org/documents /2762147-Reply-Brief-in-Support-of-Apple-s-Motion-to-Vacate.html #document/p13/a283423.

42   **"if you give a mouse a cookie":** Laura Numeroff, *If You Give a Mouse a Cookie* (HarperCollins, 1985).

43   **The All Writs Act cropped up:** In the Matter of an Application of the United States for an Order, 2:05-mj-01093-JO, Memorandum and Order, August 25, 2005. Available at: https://www.documentcloud.org/documents /3868140-12311369538.html.

43   **The government's legal argument:** "Searching and Seizing Computers and Obtaining Electronic Evidence in Criminal Investigations," Department of Justice, 2004. https://www.documentcloud.org/documents/3868141-Searching -Seizing-Computers-and-Obtaining.html#document/p172/a358622.

43   **In other words, Judge Orenstein:** "Magistrate Judge James Orenstein," USDC Eastern District of New York. Available at: https://www.nyed.uscourts.gov /content/magistrate-judge-james-orenstein.

44   **The government was not pleased:** AUSA Letter to Magistrate Judge Orenstein, September 9, 2005. https://www.documentcloud.org/documents/3868137 -1231936443.html.

44   **A week later, an outside group:** EFF Letter to Judge James Orenstein, September 23, 2005. Available at: https://www.documentcloud.org/documents /3868138-EFF-letter-to-Judge-Orenstein-Sept-23-2005.html.

44   **The dispute largely turned:** 47 U.S. Code § 1002. Available at: https://www.law .cornell.edu/uscode/text/47/1002.

44   **The government interpreted:** "Searching and Seizing Computers and Obtaining Electronic Evidence in Criminal Investigations," Department of Justice, 2004. https://www.documentcloud.org/documents/3868141-Searching-Seizing -Computers-and-Obtaining.html#document/p172/a358622.

44   **The organization felt that:** EFF Letter to Judge James Orenstein, September 23, 2005. Available at: https://www.documentcloud.org/documents/3868138-EFF -letter-to-Judge-Orenstein-Sept-23-2005.html.

45   **On October 11, 2005:** AUSA response to EFF, October 11, 2005. Available at: https: //www.documentcloud.org/documents/3868136-12312009118.html#document /p8/a358614.

45   **"Thus, as far as I can tell":** In the Matter of an Application of the United States for an Order, 2:05-mj-01093-JO, Memorandum and Order, August 25, 2005.

Available at: https://www.documentcloud.org/documents/3868139-1231998558
.html#document/p55/a358621.

45 **In 2006, the FBI created:** "FBI Announces Restructuring," FBI, July 26, 2006.
Available at: https://archives.fbi.gov/archives/news/pressrel/press-releases
/fbi-announces-restructuring.

45 **"In today's digital world":** Vanessa Thomas, "High-tech lab fights crime of digital
age," Buffalo News, September 8, 2006. Available at: https://www.rcfl.gov/western
-new-york/news/high-tech-lab-fights-crime-of-digital-age-fbis-1-5-million
-facility-can-recover-data-zero-in-on-such-offenses-as-child-pornography.

45 **In fact, the same month:** "Marcus C. Thomas Named Assistant Director of the
Operational Technology Division," FBI, January 5, 2007. Available at: https:
//archives.fbi.gov/archives/news/pressrel/press-releases/marcus-c.-thomas
-named-assistant-director-of-the-operational-technology-division.

45 **assistant director of the Operational Technology Division:** "FBI Experts Deliver Technical Tools," FBI, November 7, 2008. Available at: https://cryptome.org
/eyeball/fbi-otd/fbi-otd-eyeball.htm.

45 **By at least early 2008:** CTO Marcus Thomas: "The Wicked Problem of Going Dark." Available at: http://www.subsentio.com/cto-marcus-thomas-wicked
-problem-going-dark/.

46 **What worried Haynes and Thomas:** FBI FOIA response, December 17, 2010.
https://www.documentcloud.org/documents/3868150-20110207-Fbi-Going
-Dark-Release-Part-1.html#document/p2/a360128.

46 **In 2009, the FBI asked:** FBI Budget Request Fiscal Year 2010. Available at: https:
//www.documentcloud.org/documents/3866762-Fbi-Bud-Summary-2011
.html#document/p3/a358428.

46 **By FY 2017:** James Comey, Statement Before the House Appropriations Committee, Subcommittee on Commerce, Justice, Science, and Related Agencies Washington, D.C. February 25, 2016 FBI Budget Request for Fiscal Year 2017. Available
at: https://www.fbi.gov/news/testimony/fbi-budget-request-for-fiscal-year-2017.

46 **"We're talking about lawfully":** Charlie Savage, "U.S. Tries to Make It Easier
to Wiretap the Internet," *The New York Times,* September 27, 2010. http://www
.nytimes.com/2010/09/27/us/27wiretap.html?pagewanted=all

46 **"Many agencies that need":** Statement of Chief Mark Marshall President International Association of Chiefs of Police Before the Committee on the Judiciary
Subcommittee on Crime, Terrorism and Homeland Security United States
House of Representatives February 17, 2011. Available at: https://www.document-
cloud.org/documents/3868110-Marshall02172011.html#document/p3/a360129.

47 **For the most part, mainstream:** 2010 Report of the Director of the Adminis-
trative Office of the United States Courts on Applications for Orders Authorizing or Approving the Interception of Wire, Oral, or Electronic Communications. Available at: https://www.documentcloud.org/documents/3879529
-2010wiretapreport.html#document/p7/a360130.

47 **"The lock screen is merely":** Jonathan Zdziarski, "Your iOS device isn't as encrypted as you think," April 18, 2013. Available at: https://www.zdziarski.com
/blog/?p=2149.

47   **However, everyone's notion:** Dan Goodin, "Guardian Reporter Delayed E-mail-
        ing NSA Source Because Crypto Is a Pain," Ars Technica, June 11, 2013. Available at:
        https://arstechnica.com/security/2013/06/guardian-reporter-delayed-e-mailing
        -nsa-source-because-crypto-is-a-pain/.

47   **Within months, companies began hardening:** Sean Gallagher, "Googlers Say
        'F*** You' to NSA, Company Encrypts Internal Network," Ars Technica, No-
        vember 6, 2013. Available at: https://arstechnica.com/information-technology
        /2013/11/googlers-say-f-you-to-nsa-company-encrypts-internal-network/;
        Sean Gallagher, "Yahoo Will Encrypt Between Data Centers, Use SSL for All
        Sites," Ars Technica, November 18, 2013. Available at: http://arstechnica.com
        /information-technology/2013/11/yahoo-will-encrypt-between-data-centers
        -use-ssl-for-all-sites/; Sean Gallagher, "Microsoft to Harden Networks, Code
        Against Government Snooping," Ars Technica, December 5, 2013. Available at:
        https://arstechnica.com/information-technology/2013/12/microsoft-to-harden
        -networks-code-against-government-snooping/.

47   **"Recent press stories have reported":** Jeffrey Meisner, "Protecting Customer
        Data from Government Snooping," Microsoft Blog, December 4, 2013. Available
        at: https://blogs.technet.microsoft.com/microsoft_blog/2013/12/04/protecting
        -customer-data-from-government-snooping/.

48   **The term came from an April 2014:** Ann E. Marimow and Craig Timberg,
        "Low-Level Federal Judges Balking at Law Enforcement Requests for Electronic
        Evidence," *The Washington Post*, April 24, 2014. Available at: https://www
        .washingtonpost.com/local/crime/low-level-federal-judges-balking
        -at-law-enforcement-requests-for-electronic-evidence/2014/04/24/eec81748
        -c01b-11e3-b195-dd0c1174052c_story.html?utm_term=.a94945fb82ee.

48   **The article focused on:** Cyrus Farivar, "Judge Denies Gov't Request to Search
        Suspect's iPhone in Ricin Case," Ars Technica, March 26, 2014. Available at:
        https://arstechnica.com/tech-policy/2014/03/judge-denies-govt-request-to
        -search-suspects-iphone-in-ricin-case/.

49   **"On devices running iOS":** Cyrus Farivar, "Apple Expands Data Encryption
        Under iOS 8, Making Handover to Cops Moot," Ars Technica, September 18,
        2014. Available at: https://arstechnica.com/apple/2014/09/apple-expands-data
        -encryption-under-ios-8-making-handover-to-cops-moot/.

49   **That same day, in an open letter:** "A message from Tim Cook about Apple's com-
        mitment to your privacy." September 18, 2014. Available at: https://web.archive
        .org/web/20141112091320/https://www.apple.com/privacy/

49   **Google followed suit the next day:** Craig Timberg, "Newest Androids Will
        Join iPhones in Offering Default Encryption, Blocking Police," *The Wash-
        ington Post*, September 18, 2014. https://www.washingtonpost.com/news/the
        -switch/wp/2014/09/18/newest-androids-will-join-iphones-in-offering-default
        -encryption-blocking-police/?utm_term=.17ccabf42fca.

49   **Government officials were not going:** Brent Kendall, "FBI Director Raises Con-
        cerns About Smartphone-Security Plans," *Wall Street Journal*, September 25, 2014.
        Available at: http://online.wsj.com/articles/fbi-director-raises-concerns-about
        -smartphone-security-plans-1411671434?mod=WSJ_TechWSJD_NeedToKnow.

49   **"It is fully possible to permit law enforcement":** Craig Timberg, "Holder
           Urges Tech Companies to Leave Device Backdoors Open for Police," *The Wash-*
           ington Post, September 30, 2014. Available at: https://www.washingtonpost.
           com/news/the-switch/wp/2014/09/30/holder-urges-tech-companies-to-leave
           -device-backdoors-open-for-police/?utm_term=.324a4cd7ae49.

50   **The next month, they took:** James Cole declined the author's invitation to be
           interviewed for this book.

50   **According to the *Wall Street Journal*:** Devlin Barrett, Danny Yadron, and
           Daisuke Wakabayashi, "Apple and Others Encrypt Phones, Fueling Gov-
           ernment Standoff," *Wall Street Journal*, November 18, 2014. Available at:
           http://online.wsj.com/articles/apple-and-others-encrypt-phones-fueling
           -government-standoff-1416367801.

50   **As 2014 drew to a close:** Cyrus Farivar, "Feds Want Apple's Help to De-
           feat Encrypted Phones, New Legal Case Shows," Ars Technica, Decem-
           ber 1, 2014. Available at: https://arstechnica.com/tech-policy/2014/12/feds
           -want-apples-help-to-defeat-encrypted-phones-new-legal-case-shows/.

50   **"This Court has the authority":** In re Order Requiring Apple, CR 14-90812,
           November 3, 2014. Available at: https://www.documentcloud.org/documents
           /1372280-apple-oakland.html.

50   **"Backdoors create unnecessary":** Cyrus Farivar, "Irate Congressman
           Gives Cops Easy Rule: 'Just Follow the Damn Constitution,'" Ars Technica,
           April 30, 2015. Available at: https://arstechnica.com/tech-policy/2015/04/irate
           -congressman-gives-cops-easy-rule-just-follow-the-damn-constitution/.

51   **Echoing this lack of understanding:** Written Testimony of New York County
           District Attorney Cyrus R. Vance, Jr. Before the United States Senate Committee
           on the Judiciary "Going Dark: Encryption, Technology, and the Balance Between
           Public Safety and Privacy," Washington, D.C. July 8, 2015. Available at: https:
           //www.documentcloud.org/documents/3882428-07-08-15-Vance-Testimony
           .html#document/p17/a360447.

51   **As 2016 rolled around:** Cyrus Farivar, "Bill Aims to Thwart Strong Crypto,
           Demands Smartphone Makers Be Able to Decrypt," Ars Technica, January
           14, 2016. Available at: https://arstechnica.com/tech-policy/2016/01/bill-aims-to
           -thwart-strong-crypto-demands-smartphone-makers-be-able-to-decrypt/;
           Cyrus Farivar, "Yet Another Bill Seeks to Weaken Encryption-By-Default on
           Smartphones," Ars Technica, January 21, 2016. Available at: https://arstechnica
           .com/tech-policy/2016/01/yet-another-bill-seeks-to-weaken-encryption-by
           -default-on-smartphones/; Associated Press, "Louisiana Lawmaker Shelves Bill
           to Give Police Access to Locked Phones," *Baton Rouge Advocate*, May 3, 2016.
           Available at: http://www.theadvocate.com/baton_rouge/news/politics/legislature
           /article_bc5ea2e0-57e0-5ab6-8181-3051e2c66834.html.

52   **Later that day, Trump:** Tim Higgins and Kevin Cirilli, "Trump Urges Boycott of
           Apple Until It Unlocks Terrorist's iPhone," *Bloomberg*, February 19, 2016. Avail-
           able at: https://www.bloomberg.com/news/articles/2016-02-19/trump-calls-for
           -apple-boycott-until-company-unlocks-terrorist-s-iphone.

52   **During the Friday call:** Cyrus Farivar, "Apple: We Tried to Help FBI Terror Probe, but Someone Changed iCloud Password," Ars Technica, February 19, 2016. Available at: https://arstechnica.com/tech-policy/2016/02/apple-we-tried -to-help-fbi-terror-probe-but-someone-changed-icloud-password/.

52   **Two days later, FBI Director:** FBI Director Comments on San Bernardino Matter, February 21, 2016. https://www.fbi.gov/news/pressrel/press-releases/fbi -director-comments-on-san-bernardino-matter.

53   **The following day, February 22:** "Email to Apple employees from Apple CEO Tim Cook," February 22, 2016. Available at: https://www.documentcloud.org /documents/2716997-Tim-Cook-Emails-Apple-Employees.html.

53   **While all of this was going on:** David Kravets, "Trump Urges Supporters to Boycott Apple in Wake of Encryption Brouhaha," Ars Technica, February 19, 2016. Available at: https://arstechnica.com/tech-policy/2016/02/trump-urges -supporters-to-boycott-apple-in-wake-of-encryption-brouhaha/.

53   **The New York case:** Cyrus Farivar, "Feds: Since Apple Can Unlock iPhone 5S Running iOS 7, It Should," Ars Technica, October 24, 2015. Available at: http://arstechnica.com/tech-policy/2015/10/feds-since-apple-can -unlock-iphone-5s-running-ios-7-it-should/.

53   **Nine days later, defendant:** Guilty Plea, US v. Jun Feng, 1:14-cr-00387-MKB, October 30, 2015. Available at: https://www.documentcloud.org/documents /2499370-jun-feng-guilty-plea.html.

53   **In the government's own filing:** Guilty Plea, US v. Jun Feng, 1:14-cr-00387-MKB, October 30, 2015. Available at: https://www.documentcloud.org /documents/2711972-123111286409.html#document/p1/a277213.

53   **Later, a more senior judge:** Cyrus Farivar, "Feds: Someone Gave Us the Passcode in NY Drug Case, So We Don't Need Apple," Ars Technica, April 22, 2016. Available at: https://arstechnica.com/tech-policy/2016/04/feds-someone-gave -us-the-passcode-in-ny-drug-case-so-we-dont-need-apple/.

53   **Orenstein's conclusion largely echoed:** Memorandum and Order, In re order requiring Apple, 15-MC-1902, February 29, 2016. Available at: https://www .documentcloud.org/documents/2728314-Orenstein-Order.html.

54   **Days later, on March 1, 2016:** Josh Constine, "Obama: 'We Don't Want Government to Look into Everyone's Phones Willy-Nilly,'" Tech Crunch, March 11, 2016. Available at: https://techcrunch.com/2016/03/11/obama-says-we-dont-want -government-to-look-into-everyones-phones-willy-nilly/.

55   **"A lot. More than":** Julia Edwards, "FBI Paid More than $1.3 Million to Break into San Bernardino iPhone," Reuters, April 21, 2016. Available at: https://www .reuters.com/article/us-apple-encryption-fbi/fbi-paid-more-than-1-3-million -to-break-into-san-bernardino-iphone-idUSKCN0XI2IB?feedType=RSS &feedName=technologyNews&utm_source=feedburner&utm_medium=feed &utm_campaign=Feed%3A+reuters%2FtechnologyNews+%28Reuters +Technology+News%29.

56   **"I'm not going to describe":** Jon Brodkin, "FBI Can't Break the Encryption on Texas Shooter's Smartphone," Ars Technica, November 8, 2017. Available

at: https://arstechnica.com/information-technology/2017/11/fbi-cant-break-the
-encryption-on-texas-shooters-smartphone/.

Chapter Three

57   **By virtually ignoring data:** Arthur Miller, *The Assault on Privacy* (Signet, 1970).

57   **Sachs explained to his wife:** In re Application, US Foreign Intelligence Surveil-
lanceCourt,BR13-109.Availableat:https://www.documentcloud.org/documents
/3819997-br13-09-Primary-Order-1.html#document/p6/a356443.

58   **Sachs served as an assistant:** Gadi Dechter, "Surveillance Was 'Misguided,'"
Baltimore Sun, October 2, 2008. Available at: http://www.baltimoresun.com
/news/maryland/bal-te.md.spying02oct02-story.html.

58   **In the wake of Edward Snowden:** Faiza Patel, "Bulk Collection Under Section
215 Has Ended . . . What's Next?," *Just Security*, November 30, 2015. Available at:
https://www.justsecurity.org/27996/bulk-collection-ended-whats-next/.

58   **The new version allows:** Cyrus Farivar, "Even Former NSA Chief Thinks USA
Freedom Act Was a Pointless Change," Ars Technica, June 17, 2015. Available at:
https://arstechnica.com/tech-policy/2015/06/even-former-nsa-chief-thinks-usa
-freedom-act-was-a-pointless-change/.

58   **The 1979 *Smith* decision:** David Kravets, "How a Purse Snatching Led to the
Legal Justification for NSA Domestic Spying," *Wired*, October 2, 2013. Available at: https://www.wired.com/2013/10/nsa-smith-purse-snatching/.

59   **The legal reasoning of the third-party:** In re Application, US Foreign Intelligence Surveillance Court, BR 13-109. Available at: https://www.document-
cloud.org/documents/3819997-br13-09-Primary-Order-1.html#document/p9
/a356679.

59   **"I do not believe that I am the one":** Author's interview with Stephen Sachs,
March 6, 2017.

59   **Cardin was briefly a prosecutor:** Dan Rodricks, "In Maryland Attorney General's Race, Look Past Name," *Baltimore Sun*, June 10, 2014.
http://articles.baltimoresun.com/2014-06-10/news/bs-md-rodricks
-0610-20140610_1_brian-frosh-jon-cardin-attorney-general.

60   **"What they [had was] this nexus":** Author's interview with Howard Cardin,
March 6, 2017.

60   **"Is that right?":** Author's interview with US Tax Judge Albert Lauber, June 30,
2017.

61   **Even while Katz was working:** Nan Robertson, "Data Bank: Peril or Aid?," *The
New York Times*, January 6, 1968. Available at: https://www.documentcloud.org
/documents/3766399-110088042.html; Vance Packard, "Don't Tell It To the
Computer," *The New York Times*, January 8, 1967. Available at: https://www
.documentcloud.org/documents/3766305-83569846.html.

61   **"The presence of these records":** "THE COMPUTER AND INVASION OF
PRIVACY," HEARINGS BEFORE A SUBCOMMITTEE OF THE COM-
MITTEE ON GOVERNMENT OPERATIONS HOUSE OF REPRESENTA-
TIVES EIGHTY-NINTH CONGRESS SECOND SESSION, July 26–28, 1966.

Available at: https://www.documentcloud.org/documents/3766857-U-S-House
-1966-the-Computer-and-Invasion-of.html#document/p5/a356386.

61   **The plan was ultimately killed:** "Panel Sees Peril in US Data Bank," Associated
        Press, August 5, 1968. Available at: https://www.documentcloud.org/documents
        /3766408-79943704.html.

61   *The New York Times* **warned:** Ben A. Franklin, "Federal Computers Amass Files
        on Suspect Citizens," *The New York Times*, June 28, 1970. Available at: http://www
        .nytimes.com/1970/06/28/archives/federal-computers-amass-files-on-suspect
        -citizens-many-among.html.

61   **The book's author, Arthur R. Miller:** "Arthur R. Miller," New York University.
        https://its.law.nyu.edu/facultyprofiles/index.cfm?fuseaction=profile.biography
        &personid=20130.

62   **"Data transmissions also are more":** Miller, 183.

62   **One of the crucial elements:** INTELLIGENCE ACTIVITIES AND THE
        RIGHTS OF AMERICANS BOOK II FINAL REPORT OF THE SELECT
        COMMITTEE TO STUDY GOVERNMENTAL OPERATIONS WITH RE-
        SPECT TO INTELLIGENCE ACTIVITIES UNITED STATES SENATE, April
        26, 1976. Available at: https://www.documentcloud.org/documents/3766517
        -94755-II.html#document/p122/a356344.

62   **America had been paying:** United States,Government (2010). "Statistical infor-
        mation about casualties of the Vietnam War." National Archives and Records
        Administration. Archived from the original on January 26, 2010. Retrieved Jan-
        uary 8, 2018. Available at: https://www.archives.gov/research/military/vietnam
        -war/casualty-statistics.html.

62   **The intelligence community actively:** Nelson Blackstock, *COINTELPRO: The
        FBI's Secret War on Political Freedom*, (Pathfinder, 1975), p. 111.

62   **Other snooping efforts:** L. Britt Snider, "Recollections from the Church Com-
        mittee's Investigation of NSA," CIA, April 14, 2007. Available at: https://www.cia
        .gov/library/center-for-the-study-of-intelligence/csi-publications/csi-studies
        /studies/winter99-00/art4.html.

62   **Others, like Project Minaret, intercepted:** Matthew Aid, "Secret Cold War
        Documents Reveal NSA Spied on Senators," *Foreign Policy*, September 25, 2013.
        Available at: https://foreignpolicy.com/2013/09/25/secret-cold-war-documents
        -reveal-nsa-spied-on-senators/.

63   **On April 30, 1970, Nixon:** John M. Shaw, *The Cambodian Campaign* (Univer-
        sity of Kansas Press, 2005), p. 158.

63   **Not three months later, in July 1970:** INTELLIGENCE ACTIVITIES AND
        THE RIGHTS OF AMERICANS BOOK II FINAL REPORT OF THE SELECT
        COMMITTEE TO STUDY GOVERNMENTAL OPERATIONS WITH RE-
        SPECT TO INTELLIGENCE ACTIVITIES UNITED STATES SENATE, April
        26, 1976. Available at: https://www.documentcloud.org/documents/3766517
        -94755-II.html#document/p122/a356344.

63   **One surveillance case that preceded Nixon:** Christopher Zbrozek, "The
        Bombing of the A2 CIA Office," *Michigan Daily*, October 24, 2006. Available
        at: https://www.michigandaily.com/content/bombing-a2-cia-office.

63   **As the case moved ahead in 1969:** Sklansky, 251.

63   **In an affidavit, Attorney General John Mitchell:** Samuel C. Damren, "The Keith Case," The Court Legacy, November 2003. Available at: https://www .documentcloud.org/documents/3766851-200311-Court-Legacy.html #document/p5/a356375.

64   **The Ann Arbor case:** Ibid. https://www.documentcloud.org/documents /3766851-200311-Court-Legacy.html#document/p2/a356376.

64   **"An idea which seems":** Agis Salpukas, "Judge Reaffirms Curb on Wiretaps," The New York Times, January 26, 1971. Available at: http://www.nytimes.com /1971/01/26/archives/judge-reaffirms-curb-on-wiretaps-ruling-could-limit -power-to.html.

64   **The Department of Justice appealed:** United States v. United States District Court, No. 71-1105, (6th Cir., 1971). Available at: http://openjurist.org/444 /f2d/651/united-states-v-united-states-district-court-for-eastern-district-of -michigan-southern-division-j.

64   **The appeals court famously found:** Fred P. Graham, "White House View of Wiretap Right Denied on Appeal," The New York Times, April 9, 1971. Available at: http://www.nytimes.com/1971/04/09/archives/white-house-view-of-wiretap -right-denied-on-appeal-us-court-finds.html.

64   **"The price of lawful public dissent":** United States v. United States Dist. Ct., 407 U.S. 297 (1972). Available at: https://supreme.justia.com/cases/federal/us /407/297/case.html.

65   **In 1971, Assemblymember Kenneth Cory:** Right of Privacy California Proposition 11 (1972). Available at: https://www.documentcloud.org/documents/3678199 -RIGHT-of-PRIVACY.html.

65   **Today, California is just one:** Privacy Protections in State Constitutions, National Conference of State Legislatures, May 5, 2017. Available at: http://www .ncsl.org/research/telecommunications-and-information-technology/privacy -protections-in-state-constitutions.aspx.

65   **"For all practical purposes":** Burrows v. Superior Court , 13 Cal.3d 238. Available at: http://scocal.stanford.edu/opinion/burrows-v-superior-court-27860.

66   **"On March 8, 1971":** Betty Medsger, The Burglary: The Discovery of J. Edgar Hoover's FBI (Vintage, 2014).

66   **The group, whose members:** Michael Isikoff, "After 43 Years, Activists Admit Theft at FBI Office That Exposed Domestic Spying," NBC News, January 6, 2014. Available at: http://investigations.nbcnews.com/_news/2014/01/06/22205443 -after-43-years-activists-admit-theft-at-fbi-office-that-exposed-domestic -spying?lite.

66   **Banner replied: "I think it was legal":** SELECT COMMITTEE TO STUDY GOVERNMENTAL OPERATIONS WITH RESPECT TO INTELLIGENCE ACTIVITIES OF THE UNITED STATES SENATE NINETY-FOURTH CONGRESS FIRST SESSION VOLUME 5 THE NATIONAL SECURITY AGENCY AND FOURTH AMENDMENT RIGHTS OCTOBER 29 AND NOVEMBER 6, 1975. Available at: https://www.documentcloud.org/documents /3766735-94intelligence-Activities-V.html#document/p48/a35637.

66   **The story of *Smith v. Maryland*:** Smith v. Maryland, No. 78-5374, On Writ
      of Certiorari to the Court of Appeals of Maryland. Available at: https://www
      .documentcloud.org/documents/3762087-SUPC-USSC1978-5374-04-i1-40-1
      .html#document/p8/a356025.

67   **At the time, anonymous and:** "Albany Outlaws Threats by Phone," *The New York
      Times*, April 25, 1960. Available at: https://www.documentcloud.org/documents
      /3762241-105191721.html.

67   **In April 1965, *The Atlantic*:** Pat Watters, "Telephone Terrorism," *The Atlantic*,
      April 1965, p. 118.

67   **By 1966, the New York Telephone Company:** "Bureau is set up for Crank Calls,"
      The New York Times, April 27, 1966. Available at: https://www.documentcloud
      .org/documents/3762242-79094571.html.

67   **That same year, AT&T:** Richard D. Lyons, "Obscene Phone Calls Stir Concern,"
      The New York Times, February 26, 1967. Available at: https://www.document-
      cloud.org/documents/3762228-90272875.html#document/p1/a356026.

67   **One common way that telephone companies:** Fred P. Graham, "US to Limit
      Use of Bugging Aids," *The New York Times*, August 29, 1965. Available at: https:
      //www.documentcloud.org/documents/3762232-99463008.html#document
      /p1/a356027.

67   **In September 1970, William Claerhout:** William A. Claerhout, "The Pen Reg-
      ister," 20 Drake L. Rev. 108 (1970-1971). Available at: https://www.document-
      cloud.org/documents/3762473-Claerhout.html#document/p2/a356031.

68   **By 1971, *The New York Times*:** Robert A. Wright, "For Privacy from Cranks, Creeps
      and Crooks, Millions Getting Unlisted Phone Numbers," *The New York Times*,
      December 22, 1971. Available at: http://www.nytimes.com/1971/12/22/archives
      /for-privacy-from-cranks-creeps-and-crooks-millions-getting-unlisted.html.

68   **With this new information:** *Smith v. Maryland*, No. 78-5374, On Writ of
      Certiorari to the Court of Appeals of Maryland. Available at: https://www
      .documentcloud.org/documents/3762087-SUPC-USSC1978-5374-04-i1-40-1
      .html#document/p9/a356030.

68   **Cardin knew that he had an uphill battle:** Author's interview with Howard
      Cardin, March 6, 2017.

69   **In a 4–3 decision on July 14, 1978:** Smith v. Maryland, No. 78-5374, On Writ
      of Certiorari to the Court of Appeals of Maryland. Available at: https://www
      .documentcloud.org/documents/3762087-SUPC-USSC1978-5374-04-i1-40-1.html
      #document/p14/a356110.

69   **"everyman's master":** Ibid. https://www.documentcloud.org/documents
      /3762087-SUPC-USSC1978-5374-04-i1-40-1.html#document/p29/a356113.

69   **"Technologically, a distinction":** Ibid. https://www.documentcloud.org
      /documents/3762087-SUPC-USSC1978-5374-04-i1-40-1.html#document/p31
      /a356115.

69   **The FISC, unlike all others:** Cyrus Farivar, "America's Super-Secret Court
      Names Five Lawyers as Public Advocates," Ars Technica, November 28, 2015.
      Available at: https://arstechnica.com/tech-policy/2015/11/americas-super-secret
      -court-names-five-lawyers-as-public-advocates/.

70   **Sachs pulled a wooden chair:** Author's interview with Stephen Sachs, March 6, 2017.

71   **"I may have started in [the] Circuit Court":** Author's interview with Howard Cardin, March 6, 2017.

71   **"Mr. Chief Justice and may":** *Smith v. Maryland*, 442 U.S. 735 (1979).

72   **He also pointed out:** Robert B. Parrish, "Circumventing Title III: The Use of Pen Register Surveillance in Law Enforcement," Duke Law Journal, Vol. 1977:751. Available at: https://www.documentcloud.org/documents/3859337 -Circumventing-Title-III-Parrish-1977.html#document/p9/a356505.

73   **The Supreme Court published:** *Smith v. Maryland*, 442 U.S. 735 (1979).

74   **"Telephones, credit cards, computers":** Federal Government Information Technology: Electronic Surveillance and Civil Liberties (Washington, DC: U.S. Congress, Office of Technology Assessment, OTA CIT-293, October 1985). Available at: https://www.documentcloud.org/documents/3859634-Fgit-1985 .html#document/p12/a357129.

75   **One section of the law:** 18 U.S. Code Chapter 121. Available at: https://www.law .cornell.edu/uscode/text/18/part-I/chapter-121.

75   **Yet another portion mandates:** 18 U.S. Code § 3123. Available at: https://www .law.cornell.edu/uscode/text/18/3123.

75   **Both of these are lesser legal standards:** 396 F.Supp.2d 747 (2005) In re AP-PLICATION FOR PEN REGISTER AND TRAP/TRACE DEVICE WITH CELL SITE LOCATION AUTHORITY No. H-05-557M. United States District Court, S.D. Texas, Houston Division. October 14, 2005. Available at: https: //scholar.google.com/scholar_case?case=8980502027187529652&hl=en&as _sdt=6,38.

75   **Fundamentally, it seems quite:** US Postal Inspection Service, "Frequently Asked Questions." Available at: https://postalinspectors.uspis.gov/contactUs/faq.aspx.

76   **"It poses an untenable choice":** Lewis R. Katz, "In Search of a Fourth Amendment for the Twenty-First Century," Indiana Law Journal, Volume 65, Issue 3, Article 2 (1990). Available at: https://www.documentcloud.org/documents/3860670-In -Search-of-a-Fourth-Amendment-for-the-Twenty.html#document/p42/a356725.

76   **As Orin Kerr, a law professor:** Orin S. Kerr, "The Case for the Third-Party Doctrine," Michigan Law Review, Vol. 107-561 (2009). Available at: https://www .documentcloud.org/documents/3515439-SSRN-id1138128-1.html#document /p3/a356944.

76   **He's argued that:** Orin Kerr and Greg Nojeim, "The Data Question: Should the Third-Party Records Doctrine Be Revisited?" *ABA Journal* (August 2012). Available at: http://www.abajournal.com/magazine/article/the _data_question_should_the_third-party_records_doctrine_be_revisited.

77   **In 2012, in the case of *United States v. Jones*:** United States v. Jones, No. 10–1259 (2012). Available at: https://www.law.cornell.edu/supremecourt/text/10-1259.

77   **The following month, the FBI applied:** Fourth Superseding Indictment, US v. Carpenter, 12-20218, USDC Eastern Michigan, July 10, 2013. Available at: https: //www.documentcloud.org/documents/3861742-US-v-Carpenter-Fourth -superseding-indictment.html.

78   **Specifically, the government sought a d-order:** 18 U.S. Code § 2703. Available at: https://www.law.cornell.edu/uscode/text/18/2703.

78   **This is not a trivial distinction:** David Gray, Stephen Henderson, *The Cambridge Handbook of Surveillance Law,* (Cambridge University Press, 2017)

78   **"That's important because judges":** Author's interview with Nathan Freed Wessler, June 12, 2017.

79   **The 6th Circuit called out the ACLU's:** US v. Carpenter, 14-1572/1805 (6th Cir., 2016). Available at: https://www.documentcloud.org/documents/3861614 -Show-Temp-45.html#document/p12/a357067.

79   **"I would have felt constrained by the logic":** Author's correspondence with Stephen Sachs, June 14, 2017.

80   **In short, absent further guidance:** Author's phone conversation with Stephen Sachs, August 14, 2017.

80   **"I believe *Katz* must be replaced":** Author's correspondence with Stephen Sachs, June 14, 2017.

80   **"I think the Court will attempt":** Author's correspondence with Stephen Sachs, November 29, 2017.

Chapter Four

81   **The system was kind of:** Amanda Pike and G. W. Schulz, "Hollywood-style surveillance technology inches closer to reality," Reveal News, April 11, 2014. Available at: https://www.revealnews.org/article-legacy/hollywood-style -surveillance-technology-inches-closer-to-reality/.

81   **At one of the world's most:** Author's interview with Mike Katz-Lacabe, July 10, 2017.

81   **The 45-year-old:** Chris Soghoian, Ashkan Soltani, Ben Wizner, and Catherine Crump, "Can You Track Me Now? Government and Corporate Surveillance of Mobile Geo-Location Data," DEF CON 2012. Available at: https://www.you-tube.com/watch?v=NjuhdKUH6U4.

82   **As an experienced ACLU attorney:** Author's interview with Catherine Crump, July 13, 2017.

82   **"He struck me as an old-school":** Author's interview with Jennifer Valentino-DeVries, July 12, 2017.

82   **So, what provides the legal authority:** George Joseph, "What Are License-Plate Readers Good For?" *Citylab,* August 5, 2016. Available at: https://www.citylab .com/equity/2016/08/what-are-license-plate-readers-good-for/492083/.

83   **Katz-Lacabe attended:** S. Hick, E. Halpin, and E. Hoskins, *Human Rights and the Internet* (New York: St. Martin's Press, 2000), p. 100.

83   **"thwart armed communist insurgencies":** US Army School of the Americas, "Frequently Asked Questions," April 1999. Available at: https://web.archive.org /web/19990428095558/http://www.benning.army.mil/usarsa/FAQ/FAQ.htm.

83   **As that work evolved, he:** Niall McKay, "Hacktivists Join Activists," *Wired,* November 20, 1998. Available at: https://www.wired.com/1998/11/hacktivists -join-activists/.

83 **In 2000, Katz-Lacabe:** "Full Biography for Mike Katz-Lacabe," Smartvoter.org, 2014. Available at:http://www.smartvoter.org/2014/11/04/ca/alm/vote/katz-lacabe_m/bio.html.

84 **A few months later:** Jennifer Valentino-DeVries, "New Tracking Frontier: Your License Plate," *The Wall Street Journal*, 2012. Available at: https://www.wsj.com/articles/SB10000872396390443995604578004723603576296.

84 **On March 30, 2009:** *Denise Green v. City and County of San Francisco*, 3:10-cv-02649 (2010). Available at: https://www.documentcloud.org/documents/3892488-Green-v-San-Francisco-LPR-case.html.

85 **Later, as part of her civil:** David Kravets, "License Plate Reader Error Leads to Traffic Stop at Gunpoint, Court Case," Ars Technica, 2017. Available at: https://arstechnica.com/tech-policy/2014/05/after-being-held-at-gunpoint-due-to-lpr-error-woman-gets-day-in-court/.

85 **Fourteen years after the FBI:** "License Plate Reader Technology Enhances the Identification, Recovery of Stolen Vehicles," Federal Bureau of Investigation, 2011. Available at: https://www.fbi.gov/services/cjis/cjis-link/license-plate-reader-technology-enhances-the-identification-recovery-of-stolen-vehicles.

85 **These are essentially specialized:** "3M™ Mobile ALPR Camera P634" 3M, 2017. Available at: http://www.3m.com/3M/en_US/company-us/all-3m-products/~/3M-Mobile-ALPR-Camera-P634?N=5002385+8709322+8709393+3292106901&rt=rud.

86 **The three largest vendors of LPR:** "3M Completes Sale of Tolling and Automated License/Number Plate Recognition Business," 3M Press Release, June 30, 2017. Available at: http://investors.3m.com/news/press-release-details/2017/3M-Completes-Sale-of-Tolling-and-Automated-LicenseNumber-Plate-Recognition-Business/default.aspx.

86 **These companies routinely encourage:** "Find Out How to File for Law Enforcement Grants and Funding," Elsag, 2017. Available at: https://www.elsag.com/how-to-buy/law-enforcement-grants-guide.

86 **In 2014, for example:** "Central Marin Police Authority UASI ALRP Grant," 2014. Available at: https://www.documentcloud.org/documents/3890356-Central-Marin-Police-Authority-UASI-ALRP-Grant.html.

86 **However, there have never been:** George Joseph, "What Are License-Plate Readers Good For?" *Citylab*, August 5, 2016. Available at: https://www.citylab.com/equity/2016/08/what-are-license-plate-readers-good-for/492083/.

86 **Depending on the retention:** "Automated License Plate Readers: State Statutes Regulating Their Use," National Council of State Legislators, 2017. Available at: http://www.ncsl.org/research/telecommunications-and-information-technology/state-statutes-regulating-the-use-of-automated-license-plate-readers-alpr-or-alpr-data.aspx.

86 **Police in Oakland, California:** Cyrus Farivar, "Cops Decide to Collect Less License Plate Data After 80GB Drive Got Full," Ars Technica, August 26, 2015. Available at: https://arstechnica.com/tech-policy/2015/08/cops-decide-to-collect-less-license-plate-data-after-80gb-drive-got-full/.

86   **While many people might feel:** Y. de Montjoye, C. Hidalgo, M. Verleysen, and V. Blondel, "Unique in the Crowd: The Privacy Bounds of Human Mobility," *Nature*, 2013.

87   **To be fair, the snapshot that an LPR:** Cyrus Farivar, "Your Car, Tracked: The Rapid Rise of License Plate Readers," Ars Technica, September 27, 2012. Available at: https://arstechnica.com/tech-policy/2012/09/your-car-tracked-the -rapid-rise-of-license-plate-readers/.

87   **"The collection itself and":** Author's interview with Kade Crockford, July 6, 2017.

87   **On its website, Elsag touts:** "Greatest Hits: Kansas," Elsag, 2017. Available at: https://www.documentcloud.org/documents/3890353-17d034-ELS-Greatest -Hits-March-r2.html.

87   **In 2015, in a higher-profile example:** Cyrus Farivar, "Don't Let Roanoke Murderer Justify a License Plate Reader Rise," Ars Technica, August 31, 2015. Available at: https://arstechnica.com/tech-policy/2015/08/yes-a-license -plate-reader-helped-nab-roanoke-shooter-but-thats-a-rare-win.

87   **However, these success stories:** Mike Katz-Lacabe, "Piedmont License Plate Reader Analysis Shows 99.97% of Data Collected Is Useless," Center for Human Rights and Privacy, September 7, 2015. Available at: https://www.cehrp .org/piedmont-license-plate-reader-analysis-shows-99-97-of-data-collected -is-useless/.

87   **In fact, more than 99 percent:** Catherine Crump, "Police Documents on License Plate Scanners Reveal Mass Tracking," American Civil Liberties Union, 2013. Available at: https://www.aclu.org/blog/police-documents -license-plate-scanners-reveal-mass-tracking.

88   **The *Knotts* case is reminiscent:** Leroy Knotts and Daryl Petschen did not respond to the author's numerous requests for an interview.

88   **According to court filings:** Appellee's Brief, United States v. Knotts, 80-1952 (8th Cir., 1980). Available at: https://www.documentcloud.org/documents /3512651-80-1952-Appellee-s-Brief.html#document/p11/a361662.

88   **Petschen took Armstrong:** Appellant's Brief, United States v. Knotts, 80-1952 (8th Cir., 1980). Available at: https://www.documentcloud.org/documents /3512650-80-1952-Appellant-s-Brief.html#document/p12/a361648.

89   **This beeper—a low-range FM radio:** Oral Arguments, United States v. Knotts, 460 U.S. 276 (1983). Available at: https://www.oyez.org/cases/1982/81-1802.

89   **Armstrong took the drum to Petschen's:** Appellant's Brief, United States v. Knotts, 80-1952 (8th Cir., 1980). Available at: https://www.documentcloud.org /documents/3512650-80-1952-Appellant-s-Brief.html#document/p15/a361653.

89   **But Petschen's losing the police:** Ibid. Available at: https://www.document-cloud.org/documents/3512652-80-1952-Opinion.html#document/p2/a361657.

89   **Four days later, on March 3, 1980:** Ibid. Available at: https://www.documentcloud .org/documents/3512650-80-1952-Appellant-s-Brief.html#document/p16/a361654.

89   **"Back then the monitoring":** Author's interview with Mark Peterson, March 7, 2017.

90   **"Resolution of this contention":** Appellant's Brief, United States v. Knotts, 80-1952 (8th Cir., 1980). Available at: https://www.documentcloud.org/documents /3512650-80-1952-Appellant-s-Brief.html#document/p19/a361658.

90   **The government, in its responding:** Ibid. Available at: https://www.document-cloud.org/documents/3512651-80-1952-Appellee-s-Brief.html#document/p21 /a361663.

90   **Plus, Department of Justice lawyers:** Ibid. Available at: https://www .documentcloud.org/documents/3512651-80-1952-Appellee-s-Brief. html#document/p23/a361664.

90   **In October 1981, the 8th Circuit:** Opinion, *United States v. Knotts*, 80-1952 (8th Cir., 1980). Available at: https://www.documentcloud.org/documents /3512652-80-1952-Opinion.html#document/p3/a342530.

91   **At oral arguments, which:** Oral Arguments, *United States v. Knotts*, 460 U.S. 276 (1983). Available at: https://www.oyez.org/cases/1982/81-1802.

93   **This was a direct reference:** Opinion, *United States v. Bruneau*, 78-1526 (8th Cir., 1979). Available at: https://www.leagle.com/decision/19791784594f2d119011590.

94   **As part of its analysis:** Kara Cook, "Electronic Tracking Devices and Privacy: See No Evil, Hear No Evil, But Beware of Trojan Horses," *Loyola University of Chicago Law Journal* 9, no. 227 (1977). Available at: https://www.documentcloud.org /documents/3891952-Electronic-Tracking-Devices-and-Privacy-See-No.html #document/p22/a361950.

94   **Cook's language was echoed:** *United States v. Knotts*, 460 U.S. 276 (1983). Available at: https://supreme.justia.com/cases/federal/us/460/276/case.html.

95   **"The invasion of privacy":** Author's interview with Andrew Frey, July 15, 2017.

95   **In 1997, an officer:** Avis Thomas-Lester and Toni Locy, "Chief's Friend Accused of Extortion,"*The Washington Post*, November 26, 1997. Available at: http:// www.washingtonpost.com/wp-srv/local/longterm/library/dc/dcpolice/stories /stowe25.htm.

95   **Documents released by DEA:** e-mail, April 17, 2009. https://www.documentcloud.org /documents/3892472-33780-33791-2014-03-31-Response.html#document/p4/a362134.

95   **In 2012, the New York Police Department:** Adam Goldman and Matt Apuzzo, "With Cameras, Informants, NYPD Eyed Mosques," Associated Press, February 23, 2012. Available at: https://www.ap.org/ap-in-the-news/2012/with -cameras-informants-nypd-eyed-mosques.

95   **The following year, the NYPD:** Chris Francescani, "NYPD Expands Surveillance Net to Fight Crime as Well as Terrorism," Reuters, June 21, 2013. Available at: http: //www.reuters.com/article/usa-ny-surveillance-idUSL2N0EV0D220130621.

96   **In September 2014, an enterprising reporter:** Eric Roper, "Aug. 17, 2012: City Cameras Track Anyone, Even Minneapolis Mayor Rybak," *Star Tribune*, August 17, 2012. Available at: http://www.startribune.com/aug-17-2012-city-cameras -track-anyone-even-minneapolis-mayor-rybak/166494646/.

96   **In January 2015, through a public records:** Dave Maass and Jeremy Gillula, "What You Can Learn from Oakland's Raw ALPR Data," Electronic Frontier Foundation, January 21, 2015. Available at: https://www.eff.org/deeplinks /2015/01/what-we-learned-oakland-raw-alpr-data.

96   **Meanwhile, in November 2015:** Dakota Smith, "LA City Council Proposal Would Send John Letters to Owners of Cars in Prostitution Areas," *Los Angeles Daily News*, November 25, 2015. Available at: http://www.dailynews.com/social-affairs/20151125/la-city-council-proposal-would-send-john-letters-to-owners-of-cars-in-prostitution-areas.

96   **"I don't doubt that having":** Author's interview with Mike Katz-Lacabe, July 10, 2017.

96   **"I would feel safer":** Author's interview with Andrew Frey, July 15, 2017.

97   **Vigilant Solutions, a company:** Cyrus Farivar, "Private Firms Sue Arkansas for Right to Collect License Plate Reader Data," Ars Technica, June 11, 2014. Available at: http://arstechnica.com/tech-policy/2014/06/private-firms-sue-arkansas-for-right-to-collect-license-plate-reader-data/.

97   **"The camera affiliates":** Declaration of Todd Hodnett, *DRN v. Beebe*, 4:14-cv-00327 (2014). Available at: https://www.documentcloud.org/documents/1679018-229019843-drn-and-vigilant-v-beebe-and-mcdaniel.html.

97   **In addition, the parent:** "Whose LPR Data Is It Anyway? Vigilant Solutions Reinforces Agency Data Ownership and Offers to Migrate LPR Data at No Charge," Vigilant Solutions Press Release, 2016. Available at: https://www.bizjournals.com/sanfrancisco/prnewswire/press_releases/California/2016/10/14/DA17512.

97   **Vigilant uses the data:** Vigilant Solutions did not make any executives available for an interview with the author.

97   **Access to Vigilant's database:** "LEARN Hosted Server User Agreement July 2017," Vigilant Solutions, 2017. Available at: https://www.documentcloud.org/documents/3892602-LEARN-Hosted-Server-User-Agreement-July-2017.html#document/p3/a362163.

97   **"Woman's Life Saved":** "Woman's Life Saved Using Vigilant Solutions' License Plate Recognition (LPR) Data," Officer Press Release, 2013. Available at: http://www.officer.com/press_release/10939925/womans-life-saved-using-vigilant-solutions-license-plate-recognition-lpr-data.

97   **Another proclaims:** "Survey: License Plate Recognition Is a Valuable, Well-Regulated Technology," Officer Press Release, 2013. Available at: http://www.officer.com/press_release/11079856/survey-license-plate-recognition-is-a-valuable-well-regulated-technology.

98   **One notable example came:** "SB-893 Automated License Plate Recognition Systems: Use of Data," Bill Status, California Legislative Information, 2017. Available at: http://leginfo.legislature.ca.gov/faces/billStatusClient.xhtml?bill_id=201320140SB893.

98   **"Law enforcement will still":** "Hill Introduces Bill to Prohibit the Sale of Information Gathered by License Plate Readers," Senator Jerry Hill, January 10, 2014. Available at: http://sd13.senate.ca.gov/news/2014-01-10-hill-introduces-bill-prohibit-sale-information-gathered-license-plate-readers.

98   **In April 2014, Vigilant:** B. Shockley, "California Public Opinion Favors License Plate Readers," Vigilant Solutions, 2014. Available at: https://www.vigilantsolutions.com/california-public-opinion-favors-license-plate-reader-technology-zogby-poll/.

98   **However, under scrutiny:** Joe Silver and Cyrus Farivar, "License Plate Reader Firm Releases Dubious Poll to Show Public Support," Ars Technica, May 2, 2014. Available at: https://arstechnica.com/tech-policy/2014/05/license-plate-reader-firm-releases-dubious-poll-to-show-public-support/.

98   **Later that year, however:** "Automatic License Plate Recognition," openALPR, 2017. Available at: http://www.openalpr.com/.

98   **"I would love to":** Author's interview with Mike Katz-Lacabe, July 10, 2017.

99   **However, LPRs:** Cyrus Farivar, "'What Are You Doing in My F?!@#g House?'—A Behind-the-Lens Look at Body Cameras," Ars Technica, January 5, 2016. Available at: https://arstechnica.com/tech-policy/2016/01/what-are-you-doing-in-my-fg-house-a-behind-the-lens-look-at-body-cameras.

99   **In May 2014, in Katz-Lacabe's:** "File #: 14-002," City of San Leandro, 2014. Available at: https://sanleandro.legistar.com/LegislationDetail.aspx?ID=1739213&GUID=D1CA7A9C-4758-4BCB-AB16-6D772DB1F700&FullText=1.

99   **Less than three months:** Megan Geuss, "Obama Wants to Buy 50,000 Body Cams for Police, Monitor Military Gear Handouts," Ars Technica, December 1, 2014. Available at: http://arstechnica.com/tech-policy/2014/12/obama-wants-to-buy-50000-body-cams-for-police-monitor-military-gear-handouts/.

100   **Many agencies, like the:** "Fact Sheet: Strengthening Community Policing," White House Press Release, December 1, 2014. Available at: https://obamawhitehouse.archives.gov/the-press-office/2014/12/01/fact-sheet-strengthening-community-policing.

100   **"There's been a lot of talk":** Wesley Bruer, "Obama Warns Cop Body Cameras Are No 'Panacea,'" *CNNPolitics*, March 2, 2015. Available at: http://www.cnn.com/2015/03/02/politics/obama-police-body-camera-report/index.html.

100   **In 2013, the city paid out $80,000:** Henry K. Lee, "80K Settlement in Police Struggle Death." *San Francisco Chronicle,* December 17, 2013. Available at: http://www.sfgate.com/crime/article/80K-settlement-in-police-struggle-death-5071980.php.

100   **In an even stranger incident:** Amy Sylvestri, "City Settles in Cops Targeting Gays Lawsuit," *San Leandro Times*, October 31, 2013. Available at: https://web.archive.org/web/20160309205534/http://ebpublishing.com/index.php?option=com_content&view=article&id=6894%3Acity-settles-in-cops-targeting-gays-lawsuit-&catid=50%3Asan-leandro-news&Itemid=131.

100   **In 2007, San Leandro:** "San Leandro, CA Police Taser Wrongful Death Settlement," Lawyers and Settlements, June 7, 2007. Available at: http://www.lawyersandsettlements.com/settlements/08342/police-taser-death.html.

100   **In 2015, Baltimore, Maryland:** Keith L. Alexander, "Baltimore Reaches $6.4 Million Settlement with Freddie Gray's Family," *The Washington Post*, September 8, 2015. Available at: https://www.washingtonpost.com/local/crime/baltimore-reaches-64-million-settlement-with-freddie-grays-family/2015/09/08/80b2c092-5196-11e5-8c19-0b6825aa4a3a_story.html.

100   **In 2017, St. Anthony, Minnesota:** Sarah Horner, "Philando Castile Family Reaches $3M Settlement in Death," *Twin Cities*, June 26, 2017. Available at: http://www.twincities.com/2017/06/26/philando-castile-family-reaches-3m-settlement-in-death/.

100   **Also in 2017, Ferguson, Missouri:** Paul LeBlanc, "Settlement Reached in Mi-
       chael Brown Civil Lawsuit," CNN, June 20, 2017. Available at: http://www.cnn
       .com/2017/06/20/us/michael-brown-settlement-ferguson/index.html.

101   **But like LPRs:** Elizabeth Atkins, "#Blacklivesrecorded," Unpublished Thesis,
       Thomas Jefferson School of Law, 2016. Available at: https://www.document-
       cloud.org/documents/3894162-SSRN-id2803588.html#document/p12/a362822.

101   **Even now, a Silicon Valley startup:** Cyrus Farivar, "Meet Visual Labs, A
       Body Camera Startup That Doesn't Sell Body Cameras," Ars Technica, Sep-
       tember 3, 2016. Available at: https://arstechnica.com/tech-policy/2016/09/meet
       -visual-labs-a-body-camera-startup-that-doesnt-sell-body-cameras/.

101   **However, facial recognition doesn't:** Cyrus Farivar, "Boston Police Chief:
       Facial Recognition Tech Didn't Help Find Bombing Suspects," Ars Technica,
       April 21, 2013. Available at: https://arstechnica.com/tech-policy/2013/04/boston
       -police-chief-facial-recognition-tech-didnt-help-find-bombing-suspects/.

101   **Even the 2013 Boston bombing suspects:** David Montgomery, Sari Hor-
       witz, and Marc Fisher, "Police, citizens and technology factor into Boston
       bombing probe," *The Washington Post*, April 20, 2013. Available at: https:
       //www.washingtonpost.com/world/national-security/inside-the-investigation
       -of-the-boston-marathon-bombing/2013/04/20/19d8c322-a8ff-11e2-b029
       -8fb7e977ef71_story.html?utm_term=.0a608ddee0e3.

102   **Although, algorithms:** Cyrus Farivar, "Facebook's Facial Recogni-
       tion Will One Day Find You, Even While Facing Away," Ars Technica,
       June 24, 2015. Available at: https://arstechnica.com/business/2015/06/facebooks
       -facial-recognition-will-one-day-find-you-even-while-facing-away/.

102   **In October 2016, Georgetown researchers:** "The Perpetual Line Up Center on
       Privacy and Technology at . . . ," Georgetown Law Center on Privacy & Technol-
       ogy, October 2016. Available at: https://www.documentcloud.org/documents
       /3896102-The-Perpetual-Line-Up-Center-on-Privacy-and.html.

102   **To take one example:** Declan McCullagh, "Call It Super Bowl Face Scan I," *Wired*,
       2001. Available at: https://www.wired.com/2001/02/call-it-super-bowl-face-scan-i/.

102   **Georgetown professor Alvaro Bedoya:** Committee to Review Law Enforce-
       ment's Policies on Facial Recognition Technology, Full House Committee on
       Oversight and Government Reform, March 22, 2017. Available at: https://oversight
       .house.gov/hearing/law-enforcements-use-facial-recognition-technology/.

102   **They found that such systems:** Clare Frankle, "Facial-Recognition Software
       Might Have a Racial Bias Problem," *The Atlantic*, April 7, 2016. Available at:
       https://www.theatlantic.com/technology/archive/2016/04/the-underlying
       -bias-of-facial-recognition-systems/476991/#article-comments.

102   **For now, the most prominent:** "DMV Investigators Catch Federal Fugitive on
       the Run for 25 Years," *Nevada DMV*, 2017. Available at: http://www.dmvnv.com
       /news/17004-federal-fugitive-caught.htm.

102   **In June 2017, a Jacksonville, Florida, man:** "How a Jacksonville Man
       Caught in the Drug War Exposed Details of Police Facial Recognition," *Flor-
       ida Times-Union*, May 26, 2017. Available at: http://jacksonville.com/news

/metro/public-safety/2017-05-26/how-jacksonville-man-caught-drug-war
-exposed-details-police.

103 **An Indiana man who was:** Lauren E. Hernandez, "FBI: Facial Recognition
Software Helps ID Indiana Cold-Case Fugitive," *USA Today*, January 13, 2017.
Available at: https://www.usatoday.com/story/news/nation-now/2017/01/13/fbi
-facial-recognition-software-helps-id-indiana-cold-case-fugitive/96570250/.

103 **A year earlier, in January 2016:** David Kravets, "Enhanced DMV Facial Recognition Technology Helps NY Nab 100 ID Thieves," Ars Technica, August
28, 2016. Available at: https://arstechnica.com/tech-policy/2016/08/enhanced
-dmv-facial-recognition-technology-helps-ny-nab-100-id-thieves/.

103 **While facial recognition:** Ava Kofman, "Real-Time Face Recognition Threatens
to Turn Cops' Body Cameras into Surveillance Machines," *The Intercept*, March 22,
2017. Available at: https://theintercept.com/2017/03/22/real-time-face-recognition
-threatens-to-turn-cops-body-cameras-into-surveillance-machines/.

103 **"And there is real-time analysis":** More Weise, "Taser Thinks a Camera on Every Cop Makes Everyone Safer," *Bloomberg Businessweek*. July 12, 2016. Available at: https://www.bloomberg.com/news/articles/2016-07-12/will-a-camera
-on-every-cop-make-everyone-safer-taser-thinks-so.

104 **"We have hundreds of politicians":** Cyrus Farivar, "The Airborne Panopti-
con: How Plane-Mounted Cameras Watch Entire Cities," Ars Technica, July 10,
2014. Available at: https://arstechnica.com/tech-policy/2014/07/a-tivo-for-crime
-how-always-recording-airborne-cameras-watch-entire-cities/.

104 **For years, PSS has:** G. W. Schulz, "Hollywood-Style Surveillance Technology Inches Closer to Reality," *Reveal*, April 11, 2014. Available at:
https://www.revealnews.org/article-legacy/hollywood-style-surveillance
-technology-inches-closer-to-reality/.

104 **In 2013:** Jeremy P. Kelley, "Dayton surveillance plan delayed," *Dayton Daily
News*, February 6, 2013. Available at: http://www.daytondailynews.com/news
/dayton-surveillance-plan-delayed/I3OJCRuSkMPwcJVg4cieOP/.

104 **In the summer of 2016:** Cyrus Farivar, "Persistent Surveillance Systems Has
Been Watching Baltimore for Months [Updated]," Ars Technica, August
24, 2016. Available at: https://arstechnica.com/tech-policy/2016/08/persistent
-surveillance-systems-has-been-watching-baltimore-for-months/.

104 **"We believe":** Ibid.

105 **McNutt was likely :** Florida v. Riley, 488 U.S. 445 (1989). Available at: https:
//supreme.justia.com/cases/federal/us/488/445/case.html.

105 **In June 2017, Miami-Dade Police:** J. Iannelli, "MDPD Wants to Record Entire County from the Sky Using Iraq War Technology," *Miami New Times*, June
1, 2017. Available at: http://www.miaminewtimes.com/news/mdpd-wants-to
-record-entire-city-from-the-sky-using-iraq-war-technology-called-wide-area
-surveillance-9385950.

105 **The bill, known as Senate Bill 21:** "SB-21 Law Enforcement Agencies: Surveillance: Policies," California Legislative Information, 2017. Available at: http:
//leginfo.legislature.ca.gov/faces/billNavClient.xhtml?bill_id=201720180SB21
&firstNav=tracking.

Chapter Five

107   **The Fourth Amendment does not:** Brief for Petitioner, Kyllo v. United States, 533 U.S. 27 (2000). Available at: https://www.documentcloud.org/documents /3897367-Kyllo-Brief-for-Kyllo.html.

107   **His first thought was:** Danny Kyllo, "DANNY LEE KYLLO KYLLO vs US 2001! DSCF7027," YouTube, September 11, 2017. Available at: https://www.you-tube.com/watch?v=4eGmPAxCF04.

107   **Eventually, the agents let him:** Danny Kyllo declined the author's invitation for an interview.

108   **While infrared scans:** Author's interview with Robert Thomson, February 27, 2017.

109   **"We just kept the public back":** Author's interview with Dan Haas, July 19, 2017.

110   **"They were referring to":** Author's interview with Robert Thomson, February 27, 2017.

111   **In fact, less than two months:** Office of Legal Counsel, *Opinions of the Office of Legal Counsel of the United States*, Volume 16 (Washington, DC: Department of Justice, 1992). Available at: https://www.documentcloud.org/documents/3900045 -Op-Olc-v016.html#document/p51/a364252.

111   **But the OLC disagreed:** Ibid.

112   **"I was so happy that I got an attorney":** Danny Kyllo, "DANNY LEE KYLLO KYLLO vs US 2001! DSCF7027," YouTube, September 11, 2017. Available at: https: //www.youtube.com/watch?v=4eGmPAxCF04.

112   **"This was one of the major points":** Author's correspondence with Kenneth Lerner, October 26, 2017.

112   **Nearly immediately after sentencing:** Scott J. Smith, "Thermal Surveillance and the Extraordinary Device Exception: Re-Defining the Scope of the Katz Analysis," *Valparaiso University Law Review* 30 (1996), 1071. Available at: https://www .documentcloud.org/documents/3900048-Thermal-Surveillance-and-the -Extraordinary.html#document/p2/a364255.

113   **After years of work, the 9th Circuit:** Opinion, United States v. Kyllo, CR-92-00051-1 (9th Cir.). Available at: https://www.documentcloud.org/documents /3897368-Kyllo-Ninth-Circuit-Opinion-2.html#document/p5/a364046.

113   **Worse still, as the 9th Circuit:** Opinion, United States v. Kyllo CR-92-00051-1 (9th Cir.). Available at: https://www.documentcloud.org/documents /3897368-Kyllo-Ninth-Circuit-Opinion-2.html#document/p7/a364048.

113   **On November 13, 2000:** Brief for Petitioner to Supreme Court of the United States, United States v. Kyllo, 99-8508. Available at: https://www.document-cloud.org/documents/3897367-Kyllo-Brief-for-Kyllo.html#document/p13/ a364009.

114   **"Even if *Katz*":** Ibid. Available at: https://www.documentcloud.org/documents /3897367-Kyllo-Brief-for-Kyllo.html#document/p16/a364010.

114   **"Technological developments hold":** Ibid. Available at: https://www .documentcloud.org/documents/3897365-Kyllo-Brief-for-US.html#document /p10/a364232.

115 **"However, both** *Knotts* **and** *Smith*": Reply Brief for Petitioner to Supreme Court of the United States, United States v. Kyllo, 99-8508. Available at: https://www.documentcloud.org/documents/3897366-Kyllo-Reply-Brief-for-Kyllo.html #document/p8/a364248.

116 **"You have to figure out":** Author's interview with Kenneth Lerner, July 26, 2017.

117 **In June 2017, Dreeben was:** Joseph Tanfani, "Robert Mueller's Team Has Prosecuted High-Stakes Cases—Including Obstruction of Justice," *Los Angeles Times*, June 23, 2017. Available at: http://www.latimes.com/politics/la-na-pol-mueller -team-20170622-story.html.

117 **receding hairline:** Michael Dreeben, Oyez. https://www.oyez.org/advocates /michael_r_dreeben.

118 **In the end, months later:** *United States v. Kyllo*, 533 U.S. 27 (2001). Available at: https://supreme.justia.com/cases/federal/us/533/27/case.html.

118 **"In our hearing in the district":** Author's correspondence with Kenneth Lerner, October 26, 2017.

119 **By coincidence, months later:** Author's interview with Kenneth Lerner, July 26, 2017.

119 **More than five years after** *Kyllo*: Florida v. Jardines 569 US ___ (2013). Available at: https://supreme.justia.com/cases/federal/us/569/11-564/opinion3.html.

119 **Roughly a month later:** *Jardines v. Florida*, SC08-2101 (Sup. Ct. Fl., 2011). Available at: https://origin-www.bloomberglaw.com/public/desktop/document /Jardines_v_State_73_So_3d_34_Fla_2011_Court_Opinion?1501821269.

120 **With no trouble at all:** David Smiley, "Miami-Dade Police Dogs, Cocaine Used in 4th-Grade Science Project," *Miami Herald*, January 28, 2013. Available at: http://www.miamiherald.com/latest-news/article1946758.html.

120 **In a 5–4 decision :** *Florida v. Jardines*, 569 U.S. ___ (2013). Available at: https://supreme.justia.com/cases/federal/us/569/11-564/.

122 **On November 7, 2012, less:** Attachment B: Kansas Department of Corrections Parole Violation Warrant. Available at: https://www.documentcloud.org /documents/3914205-13-2.html.

122 **At about 8:30 AM:** *United States v. Denson*, Brief of the Appellant (10th US Circ. Ct. App., 2014). Available at: https://www.documentcloud.org/documents /3914196-Document-12.html#document/p14/a366797.

122 **Nearly a year later:** United States v. Denson, Motion to Suppress Hearing, 6:13-mj-06107 (2013). Available at: https://www.documentcloud.org/documents /3914201-Document-14.html#document/p64/a366795.

122 **Despite the fact that the Doppler:** United States v. Denson, Response to Defendant's Motion to Suppress, 13-10111-01 (2013). Available at: https://www.documentcloud.org/documents/3914203-Gov-Uscourts-Ksd-92888-15-0.html #document/p2/a366796.

122 **"Police! Come to the door!":** Attachment A: Report by Deputy Marshal Joshua Moff. Available at: https://www.documentcloud.org/documents/3914204-13-1 .html.

123   **As the case progressed**: United States v. Denson, 13-10111-01, Motion to Suppress and Brief (2013). Available at: https://www.documentcloud.org/documents /3914206-13.html.

123   **The judge did not find Denson's**: Memorandum and Order, United States v. Denson, 13-10111 (2013). Available at: https://www.documentcloud.org /documents/3914202-Show-Public-Doc.html.

123   **"Unlawful searches can give"**: Opinion, United States v. Denson, 13-3329 (3rd Circ. Ct. App., 2014). Available at: https://www.documentcloud.org/documents /3903151-13-3329.html#document/p7/a366794.

124   **Roughly midway through his 20-year career**: Author's interview with Brad Heath, May 26, 2017.

124   **After reporting for a couple**: Brad Heath, "New Police Radars Can 'See' Inside Homes," *USA Today*, January 19, 2015. Available at: https://www.usatoday.com /story/news/2015/01/19/police-radar-see-through-walls/22007615/.

124   **As of January 2018**: Christopher Soghoian, "Some Job News," Twitter, January 2, 2018. https://twitter.com/csoghoian/status/948314721316425728.

124   **Unlike an infrared scanner**: Ibid.

124   **According to an October 2012**: "Through-the-Wall Sensors for Law Enforcement Market Survey," US Department of Justice, Office of Justice Programs, National Institute of Justice, October 2012. Available at: https://www.documentcloud.org /documents/3903149-00-WallSensorReport-508.html#document/p5/a396296.

125   **These devices have been commercially**: Will Saletan, "Killer Drones that Can See Through Walls," *Slate*, September 17, 2008. Available at: http://www.slate.com /articles/health_and_science/human_nature/2008/09/nowhere_to_hide.html.

125   **According to Heath's reporting**: Brad Heath, "New Police Radars Can 'See' Inside Homes," *USA Today*, January 19, 2015. Available at: https://www.usatoday .com/story/news/2015/01/19/police-radar-see-through-walls/22007615/.

125   **If it hasn't happened already**: "Through-the-Wall Sensors for Law Enforcement Market Survey," US Department of Justice, Office of Justice Programs, National Institute of Justice, October 2012. Available at: https://www.documentcloud.org /documents/3903149-00-WallSensorReport-508.html#document/p20/a366798.

126   **"A suspect's criminal history"**: *Maryland v. King*, 12-207 (2013). Available at: http://www.leagle.com/decision/In SCO 20130603D42/MARYLAND v. KING.

127   **While the Supreme Court arrived**: Rhett Allain, "Trying Out the iPhone Infrared Camera: The FLIR One," *Wired*, August 18, 2014. Available at: https://www .wired.com/2014/08/a-review-of-the-iphone-infrared-camera-the-flir-one/.

Chapter Six

128   **The ability to store everything**: Orin Kerr, "The Next Generation Communications Privacy Act," *University of Pennsylvania Law Review* 162 (2013). Available at: https://papers.ssrn.com/sol3/papers.cfm?abstract_id=2302891.

128   **Dressed in a tank top and shorts**: Author's interview with Ladar Levison, August 18, 2017.

128   **Levison owned and operated:** Ladar Levison, "Statistics," Lavabit, 2013. Available at: https://web.archive.org/web/20130508091526/http://lavabit.com:80/statistics .html.

129   **As an e-mail provider:** Levison, "Statistics." .

130   **The d-order required:** Levison in re application US District Court for the Eastern District of Virginia 1:13 EC 254, June 10, 2013. Available at: https://www.document-cloud.org/documents/3935582-Document-21.html#document/p8/a369641.

130   **The d-order Levison had received:** Required Disclosure of Customer Communications or Records, 18 U.S. Code § 2703. Available at: https://www.law.cornell .edu/uscode/text/18/2703.

131   **However, in the digital world:** Orin Kerr, "A User's Guide to the Stored Communications Act—And a Legislator's Guide to Amending It," *George Washington Law Review* 72 (2004). Available at: https://www.documentcloud.org /documents/3924362-Users-Guide-SCA.html.

131   **While it was popularly understood:** Linda Greenhouse, "Drug War v. Deficit: The Senate Blinks,"*V. The New York Times*, October 2, 1986. Available at: http: //www.nytimes.com/1986/10/02/us/drug-war-vs-deficit-the-senate-blinks.html.

131   **This warrant requirement turned on:** Cyrus Farivar and Joe Mullin, "History by Lawsuit: After Gawker's Demise, the 'Inventor of E-mail' Targets Techdirt," Ars Technica, 2017. Available at: https://arstechnica.com/tech-policy/2017/06 /shivas-war-one-mans-quest-to-convince-the-world-that-he-invented-e-mail/.

131   **The ECPA draws a distinction:** Kerr, "A User's Guide to the Stored Communications Act."

131   **In 1991, Senator Patrick Leahy:** M. Betts, "Do Laws Protect Wireless Nets?," *Computerworld*, 1991. Available at: https://books.google.com/books ?id=_djw_FNRO4cC&pg=PA47&lpg=PA47&dq=leahy+ecpa+task+force &source=bl&ots=m5E4iXzwfM&sig=ePVBP-GcsASljPLtnwwbaroLdzU&hl =en&sa=X&ved=0ahUKEwi84filoubVAhVLwGMKHbBHAkoQ6AEITjAH #v=onepage&q=leahy%20ecpa%20task%20force&f=false.

132   **Modern e-mail, however:** M. Poole and M. Shvartzberg, "The Politics of Parametricism: Digital Technologies in Architecture," (Bloomsbury, 2015)

132   **With the pen/trap order:** *United States v. Under Seal*, Brief of the United States, 1. 13-2652(L) (2013). Available at: https://www.documentcloud.org/documents /3924368-Document-16.html#document/p11/a369627.

132   **"Safeguards were incorporated":** Author's correspondence with Ladar Levison, November 28, 2017.

133   **As a child growing up:** Tim Rogers, "The Real Story of Lavabit's Founder," *D Magazine*, November 2013. Available at: https://www.dmagazine .com/publications/d-magazine/2013/november/real-story-of-lavabit -founder-ladar-levison/.

133   **"I didn't like the idea that Google":** Author's interview with Ladar Levison, August 18, 2017.

134   **The e-mail provider then:** Declan McCullagh, "How Web Mail Providers Leave Door Open for NSA Surveillance," CNET, June 21, 2013. Available at:

https://www.cnet.com/news/how-web-mail-providers-leave-door-open-for
-nsa-surveillance/.

135 **By coincidence, prior to the FBI:** Ladar Levison, "Lavabit . . . Secure," Web Archive, 2013. Available at: https://web.archive.org/web/20130505043920/http://lavabit.com:80/secure.html.

136 **With what he later described as:** Ladar Levison, "Ladar Levison—Compelled Decryption," YouTube. Available at: https://www.youtube.com/watch?v=g _lN-RAfzRQ.

136 **"It cannot be that a search warrant":** *United States v. Under Seal* (4th US Cir.). Available at: https://www.documentcloud.org/documents/3935582-Document -21.html#document/p96/a369639.

137 **"It seemed only natural to turn that over":** Ladar Levison, "Ladar Levison— Compelled Decryption," YouTube, 2016. Available at: https://www.youtube.com /watch?v=g_lN-RAfzRQ.

137 **As he wrote:** Joe Mullin, "Ed Snowden's E-mail Service Shuts Down, Leaving Cryptic Message," Ars Technica. Available at: https://arstechnica.com/tech -policy/2013/08/ed-snowdens-encrypted-e-mail-service-shuts-down-leaving -cryptic-message/.

138 **"I was faced with the choice":** Joe Mullin, "Lavabit Founder, Under Gag Order, Speaks Out About Shutdown Decision," Ars Technica, 2013. Available at: https://arstechnica.com/tech-policy/2013/08/lavabit-founder-under-gag-order -speaks-out-about-shut-down-decision/.

138 **Levison appealed up:** Opinion, *United States v. Lavabit*, 13-4625 (4th US Cir., 2014). Available at: https://www.documentcloud.org/documents/3924369 -Document-15.html.

138 **"Even though I expected":** Author's interview with Ladar Levison, August 19, 2017.

139 **When Berkeley Nutraceuticals:** Anderson, p. 115.

139 **As complaints began to mount:** Federal Trade Commission, "FTC Charges Sellers of Avlimil, Rogisen, and Other Dietary Supplements," February 2006. Available at: https://www.ftc.gov/news-events/press-releases/2006/02/ftc -charges-sellers-avlimil-rogisen-and-other-dietary-supplements.

139 **In that message, Cossman:** Amy Wallace, "The Rise and Fall of the Cincinnati Boner King," *GQ*, September 14, 2009. Available at: https://www.gq.com/story /smilin-bob-enzyte-steve-warshak-male-enhancement.

140 **Weinberg was a good choice:** *United States v. Chadwick*, 433 U.S. 1 (1977). Available at: https://supreme.justia.com/cases/federal/us/433/1/case.html

140 **"We were alarmed to realize":** Author's interview with Martin Weinberg, August 22, 2017.

140 **When it was all said and done:** *United States v. Warshak*, Brief of Appellants, 08-3997 (6th US Cir.). Available at: https://www.documentcloud.org/documents /4114209-US-v-Warshak-Appellants-brief-to-6C.html.

141 **That's exactly what the 6th Circuit:** *United States v. Warshak*, Opinion, (6th Cir., 2010). Available at: https://www.documentcloud.org/documents/3924349 -6C-opinion-US-v-Warshak.html.

141   **The appeals court also:** Warshak did not respond to the author's request for an
        interview.

141   **Judge Keith analogized e-mail:** Leonard Deutchman, "The ECPA, ISPs, & Ob-
        taining E-mail: A Primer for Local Prosecutors," 2005. Available at: https://www
        .documentcloud.org/documents/3935621-Ecpa-Isps-Obtaining-Email-05.html
        #document/p29/a369684.

142   **Even before the 6th Circuit:** Declan McCullagh, "Tech Coalition Pushes Re-
        write of Online Privacy Law," CNET, March 29, 2010. Available at: https://www
        .cnet.com/news/tech-coalition-pushes-rewrite-of-online-privacy-law/.

142   **Within months, the House:** Cyrus Farivar, "Senate Committee Takes an
        Important Step Towards Protecting Your Inbox," Ars Technica, Novem-
        ber 29, 2012. Available at: https://arstechnica.com/tech-policy/2012/11/senate
        -committee-takes-an-important-step-towards-protecting-your-inbox/.

142   **But rather than wait for courts:** Cyrus Farivar, "Google Stands Up for
        Gmail Users, Requires Cops to Get a Warrant," Ars Technica, January 23,
        2013. Available at: https://arstechnica.com/tech-policy/2013/01/google-stands
        -up-for-gmail-users-requires-cops-to-get-a-warrant/.

142   **"In order to compel":** Ibid.

142   **"We agree, for example":** Acting Assistant Attorney General Elana Tyrangiel
        Testifies Before the U.S. House Judiciary Subcommittee on Crime, Terrorism,
        Homeland Security, and Investigations, Department of Justice, 2013. Avail-
        able at: https://www.justice.gov/opa/speech/acting-assistant-attorney-general
        -elana-tyrangiel-testifies-us-house-judiciary.

143   **"I assumed they just knew":** Author's correspondence with Orin Kerr, August
        21, 2017.

143   **"The plummeting costs":** Orin Kerr, "The Next Generation Communica-
        tions Privacy Act," *University of Pensylvania Law Review* 162, 2013. Available
        at: https://www.documentcloud.org/documents/3935636-Kerr-Next-Gen.html
        #document/p4/a370250.

144   **"Californians shouldn't be forced":** ACLU of Northern CA, *"Tech Indus-
        try Stands with Sen. Leno to Modernize Digital Privacy Protections,"* Febru-
        ary 2015. Available at: https://www.aclunc.org/news/tech-industry-stands
        -sen-leno-modernize-digital-privacy-protections.

144   **The law, which was signed:** Author's interview with Nicole Ozer, September 7,
        2017.

144   **CalECPA goes further than:** Susan Freiwald, "At the Privacy Vanguard: Cali-
        fornia's Electronic Communications Privacy Act," Research Paper No. 2017-01,
        University of San Francisco Law, 2017. Available at: https://www.document-
        cloud.org/documents/3940947-SSRN-id2939412.html.

145   **Faced with increased pressure:** Email Privacy Act, H.R.699, 114th Congress
        (2015–2016). Available at: https://www.congress.gov/bill/114th-congress/house
        -bill/699.

145   **However, when it moved to the Senate:** Jennifer Daskal, "Beware of the
        Emergency Exception Loophole in the Email Privacy Act," Just Secu-

rity, June 7, 2016. Available at: https://www.justsecurity.org/31427/beware
-emergency-exception-loophole-email-privacy-act/.

145   **Among others, then Senator Jeff Sessions:** Mario Trujillo, "Senate Amendments Could Sink Email Privacy Compromise," *The Hill*, May 26, 2016. Available at: http://thehill.com/policy/technology/281329-senators-float-amendments
-that-could-sink-email-privacy-compromise.

146   **Specifically, it wanted the federal:** Delayed Notice, 18 U.S. Code § 2705. Available at: https://www.law.cornell.edu/uscode/text/18/2705.

146   **"We believe that with rare":** Brad Smith, "Keeping Secrecy the Exception,
Not the Rule: An issue for Both Consumers and Businesses," Microsoft on the
Issues, 2016. Available at: https://blogs.microsoft.com/on-the-issues/2016/04
/14/keeping-secrecy-exception-not-rule-issue-consumers-businesses/#sm
.0001ut4dod8kidtcyuj1ufxeui8fi.

146   **In February 2017, the judge:** Cyrus Farivar, "Judge Sides with Microsoft, Allows 'Gag Order' Challenge to Advance," Ars Technica, February
9, 2017. Available at: https://arstechnica.com/tech-policy/2017/02/judge-sides
-with-microsoft-allows-gag-order-challenge-to-advance/.

146   **However, in October 2017:** Cyrus Farivar, "DOJ Changes 'Gag Order' Policy, Microsoft to Drop Lawsuit," Ars Technica, October 24, 2017. Available
at: https://arstechnica.com/tech-policy/2017/10/doj-changes-gag-order-policy
-microsoft-to-drop-lawsuit/.

147   **Meanwhile, the day after:** Joe Mullin, "After Lavabit Shutdown, Another Encrypted E-mail Service Closes," Ars Technica, August 8, 2013. Available at:
https://arstechnica.com/tech-policy/2013/08/in-wake-of-lavabit-shutdown
-another-secure-e-mail-service-goes-offline/.

147   **Silent Circle went so far:** Somini Sengupta, "2 E-Mail Services Shut Down to
Protect Customer Data," Bits Blog, *The New York Times*, August 8, 2013. Available at: https://bits.blogs.nytimes.com/2013/08/08/two-providers-of-encrypted
-e-mail-shut-down/?emc=tnt&tntemail0=y.

147   **Two companies committing:** Kashmir Hill, "Lavabit's Ladar Levison: 'If You
Knew What I Know About Email, You Might Not Use It,'" *Forbes*, August 9,
2013. Available at: https://www.forbes.com/sites/kashmirhill/2013/08/09/lavabits
-ladar-levison-if-you-knew-what-i-know-about-email-you-might-not-use-it
/#441283b1648a.

147   **He was still required:** Cyrus Farivar, "Lavabit Got Order for Snowden's Login
Info, Then Gov't Demanded Site's SSL Key," Ars Technica, 2013. Available at: https:
//arstechnica.com/tech-policy/2013/10/lavabit-defied-order-for-snowdens-login
-info-then-govt-asked-for-sites-ssl-key/.

147   **"This is just another transport":** Cyrus Farivar, "Silent Circle and Lavabit
Launch 'DarkMail Alliance' to Thwart E-mail Spying," Ars Technica, October 2,
2013. Available at: https://arstechnica.com/information-technology/2013/10/silent
-circle-and-lavabit-launch-darkmail-alliance-to-thwart-e-mail-spying/.

148   **More than four years:** "Dark Mail Technical Alliance," Dark Mail, 2017. Available at: https://darkmail.info/.

Chapter Seven

150   **Jones and eight others:** "Crime and Justice," *The Washington Post*, October
        25, 2005. Available at: http://www.washingtonpost.com/wp-dyn/content/article
        /2005/10/25/AR2005102501638.html.

150   **According to US Attorney Kenneth L. Wainstein:** "Levels Nite Club Night-
        club in Washington, DC—2022690100," ClubPlanet, 2017. Available at: http:
        //www.clubplanet.com/Venues/104019/Washington/Levels-Nite-Club.

150   **The case took years to unfold:** *United States v. Jones and Maynard*, Brief of Ap-
        pellants (US Ct. App. DC, 2000). Available at: https://www.documentcloud.org
        /documents/3983150-Jones-Maynard-Brief-for-Appellants.html#document
        /p33/a372238.

150   **At that point, GPS:** David Schumann, "Wisconsin Lawyer: Tracking Evidence
        with GPS Technology," Wisbar, May 2004. Available at: http://www.wisbar
        .org/newspublications/wisconsinlawyer/pages/article.aspx?Volume
        =77&Issue=5&ArticleID=810.

150   **One of the most prominent GPS cases:** *United States v. Garcia*, Opinion, 06-2741
        (7th Cir., 2007). Available at: http://caselaw.findlaw.com/us-7th-circuit/1046181.html.

151   **A year after Jones' original:** *United States v. Maynard*, Opinion, 08-3030 (DC
        Cir., 2010). Available at: https://www.documentcloud.org/documents/3982802
        -Bloomberg-Law-Document-United-State-C-2527-D-C.html.

151   **In March 2007, prosecutors:** *United States v. Jones et al*, Indictment, 1:05-
        cr-00386. (DC Dist., 2007). Available at: https://www.documentcloud.org
        /documents/3982985-Gov-Uscourts-Dcd-124801-344-0.html.

151   **These points of sale included:** Ibid.

151   **On May 2, 2008, Jones:** *United States v. Jones*, Judgment in a Criminal Case,
        1:05-cr-00386. (DC Dist., 2008). Available at: https://www.documentcloud.org
        /documents/3983014-Gov-Uscourts-Dcd-117572-509-0.html.

151   **"I thought he was stark-raving mad":** Author's interview with Stephen Leckar,
        May 26, 2017.

152   **Leckar wasn't convinced:** *United States v. Jones*, In the Matter of the Appli-
        cation . . . Affidavit, 1:05-cr-00386. (DC Dist., 2006). Available at: https://www
        .documentcloud.org/documents/3982974-Gov-Uscourts-Dcd-117572-144-5.html.

152   **"To have somebody subject":** Author's interview with Stephen Leckar, August
        29, 2017.

152   **"The GPS logged all":** *United States v. Jones and Maynard*, Brief of Appellants,
        (DC Cir., 2000). Available at: https://www.documentcloud.org/documents
        /3983150-Jones-Maynard-Brief-for-Appellants.html#document/p33/a372238.

153   **Citing a 2003 opinion:** *State v. Jackson*, 76 P.3d 217 (2003) 150 Wash. 2D 251
        Opinion. Available at: https://law.justia.com/cases/washington/supreme-court
        /2003/72799-6-1.html.

153   **Meanwhile, when the government:** *United States v. Maynard and Jones*, ap-
        peal, 08-3030 (DC Dist., 2009). Available at: https://www.documentcloud.org
        /documents/3983310-Gov-Brief.html#document/p16/a372402.

155   **Years later, Leckar called:** Author's interview with Stephen Leckar, August 29, 2017.

155   **The latter judge also:** T. Jay Matthews, "Operation Match" *The Harvard Crimson*, 1965. Available at: http://www.thecrimson.com/article/1965/11/3/operation-match-pif-you-stop-to/?page=single.

155   **"Prolonged surveillance reveals":** *United States v. Maynard*, Opinion, 08-3034 (DC Dist., 2010). Available at: https://www.documentcloud.org/documents/3983093-Document-30.html#document/p29/a372201.

156   **So that's exactly what:** *United States v. Jones*, Appellee's Petition for Rehearing En Banc, 08-3034 (DC Dist., 2010). Available at: https://www.documentcloud.org/documents/3983462-US-v-Jones-appeal-for-en-banc-rehearing-at-DC.html#document/p15/a372525.

156   **On November 19, 2010:** *United States v. Jones*, 10-1259. Available at: https://www.oyez.org/cases/2011/10-1259.

158   **Leckar, sitting at the other:** Author's interview with Stephen Leckar, August 29, 2017.

160   **Plus, Alito continued:** *United States v. Jones*, 10-1259, Opinion (2011). Available at: https://www.documentcloud.org/documents/3984039-10-1259.html#document/p23/a372763.

161   **"Law enforcement is now on notice":** Adam Liptak, "Police Use of GPS Is Ruled Unconstitutional," *The New York Times*, January 24, 2012. Available at: http://www.nytimes.com/2012/01/24/us/police-use-of-gps-is-ruled-unconstitutional.html?mcubz=0.

161   **The FBI put out a guidance:** "Law Enforcement Panel (Pt. 3)," University of San Francisco Law Review Symposium, 2012. Available at: https://www.youtube.com/watch?v=C5f6VDUbGXs.

161   **Within several months of Weissmann's talk:** Cyrus Farivar, "ACLU to FBI: Tell the Public How You Interpret GPS Tracking Ruling," Ars Technica, August 15, 2012. Available at: https://arstechnica.com/tech-policy/2012/08/aclu-to-fbi-tell-the-public-how-you-interpret-gps-tracking-ruling/.

162   **That's still true today:** Nathan Wessler e-mail to the author, August 31, 2017.

162   **"Technological progress:** *United States v. Garcia*, Opinion, 06-2741 (7th Cir., 2007). Available at: http://caselaw.findlaw.com/us-7th-circuit/1046181.html.

163   **By contrast, the mosaic theory:** Orin Kerr, "The Mosaic Theory of the Fourth Amendment," April 2012. Available at: https://www.documentcloud.org/documents/3515438-SSRN-id2032821.html#document/p18/a372969.

163   **In fact, in the wake of the *Jones* ruling:** "How to Define Fourth Amendment Doctrine for Searches in Public?" USvJones.com (2013). Available at: https://web.archive.org/web/20130818174432/http://usvjones.com/.

164   **In essence, it prescribes:** Christopher Slobogin, "Making the Most of United States v. Jones in a Surveillance Society: A Statutory Implementation of Mosaic Theory," Vanderbilt University Law School Public Law & Legal Theory Working Paper Number 12-29 (2012). Available at: https://www.documentcloud.org/documents/3515498-SSRN-id2098002.html.

164 **In another 2016 legal academic paper:** Kevin Bankston and Ashkan Soltani, "Tiny Constables and the Cost of Surveillance: Making Cents Out of United States v. Jones," *The Yale Law Journal*, 2013. Available at: https://www.documentcloud.org/documents/3733116-1231-jjd1qz1e.html.

165 **"Without that technology":** Ibid.

166 **In that case, Justice Sandra Day O'Connor:** *Florida v. Riley*, Opinion, 488 U.S. 445 (1989). Available at: https://supreme.justia.com/cases/federal/us/488/445/case.html.

166 **As of April 2017:** Dan Gettinger, "Public Safety Drones," April 2017. Available at: https://www.documentcloud.org/documents/3986046-CSD-Public-Safety-Drones-Web.html.

166 **By comparison, as of July 2009:** "Bureau of Justice Statistics Preview," Bureau of Justice, 2017. Available at: https://www.bjs.gov/content/pub/press/aullea07pr.cfm.

166 **A September 2016 study:** Final Report NIJ Law Enforcement Aviation Technology Program, 2016. Available at: https://www.documentcloud.org/documents/3986048-Aviation-Report-Final-09202016.html#document/p18/a373275.

166 **Case in point: in August 2017:** Elaina Sauber, "Spring Hill Police First in Williamson to Purchase Drone," *The Tennessean*, August 28, 2017. Available at: http://www.tennessean.com/story/news/local/williamson/2017/08/28/spring-hill-pd-first-local-williamson-county-police-force-buy-drone/530679001/.

166 **As of 2017, a fully equipped:** Chris Aadland, "Madison Police Are Now in the Air, Thanks to Two New Drones," Madison.com, July 25, 2017. Available at: http://host.madison.com/wsj/news/local/crime/madison-police-are-now-in-the-air-thanks-to-two/article_f7a4fefb-1024-5d52-acod-dc2c961166fb.html.

166 **(This is one:** *United States v. Jones*, Opinion, 10-1259 (2011). Available at: https://www.documentcloud.org/documents/3984039-10-1259.html#document/p23/a372763.

168 **"What the Framers wanted":** Author's interview with Paul Ohm, May 25, 2017.

168 **Unless one wishes to be a total hermit:** Paul Ohm, "Don't Build a Database of Ruin," *Harvard Business Review* (2012). Available at: https://hbr.org/2012/08/dont-build-a-database-of-ruin.

169 **"Requiring the use of surveillance":** Raymond Shih Ray Ku, *Faculty Publications Paper 274*, 2002. Available at: https://www.documentcloud.org/documents/3984710-The-Founders-Privacy-the-Fourth-Amendment-and.html#document/p52/a373077.

Chapter Eight

170 **We determine:** *State of Maryland v. Andrews*, N. 1496 (2016). Available at: https://www.documentcloud.org/documents/2780529-1496s15.html.

171 **A 2010 FBI press release:** "Hacker Indicted in Massive Tax, Mail, and Wire Fraud Scheme," FBI, April 8, 2010. Available at: https://archives.fbi.gov/archives/phoenix/press-releases/2010/px040810.htm.

171 **According to an Internal Revenue Service:** In Matter of the Seizure 08-3397MB, Affidavit, April 2010. Available at: https://www.documentcloud.org/documents/4165323-Rigmaiden-Seizure-Affidavit.html.

172 **Rigmaiden's case dates:** Kim Zetter, "Identity Thieves Filed for $4 Million in Tax Refunds Using Names of Living and Dead," Wired, April 8, 2010. Available at: https://www.wired.com/2010/04/fake-tax-returns/.

172 **Authorities identified Carter:** "Hacker Indicted in Massive Tax, Mail, and Wire Fraud Scheme," FBI, 2010. Available at: https://archives.fbi.gov/archives/phoenix/press-releases/2010/px040810.htm.

172 **In April 2008, the second:** Ibid.

172 **"Representing myself":** Author's correspondence with Daniel Rigmaiden, October 17, 2017.

173 **While StingRay:** United States v. Rigmaiden, Motion Hearing, 2:08-cr-00814 (2011). Available at: https://www.documentcloud.org/documents/3986240-Gov-Uscourts-Azd-396130-637-0.html#document/p36/a373440.

173 **The Harris Corporation:** "Harris Corporation AmberJack, StingRay, StingRay II, KingFish Wireless Surveillance Products Price List" Public Intelligence, 2017. Available at: https://publicintelligence.net/harris-corporation-amberjack-stingray-stingray-ii-kingfish-wireless-surveillance-products-price-list/.

173 **The company's 2017 annual:** United States Securities and Exchange Commission Form 10-K for Fiscal Year Ended June 28, 2013. Available at: https://www.sec.gov/Archives/edgar/data/202058/000119312513346761/d578172d10k.htm.

176 **"They had identified one":** Author's correspondence with Daniel Rigmaiden, October 17, 2017.

176 **When the FBI contacted Verizon:** Author's correspondence with Daniel Rigmaiden, October 23, 2017.

177 **Battista continued:** United States v. Rigmaiden, Status Conference, 2:08-cr-00814 (2011). Available at: https://www.documentcloud.org/documents/3986061-Gov-Uscourts-Azd-396130-451-0.html#document/p9/a373344.

177 **"Some make requests to phones":** Author's interview with Eric King, September 22, 2015.

178 **King added that he's taken photographs:** Cyrus Farivar, "Moscow Metro Says New Tracking System Is to Find Stolen Phones; No One Believes Them," Ars Technica, July 29, 2013. Available at: https://arstechnica.com/tech-policy/2013/07/moscow-metro-says-new-tracking-system-is-to-find-stolen-phones-no-one-believes-them/.

178 **In 2010, Kristin Paget:** "DEFCON 18: Practical Cellphone Spying 1/4," YouTube, 2010. Available at: https://www.youtube.com/watch?v=rXVHPNhsOzo.

178 **The Los Angeles Police Department:** Jon Campbell, "LAPD Spied on 21 Using StingRay Anti-Terrorism Tool," LA Weekly, January 24, 2013. Available at: http://www.laweekly.com/news/lapd-spied-on-21-using-stingray-anti-terrorism-tool-2612739.

179 **The Czech police:** Masha Volynsky, "Spy Games Turn Real as Eavesdropping Technology Spreads," Radio Prague. August 16, 2012. Available at: http:

//www.radio.cz/en/section/curraffrs/spy-games-turn-real-as-eavesdropping
-technology-spreads

179   **"The question is":** Author's interview with Eric King, September 22, 2015.

179   **"I had the Commodore 64":** Author's correspondence with Daniel Rigmaiden,
       October 17, 2017.

180   **"I remember thinking that it wasn't fair":** Author's interview with Daniel
       Rigmaiden, May 18, 2017.

182   **"I was going to make a million":** Manoush Zomorodi, "When Your Conspiracy
       Theory Is True," WNYC, June 18, 2015. Available at: http://www.wnyc.org/story
       /stingray-conspiracy-theory-daniel-rigmaiden-radiolab/.

183   **Once he was representing himself:** Russell Brandom, "How a Man Accused
       of Million-Dollar Fraud Uncovered a Never Before Seen, Secret Surveillance
       Device," The Verge, January 13, 2017. Available at: https://www.theverge.com
       /2016/1/13/10758380/stingray-surveillance-device-daniel-rigmaiden-case.

184   **In the penultimate box:** Pivot, "Tech Genius Exposes Secret Government Sur-
       veillance," *Truth and Power,* Episode 3 Clip, YouTube, 2016. Available at: https:
       //www.youtube.com/watch?v=NxUzqstdL30.

184   **As 2010 rolled around:** Michael Isikoff, "FBI Tracks Suspects' Cell Phones
       Without a Warrant," *Newsweek,* February 18, 2010. Available at: http://www
       .newsweek.com/fbi-tracks-suspects-cell-phones-without-warrant-75099.

184   **Years earlier, as a first-year:** Christopher Soghoian, "Facebook fun," Paranoia
       .dubfire.net, September 6, 2006. Available at: http://paranoia.dubfire.net/2006
       /09/facebook-fun.html.

184   **The next month, October 2006:** Ryan Singel, "Make Your Own Fake Boarding
       Pass," *Wired,* October 26, 2006. Available at: https://www.wired.com/2006/10
       /make_your_own_f/.

185   **The net result was that Soghoian:** Ryan Singel, "FBI Raids Boarding Pass
       Maker's House, Seizes Computers," *Wired,* October 28, 2006. Available at:
       https://www.wired.com/2006/10/fbi_raids_board/.

185   **In 2009 and 2010, Soghoian:** Kashmir Hill, "FTC Hires Hacker to Help
       With Privacy Issues. It Didn't Last," *Forbes,* December 6, 2010. Available at:
       https://www.forbes.com/forbes/2010/1206/technology-chris-soghoian-federal
       -trade-commission-agent-provocateur.html.

185   **"My reaction wasn't":** Russell Brandom, "How a Man Accused of Mil-
       lion-Dollar Fraud Uncovered a Never Before Seen, Secret Surveillance De-
       vice," The Verge, January 13, 2017. Available at: https://www.theverge.com
       /2016/1/13/10758380/stingray-surveillance-device-daniel-rigmaiden-case.

186   **On September 22, 2011:** Jennifer Valentino-DeVries, "'Stingray' Phone Tracker
       Fuels Constitutional Clash" *The Wall Street Journal,* September 22, 2011. Available
       at: https://www.wsj.com/articles/SB10001424053111904194604576583112723197574.

187   **Months later, sitting:** Author's interview with Stephanie Pell, May 23, 2017.

187   **Stingrays aside, the two:** Stephanie Pell and Christopher Soghoian, "Can You
       See Me Now? Toward Reasonable Standards for Law Enforcement Access to
       Location Data that Congress Could Enact," *Berkeley Technology Law Journal,*

2012. Available at: https://www.documentcloud.org/documents/3986065-SSRN
-id1845644.html.

187 **"If courts don't know":** Author's interview with Stephanie Pell, May 23, 2017.

187 **By the end of 2011 and into:** Christopher Soghoian, "A Recruiter for Harris . . ."
Twitter, November 10, 2011. Available at: https://twitter.com/csoghoian/status
/134726658610573312.

187 **Immigration and Customs Enforcement:** FOIA Case Number 2012FOIA5235.
Available at: https://www.documentcloud.org/documents/479397-stingrayfoia.html

187 **There was even something called:** Ibid.

188 **In the summer of 2012, Soghoian:** Jeff Stein, "New Eavesdropping Equipment
Sucks All Data Off Your Phone," *Newsweek*, June 22, 2014. Available at: http:
//www.newsweek.com/2014/07/04/your-phone-just-got-sucked-255790.html

188 **Soghoian, meanwhile:** Christopher Soghoian, "The Spies We Trust: Third Party
Service Providers and Law Enforcement Surveillance," 2012. Available at: https:
//www.documentcloud.org/documents/3986250-Csoghoian-Dissertation
-Final-8-1-2012.html.

188 **Other journalists began:** Jon Campbell, "LAPD Spy Device Taps Your Cell
Phone," *LA Weekly*, September 13, 2012. Available at: http://www.laweekly.com
/news/lapd-spy-device-taps-your-cell-phone-2176376.

189 **"What on Earth was this technology?":** Author's interview with Linda Lye,
August 23, 2017.

189 **In October 2012, Lye:** *United States v. Rigmaiden*, Brief *Amici Curiae*, 2:08-cr-
00814. (2012). Available at: https://www.documentcloud.org/documents/3987272
-Gov-Uscourts-Azd-396130-904-3.html#document/p8/a373729

190 **"This case raises highly consequential":** *United States v. Rigmaiden*, Motion
Hearing, 2:08-cr-00814 (2013). Available at: https://www.documentcloud.org
/documents/3987267-Gov-Uscourts-Azd-396130-1004-0.html#document/p44/
a373726.

190 **Judge Campbell was not:** Ibid.

190 **Ultimately, however, in early May:** *United States v. Rigmaiden*, Order, 2:08-cr-
00814 (2013). Available at: https://www.documentcloud.org/documents/3987862
-Gov-Uscourts-Azd-396129-1009-0.html#document/p8/a373741.

190 **At the end of the year:** John Kelly, "Cellphone Data Spying: It's Not Just the
NSA," *USA Today*, December 8, 2013. Available at: https://www.usatoday.com
/story/news/nation/2013/12/08/cellphone-data-spying-nsa-police/3902809/.

191 **The "defendant challenged virtually":** *United States v. Rigmaiden*, Government's Memorandum, 2:08-cr-00814 (2014). Available at: https://www
.documentcloud.org/documents/3987940-Gov-Uscourts-Azd-396129-1135-0
.html#document/p11/a373766.

191 **Soghoian continued to talk:** John Turk, "Experts Question Transparency of
Cell Phone Tracking Device Owned by Sheriff's Office at Legislative Hearing," *The Oakland Press*, 2014. Available at: http://www.theoaklandpress.com
/general-news/20140516/experts-question-transparency-of-cell-phone
-tracking-device-owned-by-sheriffs-office-at-legislative-hearing.

191   **The Republican from Rochester Hills:** Author's interview with Tom Mc-Millin, September 6, 2017.

191   **"I've been told":** Ibid.

191   **As Jennifer Granick, now an:** Cyrus Farivar, "American Spies: How We Got to Mass Surveillance Without Even Trying," Ars Technica, February 12, 2017. Available at: https://arstechnica.com/tech-policy/2017/02/american-spies -how-we-got-to-age-of-mass-surveillance-without-even-trying.

192   **In an interview years later:** Author's interview with Tom McMillin, September 6, 2017.

192   **The guide was blunt:** Linda Lye, "Stingrays: The Most Common Surveillance Tool the Government Won't Tell You About," American Civil Liberties Union of Northern California, 2014. Available at: https://www.documentcloud.org /documents/3987508-Nw-Stingrays-Guide-for-Defense-Attorneys.html #document/p5/a373841.

193   **"If they use it wisely":** Kate Martin, "Documents: Tacoma Police Using Surveillance Device to Sweep Up Cellphone Data," News Tribune, August 26, 2014. Available at: http://www.thenewstribune.com/news/local/article25878184.html.

193   **Martin's reporting quickly:** Adam Lynn, "Tacoma Police Change How They Seek Permission to Use Cellphone Tracker," News Tribune, November 15, 2014. Available at: http://www.thenewstribune.com/news/local/crime/article25894096.html.

194   **Several months later, in April 2015:** Cyrus Farivar, "FBI Would Rather Prosecutors Drop Cases than Disclose Stingray Details," Ars Technica, April 7, 2015. Available at: https://arstechnica.com/tech-policy/2015/04/fbi-would -rather-prosecutors-drop-cases-than-disclose-stingray-details/

194   **"This knowledge could easily":** Bradley Morrison Affidavit, 2014. Available at: https://www.documentcloud.org/documents/1208337-state-foia-affidavit-signed -04112014.html.

194   **In May 2015, the FBI:** Cyrus Farivar, "FBI Now Claims Its Stingray NDA Means the Opposite of What It Says," Ars Technica, May 15, 2015. Available at: https: //arstechnica.com/tech-policy/2015/05/fbi-now-claims-its-stingray-nda-means -the-opposite-of-what-it-says/.

194   **Later that same month, Washington:** Cyrus Farivar, "Cops Must Now Get a Warrant to Use Stingrays in Washington State," Ars Technica, May 12, 2015. Available at: https://arstechnica.com/tech-policy/2015/05/cops-must-now-get-a -warrant-to-use-stingrays-in-washington-state/.

194   **Rigmaiden worked on the drafting:** Kate Martin, "Stingray Snared Him, Now He Helps Write Rules for Surveillance Device," News Tribune, March 23, 2015. Available at: http://www.thenewstribune.com/news/politics-government /article26270491.html.

195   **While Washington was not:** Certification of Enrollment Engrossed Substitute House Bill 1440, 64th Legislature 2015 Regular Session. Available at: https: //www.documentcloud.org/documents/2077716-1440-s-pl.html#document /p5/a217266.

195   **"Cell-site simulator technology":** "Justice Department Announces Enhanced Policy for Use of Cell-Site Simulators," Department of Justice, 2015. Available at:

https://www.justice.gov/opa/pr/justice-department-announces-enhanced-policy
-use-cell-site-simulators.

195   **"It was the most well-researched memo":** Manoush Zomorodi, "When Your
      Conspiracy Theory Is True," WNYC, June 18, 2015. Available at: http://www.wnyc
      .org/story/stingray-conspiracy-theory-daniel-rigmaiden-radiolab/.

195   **Now that lawyers know:** Cyrus Farivar, "Appeals Court: No Stingrays Without a
      Warrant, Explanation to Judge," Ars Technica, March 31, 2016. Available at: https:
      //arstechnica.com/tech-policy/2016/03/appeals-court-no-stingrays-without
      -a-warrant-explanation-to-judge/.

196   **In June 2016, Santa Clara County:** Ordinance No. NS-300.897, Santa Clara
      County Board of Supervisors. https://www.documentcloud.org/documents
      /2854213-Attachment-149330.html.

196   **"The ordinance doesn't prohibit":** Author's interview with Joe Simitian, June
      7, 2016.

196   **In August 2016, his case:** Cyrus Farivar, "Baltimore Police Accused of Illegal
      Mobile Spectrum Use With Stingrays," Ars Technica, August 16, 2016. Avail-
      able at: https://arstechnica.com/tech-policy/2016/08/baltimore-police-accused
      -of-illegal-mobile-spectrum-use-with-stingrays/.

196   **Just three months later:** Cyrus Farivar, "Appeals Court: It Doesn't Matter How
      Wanted Man Was Found, Even if via Stingray. Ars Technica, November 24,
      2016. Available at: https://arstechnica.com/tech-policy/2016/11/appeals-court-it
      -doesnt-matter-how-wanted-man-was-found-even-if-via-stingray/.

197   **Rigmaiden's name was also:** Cyrus Farivar, "Court: Locating Suspect via
      Stingray Definitely Requires a Warrant," Ars Technica, August 26, 2017. Avail-
      able at: https://arstechnica.com/tech-policy/2017/08/court-locating-suspect-via
      -stingray-definitely-requires-a-warrant.

197   **In September 2017:** Cyrus Farivar, "Another Court Tells Police: Want to Use
      a Stingray? Get a Warrant," Ars Technica, September 22, 2017. Available at:
      https://arstechnica.com/tech-policy/2017/09/another-court-tells-police-want
      -to-use-a-stingray-get-a-warrant/.

Chapter Nine

198   **This was where David Leon Riley:** *California v. Riley*, Appellant's Opening
      Brief, D059840 (Sup. Ct. Cal.). Available at: https://www.documentcloud.org
      /documents/4046687-Riley-Aob.html.

199   **By this point, one of Dunnigan's:** Image. Available at: https://joshbegley.com
      /redlining/maps/San_Diego-hi.jpg.

199   **Ruggiero began looking:** *Riley v. California*, Brief in Opposition, 13-132. https:
      //www.documentcloud.org/documents/4046710-RileyBrief-in-Opposition
      .html#document/p6/a375655.

199   **The officers took Riley:** *California v. Riley* ("Riley II"), Appellant's Opening
      Brief, D059840 (Sup. Ct. Cal.). Available at: https://www.documentcloud.org
      /documents/4046689-RileyII-D059840-Aob.html#document/p7/a375920.

199 **But after being read his Miranda:** *California v. Riley*, Appellant's Opening Brief, D059840 (Sup. Ct. Cal.) Available at: https://www.documentcloud.org /documents/4046687-Riley-Aob.html.

199 **"Get brackin' Blood!":** *Riley v. California*, Brief for Respondent, 13-132. Available at: https://www.documentcloud.org/documents/4052238-13-132-Resp -Amcu-Authcheckdam.html#document/p15/a375983.

200 **In *People v. Diaz*, the Golden State's:** *People v. Diaz*, Opinion, S166600 (Sup. Ct. Cal.). Available at: https://www.documentcloud.org/documents/4052223 -S166600-1294077608.html.

200 **"In my view, electronic communication":** Ibid.

201 **The man who picked up the phone:** Author's correspondence with Pat Ford, October 16, 2017.

202 **"He's a charming and likeable guy":** Author's interview with Pat Ford, September 14, 2017.

202 **"Appellant does not seek":** *California v. Riley*, Appellant's Opening Brief, D059840 (Sup. Ct. Cal.). Available at: https://www.documentcloud.org /documents/4046687-Riley-Aob.html.

203 **By February 2013, the state appellate:** California v. Riley, D059840 (Sup. Ct. Cal.). Available at: https://www.documentcloud.org/documents/4052229 -D059840.html#document/p15/a375924.

203 **"In our view, allowing law":** *Smallwood v. Florida*, Opinion, SC11-1130 (Sup. Ct. Fl.). Available at: https://www.documentcloud.org/documents/4317920-sc11 -1130-1.html.

204 **Weeks later, back in California:** Author's interview with Jeff Fisher, September 13, 2017.

204 **By May 2013, Fisher:** Joan Biskupic, Janet Roberts, and John Shiffman, "The Echo Chamber," Reuters, December 8, 2014. Available at: http://www.reuters .com/investigates/special-report/scotus/.

205 **While the team was preparing:** *United States v. Wurie*, Opinion, 11-1792 (1st Ct., 2013). Available at: https://www.documentcloud.org/documents/4052232-11 -1792P-01A.html.

205 **For Fisher, this solidified:** Author's interview with Jeff Fisher, September 13, 2017.

206 **"Mr. Chief Justice, and may":** *Riley v. California* 134 S. Ct. 2473 (2014). Available at: https://www.oyez.org/cases/2013/13-132.

207 **Arguing for the State of California:** Chris Geidner, "Breaking Barriers," *Metro Weekly*, April 16, 2010. Available at: http://www.metroweekly.com/2010/04 /breaking-barriers/.

207 **"Thank you":** *Riley v. California* 134 S. Ct. 2473 (2014). Available at: https://www .oyez.org/cases/2013/13-132.

208 **"That is like saying":** *Riley v. California* 134 S. Ct. 2473 (2014) Available at: https://www.documentcloud.org/documents/4046693-Riley-v-California -SCOTUS-decision.html#document/p21/a375994.

209   "It was somehow a true mind meld": Author's interview with Jeff Fisher, September 13, 2017.

209   As Marcia Hofmann: Marcia Hofmann, "Apple's Fingerprint ID May Mean You Can't 'Take the Fifth,'" *Wired*, September 12, 2013. Available at: https://www.wired.com/2013/09/the-unexpected-result-of-fingerprint-authentication-that-you-cant-take-the-fifth.

210   In the *Riley* decision: *Riley v. California*, Opinion, 13-132. Available at: https://www.documentcloud.org/documents/4046693-Riley-v-California-SCOTUS-decision.html#document/p17/a375995.

210   "On devices running iOS 8": Cyrus Farivar, "Apple Expands Data Encryption Under iOS 8, Making Handover to Cops Moot," Ars Technica, September 17, 2014. Available at: https://arstechnica.com/gadgets/2014/09/apple-expands-data-encryption-under-ios-8-making-handover-to-cops-moot/.

210   As Ars Technica reported: Cyrus Farivar, "Here's What a "Digital Miranda Warning" Might Look Like," Ars Technica, December 29, 2016. Available at: https://arstechnica.com/tech-policy/2016/12/should-the-miranda-warning-be-expanded-to-encompass-passcodes/.

210   Months later, federal: Cyrus Farivar, "To Beat Crypto, Feds Have Tried to Force Fingerprint Unlocking in 2 Cases," Ars Technica, October 20, 2016. Available at: https://arstechnica.com/tech-policy/2016/10/to-beat-crypto-feds-have-tried-to-force-fingerprint-unlocking-in-2-cases/.

211   It turns out that such cases: Dan Terzian, "The Fifth Amendment, Encryption, and the Forgotten State Interest," *UCLA Law Review* (2014). Available at: https://www.uclalawreview.org/the-fifth-amendment-encryption-and-the-forgotten-state-interest/.

211   In 2012, the 11th US Circuit Court: In re: Grand Jury Subpoena, 11-12268 (11th Cir., 2012). Available at: https://www.documentcloud.org/documents/4052254-opiniondoe22312-1.html#document/p22/a376015.

211   In 2013, a federal judge: 13-M-449 (Dist. Ct. E. Wisc., 2013). Available at: https://www.documentcloud.org/documents/4052255-Encryption-Case.html.

211   There is a crucial exception: John Villasenor, "Can the Government Force Suspects to Decrypt Incriminating Files?" *Slate*, March 2012. Available at: http://www.slate.com/articles/technology/future_tense/2012/03/encrypted_files_child_pornography_and_the_fifth_amendment_.html.

211   Indeed, on the same day: Cyrus Farivar, "Massachusetts High Court Orders Suspect to Decrypt His Computers," Ars Technica, June 25, 2014. Available at: https://arstechnica.com/tech-policy/2014/06/massachusetts-high-court-orders-suspect-to-decrypt-his-computers/

212   In early August 2017: *United States v. Apple MacPro Computer*, etc., Opinion, 15-3537 (3rd Circ., 2017). Available at: https://www.documentcloud.org/documents/4052265-Document-35.html#document/p18/a376016.

212   According to court records: Cyrus Farivar, "Miami Sextortion Case Asks If a Suspect Can Be Forced to Decrypt an iPhone," Ars Technica,

April 28, 2017. Available at: https://arstechnica.com/tech-policy/2017/04/miami
-sextortion-case-asks-if-a-suspect-be-forced-to-decrypt-an-iphone/.

212   **While Voigt only used an iPhone 6:** *Florida v. Voigt*, F16015256 (11th
       Circ.). Available at: https://www.documentcloud.org/documents/3679649-Voigt
       -Motion-to-Compel.html#document/p2/a350984.

212   **Hours later, Victor asked:** Complaint/Arrest Warrant. Available at: https:
       //www.documentcloud.org/documents/3679198-Redacted-a-Form-1.html
       #document/p2/a351074.

213   **By May 2017, a Florida:** Cyrus Farivar, "Sextortion Suspect Must Unlock Her
       Seized iPhone," Judge Rules Ars Technica, May 3, 2017. Available at: https:
       //arstechnica.com/tech-policy/2017/05/judge-miami-reality-tv-star-must
       -unlock-her-iphone-in-extortion-case/.

213   **In the Voigt case, according:** David Ovalle, "FBI, Tech Company Help Cops
       Hack iPhone in Miami Reality TV Star's 'Sextortion' Case," *Miami Herald*,
       July 28, 2017. Available at: http://www.miamiherald.com/news/local/crime
       /article164246532.html.

214   **Caballero's federal public defender:** Cyrus Farivar, "Judge: If Feds Find Drugs in
       Your Car, Pics of Cash on Your Phone, You're Suspicious," Ars Technica, April 19,
       2016. Available at: https://arstechnica.com/tech-policy/2016/04/judge-if-feds-find
       -drugs-on-your-car-pics-of-cash-on-your-phone-youre-suspicious/.

214   **"In [fiscal year 2016], CBP":** CBP Statement regarding electronic devices,
       March 14, 2017. Available at: https://www.documentcloud.org/documents
       /3517374-Ars-Technica-Mail-Re-URGENT-Media-Inquiry-Ars.html.

214   **Under the Trump administration:** "American Citizens: U.S. Border Agents
       Can Search Your Cellphone," NBC News, March 13, 2017. Available at:
       https://www.nbcnews.com/news/us-news/american-citizens-u-s-border
       -agents-can-search-your-cellphone-n732746.

214   **In early 2017, there:** Cyrus Farivar, "Man: Border Agents Threatened to
       'Be Dicks' Take My Phone if I Didn't Unlock It." Ars Technica, May 7, 2017.
       Available at: https://arstechnica.com/tech-policy/2017/05/man-border-agents
       -threatened-to-be-dicks-take-my-phone-if-i-didnt-unlock-it/.

215   **"The border doctrine":** Cyrus Farivar, "Remember the Artist Whose iPhone
       Was Searched at Border? He's Suing the Feds," Ars Technica, September 13, 2017.
       Available at: https://arstechnica.com/tech-policy/2017/09/remember-the-artist
       -who-had-his-iphone-searched-at-the-border-hes-now-suing/.

215   **The most recent public:** "Privacy Impact Assessment for the Border Searches
       of Electronic Devices," US Department of Homeland Security, August 25, 2009.
       Available at: https://www.documentcloud.org/documents/3461785-Privacy-Pia
       -Cbp-Laptop.html#document/p7/a338498.

215   **But as Orin Kerr:** Orin Kerr, "No case," Twitter, February 14, 2017. Available
       at: https://twitter.com/OrinKerr/status/831716834529439745.

216   **Just as a stingray can:** "Endpoint Surveillance Tools (CIPAV)," Electronic
       Frontier Foundation, April 2011. Available at: https://www.eff.org/foia/foia
       -endpoint-surveillance-tools-cipav.

216   **Finally, in December 2012:** In the matter of the search of NIT for email address texan.slayer@yahoo.com, Third Amended Application for a Search Warrant, 1:12-sw-05685 (Dist Co., 2012). Available at: https://www.documentcloud.org /documents/4053665-Nit-Email-Search.html.

216   **The judge signed off on it:** Warrant Return, 12-SW-05685-KMT, USDC Colorado, February 20, 2013. Available at: https://www.documentcloud.org /documents/4053672-Gov-Uscourts-Cod-136124-9-0.html.

217   **News of the NIT:** Craig Timberg and Ellen Nakashima, "FBI's Search for 'Mo,' Suspect in Bomb Threats, Highlights Use of Malware for Surveillance," *The Washington Post*, 2013. Available at: https://www.washingtonpost.com/business /technology/2013/12/06/352ba174-5397-11e3-9e2c-e1d01116fd98_story.html.

217   **"The Government does not seek":** In re Warrant to Search a Target Computer at Premises Unknown, Memorandum and Order, 4:13-mj-00234 (Dist. Ct. S. Tx., 2013). Available at: https://www.documentcloud.org/documents/4053644 -Order-Denying-Warrant-MJ-Smith-042213.html#document/p2/a376181.

218   **At the time Judge Smith:** M. Rumold, "The Playpen Story: Rule 41 and Global Hacking Warrants," Electronic Frontier Foundation, 2016. Available at: https: //www.eff.org/deeplinks/2016/08/illegal-playpen-story-rule-41-and-global -hacking-warrants.

218   **It was around this time:** Mythili Raman, letter, September 18, 2013. Available at: https://www.documentcloud.org/documents/4053758-214950421 -AAAG-Raman-Letter-to-Judge-Raggi-Re.html.

218   **Playpen's founder, David Lynn Browning:** *United States v. Browning*, Criminal Complaint, 3:15MJ279 (Dist. Ct. W. NC., 2015). Available at: https://www .documentcloud.org/documents/3284781-Browning.html#document/p12 /a334577.

219   **Eventually, the FBI:** In the Matter of an application . . . Brooklyn, NY 11211, Affidavit, 1:15-mj-00534 (Dist. Ct. E NY, 2015). Available at: https://www .documentcloud.org/documents/2166606-ferrell-warrant-1.html#document /p12/a227161.

219   **While most of the cases:** Cyrus Farivar, "Judge Invalidates Warrant That Let Feds Hack Tor—Using Child Porn Suspect," Ars Technica, April 20, 2016. Available at: https://arstechnica.com/tech-policy/2016/04 /judge-invalidates-warrant-that-let-feds-hack-tor-using-child-porn-suspect/.

219   **For future cases, the government:** "Wiretap Reports," *United States Court*, 2017. Available at: http://www.uscourts.gov/statistics-reports/analysis-reports /wiretap-reports.

Chapter Ten

221   **"But I'm like every nine":** Author's interview with Brian Hofer, August 31, 2017.

223   **"The connection between":** Author's interview with Deirdre Mulligan, June 5, 2017.

224 **"It felt like a prerequisite":** Author's interview with Reem Suleiman, June 2, 2017.

225 **"I was a kid in the Second World War":** Author's interview with Lou Katz, May 29, 2017.

225 **"This committee has taken on":** Author's interview with Raymundo Jacquez, June 6, 2017.

225 **Rounding out:** "Saied Karamooz for Mayor," https://everyonesmayor.org/.

225 **"It might be a lost cause":** Author's interview with Saied Karamooz, June 2, 2017.

226 **Earlier that day, the OPD:** Anne Kirkpatrick, Chief's Message, May 9, 2017. Available at: https://www.documentcloud.org/documents/3765425-oak063906.html.

227 **As of late 2017, the PAC's:** "Cellular Site Simulator Usage and Privacy," February 2017. Available at: https://www.documentcloud.org/documents/4062097 -oak062903.html#document/p5/a378185.

Chapter Eleven

229 **However, in between the two:** Jeffrey Toobin, "Comeback," *New Yorker*, March 26, 2007. Available at: https://www.newyorker.com/magazine/2007/03 /26/comeback-8.

229 **Amsterdam spoke in the waning days:** Public Papers of the Presidents of the United States: Richard M. Nixon, 1972. Available at: https://books.google .com/books?id=DcHcAwAAQBAJ&pg=PA590&lpg=PA590&dq=nixon +police+peace+forces&source=bl&ots=EpJSTvEfT8&sig=kzeN2vT-JY3SJwLxDGyz8g75gDsc&hl=en&sa=X&ved=0ahUKEwjc2MKn4sPWAh-WqrVQKHbItCvoQ6AEISTAJ#v=onepage&q=nixon%20police%20peace %20forces&f=false.

230 **While Amsterdam has since:** Anthony Amsterdam declined the author's request for an interview.

231 **"Right now, we kind":** Author's interview with Raymond Shih Ray Ku, September 6, 2017.

231 **"Technology, honestly":** Author's interview with Kathryn Werdegar, September 22, 2017.

231 **"Rather than simply":** Barry Friedman, *Unwarranted* (Macmillan, 2017), p. 316.

231 **"Right now, I will tell":** Author's interview with Michael Hayden, June 5, 2017.

232 **At the federal level, the only:** Cyrus Farivar, "Surveillance Watchdog Concludes Metadata Program Is Illegal, 'Should End,'" Ars Technica, January 22, 2014. Available at: https://arstechnica.com/tech-policy/2014/01/surveillance -watchdog-concludes-metadata-program-is-illegal-should-end/.

232 **Notably, in January 2014:** "Statement By the President on the Section 215 Bulk Metadata Program," White House, 2017. Available at: https://obamawhitehouse .archives.gov/the-press-office/2014/03/27/statement-president-section -215-bulk-metadata-program .

232   **Worse still, by the time:** T. Johnson, "Watchdog Board That Keeps Eye on U.S. Intelligence Agencies Barely Functions," *McClatchy DC*, March 7, 2017. Available at: http://www.mcclatchydc.com/news/nation-world/national /national-security/article136960048.html.

232   **Back in Oakland:** Author's interview with Saied Karamooz, June 2, 2017.

ACKNOWLEDGMENTS

There are an incredible number of extraordinary individuals who have been very generous with their time and have entertained—perhaps, at times, inane—legal questions from this humble reporter. Not so many years ago, I hardly knew anything of the intricacies of our often-confounding judicial system.

These people, among others, have all influenced my thinking in some way, and have helped me. In many cases, they have also (often on deadline) responded to my questions for articles that laid the foundation for this book.

In no order, they include:

Judge Harvey Schneider (Ret.), Joseph Gunn, Catherine Crump, Nathan Freed Wessler, Ted Boutrous, Marcus Thomas, Rep. Ted Lieu, Sen. Ron Wyden, Cmdr. Sid Heal (Ret.), Susan Hennessey, Benjamin Wittes, Paul Rosenzweig, Stephen Sachs, Howard Cardin, Stewart Baker, Stephanie Pell, Louis Cohen, US Tax Court Judge Albert Lauber, US Magistrate Judge Stephen Smith, Larry Tribe, Marc Zwillinger, Alan Butler, Daniel Solove, Babak Siavoshy, Linda Lye, Christopher Soghoian, Christopher Slobogin, Tom McMillan, Ben Wizner, Jennifer Valentino-DeVries, Kade Crockford, Mike Katz-Lacabe, Freddy Martinez, Mark Peterson, Andrew Frey, Dan Haas, Ken Lerner, Lewis Katz, Tracey Maclin, David Sklansky, David Bitkower, John Martin, Robert Thomson, Ryan Calo, Fred Cate, Stephen Henderson, Elizabeth Joh, Woodrow Hartzog, Kathryn Haun, Brad Heath, Ladar Levison, Jesse Binnall, Marcia Hofmann, Stephen Leckar, James Lyons, Ashkan Soltani, Michael Hayden, Paul Ohm, Raymond Shih Ray Ku, Barry Friedman, Daniel Rigmaiden, Eric King, Kristin Paget, Jennifer Granick, Lee Tien, Brian Owsley, Sup. Joe Simitian, Nate Cardozo, Cindy Cohn, Mark Rumold, Andrew Crocker, Kurt Opsahl, Jennifer Lynch, Alvaro Bedoya, Justice Kathryn Werdegar (Ret.), Pat Ford, Jeffrey Fisher, David Ovalle, Colin Fieman, Hanny Fakhoury, Susan Freiwald, Ahmed Ghappour, Peter Bribing, Nicole Ozer, and Orin Kerr.

In Oakland, I am grateful to Brian Hofer, Deirdre Mulligan, Robert Oliver, Reem Suleiman, Lou Katz, Raymundo Jacquez, Saied Karamooz,

Timothy Birch, and Joe DeVries for their dedication to crafting sensible surveillance policies here at home.

During my 2017 reporting trip to Washington, DC, Brian Fung and Elizabeth Lamme welcomed me into their home, and Carolyn Agis was kind enough to entrust me with the key to her apartment while she was out of town. Thank you all!

At *Ars Technica*, big ups to Nate Anderson, Eric Bangeman, Lee Hutchinson, and Ken Fisher for letting me take time off to get this book done. Six years ago, I started from zero and learned everything I know about legal journalism from David Kravets and Joe Mullin.

This book began to take shape in Spring 2016, with the encouragement and support of my mentor, Samuel G. Freedman. He led me to Dennis Johnson and the incredible team at Melville House. They all believed in this book and helped it come to fruition.

My father Mehrdad, and my brother, Alex, have always constantly provided helpful guidance, even if I'm not always smart enough to realize it at the time. Also, I'm thrilled that Nena, Alan, Kiran, Martin, Stephanie, and Heidi are all here to stay.

And finally, thank you to the love of my life, Rebecca Farivar, for being the wisest of sounding boards, and patiently letting me blather on about about license plate readers.